INSIDE HIGH-RISE HOUSING

Securing Home in Vertical Cities

Megan Nethercote

BRISTOL
UNIVERSITY
PRESS

First published in Great Britain in 2022 by

Bristol University Press
University of Bristol
1–9 Old Park Hill
Bristol
BS2 8BB
UK
t: +44 (0)117 374 6645
e: info@bristol.ac.uk

Details of international sales and distribution partners are available at bristoluniversitypress.co.uk

British Library Cataloguing in Publication Data
A catalogue record for this book is available from the British Library

ISBN 978-1-5292-1628-8 hardcover
ISBN 978-1-5292-1629-5 OA EPUB
ISBN 978-1-5292-1630-1 OA PDF

Cover design: Clifford Hayes
Front cover image: iStock/Sercan Ertürk
Bristol University Press use environmentally responsible print partners.
Printed and bound in Great Britain by CPI Group (UK) Ltd, Croydon, CR0 4YY

FSC
www.fsc.org
MIX
Paper from responsible sources
FSC® C013604

Contents

Preface

> He stepped out on to the balcony and swept up the cigarette butts and broken glass, condoms and torn newspapers thrown down from the floors above. … In the elevator lobby he listened to the latest rumours. Earlier that morning there had been a serious brawl between the 9th and 11th floor tenants. The 10th floor concourse was now a no-man's-land between two warring factions, the residents of the lower nine floors and those of the middle section of the building. Despite the harassment and increasing violence, no one was surprised by these events. The routines of daily life within the high-rise, the visits to the supermarket, liquor store and hairdressing salon continued as before. In some way the high-rise was able to accommodate this double logic. Even the tone of voice of his neighbours as they described these outbreaks of hostility was calm and matter-of-fact, like that of civilians in a war-torn city dealing with yet another air-raid. For the first time it occurred to Wilder that the residents enjoyed this breakdown of its services, and the growing confrontation between themselves. All this brought them together, and ended the frigid isolation of the previous months. (Ballard 1975, *High-Rise*, Chapter 6: Danger in the Streets in the Sky, p 81)

J.G. Ballard's *High-Rise* peels back the civilized facade of the modernist tower and subverts our collective expectations of the inhabited high-rise home. New residents have scarcely filled the tower's thousand units when conviviality unravels. Social conventions crumble, proprietary gives way to base desires, and the middle-class technocrat residents mutate into the primal selves they fear most. What begins as graffiti, minor irritations and petty grievances quickly devolves into threats, intimidation and hostility. Soon enough, management disbands, building maintenance lapses and the physical surrounds deteriorate. The social fabric frays as residents fragment into clans. These clans mark out and defend their turf from rivals, they raid enemy territories – the communal swimming pool, 'enemy' floors and so forth – and mayhem ensues: skirmishes, violence, debauchery, barbarity, savagery, theft, rapes, murders, even cannibalism.

Introduction

Towers are a ubiquitous feature of contemporary urban skylines. Following the orchestrated demise of mass social housing, with its modernist tower blocks and attempts to democratize vertical living across liberal democracies, developers have ploughed city blocks for profit, often in the name of 'sustainable' urban compaction. In many cities the world over, from Melbourne to Toronto and beyond, a staggering urban metamorphosis has taken place. Thickets of towers have cropped up, many summiting dizzying heights, their vast skeletons of concrete and steel cloaked in gaudy cladding or high-sheen glazing. Indeed, this century has seen an incredible surge in the construction of tall buildings, with increasing numbers of 'supertall' towers soaring skywards some 300 metres or more (CTBUH 2019). But if the rise of vertical living has been plain to see, largely unnoticed is the way that condominium, and other analogous legal architectures that underpin this residential development, are creating new intensities of property relations (Harris 2011). And yet this vertical development involves arguably the most iconic and fastest growing permutation of residential private property on our urban horizon. As urban residents seek homes in these verticalizing cities, this book questions how those new intensities of property relations are reconfiguring their homemaking.

This book, not unlike Ballard's 1975 dystopian classic, is about everyday life inside high-rise housing. This surge in high-rise development has delivered an array of new urban homes from palatial suites in sublime 'starchitect' skyscrapers for über-wealthy elites through to densely packed small units in rather more drab tower blocks. These homes are anchored in cities at the mercy of intensifying housing financialization as global capital flows circulate into and through these and other real estate assets, concentrating wealth, property ownership and power. With urban housing systems beleaguered by affordability crises, many urban households have limited housing 'options'; if they forgo high-rise housing in its relatively high-amenity, job-rich locations, they may face weighty locational 'trade-offs', such as longer and costly commutes. Yet in some jurisdictions this contemporary high-rise development suffers design, workmanship and/or safety issues. Where investors have bought up units, renters have entered these towers in growing numbers, many seeking homes but others merely a short-stay city-break. With the proliferation of vertical urbanization, understanding how home is secured behind the faceless facades of private high-rise housing matters more than ever – and not just to distinguish reality from science fiction.

The high-rise's entrails are not unchartered terrain albeit urban scholarship has struggled to keep pace with rising skylines. High-rise towers remain ever susceptible to a 'hollowing out' that quiets the voices of those who make their homes in these vertical landscapes (Harris 2015) and in this relative silence, polysemic and polarizing urban imaginaries have taken hold. Literary, cinematic, media and academic representations run the gamut from outright vilification of high-rise housing to full-blown glorification. Modernism touted vertical living as revolutionary; it was the means to engineer a new socially progressive society through 'streets in the sky'. The modernist imperative to 'erase the traces' urged the construction of a new world on the ruins of the old (Hatherley 2009: 3). New vertical technologies such as lifts and reinforced concrete would 'lift' people into 'light and air', removing them from ground-level afflictions of pollution, disease, industrial poverty and social disorder. In some corners, associations of the high-rise with technological progress and prowess endure, though now amplified by urban compaction and verticalization tropes that laud 'building skywards' as an economic and ecological imperative (for example Glaeser 2011: 135–64).

The dystopian animation of vertical landscapes, so common as to be almost cliché in science fiction, supplies a counter-narrative. The panoptic view has again proven captivating. Early 'noir' accounts, hailing from a time when high-rise housing was largely synonymous with mass social housing, rendered modernist tower blocks as crucibles of social disorder while turning a blind eye to structural drivers. Design determinism raged, spurred at least in part by Oscar Newman's (1972) cautions about 'indefensible space' – a thesis that claimed stairwells, lifts and corridors bereft of 'eyes on the street' or any sense of ownership would harbour crime and antisocial behaviour. Soon after, Alice Coleman (1985) joined this chorus with *Utopia on Trial*, blaming the tower block for inducing crime, fear of crime and antisocial behaviour. Skip forward some three decades and these narratives have been rescripted including to account for the changing demographics of residents living in new high-rise developments.

Contemporary depictions of high-rise from critical urban geography remain somewhat bleak. Vertical development is positioned within privatization and 'gating' trends and as a site and vehicle for neoliberal urbanism (Vesselinov et al 2007; Atkinson and Blandy 2013; Graham 2016a). These narrations chronicle how high-rise housing fuses logics of security-seeking and domestic fortressing (Atkinson and Blandy 2016) with cultures of fear (Low 2004) or, at the very least, desires for social homogeneity.

Prevailing tropes characterize high-rise housing as a means for vertical ascent away from the terrestrial city that appeals to, and fosters in turn, an emergent 'bunker mentality' and secessionist impulse among the urban elite (Atkinson and Blandy 2016; Graham 2016a). High-rise housing, by these accounts, threatens writing new three-dimensional or volumetric stratifications into the city (Graham and Hewitt 2013; Graham 2016a). Ballard's depiction of a tower progressively amputated from the city below fictionalizes the assumed endgame of this trajectory whereby residents quit their jobs and fully retreat from the 'outside' world. The most 'noir' accounts suggest these buildings encode antagonistic insider/outsider dynamics through physical and social separation from city life below, while possibly tightening bonds between those living within (Pow 2015). Perhaps worse still, high-rise housing by these accounts risks leaving cities pock-marked with 'ghost neighbourhoods' as absentee owners seek sky-high 'deposit boxes' that leave this housing wastefully underused and deny the city of places of human habitation and social attachment (Atkinson 2019). Residential towers brimming with visible geographies of property, from high-tech security systems to private security guards, with their 'reassuring legibility', do not challenge these accounts (Blomley 2004a: 13–14) instead narrating something of a zero-sum game between oppressive vertical communities and the public city, between withdrawal from urban streets and meaningful participation in civic and political life. Viewed from this vantage point within critical geography, the high-rise threatens the social-spatial integrity of cities and ignites a sense of despair and hopelessness.

But these narrations do not tell us the whole story of high-rise homes. As Ballard's *High-Rise* reminds us, what goes on behind towering facades cannot be taken for granted. On Ballard's watch at least, unwanted noise and smells seep into residents' private units. Falling detritus compromises balconies. *High-Rise* residents do not cohabit seamlessly: social divisions and spatial segregations are rife, and shared home spaces are strategically deployed in high-rise politics. Clan groups devise alternative and informal property arrangements: they stake out territories – the hallways, the roof deck and so forth – and, in the process, they control how their co-residents circulate around the high-rise. Communal areas become hotspots for rising tension as roving clans assert claims over previously communal areas, such as the stairwells, lifts or recreation zones. Residents' less-than-legal territoriality establishes who belongs where and who does not. As Ballard narrates, clan territories within the high-rise are forever under threat with residents needing to re-articulate and re-assert their claims by spreading rumours and through their occupation, through locked doors and barricades and through verbal and physical confrontation. Distinct clan identities – the underdogs, the middle class, the elites – are forged only as lower-floor residents attempt to ascend the tower in the face of growing physical and social barriers. Likewise, the elites distinguish themselves only in the process of defending the tower's upper floors; the 'proletariat' only through their confinement to the lower floors. As warring ensues, the residents segregate into floors and zones in ways that both produce and reinforce these place-based identities. The physical and social space of the tower is no mere backdrop for the story Ballard tells, but rather a contingent social creation of the residents who inhabit it as they respond to the design and enforced 'community' relations of the high-rise tower (Massey 1994).[1]

The surreal high-rise landscape Ballard animates is no more than fiction, certainly. Yet this literary classic was, in part at least, inspired by the 'the most incredible trivialities' of high-rise living that Ballard (1978) witnessed while visiting his parents' high-rise flat and later experienced first-hand as a short-stay renter in a holiday apartment in Spain – the constant bickering: 'who's going to pay for the maintenance of the potted plant display on the 17th floor landing?' … 'so and so's curtains do not match'. In the decades since Ballard wrote *High-Rise*, however, lively high-rise imaginaries endure in the absence of robust understandings of vertical living and the high-rise home. We would be remiss in accepting geography's bird's-eye view accounts or paying much heed to Ballard's narrations without crossing the tower's threshold and subjecting its inner workings to closer scrutiny. We cannot assume a pre-given monolithic entity propelled by and reducible to a single coherent logic such as urban segregation, social exclusion or neoliberal privatization, somehow untethered from, and independent of, myriad other urban dynamics. To piece together a fuller story of private high-rise housing, this book asks: how is the proliferation of high-rise condominium shaping home in the verticalizing city? In responding to this question, this book explores contemporary vertical urbanization from within the tower, with this urbanization understood as a unique fusion of an architectural building type (the tower) and residential

[1] *High-Rise* is no microcosm of society and class struggle, though sometimes interpreted as such. Rather, Ballard approached the high-rise tower as a laboratory to experiment with the physical and psychological pressures on residents unaccustomed to domestic life at close proximities, and subsequent perversities induced by modernist space, at a time when UK backlash against public housing was mounting. Oscar Newman's (1972) *Defensible Space* had been published decrying the deleterious impacts of high-rise living, in which lobbies, stairs, lifts and corridors – accessible to all, but hidden from the 'eyes on the street' – would induce terror and crime. As Massey (1994) reminds us, space must be understood as political: it shapes how residents experience and perceive the world around them: space is both socially constructed *and* society is constructed spatially. Moreover, space also produces and hosts different socio-spatial/place-based individual and clan identities, shaping how identities are narrated and practised.

typology (higher-density living) within a distinct private property form (condominium).[2]

Colonize the skies

Behind the striking vertical expansion of urban skylines other changes have taken place, these ones invisible to the naked eye. In cities across common law jurisdictions, such as the US, Canada and Australia, condominium has provided the legal architecture to revolutionize the buying and selling of airspace above city lots. Traditionally, common law has been 'expansive and vague' in defining three-dimensional boundaries of ownership (Harris 2011: 700). Renowned chronicler of the common law, Sir William Blackstone remarked that land has 'an indefinite extent, upwards as well as downwards (such that whoever has the land possesses all the space upwards to an indefinite extent)' (cited in Harris 2011: 700). This ambiguity was partly addressed early in the 20th century with the advent of air rights or 'airspace parcels' – 'a volumetric parcel, whether or not occupied in whole or in part by a building', with the same legal status as conventional interests in land (*Air Space Titles Act* cited in Harris 2011: 700). Then, in the 1960s, condominium was introduced through statutory reform, mimicking the principles and legal attributes of these prior allowances such that where there was once only a single freehold title on each city lot, there could now be hundreds or even thousands of titles.[3]

With spatial units of homeownership no longer limited to the single-family home or the standard city lot, condominium provided a legal mechanism with unrivalled potential to increase the density of private land ownership

---

[2] There are no disciplinary or industry standard definitions for 'high-rise' housing. This book uses 'high-rise', vertical expansion, verticalizing (as in verticalizing cities) and vertical urbanization interchangeably to refer to urban development comprising a significant vertical dimension.

[3] Throughout this book I use the term condominium as perhaps the most widely recognized label for this legal architecture, including across North America and most Canadian provinces. Note that condominium has antecedents in French copropriété (condominium) dating back some 150 years (Webster and Le Goix 2005: 20), though its diffusion did not begin in earnest until the 1960s. Analogous legal systems include strata title (for example as used in Australia, British Columbia), common hold (UK: see Webster and Le Goix 2005) and sectional title (South Africa). On condominium in Europe, see Van Der Merwe (2015). For an early history on US condominium see Lasner (2012), for an international overview of condominium see Easthope (2019) and for additional international perspectives see Lehavi (2016) and Glasze et al (2004). Condominium's legal innovations relate to a range of housing typologies of varying residential density. However, vertical urban expansion has been a consistent response to constraints on urban land, making the stacking of ever more units a key feature of condominium's contemporary proliferation (Lippert 2019: 3).

(Harris 2011: 695). This densification of property interests appealed on multiple fronts. Developers could unlock the value of city lots through multi-unit high-rise development. Vested political interests were amenable: they saw smaller, more affordable interests in land as a means to expand the property-owning franchise to a wider base and possibly even reverse trends towards tenant living (Harris 2011: 703). Condominium also offered a means to counteract sprawl and optimize urban infrastructure and, later, as it became politically salient, this rationale was leveraged to smooth the way for more development under compact city agendas. With legislators sympathetic, developers keen and newly satisfied bank managers happy to issue mortgages on condo units, new condominium statutes precipitated a brand-new mass market in individualized ownership of multi-unit housing. To be sure, it was not that vertical subdivisions were impossible before. However, whereas units were previously sold under various arrangements such as company title, such that a company would own the building and provide its shareholders exclusive use of a single unit, condominium supposedly helped homebuyers 'achieve more concomitants of ownership' (Berger 1963: 989).

Condominium legislation passed near-seamlessly, greeted with enthusiasm but also fascination, incredulity even. For condominium essentially unfastened land, as a legal category, from the surface of the earth creating individually owned 'airspace parcels' that elicited proclamations of 'land without earth' and 'property in thin air' (Harris 2011: 693, 719). Unlike familiar freehold titles which are defined through a single geometric plane, condominium requires accounting for the third dimension. Condominium relies on the physicality of the building itself to achieve this volumetric bounding: the condo owner's individual interest encompasses everything between coats of paints on the boundary walls of the private condo unit – creating what is essentially nothing more than 'a legal fiction' (McKenzie 2011: 8; Sherry 2016). Everything in the tower besides these 'airspace' parcels is common property. This common property includes shared amenities and shared infrastructure from walls, insulation, building structures, ceilings and recessed light fittings to wiring, pipes, roofs, lobbies, hallways, lifts and fire stairs, together with any other amenities, buildings, or land. When you buy a condo unit, what you actually buy is the airspace of the private condo unit and an undivided (fractional) share in the ownership of the tower and the land it sits on.

More than just the stacking of private dwellings, condominium involves a dual property interest: the individual interest is bundled with a common interest. With common property to be managed, a collective governance structure with obligatory membership is mandatory (Harris 2011: 695, 719; McKenzie 2011: 6, 8; Lippert 2019: 105). This proprietary community differentiates condominium from other subdivisions of property interests within buildings, such as cooperatives and leaseholds. This 'community of owners' is based on a corporate form and operates according to established rules and regulations. These homeowner associations (HOA) or owners corporations (OC), to use the Australian (Victorian) terminology, exercise their power in the interest of condo owners and are responsible for day-to-day building management and maintenance, including collecting membership fees, regulating expenditure, setting and enforcing bylaws, facilities management and longer-term building maintenance planning. Owners are not only granted property entitlements but are also tasked with collective responsibilities and governed by private restrictions (Altmann and Gabriel 2018: 8–9). Even in the early days of condominium, those who understood this much recognized that condominium was a distinct form of private property ownership. Wekerle and colleagues (1980: 173) went as far as to claim condo owners may be 'comparable to tenants' on the grounds that the 'anticipated advantages of homeownership … stem not so much from "ownership" per se but from ownership of a particular form of dwelling unit – the single-family house'.

As the widespread uptake of condominium across cities has restructured the ownership of large swathes of urban land, it has reconfigured the social relationship between those who own and make their homes in high-rise towers. The supposition of a pre-formed 'community' in condominium is quixotic, though such expectations persist. Rather, condominium entails a group of owners brought together through conventional buyer-seller transactions, who are tied together as joint owners of the common property in ways house owners never would be, as a means to hold individual titles in multi-unit buildings. These condo owners must then cooperate to manage their assets and they often must comply with the whims of the majority, whether on repairs and maintenance spending or even on how their assets are disposed of. Resident relations risk being undermined by owners' incompatible lifestyles, financial means, and divergent priorities and concerns, all while sharing sizeable financial risks and collective responsibilities in residential propinquity (McKenzie 2011; Easthope 2019).

'Community' dynamics are complicated further by absentee owners who have their sights set on capital appreciation and rental revenue and by the condo renter who consequently enters the condo. With representation in formal governance based on ownership rather than residence, these renters are generally ineligible to participate or vote on matters that impact their domestic lives and home spaces and must instead simply hope their landlords participate in formal governance with their needs in mind. From the outset, this formal disenfranchisement of condo renters was deemed 'profoundly undemocratic' and associated with embedding a 'fundamental inequality' within condominium life (Barton and Silverman 1994: xii, 11). Today, such tensions and inequities present a more pressing problem, with rentership rates higher and rapidly climbing in many jurisdictions where condominium or analogous legal forms is proliferating such as Australia and the US. As this suggests, condominium is neither inherently progressive nor even inclusive as its 'community' of residents may be fragmented, policed and regulated by established power hierarchies between its owner and renter residents.

In sum, condominium's novel legal framework answered to challenges surrounding the collective ownership of common property in multi-unit developments, difficulties surrounding the vertical stacking of freehold title and the absence of both rules and a governance body to govern this vertical development (Harris 2011: 695, 989; Sherry 2016). The solution, although schematically simple was not straightforward legally, ethically and practically, as we shall see. In advanced liberal societies with traditions of individualized property ownership, the sale of condo units hinges on a long-standing deception that these units are more or less comparable to freehold property ownership inasmuch as they give owners the same bundle of rights, namely: control over their property, inviolable property rights and security of title in perpetuity. Construction hoardings hyping the latest condo development as the zenith of modern homeownership show how condo developers trade on convention in terms of homeownership alongside convenience, new-fangled designs and aspirational urbane city living. But while condominium is developed, marketed and sold to consumers on the basis that it is just another form of individualized property ownership, it is nothing of the sort. As Randolph and Easthope (2014: 213) write, such advertising 'promotes a self-assured belief that owners are buying into the pinnacle of privatised, personal urban living, in line with ideals of the neoliberal ascendency, which preferences the private over all forms of public action, with marketised private property rights reified above all else'. What these condo campaigns gloss over – conceal, even – are the finer details of property in condominium.

Property in condominium: from legal to lay perspectives

Most understand property as possession of a 'thing' such as a parcel of land over which we (ought to) have absolute control. Property, we assume, is private and exclusive. Instrumental in shaping this view is our prevailing vision of property or the so-called 'ownership model' identified by legal scholar Joseph Singer (2000: 2–3) which powerfully structures what we think property is and what it ought to do. We anticipate one determinate owner with formal title who can use their property as they wish: they have the right to exclude, the power to transfer, immunity to having it taken away and the right to be compensated if the state takes it (Blomley 2004a: 2). It is a vision that obscures property's complexity: it obfuscates how private property is more dynamic and never definitively private, as illustrated for instance by usufruct rights or tenancy law which partially limit the investor's treatment of housing as a pure financial asset (Blomley 2004a: 16, 29). It is a vision that also obscures property's diversity: although it does not deny collective forms of ownership, it considers individual private ownership rights 'anterior and superior' since collective ownership clashes with basic liberal tenets of individualized private action (Blomley 2004a: 3–4, 64, 11).

Condominium, as a form of collective private ownership, departs quite radically from the prevailing image of a solitary owner with consolidated rights over a single-family home. Legal scholar Heller (1999: 1183) has said that condominium represents 'perhaps the most significant form of social reorganization of the late twentieth-century'. But what is the significance of converting large tracts of urban land to condominium? Legal scholar Douglas Harris (2011: 721–2, emphasis added) speculates on the significance of this conversion:

> Might the sudden rise of condominium challenge deeply rooted conceptions of what it means to own property? If ... an increasingly large proportion of land is held within condominium ... then it may become increasingly difficult to think of private property solely or even primarily in terms of, in Blackstone's famous caricature, 'sole and despotic dominion'. The legal form of condominium embeds private property with community, albeit a community that excludes all but owners. *Does this embedding weaken an individualistic and detached sense of private property or enhance the detachment by limiting the community to a defined group of owners?*

Condominium constitutes a hybrid property form: it blends individual and common property interests. Common property is something of a sidekick in this arrangement, supporting the stacking of individual property titles. But it is indispensable nonetheless: without a shared lift how would the condo resident access their penthouse, for instance? But while it is easy enough to conceptualize condominium as individual titles supported by, or nested within, common property (Harris 2011; Harris and Gilewicz 2015: 292–3), the relationship that exists between these property interests is not self-evident, at least to the casual observer.[4]

[4] Indeed, private property regimes have always relied on shared forms of property – without it, private property is untenable, and its use is compromised and inefficient due to the potential resources required to secure access. Think of the pandemonium that would ensue if we stripped suburban lots of their interconnecting roadways. Much of the condominium's common property functions similarly, providing access to private property while preserving its integrity (Harris 2011). For this reason, Harris and Gilewicz (2015: 270) argue part of the significance of condominium therefore lies not just in its ubiquity but its 'capacity to reorient our understandings of property by accentuating the embeddedness of private property within community'.

Condo dissolution regimes are helpful for making explicit the hierarchy between these property interests. Recall that condominium dissolution involves the removal of individual titles (that is, the termination of interests in land and winding up of the OC) and their replacement with co-ownership interests held by co-owners. This process is of growing interest to cities where ageing condo stock is deemed ripe for 'regeneration' and it potentially interests condo owners whose co-ownership interests may exceed those of their individual interests; namely, when the exchange value of their condo unit is higher when bundled up with other owners' co-ownership interests (Harris and Gilewicz 2015: 265–6; also Easthope et al 2014). Adjudicating condominium dissolution ultimately amounts to a ruling, made in each jurisdiction, about the degree of owner consent required to dissolve condominium: either unanimity, whereby all owners must agree or supermajority whereby at least two thirds must agree, sometimes more. For some owners to dissolve condominium despite objections from other condo owners – essentially ending freehold interests without consent – represents 'an extraordinary power' (Harris and Gilewicz 2015: 266). Indeed, it amounts to a power not held by homeowners outside condominium, who cannot simply join forces to terminate their neighbour's property title (Harris and Gilewicz 2015: 266).

Normative models of property help us think about the hybrid nature of property in condominium (Schwartz 1964; Blandy 2013) by shifting our focus away from the classic 'bundles of rights' we associate with property ownership to other crucial elements of property, such as governance and relationality. Within a pluralist theory of property, which assumes property serves several competing goals such as advancing various liberal values (for example efficiency, autonomy, community, distributive justice and so on), theorists anticipate that incommensurable values will create tensions.[5] Property theorists offer several normative property models to tackle the tough choices that must be made in managing these tensions. These models suggest hybrid property regimes – property arrangements involving a blend of individual and common property interests – offer potential advantages over any of the standard trilogy of ownership forms in pure property regimes, namely private, state and common property (Lehavi 2008; Nedelsky 2011; Harris and Gilewicz 2015: 290). Note these are normative not descriptive models, with property in the real

[5] Property theorists discern two underlying rationales for property (Alexander 2012): a monistic thesis of property asserts that property law is aligned with serving one main goal or value (for example economic efficiency, individual interests or social interests), whereas a pluralist approach, which I reference here, sees property as serving several competing goals such as advancing various liberal values (for example efficiency, utility and so on).

world understood to exist along various continuums within the ideal types I review later (Alexander 2012: 1856).

Of note, Dagan and Heller (2001) posit 'liberal commons' property as private property (that is, the property form that embodies the rights of individuals, for example liberal) embedded within community (that is, commons, mutual rights and responsibilities). Within this model, condominium sits at the intersection of two important axes: a first axis based on rights allocations, spanning from commons to anticommons property and a second axis based on governance institutions, spanning from private to public (Heller 2005). At this crossroad, condominium is 'delicately poised between extremes on both the rights allocation and the decision-making axes' (Heller 2005: 329). In short, condominium is ideally positioned, unlike pure forms of property – at least as per this theory. In terms of rights allocation, condominium avoids both the overuse at the heart of the tragedy of the commons and the underuse at the heart of the tragedy of the anticommons, linked to the over-fragmentation of property interests (Heller 2008). In terms of governance, condominium likewise excels by providing conditions 'under which people can achieve the economic and social gains possible from cooperation, while also ensuring that individual autonomy exists on reasonable terms' (Heller 2005: 333).

Other normative property models turn our attention to relationships and relationality on the grounds that 'owners do not live alone but in society with others' and that property rights given to one owner necessarily deny those same rights to others (Singer, 2000: 88).[6] The focus on relationality helps us see that property is not about relations between an owner and a thing, but rather between an owner and other people with regards to a valued resource (Singer 2000: 6). Of note, property theorist Gregory Alexander (2012) posits 'governance property' as another normative model for property. Alexander juxtaposes governance property with exclusion theorists' Blackstonian 'man-in-his-castle' model of property where the right to exclude constitutes the defining feature of property and where the focus rests firmly on insider/outsider relations between owners and non-owners or third parties. Alexander (2012: 1862) argues in governance property such as condominium, internal dynamics between owners are *critical* precisely because every owner 'has some kind of property interest in everyone else property' – and indeed this is the defining feature of governance property.

[6] When it comes to the ownership of real property (for example of land and housing), the difference between a homeowner and a renter is one of power differentials between tenure groups. A residential tenancy involves ownership of a temporary right to use land/dwelling that derive from a titleholder (the landlord). The landlord surrenders some rights but retains others, including the power to evict the tenant under certain conditions (Blomley 2017).

Alexander's (2012: 1859, 1876) normative claim is that the ownership of governance property may help 'inculcate' virtues that promote human flourishing, including 'community, cooperation, trust and honesty', at least better than exclusion/Blackstonian property does.

These normative models are also telling of how legal scholars approach and understand property in condominium. This legal scholarship positions law as a 'determining force': property is assumed to yield certain advantages or values and thus the task becomes how to embed these values within the law (Cowan et al 2018: 6). Condo dissolution scholarship exemplifies this 'law first' stance with legal scholars viewing each condo dissolution regime as a statement about the status of property in condominium in that particular jurisdiction and whereby each dissolution regime expresses an alternative, even competing conception of property. A supermajority regime is thus one that 'defends property interests themselves': what is protected is the idea of the home-as-castle and property as proprietary – namely, property as 'the material foundation for creating and maintaining the proper social order, the private basis for the public good' (Alexander in Harris and Gilewicz 2015: 284). A unanimity regime is one that 'protects the exchange value of the property interest': what is protected is the notion of the owner as an investor seeking wealth maximization (Harris and Gilewicz 2015: 268). It is from this 'law first' stance that legal scholars classify dissolution regimes as a 'singularly and increasingly important site in determining what it means to hold property in condominium' (Harris and Gilewicz 2015: 289).[7]

Although this legal scholarship acknowledges that the legal sphere – legislation, court rulings and so forth – is not the lone arbiter of property or its definitions, condominium in its lived, socio-legal context is a striking absence. Harris and Gilewicz (2015: 294) concede as much, for while they emphasize condo dissolution as a critical site for understanding what property is, they also acknowledge that the 'sites that combine to construct the nature of property are diffuse and extend beyond the formal legal setting'. And indeed for these very reasons legal geographers and socio-legal scholars have elsewhere deployed a property analytic to engage with the legal fabrication of housing in their studies of 'outlier' housing typologies and tenures.[8]

[7] Under this 'law first' paradigm, the task for law then is to choose between these regimes based on what property's purpose ought to be (for critique: Ewick and Silbey 1998). If the goal of the property regime is to protect the condo as home above all else, then a unanimity regime is a preferred option for condo dissolution. If the goal is to secure the condo's exchange values above all else, then supermajority is preferable (see Harris and Gilewicz 2015).

[8] A property analytic has been deployed in studies of mobile homes (Sullivan 2018) and canal boats (Cowan and Hardy 2019) and in non-mainstream tenures such as shared ownership (Cowan et al 2018) and non-individualized ownership forms such as community land trusts, cooperatives and co-housing (Bunce 2016; Blandy et al 2018; Crabtree 2020).

A property analytic appeals in examining these 'outlier' cases precisely because sensitivity to property stands to foreground the unique property relations that underpin people's access to the places in which they dwell.

A property-sensitive perspective holds promise for understanding everyday property in condominium too. Harris (2011: 698) recognizes as much in calls for studies of condominium to 'elucidate the practices of condominium as a social space with the potential to transform what it means to own property'. Such guidance, however, has yet to be taken up despite express interest in everyday property in land in critical legal studies, though there is interest in property in multi-owned housing with notable contributions from Sarah Blandy, Susan Bright and colleagues (Blandy 2013; Blandy et al 2016; Blandy et al 2018; Blandy et al 2020). This omission comes as no great surprise given that property in everyday life, more broadly, remains a major empirical blind spot in the geographical literature too (Blomley 2016b: 225), albeit with important exceptions. Addressing this omission, however, requires establishing an approach to examining everyday property in condominium.

Condo towers as propertied space

The legal spatial category of property is socially constructed, contingent and performative (that is, it helps constitute what it describes) (Blomley 2013). Property manifests in the here-and-now through practices of appropriation, occupation, inhabitance and stewardship. Property practices express a territorial claim around individual or group access, control and use. These practices may be modest and hidden-in-plain-sight, such as a resident screening their private balcony, installing security cameras or issuing instructions to children forbidding them scootering in the condo lobby. These property claims need not mirror legal entitlements and might contravene regulation such as when a condo resident 'steals' a co-resident's private parking bay. Property practices can be everyday and routine such as ritualized garden maintenance which conveys community propriety and pride of ownership (Blomley 2013) or practical, such as negotiations between residents to upgrade their lift system or revive a neglected shared space. Other performances are representational, even intentionally persuasive, intended to convince others of the ongoing validity of that claim (Rose 1994; Blomley 2004a) such as a resident's insistence on hanging laundry to dry on their balcony in defiance of by-laws. Although tempting to see property as either strictly public or strictly private, when property is understood as 'fluid practices rather than fixed in zones', qualities associated with private interests such as privacy and autonomy entangle with qualities associated with other-regarding or 'proprietarian' interests (Blomley 2005b: 656).

Property, moreover, is a relational effect that entangles us in property relations with others, who may have greater or fewer entitlements (Blomley 2020). Put differently, property organizes hierarchical relations between people with regards to the access and use of valuable resources, such as land, conjoining us with others in interdependencies of relative vulnerability and privilege, such as the asymmetrical relationship between a landlord/owner and a renter (Bhandar 2018; Bonds 2019; Blomley 2020). Homeowners may view their home-as-castle as a 'zone of autonomy', but it is better understood as a zone of 'power and conditional relationality' with others beyond their castle walls (Blomley 2020: 40). In this transactional landscape – which Blomley (2020) terms 'property space' – property does things: it positions subjects in relations with each other, adjudicates how they interact and on what terms and communicates powerful messages to them about what property means. This transactional landscape or property space only stabilizes or 'holds up' some relations, that empower only some interests (Keenan 2015).

Property engineers this 'holding up' through 'territorialised expressions of law' (Blomley 2020) or, put another way, through the interlocking workings of both law and territory. Law, for its part, organizes 'property's relationality and power' over the access and use of any valued resource, such as land (Blomley 2020: 40). Law 'draws lines, constructs insides and outsides, assigns legal meanings to lines, and attaches legal consequences to crossing them' (Delaney 2015: 99). Beyond its institutionalized expressions and official acts such as property titles and condo by-laws, formal law is imbricated with a culture of legality that involves normative ideas and frameworks, such as the conviction that homeownership bestows full control, for instance. Legal geographers and socio-legal scholars recognize that everyday understandings and experiences of regulation and coercion are grounded not strictly in 'the letter of the law'. Rather they observe how the law is present in how we perceive the law and the assumptions we make about it, as well as other normative systems and frameworks with and through which the social world is made (Ewick and Silbey 1998: 35). Socio-legal scholars term this 'legal consciousness' which Merry (1990: 5) defines as 'the way people conceive of the "natural" and normal way of doing things, their habitual patterns of talk and action and their common-sense understanding of the world'. From this vantage point, property law and practice are not, therefore, simply imposed and legitimized through enforcement. Instead, property is 'continuously re-created and maintained by social interaction' (Blandy and Sibley 2010: 278) in a socio-legal world through diverse, modest and mundane practices involving people, things, ideas and actions at various scales and sites (Blomley 2004a; Blandy et al 2020).

Helpful in thinking about these workings of law is geographer Tim Cresswell's notion of a 'normative landscape'. Cresswell (1996: 8–9) writes that the norms and expectations governing what belongs and what does not in a given space help structure a normative landscape, whereby 'ideas about what is right, just and appropriate are transmitted through space and place'. The generic garden fence, for instance, as one ubiquitous domestic property performance, 'works' because it 'cites' many other familiar barriers, hedges and numerous other signifiers and markers of ownership and entitlement (its citational function) and aligns with prevailing ideals associated with private property, homemaking and neighbouring, including expectations of privacy (Blomley 2004a). Examining the workings of law 'on the ground' in residential contexts, socio-legal scholarship further describes how de facto rules operate above and beyond the law. For instance, Blandy (2013: 167) illustrates how co-housing residents decide over time *not* to enforce rules banning barbecues or hanging out washing since most residents wish to barbecue and air-dry their laundry. Blandy and colleagues (2018: 101) argue that over time 'de facto rules become established and may be treated as binding by new owners'. Political economist Elinor Ostrom's notion of 'working rules' helps explain this slippage between law and the property relationship *in situ*. Working rules are self-generated norms that 'assign de facto rights and duties that are contrary to the de jure right and duties' (Blandy 2013: 165) and 'are not rigid but evolve responsively to the spatial, temporal and lived dimensions of property in land' (Blandy et al 2018: 85–6). Geographer Hanna Hilbrandt's (2019; 2021) nuancing of the notion of 'obedience' to regulation as neither something simply demanded and enforced by authority nor something that agentic actors simply submit to is also helpful in considering how law works *in situ*. Through a detailed study of the everyday workings of allotment gardens in Berlin, Hilbrandt first captures how gardeners self-regulate their transgressions, to a degree. This *self-regulation* keeps officials tasked with governing the allotments off-site and on side thereby enabling gardeners to 'create a realm of acceptable tolerance within which they can get away with other offences'; it opens up some 'room to manoeuvre' in which gardeners may contravene the law in other small ways (Hilbrandt 2019: 361). Meanwhile, gardeners also engage in 'tempting pretence': they 'fake' compliance with regulation, such as erecting a tent over an illegally constructed dwelling in anticipation of an inspection. Officials are not duped but the gardeners' pretence of compliance enables officials concerned with their own workload to more readily turn a blind eye. Gardeners' self-regulation and their pretence of compliance affords them some discretion in the self-management of their allotments.

This 'room to manoeuvre' or 'wriggle room' is not limitless however, since formal law and norms interconnect, as socio-legal scholars emphasize. Blandy, Bright and Nield (2018: 102) specify that informal rules are formulated 'in the shadow of the law, which they know they can fall back on if informality doesn't work'.[9] Helping explain this 'shadow' in action, Hilbrandt identifies two mechanisms whereby formal regulation is drawn upon to contain the agency of others. First, by 'snitching', gardeners push officials to police transgressions they may previously have overlooked. Snitching suggests how subjects draw upon formal power, in this case of the officials, to constrain the agency of other gardeners. Snitching also suggests how local norms governing what is appropriate and proper take shape on the ground as subjects set limits around the transgressions they deem so inappropriate as to be reportable. Boundary work, as a second mechanism, likewise brings to the fore how opportunities for discretionary practices are shut down or closed off. However, unlike snitching, boundary work points to the way a local majority of gardeners can close off others' 'wriggle room' by designating which practices are appropriate and which are not, through 'the *collective* work of demarcating social boundaries between locally accepted and unaccepted conduct' (Hilbrandt 2019: 362, emphasis added). These various insights into the workings of law *in situ* guide my thinking about the condo as a regulated propertied landscape in which the legitimacy or otherwise of property practices is socially and situationally produced in everyday condo living through an iterative evaluative process between condo stakeholders over appropriate property practices. These various insights also guide my thinking about condo residents as agentic subjects with some capacity to shape the workings of law within the condo but outside of its formal governance structures, including through snitching and boundary work.

These workings of law interlock with the workings of territory to stabilize certain property relations. The workings of territory, for their part, provide a strategic resource for defining, inscribing and stabilizing property's hierarchical relations (Delaney 2010; Blomley 2016b). Sack (1985: Chapter 2) notes how territory assists property in three key ways. First, spatial classifications make clear what is '"ours" and "not ours" according to their location in space' (Sack 1985: 58–9) such that a territorial claim exerted over a place (for example a room or a courtyard) alleviates the need to stipulate 'an extensive list of objects governed by property rules [... instead] territory presumptively pre-assigns ownership over all objects contained within it' (Blomley 2016a: 597). Second, territory helps property by communicating these classifications to others such that others infer an intention to use, occupy and take ownership, be that through possessive signage (for example 'Keep

[9] Blandy, Bright and Nield (2018: 102, emphasis added) explain this connection with reference to the critique of Ellickson, whose influential empirical study of Montana's cattle ranchers highlighted how their work was governed by their local norms rather than the law, but yet failed to consider the extent to which the rules were informed by ranchers' status as landowners, such that 'they are creating their own rules *in the shadow of the law*, which they know they can fall back on if informality doesn't work'.

out!') or border-marking practices. Third, territory serves an enforcement function that reflects territory's exclusionary impulses. Territory, by dint of its ability to classify, communicate and control in these ways, subtends and structures hierarchical social relations, and propertied landscapes subsequently reflect (and reproduce) the hierarchical social ordering of vulnerability and privilege that property engineers (Blomley 2020). Territoriality need not mirror formal property entitlements but will instead depend on and reflect how subjects interact with and revise formal property relations. Territorial complexity and contestation is likely, with a shared courtyard, for instance 'open to shades of appropriation and imbricated claims' (Kärrholm 2007: 441–2, 447).[10] Borders are meanwhile articulated through practices and provide an essential 'legal spatiality ... embedded in and productive of dense relational geographies (normative, practical, visual, complex, social, political, and so on)' (Blomley 2016b: 252). Brighenti's (2010) notion of the boundary as an 'interaction device' usefully emphasizes how boundaries actively assist in organizing property relations.

Bringing together these workings of law and territory, the propertied space of the high-rise condo is understood as assembled and maintained not through some fixed quality of physical space nor through the enforcement of restrictions alone but rather through the dense alignment of a wide array of legal and territorial resources, under specific social relational contexts (Blomley 2016a; 2020). In the condo tower, the expectation is that territorial claims will be accepted where they reflect unspoken rules of conduct and normative understandings about how a space *should* be used (that is, local working rules) or when they reference or imitate other socially recognized proprietary practices. An additional expectation is that subjectivities, such as the 'good' or 'bad' condo neighbour, will emerge as residents practise property. In suburban settings, for instance, the 'good' neighbour emerges *through* the act of fence-building, maintaining, policing and surveilling, not before or after; namely, one's willingness to erect and maintain a fence signals one's observance with social propriety (Blomley 2013: 23–4). As this previews, how well the condo borders function as interaction devices matters for the construction of the 'good' condo neighbour.

[10] At this point, property and territory may appear indistinguishable from each other. So strong is the association of property with territory that many would conceive of territory as property itself and struggle to treat them as conceptually discrete. However, recall that property is not an object of ownership but rather a set of relations between people with regards to a valuable resource. Territory, on the other hand, is produced and reproduced through everyday property practices: it is 'a bounded social space that inscribes powerful meanings – in particular relating to spatial access or exclusion – onto defined segments of the world' (Blomley 2016a: 594).

But how do condo residents make sense of and navigate the high-rise condo's propertied spaces? Despite interest in condominium, relatively little is known about how residents interact with and revise the territorial relations inscribed in its legal architectures. Equally, despite rich accounts of formal condo governance, relatively little is known about its local working rules – the etiquette, norms and tacit codes of conduct that regulate condo residents' home lives – how these informal rules play out territorially in the condo's private and shared spaces and how residents' tenure status figures in these territorial dynamics. On the one hand, the sharing of common property, whether mail rooms or swimming pools, has long been presumed to promote 'community' through chance encounters and social interactions (McKenzie 2011: 37; Lippert 2019: 5). However, early research on common interest communities which emphasized renters' disenfranchisement from formal governance and their status as 'illegitimate' residents (for example Barton and Silverman 1994) and newer condo research that emphasizes 'internal forms of inequality' with tenure its fault line (Lippert 2019: 13), speak of a potential politics of belonging within the tower. A property perspective promises to account for the socio-territorial dynamics of condo living – noting these have rarely been explored from residents' perspectives, and never systematically from the renter's – including by foregrounding how various legal and territorial technologies function as important classifying devices.

Examining the condo home

This book approaches the condo tower as an inhabitated propertied landscape. From within my disciplinary home in urban geography and housing studies this conceptual move raises further questions. How do condo residents understand and practise property in the condo tower? And how do these understandings and practices of property inform condo residents' homemaking? The first of these questions requires observing property's everyday presence in the condo tower and calls for an analysis of residents' perceptions and practices of property. Empirically, this requires attending to how residents narrate and navigate territoriality and border-maintenance in the condo tower and it requires attending to the various things through which property is mediated, namely the workings of law and territory. In considering law, while the reflex is perhaps to think strictly in terms of the formal regulations that govern residents' home lives, property scholarship and socio-legal studies insist on the importance of everyday understandings of law rather than the letter of the law per se. A focus on law therefore involves consideration of how residents understand by-laws but also informal small 'l' law, including the tacit codes of conduct and shared expectations that govern condo living. Given the inherently social nature of property, engaging with the local working rules that surround condo neighbouring is important, especially given the residential proximities and densities of the tower typology. By design, then, an intentional omission of this book is a systematic focus on formal condo governance and the machinations of OCs – the most extensively studied dimensions of condo living – though residents' perceptions of both by-laws and building managers' implementation of these do feature. In considering territory, the reflex again is to think strictly in terms of residents' formal property titles and their legal entitlements to use and access different areas of the condo building. However, sensitivity to everyday property encourages a focus on residents' perceptions of territoriality and border-management in the context of local designs and materialities.

The second question requires understanding how residents' perceptions and practices of property then inform their homemaking. Sensitizing the analytics of home to property requires, in the first instance, a stronger conceptual grip on the way property and home interrelate. Chapter 2 takes on that task: it brings geographic understandings of home into conversation with understandings of everyday property reviewed earlier and sets out a conceptual framework for home in propertied space (Nethercote forthcoming). This framework honours recognized attributes, thematics and understandings of home in geography rather than seeking any radical departures, yet it reinvigorates the critical geographies of home by asking us to consider what propertied space does to homemaking. Of note, this framework posits *home as dominion* which includes notions of autonomy, sovereignty and freedom that pervade the geographical home literature, but adds to these an emphasis on *territorial* control associated with property. And it posits *home as belonging*, emphasizing both the intimate subject-object relationship typically framed in terms of feelings of being 'at home' and a part-whole relationship, which emphasizes notions of propriety and a politics of belonging.

Some key conceptual moves associated with my approach to home are previewed for clarity. First, home is understood as something *practised*. Home involves sedimented layers of meaning, values and ideologies that accrete over our basic need for shelter (Ronald 2008; Atkinson and Jacobs 2016). Home is inherently complex: a site with both material and experiential dimensions, and something made through everyday socio-material practices (Mallett 2004; Blunt and Dowling 2006). A performative ontology understands these practices of home as the binding of social relations, identities and materialities, that can anchor a sense of belonging, constitute and perform selfhood (Jacobs and Smith 2008: 515, 518) and configure individual and collective identities (Lloyd and Vasta 2017: 4), thereby enabling certain subjectivities to emerge (for example the 'bad' tenant: Power and Gillon 2020). Home is meanwhile never a fait accompli but rather an ongoing process of making and remaking in which home may be difficult to achieve and emotionally and physically taxing, even fraught, to sustain and forever susceptible to change (Blunt and Dowling 2006). Second, homemaking is understood as performances practised within, and circumscribed by, propertied space. As subjects move around propertied landscapes they come up against the workings of law and territory which open up and close off their capacity for homemaking. A property-sensitive approach to home attends to how these territorialized expressions of law make and unmake the condo tower as home. Third, while interest lies in understanding how condo property informs homemaking, residents' propertied ideas, ideals and expectations of home are understood to inform how they perceive and practise property too. Residents bring into the condo particular propertied imaginaries of home, such as engrained notions of control and autonomy encapsulated in tropes such as 'a man's home is his castle'. A detailed analysis of high-rise condo homemaking is advanced by drawing together insights into residents' perceptions and practices of property with evidence of how this (unevenly) opens up and closes off opportunities for different residents to make the high-rise condo home. Again, by design then, another intentional omission of this book is a focus on condo residents' homemaking *beyond* the condo, which, while clearly important, sits beyond my scope.

This book takes on this exploration of the high-rise condo home in Australia, and Melbourne and Perth specifically. The rise of vertical living in urban Australia marks a critical juncture in each city's urban growth. For although Australia helped pioneer the condominium system, unrelenting suburban sprawl largely confined this legal architecture to low-rise flats and townhouse complexes during the 20th century. Only since the turn of the century have Australian cities careered upwards in earnest, their urban morphology dramatically transforming. More than ever before, high-rise housing crams city blocks at unprecedented densities and heights. Australia now boasts incredible rates of skyscrapers per capita for such a highly suburbanised nation after becoming a global frontrunner outside of Asia in condo development. Like cities further afield, this vertical expansion has been ushered in under market-led compact city planning directives (Gleeson 2008; Nethercote 2018). Especially in the wake of the 2007/08 global financial crisis, Perth and Melbourne witnessed a significant proliferation of new high-rise condo development (Nethercote 2019). Australian high-rise condo living was still relatively novel then, especially by international standards, and has rarely been subject to systematic in-depth analysis, despite growing interest within and outside the academy. The Australian case has international relevance for urban scholarship, including because urban Australia's vertical expansion has unfolded amid conditions that similarly trouble verticalizing cities in other so-called advanced homeownership societies, such as the UK and US. One key to understanding the political economies of this contemporary condo development, which Chapter 1 reviews in detail, is a rise in condo investors and their proxies, condo renters. In Australian cities, as elsewhere, rising rates of renting sit in tension with enduring socio-political homeownership ideologies (Ronald 2008), as the 'dream' of homeownership is delayed, unattainable or 'traded off' for locational amenity and flexibility (Pawson et al 2017) and where renters now include growing shares of low- *and* high(er)-income households (Hulse et al 2018a; 2018b). These private renters endure short leases on often under-maintained properties, uncapped rents and weak tenant protections and must weigh up housing cost pressures against the threat of dislocation from well-serviced, job-rich urban locations with all the socio-spatial disadvantages that entails.

This book's empirical core derives from data collected between 2017 and 2019 under the auspices of an Australian Research Council funded project on apartment development and high-rise living.[11] *Project HOME: Housing Outcomes Metrics and Evaluation* sought to evaluate the design quality of contemporary apartments across Melbourne, Perth, Barcelona and London using interdisciplinary methods. My work on this project as a postdoctoral researcher provided the impetus for this book, which builds on my post-PhD interest in high-rise development and the lived experience of housing. Using a different dataset, I have written previously about the Australian lived experience (Nethercote and Horne 2016; Nethercote 2017) and political economies (Nethercote 2018; 2019) of vertical urbanization. This book does not rehearse those earlier explorations but rather attempts to break new ground in geographic understandings of the practices of condo property and condo homes and homemaking. This book is by no stretch of the imagination a comprehensive account of Project HOME's findings, though my analysis and conclusions speak directly to the substandard quality of Australian condo stock delivered in the wake of the 2008/09 global financial crisis. Rather, my analysis centres on a small subsection of project data: some 98 semi-structured interviews undertaken with condo residents living in Perth and Melbourne, as part of the Australian case studies. These interviews probed residents' everyday geographies and socio-material routines of apartment living through questions pertaining to architectural design and features, how residents used their private unit, their balconies and their shared amenities. Questions were also asked about residents' habitual domestic practices from laundering and cooking to socializing

[11] The term 'apartment' is used in the Australian context to denote both four-storey-plus higher-density residential developments and the units within them. This terms does not specify an ownership structure and so while the majority of these dwellings *are* private and delivered under condominium (strata title), this categorization, as reflected in the Australian Bureau of Statistics (ABS) data, would also include units in higher-density social housing and public housing. Chapter 1 provides further details on how 'apartments' are defined in Australia and its significance for local condo data and research.

and relaxing and about residents' expectations and everyday experiences living in their condo building. Interviews also included broader questions about residents' housing 'careers', plans and aspirations, and social/family and household contexts. Property was not a focus of Project HOME but quickly emerged during my data analysis. Indeed, property's tendency to appear natural and predetermined on account of the ownership model, complicates researchers' attempts to 'get at the "everyday" experiences of the "layperson" relating to property', even in fieldwork dedicated to this task (Blomley 2016b: 230). Blomley (2016b) recommends overcoming these difficulties by focusing on how people conceive of 'the normal ways of doing things, their habitual patterns of talk and action, and their common-sense understandings of the world' (Merry 1990: 5). For these very reasons, the Project HOME interviews were inadvertently sensitive to how residents interpreted and performed property. Additionally, because interviews were undertaken with multiple unrelated residents in each building, the dataset provided diverse perspectives through which to understand how residents perceived and practised property within a single condo building. The Appendix provides additional information on Project HOME and Chapter 2 provides further information on this dataset and associated fieldwork.

Melbourne and Perth are not deployed as comparative cases in the traditional sense in this analysis. Rather, as urban geographer Jennifer Robinson (2016a; 2016b: 6) advocates, they are used in the sense of 'thinking (cities) through elsewhere'. As Robinson argues, this approach opens up a revised comparative imagination that enables the experiences identified within one urban case to be drawn into conversation with other instances, in other cities, to better understand the complexity and diversity of urban life, including divergent and shared dynamics and outcomes. The cities in question, too, are not the 'usual suspects' of urban scholarship, but rather 'ordinary' cities, as Robinson (2006) also advocates. In celebrating urban diversity, such approaches also attract critiques of particularism with the risk of sliding into 'endless empirical accounts of [this] diversity, all of which may be fascinating in their own right, but which fail to … theorise back from empirical cases' (Lees 2018: 56). Thinking and theorizing between cases is essential, and so, in taking property and homemaking practices in everyday condo living as the comparator, this account embraces diversity but also does not ignore sameness where it exists (Lees 2018: 58). In this way, this book it approaches condo property and condo homemaking as locally distinct phenomena, but its approach allows for theorizations that can contribute to broader understandings of everyday property and homemaking in high-rise housing, especially but not exclusively where vertical expansion is underpinned by condominium's legal architectures or analogous legal forms.

About this book

This book argues the proliferation of high-rise condominium housing is reconfiguring home in verticalizing cities. It shows how territorialized expressions of law configure how residents make their home in everyday condo living.[12] This reconfiguration harbours two risks that threaten to unmake the condo home, especially where high-rise design and construction quality are subpar. Demanding local working rules and a distinct set of territorial constraints make satisfying private interests more difficult and threaten to undermine the condo home, and the condo *home as dominion* especially. Meanwhile, manifold property practices assist in constructing condo renters as risky and unruly condo subjects and these similarly threaten to undermine the condo home for all residents, and the condo *home as belonging* especially. *Inside High-Rise Housing* urges attention be paid to these risks as cities grow taller and as condominium and other analogous legal architectures restructure the ownership of large swathes of urban land.

The combined workings of territory and law in everyday condo living are reconfiguring urban homemaking. The *workings of territory* in the condo are characterized by a series of territorial constraints that include territorial incursions into their private units, annexations of shared spaces and circulation frictions in shared infrastructures, as the analysis details. The *workings of law* in the condo involve not only private regulations but also extensive local working rules. These unspoken rules of conduct define how the condo's home spaces ought to be used in everyday condo living and thereby regulate appropriate relations and practices of neighbouring, neighbourliness and homemaking over and above the formal rules and restrictions typically foregrounded by studies of formal condo governance. These workings of law and territory choreograph an intensive form of volumetric neighbouring in everyday condo living.[13] In terms of territory, volumetric neighbouring involves diverse, dispersed and digitized geographies of physical contact and social encounter between co-residents, whose interdependencies are extensive and formalized. Everyday condo living involves intensive geographies of physical

[12] Everyday condo living refers to the day-to-day socio-material dynamics of condo living as conditioned by high-rise condominium's legal and built architectures under contemporary condoization, the latter a term I define in Chapter 1.

[13] Contrasts with 'suburban' neighbouring – neighbouring in low-rise, low-density housing typologies rather than in suburban locations per se – risk sliding into an oversimplification and downplaying how much urban neighbouring shares in common, especially given that a systematic comparison lies well beyond my scope. These reservations notwithstanding, such contrasts *are* helpful inasmuch as they accentuate what is distinct about volumetric neighbouring so as to clarify why the expectations of volumetric neighbouring can be unreasonably demanding, especially in the context of poor design and build quality.

contact between adjoining condo units and physical proximity between adjacent neighbours, including overhead and underfoot. Yet these geographies often coincide with comparably weak geographies of social encounter and connection, including because the private unit's borders function poorly as zones of neighbouring contact, with face-to-face encounters relatively uncommon, including between adjacent residents. These geographies of contact and encounter are meanwhile heavily mediated by third-party digital security. The private unit's three-dimensional or volumetric borders are moreover relatively illegible, ambiguous and often highly pervious too which further complicates how smoothly these boundaries operate as interaction devices for regulating property relations between neighbours. Condo residents subsequently navigate a set of socio-territorial negotiations mostly 'in the dark', absent much face-to-face social interaction or rapport with co-residents. The condo's non-contiguous borders require that residents engage in collective boundary management, such as at building entrances for instance, to ensure these borders exclude 'outsiders' as expected. Shared spaces meanwhile involve far more territorial complexity, diversity and ambiguity than conceptual models of condominium capture and these tend not to function as zones of social connections, as typically presumed. Instead, residents rely on various digital communication technologies, such as condo building Facebook groups, which can give rise to uneven digital geographies of social connection in everyday condo living as we shall see.

In terms of law, volumetric neighbouring involves intensive and extensive tacit codes of social conduct that govern everyday condo living above and beyond formal private restrictions. These local working rules are locally contingent. The rules of engagement for everyday condo living are established in each condo building through a local interplay between residents' traditional propertied expectations of home, the contingencies of local building designs, materialities and spatialities and residents' understandings of by-laws and observations of their everyday enforcement. These informal rules govern how residents practise property in the condo tower: they shape how residents navigate and negotiate access and use of shared and private home spaces and they shape how residents interpret co-residents' property practices. Local working rules, moreover, reflect the way condo property come 'freighted' with social expectations and obligations to others. Residents understand these local working rules both in terms of 'doing the right thing' and as a fear of being shunned for nonconformity. Residents thus question and judge proprietorial claims on normative grounds: does a shoe rack or a doormat belong in the shared hallway? Should the kids' scooters be left by the front entrance? Given the intensive geographies of volumetric neighbouring, local working rules extensively govern everyday condo living including the sights, smells, sounds and materialities of condo homemaking, even in residents' private units.

These workings of law and of territory converge in everyday condo living as 'territorialised expressions of law' (Blomley 2020) that circumscribe condo homemaking. In the context of complex and intensive volumetric neighbouring geographies, condo residents must reconcile their private homemaking interests with local codes of conduct as they navigate their private and shared home spaces. In everyday condo living, this requires repeated and complex socio-territorial mediations which, this book argues, reconfigure homemaking in verticalizing cities. Residents do not act singularly in self-interested individualistic ways as they make the condo home. In navigating these socio-territorial dynamics, residents recognize collaborative and other-regarding property practices as essential to making the condo building 'work' as a shared home space. To be sure, residents have entered the condo with traditional propertied expectations of their condo home, and they practise property in self-regarding ways to satisfy their own private interests, such as for privacy. Yet whether motivated by a sense of reciprocity or a sense of social obligation, residents retain other-regarding concerns, including for each other's privacy and peace-and-quiet, for instance. Evidence of residents' other-regarding concerns nuances claims that the distinct socio-spatial, governance and financial interdependencies that exist between condo residents give rise to contractualized and less socially inflected neighbouring relations (for example Power 2015). The convergence of the workings of law and territory in everyday condo living need not be overly burdensome for residents nor troublesome for the condo home. These mediations may only require that residents make slight adaptations that are relatively inconsequential to their homemaking, such as prompting the resident who wishes to leave their blinds up to enjoy the view to partially draw them, aware of their neighbours' lines of sight and social expectations surrounding visual privacy. However, on occasion, mediations involve far more compromise or tolerance, and this can jeopardize the making of the condo home.

The way these territorialized expressions of law circumscribe homemaking in everyday condo living harbours two potential risks that threaten to unmake the condo home. The first risk is to the condo *home as dominion* and arises as local working rules governing condo property practices together with myriad territorial constraints (which are delineated later), significantly curtail residents' pursuit of their private interests as they seek to make the condo home. Especially where condo design and workmanship are subpar, residents find satisfying private interests while also remaining compliant with local working rules difficult and sometimes near impossible. Where residents' private interests become incompatible with local expectations, residents find neighbouring standards are more difficult to adhere to and breaches become more likely. At the same time, as co-residents breach formal or informal rules, this too can undermine residents' homemaking, including by creating perceived nuisances. Residents meanwhile interpret various territorial constraints they come up against in diverse, contextualized and sometimes conflicting ways and these can sometimes encourage a territorial apathy that sees residents disengage and even physically withdraw from their shared home spaces, notwithstanding their legal entitlements. Navigating homemaking in this context challenges residents' traditional propertied expectations of control, autonomy, security and their sense of ownership.

A second risk is to the condo *home as belonging* and arises as property practices are (mis)interpreted in ways that contribute to the subjectification of renters as undesirable condo residents. Especially in the absence of social interaction and connection between co-residents, residents interpret territorial claims and territorial tensions as deriving from co-residents' unthinking or selfish acts. Recall that the private renter is already cast as a flawed consumer by dint of their consumption 'choices' under enduring socio-political homeownership ideologies (Ronald 2008) and the prevailing 'paradigm of propertied citizenship' (Roy 2003) and that, within the condo specifically, the condo renter is moreover formally disenfranchised and delegitimized by dint of condominium's legal architectures. The subjectification of the condo renter in everyday condo living stands to reproduce these prevailing pathologies surrounding renters, such that the condo renter risks being cast not just as an illegitimate condo resident but as an unruly and risky co-resident too. Although this subjectification process involves contradictions and inconsistencies, condo renters risk hostility, discrimination and scapegoating in everyday condo living as they are blamed for various inconveniences, incursions and property breaches. This stigmatization and these exclusionary dynamics further risk hardening and compounding prevailing tenure-based power asymmetries within the condo tower by reproducing a hierarchical social ordering in which renters are demoted, further reinforcing owners and renters' uneven positioning. These socio-spatial dynamics threaten to undermine all condo residents' capacity to feel 'at home' and part of their condo's 'community'.

The aforementioned risks to condo homemaking are not new nor necessarily unique to high-rise condo living. Some comparable local working rules and socio-territorial frictions likely circumscribe homemaking in lower-rise condominium and other common interest communities too, such as gated communities. However, in increasingly dense, large and tall contemporary condo developments, such as those constructed in Australia in the aftermath of the 2007/08 global financial crisis, these risks are deemed more likely and their threat to homemaking likely more extensive and more acute. The political economies of contemporary high-rise condo development in Perth and Melbourne at that juncture trended heavily towards producing 'investor grade' densely packed, small condo units in large, poorly designed and poorly constructed towers, some with extensive building defects, as Chapter 1 details. In these specific residential settings, local working rules become intensive and extensive, and yet the content of these working rules is also oftentimes ambiguous and unsettled – after all, what type of conduct is appropriate when private domestic activities are so readily overheard by co-residents through poorly soundproofed walls, for instance? Additionally, working rules that might elsewhere be relatively well-established appear somewhat unsettled or unfamiliar, perhaps on account of Australia's relatively embryonic tradition of private high-rise living and some residents' subsequent inexperience with condo living.[14] Meanwhile, the prolific activity of property investors in this new high-rise housing stock has shifted the tenure profile of condo homes further away from condominium's conceptual ideals. With disproportionate shares of city renters entering Australian condos, the condo model of a 'community of owners' becomes ever more tenuous. High-rise condo homemaking is therefore expected to be particularly at risk, as these factors make territorial incursions and frictions likely more frequent and more invasive, and they make residents' private interests more difficult to reconcile with local working rules.

These arguments are pertinent to understanding the practices of property and home in high-rise housing in other jurisdictions beyond Melbourne and Perth. There are striking similarities in how Melbourne and Perth residents practise property in everyday condo living, notwithstanding the local contingencies of condoization in each city. This suggests the socio-territorial dynamics and risks surrounding condo homemaking may also feature in high-rise living further afield, especially where condoization has similarly produced subpar condo stock and condo renting is on the rise. On this basis, these arguments are relevant to understanding condo living in other Australian cities such as Sydney and Brisbane where condoization has similarly surged. These arguments are likely relevant to jurisdictions abroad too where condominium and analogous forms of high-rise housing has proliferated over the past decade or so and where the market share of the private rental sector is comparably significant and/or increasing too (Hulse et al 2018a). This includes other advanced liberal economies including the United States and Canada and, in the UK, some similar dynamics

[14] Most condo residents interviewed in Perth and many in Melbourne had previously lived in detached housing, for instance. Meanwhile the cultural diversity of Australia's condo residents (see Chapter 1 for overview and Chapter 2 for dataset details) may also inform differences in residents' housing and homemaking expectations. Note too, however, that despite the focus on local working rules, there is no suggestion that 'Australian' culture is in any way singular. On the other hand, and despite a relatively large dataset, without decent clusters of a particular demographic indicator, such as migrants' country of origin, there is inadequate data upon which to make definitive statements associated with any of these demographic variables.

might be expected given the steep growth in private high-rise residential development (Craggs 2018; Nethercote 2018). On the other hand, in England for instance, pending expansion of commonhold which is roughly analogous with condominium title, most flat owners are leaseholders and as such are not governed by condominium by-laws or their equivalent (see Easthope 2019). Given the interaction identified between by-laws and the formation of local working rules, which the concluding chapter specifies, further work is warranted to understand how local working rules emerge in such contexts. Conversely, some aspects of these arguments may be less relevant to jurisdictions where private high-rise housing stock is comparably better designed and well maintained since territorial constraints may be less acute; where traditions of high-rise/density living are well entrenched since local working rules may be more settled and residents more habituated with compliance; or where propertied expectations of home are more diversified and normative homemaking ideals relatively less rigid. Nevertheless, various insights into how residents practise condo property and how the high-rise home is made and unmade are likely broadly relevant to understanding vertical homemaking in the UK, Europe and other regions, such as Asia, South America and beyond.

Making the condo home

This book breaks new ground in urban geography. At a time when many cities are rapidly verticalizing it delivers a first and much-needed systematic account of homemaking in the high-rise condo. Empirically, its granular focus on homemaking and its broad focus on the tower (the private unit *and* shared amenity and infrastructures) assists in advancing an emergent international literature on the lived experience of contemporary (private) high-rise housing. Its property-sensitive analysis, which foregrounds the unappreciated role of informal working rules nuances the role of private regulation and formalized collective responsibilities in circumscribing condo residents' homemaking by highlighting how informal working rules and a set of socio-territorial dynamics circumscribe condo homemaking. The focus on Australian high-rise living provides a new perspective beyond the usual global cities that feature in much urban geography scholarship, while retaining broad international relevance for reasons just outlined. The analysis complements the broader geographic project that seeks to understand the imaginaries, perceptions, geographies and politics of urban density (for example McFarlane 2016) and, for urban geography's verticality agenda in particular, the three-dimensional rendering of everyday high-rise life contributes a major case study for understanding 'ordinary' vertical urbanisms (Nethercote and Horne 2016). This book includes novel first-hand accounts of the micro-scale impacts of contemporary vertical urbanization, including capturing the sometimes substantive personal impact of short-term letting and poor residential design and construction quality.

In terms of theory, the approach reinvigorates scholarship on the critical geographies of home by opening up the analytic terrain of home to property – a long-standing 'elephant in the room' (Blomley 2016b: 224). The approach innovates by taking seriously the legal fabrication of home, and specifically the ways the domestic domain is 'legally constituted and reconstituted' and 'legally differentiated' from other homes (Delaney 2015: 97–8). A conceptual contribution flows from this: a property-sensitive conceptual framework for home is developed that is distinguished from existing schemas, including by its centring of home *as dominion* and *as belonging*. This property-sensitive approach to home is timely given the increasingly diverse, complex and precarious legal and sublegal relations that entangle urban residents' access and use of home spaces and will likely have purchase for geographic explorations of home that seek to be more responsive to property, including its lived realities (for expanded discussion see Nethercote forthcoming).

The analysis newly pinpoints how the subjectification of renters is realized through property practices in everyday condo living. To be clear, a wide-ranging scholarship across law, public administration, political science and beyond has long identified the renter in common interest communities as disenfranchised and at risk of fraught reception and discriminatory treatment, including in condominium specifically. This account captures how relations of vulnerability manifest in and are perpetuated through territorialized expressions of law in everyday condo living. The analysis identifies that these vulnerabilities are not the result of the condo renter's formal disenfranchisement alone, however exclusionary those formal governance arrangements may be. The analysis extends Lippert's (2019) insightful account of the construction of the condo renter subject by foregrounding the importance of high-rise socio-territorial dynamics and the importance of little 'l' law in the form of local working rules in shaping everyday condo living, together with prevailing social pathologies surrounding renting. This book progresses understandings of the sway of socio-political housing consumption ideals in condo homemaking. In this, it corroborates prior accounts of vertical families' experiences of high-rise living (for example Kerr et al 2018) but extends these insights to other condo demographics and explains these with a more explicit focus on the forces of law and territory. This provides additional insights into associated intersectional dynamics by showing how renter prejudice entwines with other biases including towards youths.

This account of the plight of the condo renter represents a key instalment in the story of asymmetrical property relations inherent in contemporary urban housing systems beyond the familiar antagonisms in the tenant-landlord relationship and renters' vulnerability to radical processes of eviction and dispossession (Aalbers and Christophers 2014: 380; Blomley 2020). Shining the light on property practices nuances prior findings that condo resident relations trend toward being legalistic and depersonalized and in particular advances emergent arguments about the critical role of local condo design and materiality in structuring social relations within the condo (Power 2015). By providing a new building-scale case study of private renter/owner relations, this book contributes to the broader scholarship on renter stigmatization, which tends to make its observations from the neighbourhood- or estate-scale or focus on the dynamics between social renters and owners in mixed tenure housing developments. For housing studies, this book provides fresh evidence of the lived realities of contemporary private renting within condominium developments. This case is of value to macro-level discussions on the inequalities between tenure types under current institutional arrangements and to emergent 'tenure complexity' debates that posit conventional tenure categories as increasingly inadequate 'fault lines' for specifying contemporary housing experiences (Hulse 2008; Wegmann et al 2017; Murie 2019: np; Arundel and Ronald 2020).[15] For critical urban geography, this account of the condo renter broadens understandings of the social dynamics within private residential communities by foregrounding the distinct geographies of contact and social encounter that circumscribe everyday condo living. By showing these 'insider' social dynamics as more complex and diverse than often assumed, this account complicates the prevailing emphasis on vexed insider/outsider dynamics in accounts of private residential communities.

By virtue of its property analytic, this book also makes a secondary empirical and conceptual contribution to legal geography and socio-legal studies. It provides the first in-depth account of the everyday legal geographies of condominium and of the high-rise condo as a propertied landscape, to my knowledge. In so doing, the book's remit directly responds to calls to advance socio-legal and legal geography scholarship on property in everyday life into under-researched urban spaces (Braverman et al 2014). Its focus on property in condominium diversifies legal geography's remit to include collective private ownership thereby broadening its routine focus on either individual private property, such as single-family homes and private gardens, or public property, such as public streets and parks. Its insights complement emergent critical socio-legal inquiry into hybrid property forms

[15] As Murie (2019: np, emphasis added) argues, based on the UK housing system, 'there have been significant changes in housing tenure … key fault lines are *within* tenures rather than *between* them' and that this requires reflection on those 'households and processes that remain invisible to tenure-based analysis'. This book highlights condo renting as a case in point.

and multi-owned housing as forwarded by legal scholars Douglas Harris, Dave Cowan, Sarah Blandy, Susan Bright, Sarah Nield and others. Through its focus on everyday perceptions and practices of property, the analysis cracks open condominium's private property 'shell' and begins to reveal the messy *in situ* operation of property in condominium. It captures, in particular, how the neat private/common delineations implied in the schematics of conceptual property models are far more complex, ambiguous and locally contingent in everyday condo living. The analysis also offers insights into the various social meanings and practices of private and common property in everyday condo living and insights on how residents perceive and assert their ownership. In accounting for local working rules, the analysis provides insights into their origins, content and reach that corroborate recognized connections between private regulation and local working rules (Blandy et al 2018)[16] and advances conceptual understandings by specifying this connection as situationally and materially contingent, including on the design and materialities of each building and on the everyday enforcement of private restrictions. Finally, the focus on the condo tower's propertied landscapes as complex three-dimensional home spaces encourages a break from the temptation of thinking about territory as two-dimensional bounded space and associated conceptualizations may have applicability at other geographic scales and empirical sites. In particular, the notion of 'circulation frictions' residents encounter in using shared infrastructure (see later and Chapter 5) departs from the usual focus on movement and flows across borders by considering how mobilities around the condo are differentially constrained and enabled *within* territories.

Book structure

This book embarks on a tour of the high-rise condo to understand everyday property in the making and unmaking of the condo home. The next two chapters provide background context and theoretical frameworks to guide this exploration. Chapter 1 contextualizes the rise of Australian high-rise condo living in international trends involving intensive vertical urbanization and the proliferation of condominium development. It introduces condoization to underscore that how condos are produced, consumed and governed is important to the property practices of residents living within, including because it recognizes condoization as inherently accountable for condo governance outcomes that circumscribe everyday condo living. It overviews the history, geographies and housing submarkets behind the remarkable contemporary surge in local condo development in Australian cities,

16 See footnote 9 for details of this relationship.

especially in the wake of the global financial crisis. To further contextualize everyday condo living, it documents issues surrounding condo governance, highlights how by-laws govern residents' home lives and explains how formal governance enables condo owners to exert power over condo renters. Chapter 2 sets out a property-sensitive conceptual framework for examining home that better accounts for the way home is practised in propertied landscapes. Drawing on legal geography's understanding of everyday property, the framework aims to capture how residents' perceptions and practices of property inform homemaking. It then provides a revised conspectus of contemporary high-rise condo living by rereading relevant housing and urban literatures through this framework. This review serves two purposes. First, it synthesizes understandings of the lived experience of (high-rise) condo housing and identifies various omissions, including in relation to the socio-territorial dynamics of everyday condo living. Second, it tables evidence of condo owners' and condo renters' divergent homemaking experiences. It shows that despite some recognition that tenure-based inequalities riddle condo life these have not been systematically explored from both owners' *and* renters' perspectives, leaving unknown their implications for the condo home. The condo tour then begins with the focus centered on how residents' perceptions and practices of property circumscribe their homemaking, and the sometimes-stark differences between residents' accounts. Each of four empirical chapters takes in a different component of the condo building and introduces another pressure point for condo homemaking. These pressure points on condo homemaking reconfigure the condo home.

Chapter 3 enters the private unit and introduces *local working rules* as a pressure point for condo homemaking. It identifies how locally contingent informal expectations about appropriate everyday conduct circumscribe residents' homemaking as they do laundry, store personal possessions, undertake minor renovations and manage maintenance issues. This chapter complicates the perceived role of formal private restrictions and private interests in regulating property practices in everyday condo living by capturing how residents self-regulate to conform with local working rules, including engaging in 'faux compliance' to satisfy private interests and other-regarding concerns. These practices variously support and undermine homemaking in the private unit, including challenging residents' traditional propertied expectations of these private domains as places of relative autonomy and control. Staying in the private unit, Chapter 4 explores the private unit's borders and introduces *territorial incursions* as another pressure point for condo homemaking. It identifies how residents engage in boundary-management in response to repeated visual, acoustic, olfactory and material breaches into their private units, ranging from innocuous cooking smells to harmful smoke infiltration. This chapter shows these private borders operate as intensive, often porous, zones of physical contact between condo units, especially where design and construction are subpar, but as poor zones of social interaction. Residents' subsequent interpretation of co-residents' territorial incursions as unreasonable private 'takings' contribute to the construction of co-residents, and renters especially, as 'bad' neighbours. Together these bordering dynamics undermine the condo home, including by creating perceived nuisance and diminishing residents' (sense of) territorial control. Meanwhile, as residents mediate their private interests with what they deem non-invasive to co-residents, their recourse to formal governance's rules and agents remains relatively limited, thereby corroborating the importance of informal local working rules, in particular, in circumscribing condo homemaking.

The tour then turns to the high rise tower's common property elements. Chapter 5 examines the shared infrastructure that makes private units accessible, functional and comfortable homes and introduces *circulation frictions* as another pressure point for condo homemaking. It identifies how the circulation of people, non-humans, objects and matter around the condo's shared infrastructures – its entryways, lifts, cables, rubbish chutes and so forth – is variously stalled, obstructed or otherwise compromised. Residents find the collective management of these everyday condo mobilities complex and sometimes fraught, with the mobilities of visitors, rubbish, parcels and so on variously facilitated *and* thwarted by multiple high-rise agents, including co-residents and building managers, and diverse digital security and communication technologies. While owners are relatively better placed to navigate and respond to these frictions in ways that support their homemaking, circulation frictions generally and residents' role in making and exacerbating these meanwhile present another means through which the condo renter is constructed as an unruly condo resident. The last stop on this tour is the condo's shared amenities. Chapter 6 examines the condo's shared amenities and introduces *territorial annexations* and *territorial withdrawals* as final pressure points on condo homemaking. It identifies how residents perceive and assert multiple territorial claims over these shared home spaces, some as innocuous or temporary as a Christmas wreath hung on a unit door or a pram left in the lobby and others which are more overtly proprietorial that can lead co-residents to forgo their legal entitlements to use these spaces in response. Condo governance actors legitimize and delegitimize residents' territorial claims as their (in)action partly informs what residents understand as locally accepted and acceptable. Residents likewise influence which territorial claims are sanctioned as their 'snitching' forces management to police practices they might otherwise have overlooked. Absent much social interaction or rapport, residents can interpret co-residents' claims as private 'takings' with this fuelling frustrations, resentment and (perceived) exclusionary dynamics that undermine condo homemaking and further assist in constructing condo renters as unruly condo subjects. Moreover, while residents display a territorial apathy towards shared home spaces that is suggestive of a weak sense of ownership, residents' sense of ownership is nonetheless ambivalent, with even poorly frequented shared spaces still valued for their perceived financial value as residents envisage their condo homes as financial assets.

With the book's evidence in hand, the concluding chapter first synthesizes how everyday condo living harbours risks for the high-rise condo home, especially where condo design and construction is substandard. Besides appraising the two previously noted risks, Heller's (2008) anticommons thesis – which describes a tendency towards the underuse of valuable resources when ownership is fragmented between too many owners – provides a way to conceptualize an additional potential risk associated with the 'sharing' of some common property elements in condominium, again especially where condo design and construction is substandard. Thereafter, and to take stock of this fine-grained account of everyday condo living, the book concludes by stepping back to consider the prospects for high-rise condo futures in light of these risks. In so doing, the conclusion presents two sets of provocations, informed by this book's findings on how homemaking is impacted by the subpar quality of this high-rise housing stock and renter/owner relations. These provocations are intended to promote discussion, and perhaps action, on brighter urban condo futures. A property perspective is necessarily open to the possibilities for more hopeful and productive rearticulations of property and subjectivity – after all, since property must be performed other articulations of condo property more amenable to home are imaginable. However, as the Conclusion sets out, the task is far from straightforward. Ultimately, meaningful resolution of the risks that beset the condo home require revisiting the political economies of contemporary condoization and confronting anew knotty questions surrounding the function of private property in contemporary society, much as debates around condo dissolution regimes are requiring. The condo renter's plight speaks to broader challenges surrounding securing renters' rights to a home in the city in the face of increasingly limited and problematic housing 'options'. Considering these hurdles, recent optimism expressed by urban scholars about the condominium as a crucible for 'positive change in modern cities' (Easthope 2019: 156) may be premature or potentially misplaced.

1

Verticalizing Cities

In many cities around the globe, urban skylines have risen at faster rates and to higher heights than ever before over the past two decades. Large, tall and often gaudy tower development has become a hallmark of 21st-century urban change from Melbourne to Tel Aviv and from London to Vancouver (Nethercote 2018). Globally, this vertical expansion has not followed a single universal pattern: it is neither linear nor uniform in its scale, its target neighbourhood types, nor its design. Even so, much of this high-rise development has been residential rather than commercial, making this the latest instalment in a stunted history of vertical living in many cities. Unlike their much-maligned modernist forebears with their lofty aims to democratize the skies, some new skyscrapers are unashamed beacons of decadence designed by 'starchitects'. These sometimes spectacularly vertiginous new additions shun local housing needs in favour of providing what have been described as 'eyrie-like refuges for the world's super rich' or worse, merely places for these elites to 'park' their capital (Graham 2016a: 215, 192; Atkinson 2019). Other new housing developments, which stand in the shadows of this conspicuous luxury, are decidedly more prosaic though by no means affordable. Neither avant-garde nor pioneering, this latter stock might be thought of as the stacking of 'highly fungible and slickly marketed investment commodities' (Peck et al 2014), development that has been driven by intensifying housing financialization.

Prompted by this remarkable urban verticalization, urban and political geographers have challenged the pervasive horizontalism of urban scholarship on the grounds that this way of seeing limits full interrogation of these changing urban morphologies and their implications. A dedicated strand of research singularly or largely dedicated to urban vertical expansion is only just emerging, encouraged by the impetus to explain this stark rise of city skylines, including amid economic turmoil (for discussion: Nethercote 2018; also McNeill 2005; Graham 2016a; Drozdz et al 2018). This 'vertical turn' in urban and political geography calls upon scholars to attend to the verticalizing urban topography and volumetric profiles of cities (McNeill

2005; Graham and Hewitt 2013; Harris 2015). Recent contributions identify skyscrapers as important cultural artefacts in intercity competition and geopolitics, foregrounding their performative function as 'signifiers and logos of "global cityness"' (Acuto 2010; Graham 2016b: 755) and iconographies of power (Kaika and Thielen 2006). They highlight the tower's constitutive function, enabling political, planning and real-estate elites to orientate host cities outwards by providing means for attention-grabbing, differentiation and identifiability whether through iconicity (Kaika 2010; Sklair 2017) and starchitect designs (Charney 2007; McNeill 2009) or whether by projecting dynamism, innovation and progress (Ong 2011). Recent accounts of the political economies of these rising skylines meanwhile capture how vertical urbanization's local contours are shaped by a complex array of political, economic, geographic and temporal contingencies that derive from myriad factors, including intermediaries, states and local opportunity structures (for example London: Craggs 2018; Chicago: Weber 2015; Melbourne: Nethercote 2019). Such accounts corroborate that planning regimes do not single-handedly steward this development with developers' influence unmistakable (North America: Lippert and Steckle 2016; Rosen 2017; Australia: Nethercote 2019; Troy et al 2020).

Condominium's role in this vertical expansion has not gone unnoticed in urban geography (Kern 2010; Lehrer et al 2010; Harris 2011; Rosen and Walks 2013; Webb and Webber 2017). On account of their distinctive legal architecture, these towers have been interpreted as an accelerant of urban privatization as towerscapes revise public/private boundaries through new vertical forms of exclusive, privatized and securitized residential gating (for example Hong Kong: La Grange 2014). For many, this condo-backed urban privatization accords with a deepening urban neoliberalism (Kern 2011; McKenzie 2011: 3; Graham 2016a: Chapter 8) and it reflects and produces gentrification (Rosen and Walks 2013; Rosen 2017: 606). So-termed 'condoification' is deemed, by some, gentrification's latest phase (Lehrer and Wieditz 2009), prompting processes of displacement, urban segregation and polarization. Much of this work positions the diffusion of condo development as a collision of economic and cultural/demographic forces – a dynamic Rosen and Walks' (2013; 2015) neologism 'condo-ism' deftly encapsulates. Based on the rapid rise of Toronto's skylines, condo-ism points to the vertical expansion wrought by development industry and state interests *and* 'new urbane yet privatized residential preferences, lifestyles, and consumption interests amongst consumers' (Rosen and Walks: 2013; 2015: 290). Extending this framing, Lippert (2019: 13, Chapter 3; also Lippert and Steckle 2016) has insisted on the importance of condominium's legal architectures in condo-ism and in doing so revamped 'condoization' to reference 'a constitutive process that … relies upon various processes, agents, technologies – especially knowledges – to bring governing relations, and thus the condo itself, into being'.[1] This reworking emphasizes profit-seeking agents' 'takeover' of the condo tower and condo governance by condo law, insurance, security and property management firms, as well as by absentee condo owners (Lippert 2019: 8, 13).

'Condo-ism' and Lippert's reworked 'condoization' are complementary processes: condo-ism gives weight to 'supply-side' and 'demand-side' factors in vertical expansion, while condoization pays heed to governance (Lippert 2019: 13). However, to see condoization as focused on the inner workings of condo is to misinterpret – minimize, more specifically – how condo development and governance intermesh in 'a governing, constitutive process in cities that enlists a wide but mutually supporting army of agents, processes, knowledges and other elements' (Lippert 2019: 3–4). In this sense, condoization offers a summary term to refer to this condo-backed vertical urbanization, indicating 'all the agents, knowledges and logics, and processes that have arisen, been repurposed, or continue to emerge and are assembled in spaces and times to make the condo and its governance possible' (Lippert 2019: 3–4). To grapple with contemporary condoization is to appreciate that *how* condo towers and their residents come to be governed is as much a defining feature of this vertical expansion as the economic and cultural forces that bring these towers into being. Framings of condoization via concepts such as gentrification or neoliberal development fall short, in this sense, by glossing over the complex urban governance arrangements at play, and particularly the way 'the growth of condo development investment leads to conflict … that occurs within condo governance *in buildings* rather than only across urban neighbourhoods' (Lippert 2019: 237, emphasis added).[2] This is a point Lippert (2019: 237, emphasis added) doubles down on in closing remarks in his recent book *Condo Conquest*:

> The critical political economist Mike Davis is correct when he writes that 'we are dealing with a fundamental reorganisation of metropolitan space, involving a drastic diminution of the intersections of the lives of the rich and the poor, which transcends traditional social segregation and urban fragmentation' (Davis 2007: 119). In Toronto, New York and undoubtedly other cities, this transcendence is not merely about walling off or gating urban enclaves to reflect the growing divide in cities; *the condo is currently assembled in ways that enable this to happen inside*

1 'Condoization' is not a neologism. It entered circulation in 1970s to reference the increasingly prevalent processes of 'going condo': namely, readying North American rental apartment complexes for private sale (Lippert 2019: 3).

2 As Lippert (2019: 237) qualifies, this reasoning does not deny the relevance of such concepts to understandings of condoization but clarifies their association. For instance, condoization often features in gentrification, but condoization may occur without gentrification.

> *residential, vertically arranged urban spaces*. In condo conflicts, resident owners from the dwindling middle class seeking long-term community and building integrity are pitted against non-resident investors (who may never set foot in condo buildings and who seek low maintenance fees and a better aesthetic for profitable unit flips), developers typically armed with high-priced legal knowledge, and lower-income renters with nowhere else to live but whose presence investors demand.

Condoization, in this framing, insists then on the importance of how condos are produced, consumed and governed in shaping the property practices of those living within, including because it recognizes condoization as inherently accountable for condo governance outcomes that circumscribe everyday condo living. It is from this vantage point and on these grounds that this chapter provides essential context for understanding how residents make their homes in high-rise condos. After briefly mapping out the histories, geographies and consumer submarkets of condoization in Melbourne and Perth, this chapter reviews two sets of known outcomes associated with condoization. The first set relate to the urban-scale outcomes of condo development and the second set to issues surrounding condo governance. These issues are plotted separately for clarity, though the forces of development and governance are understood as indivisible in condoization as tabled earlier. The political economies and outcomes of condoization are necessarily locally contingent (Nethercote 2018), yet Perth and Melbourne's trajectories and outcomes share parallels with other cities beyond Australian shores, and an international evidence-base surfaces some important connections as well as divergences. My discussion of governance issues meanwhile marshals international evidence to complement and expand the Australian account, on the basis of similar legislative and governance arrangements (Easthope 2019; Lippert 2019: 8).

Verticalizing Melbourne and Perth

Australian cities are renowned for sprawl rather than soaring towers, and yet, over the past two decades these cities have grown noticeably taller as condoization has ushered in once unthinkable vertical development. Certainly cities such as Toronto and Vancouver sit at the 'cutting edge' of condoization trends (Harris 2011), but condoization has succeeded further afield in land-scarce city states such as Singapore and Hong Kong (Pow 2009a; La Grange 2014) and in Australian cities too. In Australia, the number of apartments[3] built each year has tripled since 2009 with more apartments

[3] In this and the following section, I use the term 'apartment' to accurately reflect Australian Bureau of Statistics (ABS) data categories and terminology. The ABS's 'apartment'

being built than houses by 2016 (Reserve Bank of Australia [RBA] 2017: 1; RBA 2019). This century some 667,000 apartments have been built in Australian cities with Brisbane, Melbourne and Sydney especially prolific in this regard, alongside some 40,000 new apartments in Western Australia, there were some 175,000 new apartments in Victoria (Nicholls et al 2019). Most apartments have been built in inner- and to a lesser degree middle-ring suburbs positioning condoization as part of a three-decade-long process of socio-spatial restructuring involving the revaluation of inner-city areas and the progressive shunting of the lower-income households to increasingly distant suburban peripheries, with familiar international parallels (Randolph 2020: 76–9). These apartments, at least half of which are rented, now house some one in ten Australians and much higher shares in some urban neighbourhoods (Easthope et al 2018).

Condoization in Perth and Melbourne has overlapped, but with asynchronous peaks. Melbourne's skyline was transformed in the aftermath of the global financial crisis, while Perth's peak came earlier, heralded by its natural resource boom and trailed Melbourne in its intensity, as we might expect from a city with half Melbourne's population. For everything that separates these two cities, including some 2,700 kilometres or the distance between London and Moscow, Melbourne and Perth share important commonalities. In both cities, densification via private development began in earnest in the 1960s when condominium (strata title legislation) was introduced. Only this century, however, has this development soared to historic highs (RBA 2017) facilitated by performance-based planning regimes, inner-city site availability, favourable land price dynamics, and booming populations (for discussion: Nethercote 2019). Condoization has coincided with shifting social dynamics too: significant international migration, an ageing population, decreasing household size, shifting and diversifying urban lifestyles, acute housing affordability pressures and rising rates of private renting. Alongside the safeguards provided by Australia's relative economic and political stability, these cities offered local and

categorization includes flats and units and excludes townhouses. At the 2016 census, there were around one occupied apartment for every five occupied houses. 'Apartment', in Australian usage, does not specify an ownership structure. While the majority of these dwellings *are* private and delivered under condominium (strata title), this categorization also includes other ownership structures such as social housing. A further note on classifications and available Australian condo data is also needed. Within the 'apartment' categorization further disaggregation of building type is generally not available, with only exceptional instances of subclassifications referencing 'high rise apartments', which the ABS defines as all apartments in residential buildings of four storeys or more. Although 'apartment' data is used to describe condoization in Australia, it is often fairly uninstructive in specifying the *vertical* character of recent development since it does not specify building scale.

international condo developers and investors development opportunities that were backed by strong housing demand, this, underpinned by record migration into the city and property expert and bank reassurances that real rises in income throughout the 2000s and rising prosperity were fuelling its hot property markets (Birrell and Healy, 2013). These developers in turn delivered to a thriving investor market predominantly small, undifferentiated, one- and two-bedroom units in large condo towers, many beset by design and build quality issues, as we shall see, alongside a smattering of premium condo homes, some in super tall towers.

In Melbourne, the genesis of this condo development dates to the 1990s when the City of Melbourne's *Postcode 3000* programme incentivized developers to undertake new-build projects and conversions of high-rise office buildings left vacant by the 1991 recession. This spawned a wave of development, although Melbourne's higher-density housing stock remained modest. Only later, in the wake of the GFC, did condoization accelerate, rapidly transforming Melbourne's skyline. Victorian Planning Minister Guy's 'Grand CBD' plan aimed to 'Manhattanise' Melbourne by expanding its high-rise footprint fivefold. In the absence of coherent metropolitan governance, and under the Central City Zone designation, state government gained unbridled executive power over all large developments and inner-city sites – in contrast to Perth's comparatively centralized, stable and predictable planning system (Bunker et al 2017: 386). Almost 100 towers were approved with limited local government consultation during Guy's ministerial term (2010–14), syphoning unprecedented investment into Melbourne (Shaw, 2013; Buxton et al 2016: 141–2). Residential high-rise, uncommon even at the turn of the century, now crams inner-city blocks at record densities and heights and has made the City of Melbourne one of the fastest growing local government areas in the nation. Since 2009, Melbourne's apartment stock expanded by some 30 per cent (RBA, 2017: 3, Graph 4) with some development into middle-ring suburbs and along arterials too. Development has fallen from its peak, but not without first positioning Melbourne as 26th in the world in a count of buildings over 150 metres, trailing closely behind renowned 'skyscraper' cities, such as New York and Hong Kong (CTBUH 2020).

Melbourne's condoization translated to record annualized rates, with its construction sector a 'bright light' of the Victorian economy (Birrell and Healy, 2013: 5). This development parallels a national urban story over the past decade or so, in which the federal and state government have buttressed the urban development industry in the name of stimulating the economy. Most memorably, this included the National Rental Affordability Scheme (2008–13), which provided tax incentives to housing providers to deliver below-market rate rental units. Recall that Australia avoided the deep recessions that plagued most major advanced economies following the GFC, but its economic growth slowed, unemployment rose and the country faced heightened economic uncertainty. Business and consumer anxieties were eased in part by conspicuous building activity, together with macroeconomic strategies and sharp actual and forecast population growth. Melbourne's population expanded by one million in the decade to 2016, and is now at 5 million with substantive ongoing growth forecast prior to the COVID-19 pandemic. Later, as the resource sector contracted and commodity prices fell, events we will return to in discussing Perth, the 2013 coalition government restated the role of cities in a transitional post-resource boom economy and as drivers of state economies. In the decade to 2016, higher-density dwelling investment doubled from less than 1 per cent of GDP to almost 2 per cent, with Melbourne a key contributor (RBA 2017: Table 2).

Travelling west from Melbourne lies Perth, a sprawling, remote city whose suburbs stretch some 150 kilometres along the neighbouring coastline. Not so long ago Perth was disparaged as not a 'real' city because of its smaller population and economy, its geographic isolation as one of the world's most remote capital cities and its low residential densities (Maginn and Foley 2017). But its mining-fuelled economic and population booms have quashed this perspective, transforming Perth from a 'large provincial city' to a 'globalising city', in some accounts at least (Maginn and Foley 2017). Unlike Victoria, natural resources are at the heart of the Western Australian economy and, between 1995 and 2013, iron ore mining flourished with growing international demand as part of a global resource boom. The two decades to 2015 saw Western Australia's contribution to the Australian economy climb, enabling the state to emerge relatively unscathed post-GFC (Bunker et al 2017: 387). Perth's population expanded as a result of the exponential rise in employment opportunities in mining, construction and related sectors leading to a surge in interstate and international migration that in turn positioned Perth as Australia's fastest growing city in the decade to 2011 (ABS 2011).

As Perth's economy boomed and its population grew, higher-density housing stocks expanded. As in Melbourne, much of the new high-rise development occurred in the inner city where most of Perth's lower-rise higher-density housing is also located (ABS 2010; Maginn and Foley 2017). Off an exceptionally lean base, higher-density development approvals doubled between 2005 and 2008 (ABS 2010), and though these dipped as the GFC unfolded, they quickly rebounded (RBA 2017: 20). From 2013 to 2015, the city witnessed a record number of new higher-density construction projects with these making up almost a third of all approvals by their peak in 2014/15, before then plummeting to less than a fifth (Housing Industry Forecasting Group [HIFG] 2016: 8; Rowley et al 2017: 34). This tapering coincides with the end of the resources boom in late 2013, albeit with a lag effect reflective of the long project lead times in condo development (HIFG 2019). Unemployment and economic uncertainty rose, migration declined, population forecasts were downgraded and the local housing market reeled (Department of Planning, Lands and Heritage [DPLH] 2019). Perth's vertical expansion never rivalled Melbourne's in scale or intensity: Perth's tallest towers are still commercial office skyscrapers, many built decades prior, and detached homes are still the mainstay of its housing stock. Perth's condoization nonetheless expanded higher-density stocks by some 50 per cent this century and has delivered several 30-plus-storey towers, whose heights are somewhat incongruous in a city of Perth's low density and sub-2 million population. Note that while Melbourne's apartment market remained relatively strong in the lead-up to the COVID-19 economic downturn, Perth's house prices and rents declined from 2015 as population and economic growth slowed, albeit substantive affordability pressures persist (Rowley et al 2017: 32–4).

Condo residents

Paying for housing in Australian cities has never been more costly. House prices and rents have surged ahead of wage growth, and household debt is among the highest in the OECD (Pawson et al 2020). For growing numbers, homeownership is out of reach and affordability pressures acute, in what is now a familiar international story (Wetzstein 2017). In Perth, between 2000 and 2015, house prices soared by some 250 per cent, with the rise especially steep pre-GFC (Maginn and Foley 2017: 128). With only one in ten households benefiting from high mining-related income, a two-speed economy emerged in which many Perth households struggled with living costs and took on significant housing debts (Maginn and Foley 2017: 127–8). In Melbourne, affordability pressures push households seeking affordable homes into outer suburbs which now sprawl some 50 kilometres or more beyond its core. Median house values have risen tenfold in some suburbs since the 1990s: in Box Hill, which is similar to the middle-ring neighbourhoods in which some of the condo residents that were interviewed lived, median house prices are tenfold higher, soaring from $150,500 in 1993 to $1,755,000 in 2018 (CoreLogic 2018). Apartment prices have also risen, but less sharply. In the City of Melbourne, where many other condo residents that were interviewed lived, prices have more than doubled between 2000 and 2016, rising from $240,000 to $538,000 (City of Melbourne 2020). These apartments are less expensive than neighbouring housing typologies, with the median apartment price typically 30 per cent cheaper or more than houses in the same neighbourhood, both because they are usually smaller and because condo developments use land more intensively (RBA 2017: 2). Meanwhile family-friendly larger condo offerings of $80m^2$

are comparatively rare and usually attract a premium (RBA 2014; Birrell and McCloskey 2016: v).

Residents in Perth and Melbourne navigate these housing markets in the context of persistent socio-political homeownership ideologies, in which the owned home, and owned *house* especially, is aspirational – again with evident international parallels (see: Chapter 2). This ideal has persisted since the postwar, supported by, and producing in turn, a suburbanized, car-dependent urban form. Unlike land-scarce city states such as Singapore and Hong Kong, for instance, where condo living is the default housing option for all but the very wealthy, in Australia detached housing remains the dominant housing typology. Measured against the 'Great Australian Dream' of owning a 'quarter acre block', condo living is still far from widely embraced or even widely accepted (Kelly et al 2011). Antipathy may slowly be thawing, as consolidation tropes proffer permissible alternatives centred on shifting and diversifying urban lifestyles. However, higher-density living, and the high-rise condo specifically, is typically viewed as a transitional step on the way to 'bigger and better' housing or as a 'downsizing' option. The former reflects growing international associations of higher-density with young adults (for example Moos 2016) and the way condos continue to be perceived as an inferior, undesirable and even 'inappropriate' form of housing, such as for families with children (Troy 1996; Gleeson and Sipe 2006; Kelly et al 2011). Australian condominiums are usually, though not exclusively, purchased and rented over detached houses in the context of acute affordability pressures that force householders to make 'trade-offs' between domestic space and locational advantages, such as employment opportunities, amenities and conveniences such as reduced commutes (RBA 2017: 3).

A majority of those who buy Australian apartments are investors, typically local 'mum and dad' investors alongside some non-resident investor (Nethercote 2019). This investor presence is not surprising given that investors own over a quarter of Australia's housing stock and around one in seven Australians own an investment property, attracted by rental yields, capital gains and generous tax concessions. Even so, investors are especially active in higher-density housing. In Melbourne, for instance, investors own almost two thirds of all apartments (CoreLogic 2016: 16), compared with only one in five detached houses (based on 2016 census data, RBA 2019: np). In some neighbourhoods, investors are especially prolific: between 2009 and 2013, investors purchased upwards of 85 per cent of Melbourne's new inner-city high-rise apartments and some 75–80 per cent of new apartments beyond this urban core (Birrell and Healy 2013: 13). The treatment of apartments as assets aligns with international trends towards the intensifying financialization of real estate (Aalbers 2016).

As investor consumption of the condo foretells, renters make up a disproportionate share of condo dwellers. At least half of Australian apartments are rented, with higher shares in many neighbourhoods (Easthope et al 2018). Indeed in lockstep with condoization and the aforementioned housing affordability pressures, Australia's private rental sector has expanded by some 38 per cent over the past decade, to make up a quarter of all households and far higher rates in some urban neighbourhoods (Hulse et al 2018a: 8; 2018b; Pawson et al 2020: 177–215). As noted in the Introduction, this reflects a broad tenurial shift towards renting that parallels the expansion of the UK, Irish and US private rental sectors following the financial crisis, albeit with divergent national drivers (Martin et al 2018; Byrne 2019). Private rental in Australia is also diversifying, as it is in other advanced homeownership societies. Once a route to homeownership, private rental is now a tenure destination, with homeownership delayed, unattainable, or 'traded off' for locational amenity and flexibility (Pawson et al 2020) and social housing opportunities few and far between within highly residualized social housing sectors (Martin et al 2018). Private rental sector (PRS) households are becoming more diverse too. Australia's PRS contains growing shares of lower *and* higher income renters, more longer- (ten+ years) and mid-term (five to nine years) renters, more midlife renters and more families with children than ever before (Hulse et al 2018b). Private renters typically face uncapped rents, weak tenant protections, little security of tenure in often under-maintained properties and involuntary house-moves (National Shelter 2018).

The profile of Australian private rental stock differs from its North American and European counterparts. With only an embryonic local multifamily or build-to-rent sector, there are very few private purpose-built rental apartments, beyond purpose-built student accommodation, aged-care communities and serviced apartments (Holton and Mouat 2020; Nethercote 2020). Even so, the tenure profile of Australian condos is not dissimilar to these other jurisdictions with growing numbers of private renters making their homes in condominium internationally too; for instance, in New York, over 40 per cent of condo units are rented and in Toronto over 30 per cent are rented (Treffers and Lippert 2019: 1038). Indeed condoization is broadly considered in North America as 'the de facto method for producing rental housing … symbolising reduced public control and regulation over the provision of rental housing' (Rosen 2017: 617).

Melbourne and Perth have their own distinct high-rise apartment housing submarkets though the contours of these markets are not well delineated due to a lack of fine-grain data. Available evidence suggests high-rise apartments in both cities house diverse populations of owners and renters that are likely skewed towards: the young, employed or studying, and childless (for example single- and dual-income households with no children); students, especially in Melbourne on account of its large education sector; mid-age households in professional and managerial occupations; and retirees including downsizing 'empty-nesters' (Randolph and Tice 2013; ABS 2016; Easthope et al 2018). Despite the relatively undifferentiated nature of most of the apartment stock in Melbourne and Perth, these apartments nevertheless house a diverse mix of household types: single and couple households, families with children, intergenerational households and share/group households – not dissimilarly to condo demographics found abroad (Easthope 2019: 32–3) – though weighted towards the 20–40 age bracket (ABS 2016). As previously noted, Australian condo residents include high shares of (non-Anglo) migrants, reflecting the diverse nature of Australia's population at large (Liu et al 2018).

Problematic condo towers

Australia's condoization has been legitimized by policy elites' wholesale subscription to the compact city consensus. Since the late 1980s, metropolitan planning agendas advocated for a more consolidated urban form in response to an emergent suburban critique (Forster 2006). This policy positioning proffered higher intensities of land use, and especially higher residential densities, as an environmental and socially sustainable antidote to sprawl (Troy 1996; Searle 2004). In now familiar international tropes, urban compaction is lauded as a fix-all: a panacea for sprawl, a precondition for environmental and social sustainability, an end goal for planning practice – a seldom-questioned normative objective (Keil 2017). The traction behind these discourses in Australia, much as further afield, betrays just how entrenched this density fetish, and its twin, suburban pathologization, has become. Density, to be sure, is neither inherently 'good' nor 'bad'; but it can concentrate wealth and power and, just as adeptly, poverty and oppression – outcomes are context-dependent after all (Charmes and Keil 2015; Keil 2017: 159). Perth and Melbourne may score exceptionally well in global liveability rankings and yet a compact urbanism agenda has failed to deliver on many of its lofty promises, producing some less-than-ideal urban and housing outcomes. A brief review of these challenges, considered alongside the condominium governance challenges which follows afterwards, provide background for examining how home is practised in high-rise condominium.

High-rise condo development has at times drawn public and academic condemnation and prompted growing unease. On the surface, this prolific development may give the impression of an ostensibly 'winning formula' of density, liveability and sustainability (Peck et al 2014). But in Australia as elsewhere it has reflected a real-estate complex that remains out of kilter with local housing need – a real estate complex that often provides little reprieve to growing socio-spatial divides as lower-income households are relegated to sprawling urban fringes (Dodson 2012). Providing high-rise housing only in areas with high amenity and job access not only defies metropolitan planning ambitions for medium-density, middle-ring development but, without affordable or social housing stipulations, this density is 'effectively "wasted"'(Dodson 2012: 29), since high land prices translate to relatively high-cost apartments that cater only to the housing and investment needs of relatively better-off households.

Melbourne especially has been criticized for succumbing to a resource- and energy-hungry vertical sprawl that has produced a local legacy of small, undifferentiated, poorly designed, poorly constructed, investor-focused 'dog-box' condominiums with limited prospects for fostering environmentally sustainable vibrant communities (Dodson 2012; Horne and Nethercote 2015; Buxton et al 2016; Gleeson 2017a). In terms of design quality, Melbourne's condoization has delivered huge tower developments, with two thirds containing upwards of 200 private units each (Birrell and Healy 2013). Units have poor light, poor passive ventilation and compromised visual and acoustic privacy (City of Melbourne 2013). Many also feature excessively deep floor plans and 'snorkel bedrooms' – both unfavourable design arrangements. Another assessment of Melbourne's new high-rise condos found that only 16 per cent were 'good' quality, while 48 per cent were 'average' and 36 per cent 'poor', and that almost a quarter had bedrooms reliant on 'borrowed light' from adjacent rooms (City of Melbourne 2013). At the precinct level, condoization is also blamed for creating wind-swept, uninviting and sometimes desolate urban precincts (Shaw 2013). Design issues plaguing Perth's condos have received relatively less publicity, but include poor internal amenity, inboard bedrooms, single aspect units without cross ventilation, inadequate site setbacks, which may be indicative of privacy issues, and poor public realm interfaces (SGS 2018: 3).

Alongside design concerns, high-rise condos are plagued with systemic build quality issues. Recent investigations reveal a litany of defects including leaking, cracking, and creaking buildings, poor workmanship and concerns about facade flammability (Johnston and Reid 2019). A recent academic study of Australian apartments found that in a sample of towers in each capital city built between 2008 and 2017, some three in four had defects (Johnston and Reid 2019). There have been several high-profile structural 'cracking' debacles in Sydney, other defects cases in Perth and ongoing concerns nationally about cladding standards especially in the wake of London's Grenfell tragedy and several large fires in Melbourne's high-rise condos. Publicity surrounding the aforementioned defects report and other incidents have encouraged a broader crisis of confidence in the quality of Australian condos. A 2019 article from the national broadcaster read: 'A legacy of defects' with the derisive by-line '667,000 apartments in 18 years. What could go wrong?' (Nicholls et al 2019). Many more cautionary headlines were generated before and since. These design and construction quality issues create unknown headaches, heartaches and financial costs for residents (see Johnston and Reid 2019: 51–4).

When not dissimilar intensive vertical urbanization is described in other global cities it is implicated in a trajectory towards a 'minimum city' – a city characterized by gentrification, transience, flailing local allegiance and lifeless/'dead' dwellings as condos are bought up by those who rarely or never take on local responsibilities, whether economic, social or environmental (Forrest et al 2017; Atkinson 2019). The political rhetoric that 'more houses' will relieve urban housing pressures does not add up: condos delivered in coveted high-amenity locations translate to higher rents, if they are rented out at all, and luxury residences to prohibitive rents. Decadent pieds-à-terre are described as playgrounds of the super-rich, used only sporadically as they flit the globe on their private jets. Some condos languish vacant, used only as sky-high deposit boxes to park surplus funds, and others, more insidiously still, as cover for laundering dirty capital (Atkinson 2019; Tel Aviv: Alfasi and Ganan 2015). In many global cities, condoization is subsequently blamed for new forms of verticalized segregation and elite secession – a 'luxification' and 'elite takeover' of our urban skies – that Graham (2016a: 197), Atkinson (2019) and many others have condemned. Meanwhile, developers capitalizing on prevailing fears of the 'other' and tenure-based prejudices have produced lamentable designs such as 'poor doors' in the UK that segregate wealthy co-residents and social renters using separate entrances and lifts.

Australian condos are not immune to all these risks, but seem to have avoided the worst extremes with ultra-luxury condos a minor submarket. All the same, flashy penthouses and, more exceptionally, exclusive towers filled with super-luxury units, have broken local sales records with price tags in the tens of millions of dollars. Additionally, Melbourne's inner city high-rises have been compromised by 'zombie' apartments left vacant, with indications of a reported 19 per cent rise in property vacancies over five years (Pawson 2017), raising concerns about the vibrancy of urban neighbourhoods and neighbourhood community. These super-luxury residences and empty condos are hugely problematic but are neither mainstays in the local condo stock nor its biggest problem.

In many global cities, architectural renderings of high-rise towers showcase an array of shared amenities ranging from the extravagant to the sublime – from 'world-first' swimmable bridges stretching between high-rise towers and forest parks carved into soaring facades to sky-scraping tennis courts-cum-helipads. Many of these often-grotesque extravaganzas are nothing more than clickbait marketing stunts, but those that see the light of day are hallowed frontrunners in an 'Amenities Gone Wild' trend (PwC & ULI 2019: 9–10). This 'amenity creep', witnessed in much new condo development follows in the footsteps of, and borrows the term used by, hotel developers who have for some time witnessed the ratcheting up of amenity provision (PwC & ULI 2019: 9–10). If in part a trend that broadcasts rising consumer expectations and elite purchasing power, these offerings also give developers an 'edge' as they vie for buyers, including offshore investors. Developers rely on slick marketing campaigns to set their latest vertical offering apart from the competition in a futile game of one-upmanship. Such amenity creep epitomizes both the growing 'hotelization' of home, a trend towards hotel- or resort-style residential development as well as the related 'luxification of verticality' following the high-rise's modest debut in 1960s modernist public housing estates (Zukin cited in Graham and Hewitt 2013: 81). Developers who once enticed condo buyers with no-frills gyms and pools now coax buyers with a startling array of facilities, sometimes packaged up with white-glove concierge services, that might include dog spas, resident-only bars, helipads, basketball courts, rooftop running tracks, outdoor cinemas, climbing walls and ice-skating rinks, workspaces, bike repair stations, rooftop gardens and wine cellars. While more lavish offerings are the purview of super-luxury condos alone, middle-market condos have not bucked this general trend and their marketing campaigns similarly brandish 'novel' and 'cutting-edge' hotel-style lobbies, lounges, gyms, roof terraces and swimming pools as increasingly standard accoutrements of high-rise living.

Somewhat in contrast, in cities such as Melbourne and Perth, developers have frequently pursued a 'volume' strategy aimed at 'mum and dad' investors. Developers have maximized how many units they squeeze onto each site, minimizing ceiling heights and shrinking dwelling sizes. The result has been 'investor grade' condo stock (CoreLogic 2016) that faces its own challenges. These small, boxy, standardized condos are ill-equipped to meet the housing needs of diverse households and life-stages, including those of larger households, families with children and those living in share-house arrangements. In a sample of 10,373 new Melbourne apartments less than 5 per cent had three or more bedrooms, 43 per cent had one bedroom, and over two thirds of these homes were deemed small, at between 41 and 50m^2, and another 7 per cent, very small at under 40m^2 (Department of Environment, Land, Water and Planning [DELWP] 2015). Insofar as developers catered to city residents, they initially anticipated an 'imagined community' of consumption-orientated, childless young professionals and downsizing empty-nesters (Australia: Fincher, 2004; 2007). Such stale and patriarchal views (Fincher 2004) may no longer dominate, with developers recognizing women, if not their families, as an important submarket.[4] Yet

[4] Kern (2010; 2011), writing about condoization in Toronto, suggests how developers and real estate agents have adopted gendered marketing with 'Sex and the City vibes' intended to entice women to the 'excitement' of the city, with its 24/7 access to consumption and leisure. Meanwhile, to draw women into 'up and coming' neighbourhoods – namely, previously stigmatized neighbourhoods – developers appealed directly to women's safety and security fears, advertising 24-hour security and concierge, high-tech security features such as biometric fingerprint door locks, CCTV and alarm systems.

evidence suggests Australian developers continue to overlook how women use and experience high-rise spaces, and thereby undermine women's lived experience as Chapter 2 elaborates (Reid et al 2017b). Meanwhile as towers have filled with private renters whose tenancies are necessarily insecure under current arrangements, this has translated to high residential turnover. In Melbourne, for instance, only 30 per cent of those living in the inner city in 2006 stayed put until 2011, compared to the statewide average of 80 per cent of households 'staying put' (Birrell and Healy 2013). Meanwhile the uptick of unregulated short-stay rentals has raised new concerns about the disappearance of longer-term rental stock, albeit local data is patchy. These short-stay renters introduce other concerns, which I detail later.

The fallout of condoization appears bleak; Gleeson (2017a: np) cautions that, left uncorrected, these 'transformational "furies"' will drive Australian cities further from achieving the ideals of compact urbanism. The Victorian government acknowledged some of these challenges, with euphemistic references to the 'natural "growing pains"' of vertical expansion (DELWP 2015: 5). Both in Perth and Melbourne state governments, alongside federal government, have intervened often to smooth the way for property interests and to restore condoization's legitimacy. State interventions have included new apartment design guidelines, 'stricter' planning controls, and vacancy/absentee owner surcharges. The impact of these is not well documented. Gleeson (2017b: 202) argues this market-driven compaction has led to 'a fracturing and ransacking of urban value and amenity and of human wellbeing by development capital that has worn the thin robe of legitimacy provided by the compact city ideal'. Elsewhere, Gleeson (2017a: np) characterizes this development as a form of 'urban fracking' that is altogether parasitic in the way it depletes existing amenity 'even for some affluent areas (especially towerscapes)'.

Governance problems within

As condoization quietly transforms how tracts of city land are owned, it complicates the governance of urban homes. Namely, it tasks condo owners with responsibilities and restrictions in addition to their property rights and entitlements (Altmann and Gabriel 2018: 8–9). Responsibilities are the duties owed to co-residents that enable the condominium to function, including acting and voting in the collective long-term interest (Altmann and Gabriel 2018: 8–9).[5] Private restrictions concern additional regulation imposed on

[5] OC committee members, as elected representatives of all co-owners, are tasked with exercising power in the interest of the condo owners. They have responsibility and control over general upkeep, everyday management, building security and longer-term building maintenance, servicing and upgrading. The OC operates through an executive

condo owners above and beyond those placed on all homeowners by civil society and other regulating agencies (Sherry 2018). These responsibilities and restrictions raise additional concerns about condoization's impacts for those living within the condo tower. In this review, it will be immediately apparent that issues are often raised in the context of studies of condominium in potentially low-rise settings, rather than in the context of high-rise condo settings. Cited issues nonetheless logically apply to the high-rise typology too. Indeed these issues are likely to be exacerbated in the high-rise condo under contemporary condoization, including due to some of the features and problems associated with this development, as documented in preceding pages. The intersection of issues of residential scale, density and proximities, poor-quality residential settings and the distinct renter-intensive tenure profiles of these buildings is summarized in the Introduction.

Theoretical models of property in condominium expect a great deal from collective self-governance which condo housing does not readily achieve in practice. Structurally, OCs are not optimized for success: their make-up is random with the onus automatically and exclusively falling to owners, as 'reluctant democrats', who must participate in governance 'few understand or are prepared for' (Randolph and Easthope 2014: 213). The quality of these owners' contribution hinges on their knowledge, experience and competency as well as their private resources, including their time, energy and loyalty (McKenzie 2011: xiv). Meanwhile, these owners are unpaid, untrained, inexperienced and even unqualified for this onerous task. Participation rates can be 'alarmingly low' (McKenzie 2011: 27) and lower still for absentee owners (Easthope 2019: 87), whether due to apathy, self-, group- and proxy-efficacy beliefs (Yau 2018) or other constraints. Representation is skewed too: renters typically cannot participate or vote and therefore cannot 'avail themselves of these privileged spaces of influence' (see Lippert 2019: 225),[6] and cultural diversity and social mix are ignored in board composition (Liu et al 2018; also Yip and Forrest 2002). Governance thus amounts to something of a 'shareholder democracy' with owners', rather than residents', interests protected (Glasze 2003: 92). This

committee, with an annually elected chairman, treasurer and secretary, who typically delegate some of their powers and responsibilities to a condo managing agent or building manager. Condo governance therefore also involves building management (an on- or off-site building manager who is either a caretaker or, in larger complexes, more akin to a facilities managers) who is responsible for things such as rubbish removal, safety and security, fire safety, cleaning, general maintenance and so forth.

6 In some parts of the US, Canada and Australia, renters *may* potentially qualify to participate and vote in condo governance, if elected as board members. In New South Wales, Australia, for instance, legislative reform newly allows for the election of a tenant representative to boards in condominiums where half of all households rent, albeit these allowances are not well known to condo residents (Easthope 2019: 89).

can amount to a 'profoundly undemocratic' arrangement (Barton and Silverman 1994: xii): by-laws can be designed and enacted undemocratically and enforced inconsistently (Low et al 2012), OCs can face accusations of oligarchic rule (Yip and Forrest 2002) and, with few checks and balances, civil litigation between OCs and owners often becomes a primary check on their power (McKenzie 2011: 14; Lippert 2019).

The collective self-governance of something as emotionally charged as one's private home is vulnerable to fraught micro-politics too. Condo professionals abbreviate to 'CRAP' the main sources of tension: cars, renters, animals and parking (Sherry 2008: 15). Contrast this with the somewhat tongue-in-cheek 'ABC' of the suburbs: adultery, barbecues and children/crabgrass and sometimes an added 'D – dogs', the latter 'both as glue or solvent' (Perin 1988: 108). In condo living, disputes also arise from rule violations, nuisance and contention over the limits of collective and individual responsibilities, including because common/private property boundaries are unclear (Sherry 2008: 10; McKenzie 2011: 10). Frictions arise from owners' diverse and conflicting interests and because owners are drawn into situations where they are expected to put those private interests aside and act in the collective interest. Such frictions are exacerbated because owners are bound together financially and, in the case of resident owners, spatially, but rarely socially as will soon become evident (Lippert 2019: 226–7).

Doubts have long overshadowed the promise of 'community' in condominium (Barton and Silverman 1994), and these endure (McKenzie 2011: 38; Lippert 2019: 5). Relations can be less-than-cordial within OCs and between OCs and residents, sometimes devolving into threats of litigation. Foucauldian-inspired studies of multi-owned property, for example, link contractualized self-governance with more legalistic, depersonalized, less socially inflected neighbour relations (Blandy and Lister 2005; McGuirk and Dowling 2011; Power 2015). Some recognize these tensions as *inherent* to condominium, pointing to the problematic assumption that condominium begets democratic governance. Barton and Silverman (1994), for instance, argued that common interest communities would fail as 'democratic communities' because the dominant private property interest obscures any collective role and function and, moreover, that the private property interest intensified conflict as residents asserted their property rights against each other (also McKenzie 2011: 38). These inherent tensions are evidenced in the sometimes-incompatible priorities of absentee condo investors and resident owners, with one safeguarding an asset, the other a home (and asset too). Each potentially has differing interests in the 'health' of the community (Treffers and Lippert 2019: 1038) and differing enthusiasm and capacity to invest in proactive maintenance and upgrade programs (Yip and Forrest 2002). We should expect all this to have financial, material and social repercussions for everyday condo living.

Meanwhile, OCs are nowhere near as powerful as generally assumed. They lack mechanisms for even basic rule enforcement with this often too costly and complex to administer (McKenzie 2011: 20; also Sherry 2008: 10–11; Treffers and Lippert 2019: 1039–40). Illustrating this, Lippert (2019: 125) describes property managers' cumbersome attempts to police a ban on short-term letting using custom software and algorithms, such as BNBShield, and conducting manual online searches of sharing platform databases to identify listings in their buildings. The professionalization and commodification of condo governance also diminishes an OC's power. OCs rely heavily on a host of condo 'experts', from lawyers and building managers to private insurance representatives and security personnel – all purporting to support self-governance. So great is this reliance that some argue self-governance in condominium is 'increasingly fictional … more fantasy than reality' (Treffers and Lippert 2019: 1026). North American OCs are shown to be stymied by 'contracts and financial realities': relatively powerless in the face of private condo insurers and management firms whose interests are better protected than owners and influenced by 'property managers, myriad legal knowledges, processes of risk avoidance and securitisation' (Lippert 2019; also McKenzie 2011: 20). Without adequate regulatory oversight, an OC's dependencies on other condo agents increases the chance of conflicts of interest and other forms of fraud (Lippert 2019; Treffers and Lippert 2019: 1032–3). More cynically, Lippert (2019: 138) suggests many private restrictions in the condo exist not only to promote resident safety, security and wellbeing but simply to demonstrate to third parties that adequate steps had been taken in the event of future accidents, injury or loss. This suggests real limits on the prospects of condo governance as a so-called 'fourth tier' order of governance positioned beneath federal and state government, as some endorse (see Easthope 2019).[7]

---

[7] Condo governance is conceptualized as a vehicle for the privatization of local government services and amenities. This 'fourth tier' is conceived as operating below or alongside municipal or local government, albeit as a *private* rather than public institution and bounded by legislation (for example Rosenberg cited in Harris 2011; Easthope 2019). For some, this fourth tier represents a substitution of local government (akin to discussion of civic 'secession' from public government in gated communities, for example Blandy 2008): what McKenzie (2016: 52) terms 'a form of local government privatisation' or Rosen and Walks (2013) describe as an 'offloading of state responsibilities to private collectivities' with the expense and logistics associated with high-rise maintenance heightening the risks to neighbourhoods (for example Israel and Florida: Alterman 2010). Others still, such as Lippert (2019: 223–4), critique this framing, challenging its helpfulness, beyond emphasizing 'a smaller scale and population to govern'. Lippert suggests condo governance is more accurately positioned as 'operating alongside, borrowing from, and contributing to other levels and tiers (especially municipal) rather than "below" or at the bottom of urban life'. I will not summarize all of these engaging debates. Suffice to say these problems

Moving from responsibilities to restrictions, private rules are another important source of contention and controversy within the condo. These regulations prescribe what residents can and cannot do in the development, intervening in aspects of residents' domestic lives ordinarily assumed to be off limits to government (McKenzie 2011). These rules range from the common sense to the seemingly petty, governing aesthetic and behavioural aspects of everyday condo life. These restrictions are unparalleled in freehold homeownership and are typically modelled on standards provided in legislation or formulated for a specific condo development site. These private restrictions often challenge owners' traditional propertied expectations of freedom and autonomy by regulating activity within their private homes. This might include bans on pets or on smoking for instance, with bans on political expression such as the use of signs and flags, especially controversial (McKenzie 2011: 7, 27). Writing about gated communities, Cowan (2010: 340) suggests these restrictions represent the 'apotheosis of the logic of property law – a community divided off from the outside by its own relational "local law" and norms'. Legal scholar Cathy Sherry (for an excellent discussion: 2008; 2013) takes a normative view, cautioning that by-laws may well be too far-reaching. Sherry questions under what conditions private citizens, acting in their own self-interest, should be allowed to enact binding regulations over the homes and lives of people they co-own with or who rent from them. Development-specific by-laws are of the greatest concern, Sherry (2008: 11–12) argues, because they effectively provide lawyers with 'carte blanche on bylaw content' and even while we anticipate lawyers acting in good faith, there are cases of by-laws banning children from playing on shared lawns that are indicative of the potential social risks. In Australia, weak legislature surrounds by-law content, which occurs, in the first instance, under the auspices of the developers. Owners risk facing onerous obligations and restrictions and, at worst, stand to be stripped of their vested rights. By endorsing the private values and interests of owners rather than the interests of civil society, by-laws risk being 'economically inefficient' and 'socially regressive' and/or conflictual with public legislation (McKenzie 2011; Sherry 2016; 2018). At the same time, by-laws that govern activities that 'do not

raise interesting questions about efficiencies and accountabilities at the neighbourhood scale (McKenzie 2011; also Le Goix 2005; Webster and Le Goix 2005; cf. Webster 2002) and conceptual arguments about the 'double taxation' of condo residents via municipal and condo fees. From this vantage point, poor condo governance poses risks not just to residents and owners, but also to municipalities tasked with responding to OC failures be that, for instance, when an OC fails to maintain its rooftop pool and it turns into a mosquito infested public nuisance, when an OC fails to maintain high-rise structures and these become hazardous or when an OC mismanages finances and becomes insolvent (McKenzie 2011: 20–3).

cause meaningful harm to others' clash with the foundational principles of liberal society, namely 'negative liberty' (McKenzie 2011; Sherry 2018).

Discussion of the issues surrounding condo governance are incomplete without returning to the vexed case of the condo renter. Lippert (2019: 109, 128; 2012) argues condo governance actively constitutes the risky and unruly renter subject as a distinct category of governance. This construction takes place as legal, insurance and property management firms navigate 'renter risk'. These agents assume renters are 'variously immoral, risky, unsafe or transient' (Lippert 2019: 128). Property managers associate renters with increased property damage and wear and tear, by-law breaches and security issues (Altmann 2015; Easthope 2019: 115; Lippert 2019). In Australia, condo renters have been linked to illegal subletting and subsequent overcrowding issues (Altmann 2015) and with illegal activities, including drug trafficking and prostitution (Easthope, 2019: 121). In Sydney, short-term rentals and overcrowding in condo buildings are in turn blamed for nuisance noise, increased water consumption, parking shortfalls, added wear and tear and increased fire risks, including as a result of poor safety procedure knowledge (Altmann 2015; Easthope 2019: 121). With building-level renter stigma seen to lower condo property values in North America, Australia and beyond (Easthope 2019: 115; Lippert 2019: 77), some OC manuals advise risk mitigation strategies, such as deploying rental management companies to screen tenants (Lippert 2019: 122). More insidiously, concerns about renter 'saturation' have led to attempts to cap (for example in New York City: Lippert 2019: 110) or ban (for example in Florida and Massachusetts: Easthope 2019: 115–16) condo renters.

Condo insurance firms in North America perceive the renter as a risk factor and this has led to 'renter' premiums, higher overall premiums in buildings with higher renter-to-owner-occupier ratios, and threshold ratios above which some insurers will decline insurance out of fear of the 'renter complex' (Lippert 2019: 112, 120–1, 129). Condo insurance agents claim this risk bears out in actuarial data on the 'better care' observed in buildings with higher levels of owner occupation (Lippert 2019). Read critically, constructing the renter as risky represents a profitable income stream for condo insurance agents since these risky renters justify higher premiums (Lippert, 2019: 112, 129). Indeed condo stakeholders have refuted such risks as mischaracterizations of condo renters in everyday condo living. A property manager Easthope (2019: 115) interviewed, for instance, conceded that while 'renters are hated [...] and don't have as much skin in the game', they found most problems stemmed from owners who fail to participate or pay fees, and who 'needlessly' sue the board.

Condo governance studies position short-stay renters as even more problematic. In addition to the aforementioned criticisms, the peak body for condominium in Australia cites concerns about condo insurance coverage and about short-stay renter compliance with building security, emergency and safety protocols in buildings designed for residential use. For instance, in the event of a fire, short-stay renters would be without the usual illuminated green 'EXIT' signs, as usually required in settings where patrons are likely to be less familiar with their surrounds, such as hotels (Owners Corporation Network of Australia Limited [OCN] 2015: 3–4). The peak body also associates a rise in short-term letting with increased overcrowding, antisocial conduct including nuisance noise and drunken behaviour, waste disposal issues, parking violations, increased wear and tear, and increased use of lifts and higher rates of water consumption, alongside threats and bullying of owners who attempt to intervene (OCN 2015: 3–4). OCs blame short-stay renters for increased administrative and governance workloads (Easthope 2019: 122). OCs are meanwhile poorly placed to charge landlords, renters or their leasing agents with associated costs, including because OC fees do not account for how units are actually used. With high shares of renters, there are also fewer longer-term residents to object to any nuisance. Restricting condo investors from operating short-stay lettings in their condo units has been difficult, including because large numbers of non-resident owners already taking advantage of lucrative short-stay lettings make achieving majority votes in favour of such restrictions, as needed to change by-laws, unlikely.

There is an evident but poorly recognized disconnect between condo legislation and tenancy legislation, as this discussion captures (Altmann 2015). The OC plays no part in the leasing process or in tenancy management. Indeed, the condo renter has no direct legal relationship with the OC nor other condo owners, and no established formal communication channels either. Tenancy agreements may make no mention of the collective responsibilities and private restrictions imposed under condominium legislation and landlords may exacerbate the renter's formal disenfranchisement by not relaying relevant information to their tenants at the start of their tenancy, such as communicating the content of by-laws, nor pass on relevant updates throughout their tenancy. With no formal relationship between the condo renter and their OC and weak and circuitous renter-landlord-OC communication channels, it is not difficult to imagine some of the problems and delays tenants may face in dealing with issues they encounter while living in their condo. Renters in Victoria, for example, *do* have recourse through state administrative tribunals to pursue issues directly with the OC, but tolerating poor amenity or moving out of their rental unit are more likely reactions (Stone et al 2015).

The workings of law

This century, condoization has transformed the urban form and housing stock of Australian capital cities. Melbourne's and Perth's skylines have risen steeply, albeit asynchronously with differing intensities and drivers. Ushered in by market-led planning regimes and legitimized by entrenched urban compaction planning orthodoxies, this development presents challenges for these cities, for the governance of this new housing stock and for the residents who make their homes within it. At the urban scale, condoization risks a form of 'urban fracking' (Gleeson 2017b). In terms of the built environment, condoization may yield, at worst, thousands upon thousands of undifferentiated, poorly designed, constructed and performing homes crammed into vast towers that cluster to form inactive, windy and overshadowed streetscapes. In terms of urban socio-spatial dynamics, condoization may contribute to a more unequal, physically segregated city as condo residents cocoon themselves away from the city below in private, securitized towers. In terms of condo governance, neighbourhoods and those residents living within face potentially wide-ranging issues from poor maintenance to fraught micro-politics. OC committees may meanwhile find themselves relatively powerless, unable to enforce by-laws and reliant on condo stakeholders purporting to facilitate their self-governance. Condominium as a legal institution of private property and condoization as the process of development and governance that bring this institution to life have different iterations and local contingencies, yet this snapshot overview raises significant doubt about unqualified praise and about lauded urban and housing outcomes this development is argued to secure (for example Glaeser 2011: 135–64).

This chapter provided insights into the 'workings of law' in the high-rise condo with this review foregrounding the almost singular focus on formal law, rather than small 'l' social norms and etiquette that are also understood to circumscribe everyday property practices. Nonetheless, two governance arrangements appear instrumental to understanding how the practice of condo property informs the making of the condo home. A first issue is the unusual degree to which by-laws intervene in aspects of residents' domestic lives and challenge residents' propertied expectations of their home spaces. A second set of issues concerns how condominium disenfranchises the condo renter and further institutionalizes the condo renter in positions of vulnerability in the property space by valorizing the interests of the condo investor over the renter's need for home. In the context of prevailing renter pathologies, the condo renter risks stigmatization and exclusionary dynamics in the condo home. To be sure, protections exist outside condominium to safeguard private renters within their tenurial arrangements, but in Australia, as in other advanced homeownership societies, these protections are relatively weak and do nothing to remedy the renter's formal disenfranchisement from condo governance. As noted, insights into residents' experience of this institutionalized 'othering' remain surprisingly sparse.

Meanwhile, approaching the high-rise condo as a propertied space we understand that how residents practise condo property is not singularly shaped by these workings of law but also by the workings of territory in the condo's propertied landscapes. These socio-territorial dynamics are very much in the background in this chapter, though the distinct spatialities and materialities of the high-rise home are outlined here and problems surrounding these, including poor design and construction quality will prove important going forward. In the chapters that follow, a key task then will be to excavate those hidden workings of territory in condominium and to capture how these reflect and inform residents' everyday property practices and, in turn, the making and unmaking of the high-rise condo home. Before entering the condo to explore these workings of law and territory in earnest, however, a necessary first step is to clarify the link between how residents practise property and how residents make their home. The next chapter takes on this task by establishing an approach to the high-rise condo tower as a propertied home space.

2

The Condo Home

Home is familiar – omnipresent even – yet hard to pin down (Mallett 2004). Although geographic scholarship tells of 'home' encompassing scales from the domestic to the neighbourhood and beyond (Blunt and Sheringham 2019), we instinctively associate home with the private dwelling. Home is a relational process: the binding of the material and the affective; neither just a physical site nor feeling alone but rather the relationship between these (Blunt and Dowling 2006: 22). A place called 'home' is made through social and psychological meanings we attach to these dwellings (Massey 1992; Easthope 2004) from notions of distinction, pride, status, self-expression and identity to notions of agency, control and autonomy, as well as notions of belonging and attachment (Somerville 1997; Saunders and Williams 1988; Kearns et al 2000; Mallett, 2004; Clapham 2005; Blunt and Dowling 2006). Home can have other symbolic meanings too as a site of exclusion, fear, alienation, danger and violence (Blunt and Dowling 2006). Moreover, while the experience of the dwelling as home is usually deeply intimate, home is not inviolate of social, economic and political relations, however compelling the impression of its boundedness (Massey 1992). Home, moreover, is *practised*: homemaking binds social relations, identities and materialities, anchors a sense of belonging and constitutes and performs subjectivities (Blunt and Dowling 2006).

Homemaking practices may be habitual, routinized and practical such as cooking, washing, cleaning, gardening, or undertaking maintenance, decorating and DIY. Homemaking also includes all manner of other practices such as socializing, hosting friends and other caring and self-care activities, in and through which we forge connections, create order and establish a sense of belonging (Blunt and Dowling 2006). Homemaking meanwhile comprises a critical set of practices through which subjectivities and social relations (gender, family, class and so on) are reflected, reproduced and also contested (Blunt and Dowling 2006). Approaching home as something that we do, as proposed here, has multiple rich antecedents in the critical geographies of home research from early conceptualizations of home-*making* (Blunt and

Dowling 2006) and more recent calls for conceiving the home as 'practised' (Lloyd and Vasta 2017: 4), as 'quite literally a fabric-ation' (Jacobs and Smith 2008: 516), as 'performed' (Roelofsen 2018) or as 'performance' (Richardson 2018) and as assemblage (Soaita and McKee 2019; Harris et al 2020).

While approaching home as a verb in this way, home is never a fait accompli. Rather, home is understood as an ongoing process of making and remaking whereby home may be difficult to achieve and emotionally and physically taxing, even fraught, to sustain and forever susceptible to change (Dowling and Mee 2007). As the material or immaterial dimensions of home are divested, damaged or destroyed, whether intentionally or accidentally, home can be undermined or 'unmade', briefly or permanently (Baxter and Brickell 2014: 134). This process of unmaking need not involve the dramatic destruction of housing through exceptional events such as forced evictions; it may be altogether more prosaic. Moreover, home unmaking is not about 'obstacles' that stand in the way of homemaking; rather experiences of unmaking are varied and expansive, including 'more mundane and unreported happenings of domestic life and times passing' (Baxter and Brickell 2014: 135). Homemaking and home unmaking are not mutually exclusive, indeed they can occur in concert and, what's more, home, through its unmakings, can be simultaneously recovered and renewed (Baxter and Brickell 2014; Nowicki 2014; Brickell et al 2017). As this intimates, the meanings and material and social realities of home are susceptible to multiplicity and contradiction, involving conflicting feelings of comfort and hostility, of constancy and insecurity, of belonging and alienation, and of homeliness and unhomeliness (Blunt and Dowling 2006; Mee 2007).

Property keeps a low profile, if it is perceptible at all in these renderings of home. And yet, wherever and however we dwell in the world, we are all inescapably entangled in property relations and nestled in propertied landscapes (Blomley 2020: 36), as the Introduction previewed. To recognize that home is unavoidably practised in propertied landscapes is to pay more attention to what territorialized expressions of law do to homemaking subjects and to their homemaking capacities. To this end, this chapter intervenes in the well-traversed terrain of home in geographic scholarship to take on this task, setting out in the first instance a conceptual framework for home that is sensitive to property. I develop a framework that at once takes seriously those attributes, thematics and conceptualizations of home noted earlier, with which geographers and housing scholars are familiar, but additionally seek to centre home as imagined and practised in *propertied* landscapes. In particular, I engage with the notion of property space outlined in the Introduction in structuring this framework around two key modalities of dwelling as home: *home as dominion* and *home as belonging*. *Home as dominion* encompasses notions of autonomy, control and freedom that saturate the home literature

(Saunders and Williams 1988; Kearns et al 2000) and additionally attends to how propertied space legitimates and hardens imaginary and material territorializations of home as private and exclusionary. *Home as belonging* meanwhile reflects geographers' understanding of belonging's importance to home (Probyn 1996; Yuval-Davis 2006; Mee and Wright 2009; Antonsich 2010) and additionally attends to the way a politics of belonging imprints a hierarchical valuation system that delineates some social relations of home as more 'appropriate' and 'proper', subtending and structuring in turn territorialized expressions of law that reticulate propertied landscapes. In homemaking – in practising home – these two modalities of home are synchronous and intertwine. In the synergies and interactions between these modalities, the framework centres the overarching calculus of property which infuses home, including the way propertied space unevenly 'disorientates' subjects in property relations of vulnerability, threatening their ability to feel 'at home'.

After setting out this conceptual framework, this chapter sets its sights on the making of the *vertical* home in particular. The high-rise home has rarely taken centre stage in geographic explorations of home. Historically, home often slipped from view as scrutiny of the 'failures' of modernist tower blocks that dominated the 'western' 20th-century history of high-rise living focused upon the presumed role of vertical shared spaces in crime and antisocial behaviour. Thereafter, human geographers tended to privilege material ontologies and actor network theories, in their consideration of high-rise towers within work on the critical geographies of architecture. Their ethnographic geographies of vertical architecture foregrounded the relational effects and performative agency of things, on the basis that semiotic and symbolic readings of architecture failed to account for 'all that matters' (Jacobs et al 2012). Since then, calls urging more conceptual balance between the material and the immaterial to better acknowledge the 'human imbrication in building events' (Lees and Baxter 2011: 109) and rising interest in the socio-material, affective and emotional geographies of high-rise living have begun yielding rich insights into high-rise living. In revisiting the vertical home through this revised property-sensitive conceptual framework for home, it is this small but growing empirical record on the lived experience of contemporary high-rise condominium that I revisit, alongside urban and socio-legal studies of condo governance and common interest communities, as relevant. For clarity, the condo home as dominion and as belonging are considered in sequence, but the framework understands these modalities as necessarily intertwined in everyday condo living in ways that variously support and inhibit residents' homemaking capacities. This propertied conspectus of the high-rise home establishes current understandings and omissions surrounding homemaking in the propertied landscapes of the high-rise condo.

Positioning home in propertied space

Home as dominion foregrounds well-rehearsed geographical thematics of autonomy and control but additionally brings into view the way propertied imaginaries of home as a private and exclusive domain are legitimated and cemented through prevailing territorialities of home, both real and imagined. As the Introduction highlighted, in 'western' liberal democracies (and beyond) the so-termed ownership model powerfully structures what we think about property. This vision embodies something of chronicler of the common law Sir William Blackstone's (1786 cited in Singer 2000: 3) pronouncement that property was 'that sole and despotic dominion which one man claims and exercises over the external things of the world, in total exclusion of the right of any other individual in the universe'. This vision infiltrates how we think about home too. Prevailing propertied imaginaries of home, as encapsulated in the aphorism 'a man's house is his castle', convey the pervasive expectation that owners, akin to lords, may do as they please within their castle. This propertied vision of home likewise invokes prosaic physical and symbolic markers that defend the metaphorical moat and sequester sacred private domains from threatening worlds beyond. This aphorism also emphasizes spatial integrity and control with a safe and secure 'inside' delineated by 'sharply bounded spatialities of individualised title' (Blomley 2020: 37), neighbours with settled parcels of land, and a 'dense landscape of prohibition, exclusion and security' (Blomley 2006: 3). Housing scholars Saunders and Williams (1988: 83–4) thus describe an implied partitioning of home from the world beyond operationalized through 'fences, front doors, net curtains, private hedges, spy holes, burglar alarms, gates and signs – and socially – by rules governing "dropping in"' and so forth.[1] Likewise, and just as the castle aphorism anticipates, homeowners *do*, increasingly, use aggressive signalling markers to ensure the 'impregnability of the physical and social boundaries' of their dwellings (Low 2008: 57). Fearful, the middle classes increasingly securitize and fortify their homes such that a growing 'defensive homeownership' sees owners resorting to safe-rooms and nanny-cams and retreating into gated enclaves (Low 2008: 57; Atkinson and Blandy 2016: 44).

Indeed when home is considered in terms of territory, territoriality and territorial behaviours, it is often envisaged '*as* territory', and more specifically as a 'primary territory': a place of maximum control and freedom, of security,

[1] Undoubtedly, this representation denies the realities of shifting conventions, borders and forms of these spheres (domestic/'parochial'/public) associated with late modernity in *all* forms of housing (Bauman 1993: 149). Yet the home, at least symbolically, endures as *the* locus for intimate relations, with the preference for encounters with neighbours, acquaintances, and strangers to take place 'out there'.

privacy, identity and so on (Altman 1975; Fox O'Mahony 2012: 162, emphasis added). But home is itself more territorially complex than this. Domestic territorialities, if perhaps unexceptional and quotidian, overlay the home space; think of the out-of-bounds study, a treasured vegetable patch annexed by a green-fingered householder or a humble filing cabinet drawer colonized for one's private use. Even these mundane territorialities hint at socio-spatial negotiations between householders (Sack 1985) and these are reflected, for instance, in studies of the micro-geographies of families with children, for instance, which observe how parents deploy space- and time-zoning negotiations and scheduling strategies (Munro and Madigan 1999), including in high-rise condos (Nethercote and Horne 2016). Domestic territorialities also surface in accounts of the socio-spatial negotiations that occur when relative 'strangers' enter the home space, for instance when paid care providers enter the home as a site of care and navigate their professional roles in the care recipient's private domain (Dyck et al 2005) or when AirBnB guests enter dwellings operating as AirBnB rentals and navigate their fee-paying-guest status with their host in the host's private domain (Roelofsen 2018). Some 'strangers' in the home space arrive uninvited, including the non-human kind, such as plants and animals, and other research documents their territorial incursions of home spaces and how householders navigate their territorializations (Power 2009a; 2009b).

These territorial incursions of home spaces are understood to undermine residents' sense of home in diverse ways, including diminishing their sense of autonomy and privacy, but the evidence also indicates that these need not necessarily undermine homemaking. Furthermore, research examining border-making and -marking practices at home, such as dressing one's windows (Garvey 2005) or tending to one's front garden (Blomley 2005b), for instance, shows how homemaking practices communicate and reproduce material and symbolic boundaries that bound the private dwelling. Certainly, these homemaking practices reflect, and reproduce in turn, propertied imaginaries of home such as those conveyed by the home as castle trope but as Garvey and Blomley also identify, these border-marking practices also variously assert and reflect notions of propriety too. For instance, in these examples, bordering practices at the interface between the private and public domain of the street, whether plant- and candle-adorned windowsills or well-trimmed hedges and neat lawns, suggest how homemaking practices, when read as performative of normative notions of 'homeliness' or of 'neighbourliness' and civic responsibility, mediate – through the social gaze, in these instances – relations with proximate others, such as neighbours and passers-by. In this latter sense, we can see in homemaking practices property's social nature, which the Introduction previewed. Such research complicates our understanding of the ambitions behind the domestic territorialities performed in and through homemaking and helps steer our approach to home as dominion. In particular, we should expect various concerns to drive homemakers' territoriality and their territorial negotiations: autonomy, control and privacy, certainly, but also manifold more relationally inflected issues, including propriety and conformity with local expectations for neighbouring and homeliness.

The sometimes-unremarkable domestic territorializations that home as dominion centres will not all be formal or mainstream forms of property. Rather, as the law sets forth one arrangement, including those formalized through property titles, tenancy contracts or by-laws, territoriality *in situ* will depend on, and reflect, everyday interpretations and interactions with these. We do not have a discrete vocabulary for these domestic territorializations of the home space nor indeed a specific vocabulary for describing territorializations of *private* property, besides territorial terms such as trespass and incursion. However, legal scholar Carol Rose termed a similar layering of private individual ownership claims on *public* property, 'unreal estate'. Unreal estate describes, for instance, the way the avid suburban gardener created complex informal property relationships with passers-by and other neighbours as they tended to the kerb beyond their picket fence, irrespective of any overt agenda on their part to gain formal ownership (Blomley 2004b). This is a concept we can return to and refine as we engage with the domestic territorialities home as dominion centres.

Home, however, is irreducible to questions of autonomy and control, critical though these are. Also important is *home as belonging*, as the second modality of home in propertied space. Home as belonging attends to geographers' long-standing awareness of belonging's formative importance to home (Yuval-Davis 2006; Antonsich 2010) and additionally attends to how a politics of belonging subtends, and structures in turn, territorialized expressions of law that reticulate propertied space. Geographers and socio-legal scholars alike (see Cooper 2007; Keenan 2015) draw upon a bipartite conceptualization of belonging involving a subject-object relation and a part-whole relation. The subject-object dimension appears initially to reference what we own – 'the house that belongs to me' – but in fact concerns the affective dimensions of belonging. This includes feelings of being 'at home' as well as the practices used to signal that people are 'meant "to be" in a place' such as boundary-marking and inhabitation, and the sense of yearning to achieve or maintain this sense of belonging (Mee and Wright 2009: 772; also Probyn 1996). These relations of belonging are what geographer Antonsich (2010: 646–7) calls feelings of being 'at home in a place' or 'place belongingness' or what geographer Gorman-Murray (2011: 212–13) refers to as an 'emotional binding between subject and space', a 'right fit' between person and place. Note that the absence of these relations is not exclusion but rather 'loneliness, isolation, alienation, and displacement' (Antonsich 2010: 649).

However, while these feeling of being 'at home' reference an intimate personal experience, home as belonging cannot ever be just that, since belonging (like property itself) is inherently a social matter (Probyn 1996: 13; Antonsich 2010). This brings us to the second dimension of home as belonging which concerns a part-whole dimension of belonging, such as the relationship between a condo resident and their condo 'community'. This politics of belonging delineates particular social relations as appropriate or more desirable (Yuval-Davis 2006). Part-whole belonging therefore references an hierarchical valuation system in which some social relations of home are upheld as more desirable or more appropriate. This is a valuation system through which people claim and judge their own and others' belonging to a place and a valuation system through which some subjects are classified as legitimate while others are cast as illegitimate or deficient. By foregrounding propriety in this way, home as part-whole belonging subsumes the social dimensions of distinction, pride and status that permeate the geographic scholarship on home. The critical relational geographies of home scholarship attends to 'difference and the possibilities of "becoming"' and the way dominant ideologies and practices of home – which are understood as reproduced through political, social, economic and cultural processes – valorize some social relations and marginalize others such that some places are cast as homes while others are not, some identities are cast as 'homely' while others are not, and some practices are cast as obedient while others are not (Blunt and Dowling 2006: 26, 255). This rich scholarship informs understandings of the prevailing valuation systems that surround the 'ideal' home and 'appropriate' homemaking that home as belonging foregrounds.

Positioned within propertied space, a politics of belonging moreover foregrounds how property, infused with manifold rules, regulations and social norms, inscribes hierarchical social schemas through particular propertied imaginaries and socio-legal practices of home. We can anticipate law to be present in an explicit way, such as in renters' tenancy contracts, condo by-laws and neighbourhood ordinances but also recall from the introductory discussion of property that, with little 'l' law far more expansive, everyday and subtle than these formal expressions of law, law will also be present in various dwelling- and home-related social norms. In sum, home as part-whole belonging asks us to pay attention to the socio-political ideals and imaginaries of home, homeliness and homemaking that make apparent which social relations are (de)valued. In considering how social relations come to be valued, a wide array of ideals that infuse housing consumption and neighbouring norms warrant further commentary to support the exploration at hand. As we later review how these various ideals infuse home with a politics of belonging, it is helpful to think of part-whole belonging 'as a process (becoming) rather than a status (being)' (Mee and Wright 2009; Antonsich 2010: 652) as this better attunes us to the relations of domination that may constrain and condition the possible performances of belonging – the possible forms of belonging for each subject.

The socio-political ideal of the owned home provides a first and pertinent illustration of the way certain social relations of home are valued – a valuation that home as part-whole belonging seeks to foreground. In advanced liberal democracies, the 'homeownership dream' is a socio-political construct built on distinct convictions about private property, individualism and the role of the state (Ronald 2008). This politicised ideal of the *owned* home betrays the extent to which citizenship has become predicated on private consumption and the ownership of residential real estate in particular.[2] Homeownership and renting have become socially sanctioned consumption 'choices' infused with contrasting aesthetic and moral judgements about our conduct as dutiful citizens and consumers such that whether we own or rent, in turn, acts as a status marker. In simple terms, homeownership ideologies position the social relations of homeownership as superior and aspirational. Moreover, with homeownership 'king', home has become 'semantically hijacked and bound up' with owner-occupied dwelling as a site of security, privacy, autonomy, permanency, status and identity and as a financial asset (Ronald 2008: 51). Homeownership, some have claimed, structures a *special* relationship with one's dwelling (see Blunt and Dowling 2006); Saunders and Williams (1988), for instance, alleged homeownership was exceptional in heightening feelings of ontological security, belonging and control. The rented home was meanwhile relegated as antithetical to home: judged inferior, inherently transitory – the antithesis of homeownership's privacy, autonomy, freedom and independence.

Homeownership ideals often interlock with housing typology biases, as has been the case in the heavily suburbanized Australian context, where

---

[2] This ideal, Ananya Roy (2003) argues, is rooted in the prevailing 'paradigm of propertied citizenship' – both a model in the sense that it defines the elements of model citizenship and a model to be emulated. This paradigm has been systematically sponsored via state policy and practice, including through the idealization, normalization and mainstreaming of homeownership with phenomenal, systematic, stigma-free and indeed largely unnoticed subsidies for private homeownership (Nethercote 2018). Foucauldian-inspired scholarship on contemporary governmentality provides another theoretical basis for explaining how consumption is bound up in citizenship and classified as aspirational or flawed. By these readings, late modernity coincides with a revised regime of political power based on a new politics of conduct, what Nikolas Rose (2001: 7) termed ethopolitics. Through ethopolitics, Rose (2001: 18) emphasized how 'the sentiments, moral nature or guiding beliefs of persons, groups and institutions – has come to provide the "medium" within which the self-government of the autonomous individual can be connected up with the imperatives of good government'; ethopolitics concerned 'self-techniques by which human beings should judge themselves and act upon themselves to make themselves better than they are'.

ownership of a detached house within the suburban idyll, replete with privacy and space, came to constitute the 'proper' setting for family life (Dowling and Mee 2000). The high-rise condo, by default, is devalued as unsuitable for families, dangerous, deviant even (Raynor et al 2017; Raynor 2018). These ideals likewise distinguish the desirable, proud and responsible owner subject as someone with a stake in the property-owning democracy, from the renter whose flagrant 'rejection' of this home-owning ideal provides grounds for suspicion and disdain. The renter, afflicted with the 'serfdom of tenancy' (Yip and Forrest 2002: 703), is thus pathologized as an irresponsible, undeserving, feckless and 'flawed' consumer with no stake in their community (Bauman 2005; Ronald 2008; Cheshire et al 2010), even an incomplete citizen, an 'outsider' (Elias and Scotson 1994). Homeownership ideologies reflect and inform property laws which structure and reproduce subsequent material differences between housing tenure types. These dynamics in turn embed associated tenure inequalities, including well-rehearsed state-sanctioned asymmetrical landlord-tenant power relations. Previewed already in such ideals is the relative vulnerability of the renter within the housing system at large and, together with issues surrounding formal condo governance which Chapter 1 overviewed, the possible ways condominium's legal form potentially risks amplifying those vulnerabilities.

Housing consumption ideals, however, are not the only norms permeating the home space. Also foregrounded by home as part-whole belonging are neighbouring norms as another set of norms that govern the socio-spatial dynamics that surround homemaking. As noted, neighbouring is especially instructive in the condo setting, given property's inherently *social* character and the distinct geographies of volumetric neighbouring. Again, the particular interest here is the way neighbouring norms or local working rules come to operate as valuation devices classifying various homemaking practices as appropriate (or not) and how these norms operate as part of the politics of belonging that subtends the propertied home space. Geographic and sociological inquiry into suburban neighbouring practices observes tacit codes that delineate expected neighbourly responsibilities and interactions, such as maintaining suitable social distance (Laurier et al 2002: 350). These studies insist on the way these neighbouring norms rely upon the symbolic line between 'in' and 'out' denoted by gates, fences and gardens in communicating spatial territories and boundaries and in developing neighbourly relations. These symbolic territories are familiar in the traditional framing of a private interior for intimate relations, the garden as a buffer zone and the urban public realm beyond as the 'rightful' place for everyday encounters with strangers (Stokoe 2006; Van Eijk 2011: 6). All the while, these domestic boundaries involve 'locally produced, contingent understandings' of where public spaces stop and private spaces start, with private gardens or 'over the fence' deemed legitimate sites for interaction (Stokoe 2006: 5–6, 8).

What is 'appropriate' or not in these neighbouring dynamics is locally contingent. For instance, in Stokoe's (2006: 8) UK-based study, neighbours articulate a list of normative rules about 'proper' conduct in their suburban gardens including not talking loudly or profanely, nor about personal topics such as finances within earshot of neighbours, keeping doors and windows shut to buffer private sounds and so forth. Neighbours are likewise expected to understand 'the different symbolic functions of fences, and their permeability, and adapt their behaviour accordingly' (Stokoe 2006: 8). Adherence to socially constructed 'private' boundaries not only preserves the sanctity of home but constructs the 'good' neighbour (Stokoe and Wallwork 2003; Stokoe 2006). This role of boundary-maintenance and transgressions in constructing neighbouring subjects is suggestive of the property perspective at the heart of this book which, as outlined in the Introduction, understands property practices as subject-making acts. Stokoe and Wallwork's (2003: 551) work on neighbourly disputes, for instance, refers to 'the moral-spatial order' suggesting how 'good' and 'bad' neighbouring subjects emerge through interactions in and around the domestic domain: the bad neighbour is one who transgresses private boundaries, the good, one who maintains privacy and distance. Being a 'good' neighbour is not necessarily straightforward, however; Perin (1988: 4, emphasis added) writes 'of all the relationships we have, those with neighbours probably have the *least clear lines* around them'. The 'good' neighbour provides 'functional and managed contact ... must be friendly but not *too* friendly' and must engage in 'contact at the edges of, or outside, private spaces' (Stokoe 2006: 5–6, emphasis added).

Home as belonging foregrounds these various politics of belonging surrounding the home and the home space, as value statements about (un)desirable social relations and socio-territorial dynamics. Moreover, home as belonging asks us to appreciate both dimensions of belonging: the intimate matter of being 'at home' and these politics of belonging 'in that very place and which inexorably conditions one's sense of place belongingness' (Antonsich 2010: 649). Namely, home as belonging asks us to attend to how part-whole belonging protects – or indeed fails to protect – one's ability to feel 'at home'. Recall here that belonging is performed; as Antonsich (2010: 649–50) writes 'the exclusive link between a group of people and a portion of the Earth is, in fact, not only activated in identity terms [belonging to a group] but also in terms of exclusive territorial "possession" or ownership'. Belonging is practised through individual or collective socio-spatial practices that signal that people are 'meant "to be" in a place': this involves inhabitation certainly, but also the dirty work of boundary-marking and -maintenance (Mee and Wright 2009: 772). The intimations of belonging's socio-territorial dimensions in the discussions earlier reroute us back to the territorial exclusivity home as dominion underscores and hints at the likely interactions between these two seemingly contradictory modalities of home this property-sensitive schema for home brings together. Put another way, every politics of belonging also involves a spatiality (Antonsich 2010: 649–50), such that the inscription of this valuation system subtends and structures particular territorialized expressions of law that reticulate propertied landscapes. As we shall see, as subjects make their homes in propertied landscapes, those subjects who conform with ideals and practices that reflect hegemonic understandings about what constitutes a 'proper' home and 'appropriate' homemaking find the property space 'holds up' their smooth 'orientation' in ways that supports their homemaking. Meanwhile, those who do not or cannot conform come face to face with various territorialized expressions of law, such that these subjects find themselves disorientated and their capacity for homemaking destabilized.

Bringing together these two modalities of home then, the synergies and interactions between home as belonging and as dominion can be further specified. First, we should understand how home as part-whole belonging operates as a valuation system that produces blueprints for the 'ideal' home and for 'appropriate' homemaking that home as dominion protects and asserts. Second, and relatedly, we can anticipate the way home as belonging's valuation devices and home as dominion's territoriality may be self-reinforcing and auto-legitimizing. For while a politics of belonging informs the territorialized expressions of law that reticulate propertied landscapes, this valuation system also relies upon that very assertion of territoriality, both material and visceral, to ensure that certain property relations are actually 'held up' while others are denied. Third, home as dominion's territoriality performs essential classificatory and communication work in the service of prevailing frameworks of belonging. Crucially, territorial transgressions identify transgressive subjects and practices: homemaker subjects who do not or cannot conform within normative landscapes are cast as inappropriate or even unlawful and their associated homemaking practices cast as illegitimate. Fourth, one's capacity to be 'at home' meets its limits in the material and visceral territorializations of dominant frameworks of part-whole belonging. Or, put differently, homemaking meets its limits as subjects come up against material and visceral territorialities within propertied home spaces. At these limits, propertied space 'disorientates' subjects, what I elsewhere call 'unhoming' (Nethercote forthcoming), threatening a subject's capacity to feel 'at home'.

The condo home as dominion

The depiction of condoization as simply extending the private 'front door' (for example Le Goix and Webster 2008) *is* accurate in that it alludes to the way condoization privatizes urban space, extending the private domain's threshold out to the heavily securitized doors of the condo's lobby. It also reflects propertied scripting advanced by condo marketers that primes potential condo buyers to expect the concomitants of individualized private property, as the Introduction noted. It is a representation of the condo that depicts the tower as a single impenetrable privatized zone characterized by social homogeneity and familiar, familial and intimate relations. But this narration of the condo tower is a totalizing perspective that says little about questions of control, social heterogeneity and contested territorialities *within* the tower. Meanwhile, etymologically, condominium might mean *dominium* jointly (con) with other owners (Wekerle et al 1980: 170–1) but condo owners face private restrictions and collective responsibilities, as Chapter 1 detailed. These place greater demands on owners to cooperate with co-residents and they place constraints on personal freedoms. This, and the subsequent lack of autonomy, run counter to propertied expectations entrenched through the ownership model. This disjuncture bears out in the empirical data which reveals condo owners' sense of autonomy to be compromised in at least four ways relative to traditional forms of homeownership, with implications for residents' achievement of home. As a review of these shows, much less is known about how either autonomy or ownership play out spatially and territorially in everyday condo living, nor the renters' perspective on these.

First, condo owners demonstrate a relatively weak grasp of their rights, responsibilities and restrictions. In advanced homeownership societies especially, resident confusion derives not only from the complexities of condo owners' property rights but from flawed assumptions that condo ownership bestows much the same rights as freehold ownership. An Australian survey conducted by Easthope and colleagues (2012: 72–5; Easthope and Randolph 2018; also Reid et al 2017a) found that first-time condo owners, in particular, were frequently unaware of their rights and responsibilities, such as their need to abide by by-laws, pay levies and contribute to condo governance. Condo owners were naive and confused about the OC, its role and its legal basis and the control exercised by managing agents. North American condo owners may be comparably ill-informed. McKenzie (2011: 5, 9; also Lippert 2019) writes of US condo owners who 'seem to bring with them expectations of dominion and control more suited to detached single-family homeownership' and indeed who may choose a 'condominium unit with little awareness – much less understanding – of the quasi government that comes with it other than the notion that somebody else is responsible for maintaining the common areas'. Moreover, while *caveat emptor* ('buyer beware') places the onus on homebuyers in the property transaction, prospective condo buyers may struggle to do so. Lippert and Steckle (2016: 139–40), for instance, identify how Toronto condo marketing materials systematically fail to mention condo governance responsibilities, instead enticing buyers with a 'close the door and forget your worries' lifestyle and low first-year fees (for point-of-sale ambiguities and inaccuracies in multi-owned properties, also see: Blandy et al 2006: 2376–8; also Blandy et al 2016).

The role of private regulation in supporting homemaking is not well established, with data on the lived experience of condo residents patchy. On the one hand, the physical attributes of higher-density housing are seen to legitimize heavy regulation with a swathe of rules deemed necessary to mitigate potential nuisance whether from obstructions to circulation spaces, from 'nuisance' noise such as drumming (Lippert 2019: 154) and barking dogs (Power 2015), or from 'nuisance' smells such as smoke drift (Lippert 2019: 154). Lippert (2019: 156, 159) writes that 'the inevitable features of conduct due to shared spaces tend to flow horizontally and vertically', citing water leakages, garbage, visitors' access and egress, legal and illegal businesses, pets and parties and their relentless 'residues'. Residents can be disappointed to find homemaking circumscribed by rules governing interior decor such as detailed requirements for noise-dampening floor coverings or prescriptive guidelines for the colours of window coverings (Easthope et al 2012: 72–5). Unlike in a detached house, condo owners generally need OC approval for all exterior changes, such as changes to window frames or unit doors and for all interior renovations of bathrooms and kitchens. On the other hand, these very restrictions can protect residents against nuisance. Blandy and Lister's (2005) study of English gated communities, for instance, illustrates how private regulation underpins residents' sense of home, ensuring neighbours are kept 'in check', especially those whose social values they fear may differ from theirs. Then again, residents' strict adherence to regulation is not a given, with residents citing unintentional and deliberate breaches, both benign and spiteful, that risk causing nuisance to others. Ghosh's (2014) contemporary study of low-income private renters in residentially segregated mass-produced 1960s Toronto high-rise buildings, captures, for instance, how residents 'routinely ignored' and flouted regulations as a means of re-establishing their autonomy and achieving a sense of home.

Wekerle and colleagues (1980) argued early on that condo living might encourage a sense of alienation. Drawing on Peter Marcuse's writings on homeownership and his account of residential alienation, Wekerle and colleagues emphasized three tensions: residents' inability to shape their own dwelling and express their individuality in it; the subjection of the dwelling to outside powers; and residents' inability to mark or signal their private ownership. In more recent research, this alienation is perhaps most tangible where majority rules force condo dissolution, especially in the case of urban 'renewal' of older condo buildings. At one extreme, though by no means rare, is the ultimate loss of control over one's condo home, as in the case of the Wang family whose unit was taken from under their feet when their tower was sold 'en bloc' to enable redevelopment (Chang and Peng 2018). Although the distinct experiences of condo renters are often unaccounted for in such studies, private renters likely experience additional restrictions through their tenancy agreements and more generally are susceptible to experiencing a lack of control over their housing, including due to increased financial pressures and uncertainties associated with their insecure tenancies under landlord-favouring arrangements, such as heightened anxieties about lease renewals, threats of rent hikes and evictions (Morris 2009). The thin evidence available on multi-occupancy housing supports such claims (for example Altmann and Gabriel 2018: 4).

Second, condo governance itself is potentially fraught as Chapter 1 previewed. Owners, as volunteer and amateur committee members, lack adequate technical, legal and managerial skills and knowledge, including to manage contracted specialists (Australia: Reid et al 2017a; Easthope and Randolph 2018 and in masterplanned estates McGuirk and Dowling 2011: 2621–2). Wekerle and colleagues (1980: 183) argued condo governance arrangements were 'inherently elitist' and alienating and that it was unrealistic to expect residents to want to participate in, or be successful at, self-governance. Appearing to confirm this, self-governance duties fall to a minority of owners whose motivations range from the altruistic and community-minded to self-interested and instrumental (Reid et al 2017a). Relatively little is known about those condo owners who do participate nor how well they represent the condo's diverse resident body, be that socio-economic, demographic or cultural (for review, see: Liu et al 2018). Renters are typically excluded by default and, in rare instances where they need not be fully excluded, evidence suggests renters and condo boards alike may be unaware of opportunities for their inclusion in formal governance (Easthope 2019: 89). Condo renters typically have no formal say in matters that shape their domestic domain and are not consulted on new private restrictions nor on how their fees (rent) are spent on legal, insurance, security and property management costs (Lippert 2019: 128). Any disparities in representation stand to be significant since interviews with condo owners confirm that owners bring their own personal interests to bear on their OC participation, including their vested interests in matters ranging from aesthetics to community composition and real estate values (Lippert and Steckle 2016: 141).

Non-participation in formal condo governance is rife including due to apathy as a result of ignorance, complacency or other constraints. Condo owners see committee participation as 'arduous and time-consuming' and many residents have 'expressed no sense of community duty to rotate in [participate]' (Lippert, 2019: 46–52). Over a third of Australian condo owners surveyed by Easthope and colleagues (2012; Easthope and Randolph 2018: 182) believe their co-owners' general understanding of their responsibilities was 'less than satisfactory'. Some confirmed their apathy and others felt unable to participate. Nearly one in five suggested 'there was little or no cooperation' with follow-up interviews detailing blame games, bullying and intimidation and a perception that 'their vote would not make a difference' (Easthope et al 2012: 10). Residents deemed participation on committees time-consuming and reconciliation of community betterment with private interests fraught (Easthope et al 2014). Some owners suffered ill-health 'as a result of all the unpleasantness' of resident politics (Easthope et al 2012: 72–5). Easthope and Randolph (2018: 183) also link the 'off-loading' of governance commitments onto a minority of co-owners to high rates of absentee owners, many of whom may not live locally.

Third, condo governance could undermine neighbourly relations. Tensions arose between OC committee members and other residents, with these often compounded by residential propinquity in the emotionally charged setting of their private domain. Owners criticized OC committee members for being self-serving (Easthope and Randolph 2018), while OC members frowned upon their 'free-riding' apathetic neighbours for failing to share their communal ethic or sense of reciprocity (Reid et al 2017a: 445). OC members also lamented the 'incessant invasion' of their private sphere as residents approached them with complaints and sent aggressive emails. In stark contrast to the carefree living sales pitch, owners experienced subsequent discomfort, alongside frustrations, stress, burnout and other health issues brought about by committee workloads (Reid et al 2017a: 447–8). Repair and maintenance work was a common source of contention, especially 'big ticket' common property items. Apportioning costs between parties could be fraught, with owners confused about private lot boundaries and loath to fork out for anything they 'did not use or that did not affect their lot' (Easthope and Randolph 2018: 187). Owner-occupiers and absentee owners' differing priorities presented an additional source of tension, with the former invested in their home and the latter assumed to be invested only in returns on their asset (Guilding et al 2005; Fisher and McPhail 2014). Owner-occupiers generally frowned upon subletting, with short-term rentals especially contentious.

Condo governance could undermine neighbourly cooperation and trust. Poor management or the perception of poor management left residents dissatisfied, disengaged and even resentful towards their OC (McKenzie 2011: 27) and distrusting of its activities (Lippert 2019: 51–2). Lippert (2019) reports how owners perceive OC members as akin to building sheriffs. Moreover, residents could feel trapped with owners not expected to challenge their OC and those who did put themselves at risk of being labelled as 'trouble-makers' (Lippert 2019: 53). Poor OC management could impact condo residents financially too, with poor management of reserve funds leading to the 'blacklisting' of condo buildings, making it difficult for potential condo buyers to get mortgages and therefore for owners to sell (Lippert 2019: 84). In early condo research, Wekerle and colleagues (1980: 176) also identified how neighbourly relations were undermined by regulations that were 'complex, vague, or basically unenforceable' without resort to court. In the US in particular, this has eventuated in lengthy, complex and expensive litigation and disputes, ranging from 'significant intrusions on basic civil liberties to incredibly petty neighbourhood squabbles' (McKenzie 2011: 27; in Australia: Easthope et al 2012; Leshinsky et al 2012).

In Australia, Sherry (2008: 18) deftly illustrates just how residents can weaponize by-law compliance in neighbourly disputes with a legal case that shows the weighty fallout for the accused. The case involved a new mother photographed breaching by-laws prohibiting the hanging of washing on her third-floor balcony. In a written statement, the mother describes the ordeal as 'nothing short of a nightmare … legal action and the threat of a huge fine is not only extreme, it also strikes me as cruel and insensitive. As it is, this farce has caused us to commence seeking alternative accommodation' (Sherry 2008: 18). One of the tribunal members reflected on the potential weaponization of by-laws: 'The potential for mischief is very great indeed. It is quite clear that parliament did not intend the "notice to comply" application for a penalty procedure to be used as a weapon in personal vendettas or banal neighbourhood disputes' (Sherry 2008: 18). Renters are potentially most vulnerable, as the tribunal member recognized, due to the 'distinct preponderance of applications of that type against people who are renting the premises, ie, tenants' (Sherry 2008: 18). The fallout of neighbourly relations echoes findings on multiple-ownership property and common interest communities more broadly which shows that with community self-governance, neighbourly relations can acquire legalistic overtones, including as residents defer to the OC to manage disputes and police each other's infringements (Blandy and Lister 2005; McGuirk and Dowling 2011).

Fourth, residents encounter multiple issues with the management of their buildings. Alongside more favourable accounts, residents reported a litany of (perceived) management incompetency, inefficiencies and outright failures to deliver contracted services. Complaints include subpar cleaning and maintenance, delayed or neglectful responses and management refusal to attend to complaints including nuisance and trespassing (Fisher and McPhail 2014; Reid et al 2017a). Management inconsistencies and favouritism are also cited such as irregular dispensations and management partiality, with renters disproportionately blamed for building nuisance, property damage and security issues (Reid et al 2017a; Lippert 2019). Owners protested management's dominance, albeit some owners acknowledged their own knowledge 'deficit' as a cause of this asymmetrical working relationship. For instance, Lippert and Steckle (2016: 139–40; also Lippert 2019) cite OC committee members in Toronto condos who concede a 'general deference' to lawyers with condo expertise ('to tell me what I need to know'), including employing them to chair their AGMs.

Wekerle and colleagues (1980: 177, 175) forewarned that condo governance structures encouraged this deference – which they characterized as a tendency for condo owners 'to act more like tenants than owners' – by failing to adequately empower condo owners, mocking self-governance as 'hardly noteworthy as successful experiments in modern-day participatory democracy'. Wekerle and colleagues (1980: 176) cited, for instance, the 'extraordinarily high majorities' owners required to make changes, suggesting that although this protected the individual owner's ownership rights against the tyranny of the majority, it also made for a 'conservative and inflexible' form of governing. The arrangements were traced to the legal complexity of the ownership form and to the tensions between the individual and the collective, whereby the owner's power as an individual consumer was deemed 'extremely limited'. Wekerle and colleagues (1980: 175) conclude that condo owners have not only less control than freehold homeowners but moreover are more alienated than renters living in multifamily rental with institutional landlords (that is, build-to-rent). In Australian mixed-use residential/tourist condominiums, OC committee members corroborate this general sentiment, conceding they 'didn't have a say and numbers were stacked against them' (Fisher and McPhail 2014) and that they had been excluded from operational issues and 'ridden roughshod' by managers using 'loopholes' to evade their obligations (Reid et al 2017a: 449–50). Owners' perception of management as 'all-powerful' indicates owners' relative naivety to the way management is itself hamstrung by other condo stakeholders, as discussed in Chapter 1.

Owners' working relationship with management could risk devolving into 'us vs. them' dynamics. This imbalance of power is epitomized in the alarming albeit comic anecdote shared by Lippert (2019) of a condo manager who DNA tested dog excrement to identify the offending pet-owning resident (also Wekerle et al 1980: 182). Research on residential/tourist high-rise condominiums on Australia's Gold Coast likewise captures an acrimonious relationship (Reid et al 2017a) with management intentionally unreachable, 'obstructive', 'antagonistic' and even unethical (for example: alleged attempts to sway AGM voting), with residents subject to 'bullying tactics' and legal threats (Fisher and McPhail 2014). These and other accounts link high ratios of absentee owners to resident owners to increased conflict. Owners' perceived lack of control over building management triggered resentment, distress, dissatisfaction and feelings of powerlessness (Fisher and McPhail 2014) and, for some residents, such as those in Reid and colleagues' (2017a: 451) study, these residential politics escalated into 'an untenable living situation'. This echoes other common interest community research findings that highlight how owners' perceived lack of control over building management impinges on residents' 'liveability' (Blandy et al 2006: 2370; also Blandy et al 2016).

The condo home as belonging

Studies of the affectual geographies of high-rise homes foreground how the experiential dimensions of high-rise living shape residents' sense of attachment. These are informative for our purposes in understanding subject-object belonging in the condo home. These studies capture how verticality and vertical elements expose residents to (novel) bodily experiences and emotions that both promote and undermine feelings of being 'at home'. Several studies of contemporary lived experience in older/modernist public housing towers capture negative bodily experiences and their detrimental impacts on residents' sense of belonging (Lee and Baxter 2011; also Arrigoitia 2014). However, residents' experiences are diverse; for instance, tenants enjoyed a sense of being in their 'own world' because of the seclusion afforded by elevation, good insulation and airiness and vistas enabled by the relative geographic dispersal of high-rises under modernist planning (Baxter 2017). Baxter (2017: 350) argues that verticality can 'construct novel experiences and intensify home', but moreover that it 'can be central in [residents'] "being" at home'. Geographic studies of affect in private high-rise housing specifically are comparatively rare but corroborate how novel experiential dimensions of vertical living contribute to residents' attachment to their homes. These show for instance how perceptions of security, safety and privacy enable residents to feel 'at home', including women specifically (see Reid et al 2017b). Shilon and Eizenberg's (2020) account of high-rise residents in Petach Tikva and Natania, Israel, highlights the ambivalent role of digital technologies, such as WhatsApp, in mediating the high-rise's affective atmospheres. These technologies are associated with fear, insecurity and dissatisfaction including, for instance, because they alert residents to building issues they might otherwise have failed to notice, such as poorly cleaned spaces. On the other hand, digital technologies are also shown to create 'a sense of belonging and a shared atmosphere of communality and social cohesion', including through shared negative experiences, such as unifying residents against a developer who has under-delivered (Shilon and Eizenberg 2020: 133). In a socio-material analysis, Horne and I illustrated how living closer, higher and smaller shapes how young families engage in distinct socio-spatial negotiations that can stall, complicate or obstruct their capacity to feel 'at home' and can lead some families to eventually abandon condo living (Nethercote and Horne 2016). Other research with Dorignon (Dorignon and Nethercote 2020) presents a fairly sombre picture of single men whose disorientation relating to restlessness, frustration and disappointment unmakes their new Melbourne and London high-rise condos as home, despite their initial high hopes.

Moving on to residents' experience of the condo home from the vantage point of a politics of belonging, insights are gleaned from research that engages with housing consumption ideals and neighbouring norms. In terms of housing consumption, historically high-rise housing in advanced homeownership societies was associated with social disadvantage. The tower and its residents were widely stigmatized and this stigmatization endures in a sometimes-extreme pathologizing of high-rise public housing which is now 'implicated in a finite and extreme unmaking of home' in the 'regeneration' of housing estates, especially but not only in the UK (Baxter, 2017: 350). Even so, high-rise social tenants' lived experiences are mixed, sometimes defying representations of their vertical home spaces as undesirable, unhomey and alienating, albeit stigma remains undeniably challenging for tenants. Private high-rise housing has not suffered the same stigmatization and yet tenure-based prejudice towards private condo renters surfaces at both the building- and individual-level.[3]

Lippert's (2019: 110–24; also Lippert and Steckle 2016: 138) interviews with condo owners and management in New York and Toronto reveal how perceptions of high rates of renters in a condo building compromises a building's reputation, desirability and property value, with this prompting condo owners to attempt to limit absentee owners' rights to lease, especially to short-stay visitors. Owners and managers Lippert (2019) interviewed believed condo renters lacked owners' 'propensity to care' for their homes

[3] The stigmatization of private renters has received attention in the context of suburban neighbouring. This work has often centred on social attitudes that cast renting as 'inferior' or attitudes towards (perceived) concentrations of renters in suburban neighbourhoods. A range of issues are cited in Perin's (1988) *Belonging in America* including concerns about unexpected high shares of renting beyond what some considered 'reasonable' and 'acceptable' levels and general unspecified antipathy towards renters. Other concerns included renters' inferior home space aesthetics such as poor maintenance of gardens, which homeowners interpreted as a sign of renters' lack of pride and respect; renters' inconsiderate conduct and deficient community ethic including because renters were transient, unwilling to invest in neighbourly relations and because owners also deliberately excluded them on that basis; and concerns about undermining property values or street appeal. Rollwagen's (2015) interviews with low-rise homeowners in neighbourhoods across Calgary had some similar findings including that all owners saw private rental housing and private renters pejoratively. They cited a range of risks including associations with transience, lack of trust, difficulties forming rapports, lack of care and even some questioning of renters' moral character. In an Australian master-planned estate, Cheshire and colleagues' (2010: 2604; also 2019) interviews, almost all with homeowners, show how private renters are viewed as failing across three domains: aesthetics, ethics and community by undermining the aesthetic value of the neighbourhood and by failing to demonstrate an ethic of care for themselves and others.

and they disproportionately blamed renters for multiple problems including nuisance (178), high residential turnover, (perceived) over-occupancy (119), a poor 'community' feel (118), increased safety concerns (111) and higher overheads from increased maintenance costs through wear and tear and higher insurance premiums (127). Longer-term renters were presumed to have a relatively greater stake in their home, if not their communities, whereas short-stay renters were deemed 'absolute strangers' who, at worst, wreaked havoc, defied by-laws, caused nuisance and raised security concerns (Lippert 2019: 23, 122; also Reid et al 2017a). Ironically, some of these very characteristics deemed to make renters so undesirable, such as itineracy, may well be those encouraged by condoization. Kern's (2011: 91) interviews with female condo owners in Toronto revealed many had 'short-term intentions' and developers sought to capitalize on these, with relatively more affordable condos enabling women to enter the property market, including by opening up 'sometimes "sketchy" neighbourhoods' as developers assured women the condo's security features would keep them safe. Kern (2011: 91) elaborates: '[this] suggests that the city is courting a highly mobile, transient population of city dwellers who may not make long-term commitments to the city or seek out ways to participate in civic life'.

In Australia, residents in Reid's (2015: 443–4) study of Brisbane condos perceived a 'social divide' between owners and tenants and 'a generalised prejudice towards renters'. Renters were associated with transience and a limited commitment or inclination to invest in neighbouring relationships, albeit owners meanwhile also confessed to being unwilling to invest in fleeting relationships. This undermined trust, encouraged 'us-and-them' dynamics and perpetuated a 'cycle of anonymity and disconnection, which could impact residents' sense of safety and security, as well as belonging' (Reid 2015: 444). Another study by Reid and colleagues (2017a: 452, 454), this time focused on Gold Coast condominiums, captured how owners also perceived short-stay renters as having 'no sense of reciprocity' and 'minimal moral or communal obligation' towards their buildings and as lacking in accountability for subsequent damage, nuisance and repairs and maintenance. On the other hand, longer-term residents' shared frustration at the costs, inconveniences and perceived injustices of the short-stay renter 'takeover' could unite condo residents against these 'outsiders' within their home spaces.

Residents in Baker's (2013: 274) study of condos in Newcastle, Australia, also perceived a 'palpable distinction' between owners and renters. Owners, who viewed themselves as 'house proud', saw renters as careless and lacking pride: renters purportedly scuffed walls, left balcony planters untended and entranceways strewn with shoes (Baker 2013: 274–5). Renters, on the other hand, saw owners as entitled and condescending, including for looking down on them as 'less legitimate residents' (2013: 275) and this made them feel as though the condo was less 'theirs' (2013: 278). Baker (2013: 274) suggested renter prejudice encouraged an antagonistic relationship – 'almost an "us vs. them" dynamic' – that was aggravated by residential propinquity. Notably, with tenure not visible, owners often used youth or 'poor' behaviour as (an unreliable) proxy. Meanwhile, renters' perspectives are largely missing from the empirical record making it unclear how such prejudicing, coupled with their formal disenfranchisement from condo governance, undermines condo renters' sense of part-whole belonging and in turn, their capacity to feel 'at home'.

Everyday condo living is also conducted in the shadows of other normative housing ideals, including those that position high-rise living as an undesirable, even unsuitable, setting for family life (Fincher and Gooder 2007; Easthope and Judd 2010; Easthope and Tice 2011; Raynor 2018). Kerr and colleagues' (2018) study of parents living in Sydney condos describe parenting in close physical proximity to neighbours as stressful, especially in terms of managing the noise children make. One parent, for instance, recounts the dilemma of managing their baby's nocturnal crying, after being criticized by their neighbour, in terms of having to either prioritize 'sleep training' in their family's best interest or prioritize noise minimization in order to be a 'good' neighbour. In subsequent work, Kerr and colleagues (2020: 432) describe the emotional toll condo parents face living under the 'critical gaze' of family, friends and strangers as they appear to flout suburban family/parenting ideals, including middle-class expectations regarding aesthetics, space, privacy and child-adult spatial separation and privacy. Condo parents described friends and family who were dismissive of their housing 'choices' as non-aspirational, variously casting condo living as 'settling [for less]', as forced through financial constraint, as an unwise investment over traditional homeownership, and as unacceptable for nuclear families, though perhaps admissible for single parents. Sensing this, parents experienced parenting guilt, embarrassment, discontent and frictions within their social networks and this in turn diminished their sense of home and rendered uncertain the longer-term prospects for making and maintaining the condo as home. Although some parents adjusted, parents remained wary of judgement: 'defensive' and quick to 'point out the good bits' including location, lifestyle, affordability, security and low maintenance (Kerr et al 2020: 434; also New Zealand: Carroll et al 2011). Parents also internalized family and friends' judgements and 'second-guessed' their housing 'choices' even when condo living was a 'proactive and positive choice', and even as they rationalized the lifestyle benefits or financial necessity of condo living (Kerr et al 2018; 2020).

This work on condo families productively previews how experiences of subject-object belonging – of feeling 'at home' – and part-whole belonging – of belonging to a community – collide to make and unmake the condo home. Of note, it shows how this can cause diverse, contradictory and simultaneous feelings of being 'at home' and of not being 'at home'. The way family living ideals interacts with homeownership ideals remains unresolved. Kerr and colleagues (2020: 19, 11) interviewed mostly renters and explicitly state they found no marked differences in resident experiences between tenures, including notably, that owners *and* renters can perceive the condo as a temporary home.

Understandings of how a politics of belonging might operate within everyday condo living are further gleaned by shifting focus from tenure ideals to neighbouring norms. A set of studies of privately governed housing inspired by (post)Foucauldian governmentality are insightful, with these observing social norms and expectations in the context of a rising politics of conduct. This politics of conduct or so-termed 'ethopolitics' is understood to mobilize citizens to monitor and self-regulate their conduct on the basis of their allegiance and duties to communities, neighbourhoods or other social groupings rather than 'society' writ large and to regulate their conduct out of a sense of 'obligation, reciprocity, mutuality, cooperation, belongingness, and identity' (Rose 2000: 1389). These studies detail how contractualized self-governance mobilizes residents to self-regulate their behaviours in compliance with valued middle-class social norms and aesthetics (Low 2004; Walks 2006; Pow 2009b). This research helps explain how potential slippage between formal rules and 'working rules' occurs as formal governance fails to adequately regulate for all social expectations or potential nuisance. These studies suggest by-laws 'merely' codify otherwise common-sense 'material and behavioural elements of middle-class respectability', but that residents' self-governance can be inconsistent and contradictory, and even rejected outright at times (McGuirk and Dowling 2011: 2623). Easthope and colleagues' (2012; also Easthope and Randolph 2018) findings appear to corroborate this as they describe condo owners who fail to accept legislated responsibilities, identifying that one in ten residents, in a dataset of some 120 respondents, cite breaches and other unacceptable behaviour. The broad or ambiguous scope of by-laws and regulatory oversight of other valued dimensions of domestic life may contribute to this non-compliance. Other research meanwhile suggests by-laws may be incomplete in terms of adequately governing consequential dimensions of everyday condo living. For instance, in a survey of condo residents in Ljubljana, Slovenia, Mandič and Hrast (2019: 417, emphasis added) find residents also 'interact and try to establish some control over ad-hoc issues that are *too small* to be covered by formal provisions'.

Foucauldian studies, by highlighting the moral undertones associated with social codes, also demonstrate the role of these tacit norms in the construction of the 'good' neighbour as well as in structuring neighbourly relations (for example Blandy and Lister 2005; Cheshire et al 2010; McGuirk and Dowling 2011). Contractualized self-governance is argued to alter neighbouring dynamics by prompting legalistic, distanced and depersonalized relations and the demise of 'socially inflected, negotiated neighbouring' (Blandy and Lister 2005; McGuirk and Dowling 2011; Power 2015: 256). Nuancing this, Power (2015: 259) has argued that, in 'apartments' specifically, these kinds of neighbouring dynamics may be as much a product of the physical setting as a product of formal governance per se, since the 'apartment' setting limits residents' possible responses to nuisance and neighbouring disputes. For instance, a resident can play music with relative anonymity – since the architectural typology renders them relatively 'invisibilised' and unreachable – and so, might persist in playing their music loudly despite knowingly disturbing their neighbours. Neighbours meanwhile may struggle to pinpoint the source of the music and may also be physically unable to reach the music-playing resident to resolve the matter informally, since residents are unable to access each other's floors. Power (2015: 259) argues the materiality and spatiality of multi-storey condos may therefore disrupt self-governance which relies on a sense of duty, by undermining 'the capacity for affects such as guilt and obligation to act on residents' and in turn may push residents to pursue more 'legalistic interventions'. This noted influence of physical design represents an important qualification, as it positions self-governance as working *in combination with* the spatial and material environment in structuring neighbouring relations and more contractualized neighbourly relations, in particular. This focus on the materiality of the condo tower is advanced in this book's property perspective through its socio-territorial focus. Like Power's approach, this constitutes a productive shift away from common treatment of the spatial and material environment of the high-rise as a backdrop for high-rise living. This has every potential to shed light on everyday condo living, especially when held in frame with the aforementioned focus on socio-symbolic dimensions of belonging, such as exclusivity and stigma, which inform home as belonging.

Still, we know relatively little about neighbourly relations in the condo, perhaps in part due to long-held assumptions about the condo's social homogeneity (for example Australia: Dredge and Coiacetto 2011: 422). Verticalities and gating literature, for its part, says little about relations *within* buildings, emphasizing instead the exclusionary dynamics between 'insiders' and 'outsiders'. When social difference *within* towers has been acknowledged within this literature, hierarchical class relations have often been mapped in a linear fashion, with greater height associated with greater prestige, status and cost premiums (for example Graham 2016a; 2016b). On the other hand, Australian condo buyers are reported as listing 'who you have as your neighbour' as a primary concern (Yuen et al 2006: 594) and concede their condo purchases were based on an expectation of 'living in a community with people who formed a "relatively homogeneous group"' (Fisher and McPhail 2014: 794).

Everyday condo living may challenge these expectations and aspirations. Lippert (2019: 138) captures how governance arrangements in large North American condos foster 'mutual surveillance and, at times, suspicion-raising among condo neighbours', and cause distrust, fear and precaution between neighbours (cf. Blandy and Lister, 2005; McKenzie 2011). Lippert (2019: 5) subsequently concludes that the promise of condo 'communities' appears 'increasingly dubious, though perhaps not yet beyond hope' (also Blandy and Lister 2005). Again, high-rise design is implicated. In the first instance, condo residents are described as trying to 'strike a balance' between privacy and social contact to manage the 'intensities of contact' associated with higher-density living, albeit in a small survey of 73 condo residents in Newcastle, Australia, over half reported 'minimal to no contact' with neighbours (Baker 2013: 276). In the second instance, design could impede co-resident interactions such as by making chance encounters with neighbours unlikely. Baker (2013) also notes residents' other rationales for limited neighbourly interactions including conflicting daily schedules and lifestyles, intentional avoidance of others, residents' selective interactions with owners and disinterest in engaging with high-turnover renters. Feminist materialist research, such as by Reid and colleagues (2017b: 20; also Kern 2011) similarly captures how design inhibits social connections, especially for women with children who can experience the high-rise as a 'space of social isolation'. Women describe units as too small to entertain, amenities poorly suited to children's play, lifts limiting opportunities for chance interactions and units providing no clues as to 'common interest/value that could be a starting point for a relationship' (Reid et al 2017b: 20).

Critically, the emergent evidence suggests high-rise living may involve distinct neighbouring norms. Insights into condo residents' experiences of making and hearing noise not only highlights concerns about noise, but particular social expectations surrounding noise production. For instance, the allegations made against the 'noisy' family in Sherry's legal case referenced previously would not only have had no legal redress in a suburban setting but also would likely have been a non-issue to begin with (Sherry 2008:16–17). Noise-related norms are likely complex too with noise volume not the sole determinant of nuisance; in Sherry's case, the 'hammering, banging, yelling and door slamming' constituted a by-law breach while the crying children, thankfully, did not.

The content and workings of informal high-rise neighbouring rules and expectations have received little systematic attention, however. Even so, available evidence offers several insights: first, that physical proximities between residents exacerbate residents' experience of nuisance noise; second, that residents can be highly attuned to the noises produced in their units, whether by crying babies (Kerr et al 2018) or barking dogs (Power 2015); and third, that residents may subsequently self-regulate their homemaking practices in response. It appears these high-rise neighbouring norms also intersect with other housing-related politics of belonging to shape and accentuate distinct social expectations in the condo tower. Kerr and colleagues (2018), for example, capture how some condo neighbours' disdain for young children's noise, whether their crying or rowdy playdates, stems not just from the auditory disturbance itself but from a view that families do not rightfully belong in the condo. In this Australian case, quite evident is a distinct housing typology-based politics of belonging which envisages families' rightful place in the city as somewhere other than the high-rise condo. Condo parents, for their part, reported self-regulating to meet these perceived social expectations: banning kids from running around inside, limiting activities such as singing and dancing to rooms without party walls, socializing outside the home and making material changes to their unit to minimize noise transmission to neighbours such as redesigning, installing carpets and covering air-vents. These self-regulatory practices could, in turn, undermine parents' sense of home. Conversely, other accounts capture how residents' failures to meet unspoken social norms could undermine their sense of home, as evidenced by residents who were troubled by short-stay renters' 'unsavoury' behaviour (see Reid et al 2017a).

Touring the condo tower

Revisiting the literature on condo living through the framework of *home as dominion* and *as belonging* highlights that understandings of the condo tower as a lived propertied space remains embryonic, despite a rich emergent literature on condo living. There has been little systematic consideration of how residents practise condo property in everyday condo living and relatively little examination of how amenities and infrastructure are shared. Additionally, little is known about the local working rules that govern residents' property practices though socio-legal scholarship primes us to anticipate slippage from condo by-laws (Blandy et al 2018). A property perspective anticipates that private and other-regarding concerns may inform how residents perceive and practise condo property, and indeed some evidence around nuisance noise appears to partly corroborate this. Power (2015) comes closest in capturing something of the distinct socio-spatial dynamics of condo living when she links 'good' and 'bad' condo neighbouring to the material specificities of higher-density living. Still, little is known about condo borders, including how these function as interaction devices that construct neighbouring subjectivities, the kinds of incursions in play, the border-maintenance and -management practices involved in managing those incursions and the implications of these dynamics for condo homemaking. All the while, evidence of potential inequalities within condo life between owners and renters (Lippert 2019: 13) and renters' disenfranchisement from formal condo governance speak to an underlying politics of belonging, with the potential to unsettle condo home as belonging. Lastly, this review considers each modality of home (as belonging and as dominion) sequentially and yet there are synergies and interactions between these sometimes conflicting modalities of home that open up and close off opportunities for residents to make themselves 'at home'. This is evident in Kerr and colleagues' (2018) sensitive accounts of condo parenting where questions of territorial control and autonomy and a politics of belonging are self-reinforcing and undermine residents' capacity to feel 'at home', for instance.

The condo tour designed to explore these issues draws upon some 128 interviews conducted with condo residents in inner and middle-ring Melbourne and Perth. Interviews were conducted with 68 Melbourne residents living in 14 different buildings and with 60 Perth residents living in 17 different buildings. These condo developments, which were all built between 2009 and 2017, are typical of Australia's post-GFC condo development; many comprised small units, many were poorly designed and/or poorly built, and some had significant defect issues. In each condo building, building managers were charged with managing shared amenities, though the designs, size, features and quality of these amenities varied. All residents had access to a (basement) car park, usually a gym and a rooftop terrace or (podium-level) outdoor/green space. In larger high-end condo buildings, they often had access to resident lounges, larger and better-equipped gyms and swimming pools too. Given the high-rise focus, this analysis centres predominantly on the accounts of 57 Melbourne residents and 41 Perth residents living in condo complexes of seven or more storeys and comprising upwards of 50 units and many closer to 200 units. The Appendix details the selection of urban sites and condo buildings and researchers involved.

These residents reflect the demographic profiles of each city's 'apartment' housing stock and submarkets, which Chapter 1 detailed. In Perth, 52 per cent of residents rented and 48 per cent owned, almost all with mortgages, and in Melbourne, 20 per cent owned, a few outright, and 80 per cent rented. Information on the tenure profile of each condo building is not publicly available, but these high shares of renters reflect the prominence of investors in Australia's condo market, especially in inner Melbourne. Most residents lived in one- or two-bedroom units. A tiny minority who lived in three-bedroom units were single and couple retiree households, reflecting the local rarity of new three-bedroom units and associated price premiums. All residents lived in relatively small households, most alone or with a partner. The largest households comprised only four people, though some residents regularly hosted family visitors, sometimes for months at a time. These larger households consisted predominantly of flatshares. In Melbourne, around a quarter of residents lived in two-bedroom shared households, comprising various combinations of couples and/or singles, most aged 35 or younger. A small minority of large households were young families with one or two caregivers and one or two (most pre-school aged) children or small intergenerational families, such as a parent with an adult child. Slightly more residents identified as females (some 60 per cent) than males and most residents were aged between 25 and 65 years old. Owners were generally older than renters: roughly half were over 50 years old whereas a relatively greater share of renters were younger than 50. For the most part, renters and owners comprised similar household types; however, renter households included slightly more young families (noting these were a minority cohort) and flatshares exclusively. These residents likewise reflect Australia's cultural diversity to the extent this features in these housing submarkets, including significant shares of migrants and, in Melbourne, international students (see Chapter 1; Fincher and Shaw 2011), noting that over 50 per cent of Australian 'apartment' residents are migrants (Australian Bureau of Statistics [ABS] 2016).

These residents' accounts of condo living are captured through vignettes and verbatim quotations in the chapters that follow. There is no one-size-fits-all approach to preserving participants' anonymity, and associated decisions necessarily involve compromise (Saunders et al 2015). A careful balancing act was required in this case between preserving residents' anonymity (including in anticipation of future research team outputs) and maintaining data integrity. A series of decisions taken in this regard include: assigning pseudonyms to participants to assist in reconstructing personal accounts, presenting only select personal details as required, carefully amending idiosyncratic details on occasion and not providing a pseudonym where linking together two data extracts from the same resident might compromise their anonymity. To protect the identity of residents' homes, further decisions were made to amend and/or be non-specific with some building descriptions including exact building heights and neighbourhoods and to rename buildings on occasion where names facilitated this account.

The following four chapters chart a tour through the condo tower to chronicle how home is being made and unmade under contemporary condoization. This detailed account of condo homemaking brings into conversation understandings of how condo residents perceive and practise condo property with evidence of how they make the condo home as dominion and as belonging. In practical terms, the tour approaches the condo as a propertied landscape comprising private *and* common property elements and it provides a volumetric rendering of the socio-territorial dynamics of everyday condo living that is attuned to the materialities and spatialities of the condo tower's home spaces and borders. To this end, each chapter examines a different home space and foregrounds another aspect of the territorialized expressions of law that reticulate these propertied landscapes. These territorialized expressions of law are conceptualized as a series of pressure points for condo homemaking. In visiting the private unit, the analysis foregrounds *working rules* (Chapter 3) and *territorial incursions* (Chapter 4); in circulation zones, such as shared hallways, water pipes and rubbish chutes, it foregrounds *circulation frictions* (Chapter 5); and in the shared amenity spaces, such as swimming pools and rooftop decks, it foregrounds *territorial annexations and withdrawal* (Chapter 6). The tour sets off, however, in the private condo unit – an ostensibly private domain – to understand how this home space is intensively governed, including by informal social norms that variously inform residents' homemaking.

PART I

The Private Unit

3

'You're Not Supposed to Do That'

Condo governance research emphasizes how private restriction potentially reduces condo residents' autonomy and control over their home lives. As this tour takes in the private condo unit, the significance of private restrictions is considered anew by examining how residents perceive and practise property in these private home spaces and how this makes and unmakes the condo home. Hilbrandt's (2019; 2021) contributions, as set out in the Introduction, guide us to think about how condo residents might stake out or reclaim some autonomy amid the formal rules and regulations that govern everyday condo living. To what extent do residents carve out 'wriggle room' or 'room to manoeuvre' through self-regulation and fake compliance? And how do snitching and boundary work in turn act as *limits* on any discretion such practices afford residents? Drawing on condo residents' accounts, this chapter considers these questions by examining how residents do their laundry and decorate their units and how they manage personal possessions and everyday home maintenance. In so doing, this condo tour begins with a perhaps unexpected focus on laundering practices. Laundering and other everyday and mundane domestic practices shed light on how social norms and expectations govern condo homemaking, over and above private restrictions.

Following the invention of tumble dryers, the consumption of these energy-guzzling machines skyrocketed. In the US, for instance, the humble clothesline came to be viewed as unsophisticated, anti-progress, even a sign of frugality and, worse, of poverty and blight, marking out households too impoverished to purchase a dryer. Gardens liberated of 'unsightly' laundry signalled respectable household consumption. With this stigma, the simple clothesline became a class issue. The ideal neighbourhood was clothesline-free: devoid of visible markers of economic hardship, devoid of property-devaluing eyesores. In private residential communities, OCs rallied to ban line-drying on aesthetic grounds, encouraged by rising national consensus of its detrimental impact on 'curb appeal'. Some 50 million US households remain subject to such bans, reliant instead on tumble dryers or indoor clothes racks to dry their laundry (Drying for Freedom 2012). Even without outright bans, enduring stigma surrounding clotheslines means they remain frowned upon by some neighbours, albeit attitudes are changing.

On the other side of the Pacific Ocean in Australia, the humble clothesline did not succumb to an image problem of comparable magnitude. Indeed far from maligned, the Hills Hoist rotary clothesline developed in the 1940s is still sometimes a fixture of Australian backyards and is nowadays something of an ironic national icon. And yet with the recent surge in higher-density living in Australian cities, laundering practices *are* the subject of renewed public scrutiny. For some, high-rise balconies and laundry are immiscible. Unlike clotheslines in suburban backyards, high-rise clotheslines are more readily visible, and to far more people. Australian media has reported on city residents' intolerance of 'unsightly' clothes racks on balconies, sometimes condemning these as neighbourhood 'eyesores'. Others ridicule this assessment and the way some have 'become apoplectic when they get so much as a glimpse of a neighbour's smalls fluttering on a balcony' (Thomson 2018). The humble clothesline ban in private residential communities turns mostly on a question of aesthetic sensibilities, though in the high-rise condo perhaps some might also make an argument on safety grounds following several fires in high-rise condos originating on balconies housing flammable personal property.[1]

These laundry debates begin to suggest how private regulation, such as those governing condo balcony usage, might variously reinforce and conflict with other social expectations about appropriate and desirable conduct. As this chapter explores everyday homemaking practices including laundering, it pays attention to the way formal restrictions intersect with social expectations to inform locally contingent working rules that govern resident property practices in their private units. A picture begins to emerge of how residents perceive and practise property that nuances condo governance research's strong emphasis on the way private restriction circumscribes residents' home lives. In the first instance, the analysis shows that while residents comply with by-laws in everyday condo living they also sometimes fake compliance and brazenly flout these rules. Moreover, this analysis foregrounds an interplay between formal by-laws and social expectations and norms in everyday condo living that gives rise to local working rules which are informal and based on social rather than legal terms of reference, but nonetheless significant to the governance of condo home lives and home spaces. In so doing, this chapter

1 In Melbourne, following several recent fires in condo towers for instance, the Metropolitan Fire Brigade issued new safety advice to keep all clothes racks at least one metre away from balcony air-conditioning units to mitigate risks (Metropolitan Fire Brigade [MFB] & City of Melbourne nd).

shines light on the importance of local working rules in circumscribing how residents practise property in everyday condo living and it emphasizes the rarely considered role of these informal rules in circumscribing condo homemaking. It captures how residents variously self-regulate as they mediate their individual private interests in the face of social expectations and their other-regarding concerns. Residents find this mediation trying at times, having entered the condo with traditional propertied expectations of these home spaces as a place of personal autonomy and freedom. While this mediation need not undermine the making of the condo home, it sometimes does, as we shall see.

'The washing police'

Most residents saw their private units as a zone governed by formal regulations. These restrictions included a perceived ban on hanging items to dry on their private balconies – a ban that residents variously attempted to comply with.[2] Residents had no separate laundry, as is typical in other housing typologies in Australia, but instead 'European-style' laundries either in their kitchen or bathroom. They usually had no built-in dedicated drying racks or lines within their private unit and rarely had access to a communal clothesline, as commonly found in lower-rise higher-density housing such as flats and townhouses. Many residents conceded they may not use a communal line in any case, expressing reluctance about having their laundry *that* "on show". Poor design, and especially poor ventilation in windowless bathrooms compounded the impacts of this balcony by-law. One resident installed a clothesline over their bathtub but this was never going to be ideal since bath towels were already slow to dry in their stuffy bathroom. More commonly, residents purchased clothes racks and kept these out in their open-plan lounges or in their bedrooms most of the time. As Max, a 60-year-old Melbourne owner, explained: "I've got a little thing I can put in the corner over there that I can hang my things on, but if I want to do, say, a couple of bedsheets, I'll do them on separate days so that I can hang them over to dry properly." Residents resented these "unsightly" clothes racks and though they became accustomed to them they still hid them away under beds and behind doors when guests visited. Many residents came to rely on tumble dryers, seeing few alternatives; as one first-time condo resident

2 As noted in the Introduction, this analysis concerns only residents' *perceptions* of by-laws and *perceptions* of by-law breaches. References to by-laws and breaches in discussions of residents' accounts hereafter should be taken to mean residents' personal impression of by-laws and by-law breaches rather than as statement of facts about the content of actual by-laws that governed their buildings.

exclaimed: "What the hell do you do with sheets?" Besides their financial cost and environmental burden, dryers also created additional problems in the private condo unit by exacerbating condensation and damp in residents' small, poorly ventilated windowless bathrooms. Most residents left bathroom doors open to counteract the moisture and humidity, though designs meant this left the toilet in view from the lounge, and some bought moisture-absorbing products, such as crystals. In two-bedroom flatshares where each housemate had a designated private bathroom, having the laundry in the main bathroom forced the flatmate who ordinarily used the ensuite bathroom to trespass into their housemate's dedicated bathroom to use the washing machine and dryer, compromising both flatmates' privacy.

Besides these compliant residents whose laundering practices were quite obviously mediated by balcony washing bans, there were many other residents who admitted flouting washing bans to dry their clothes. These residents mostly rehearsed engrained Australian social norms around air-drying, especially given its conducive climates. As many residents rationalized, balcony drying "just made sense", particularly since they often found space limited within their private units even without setting up clothes horses. These residents rejected or limited their use of energy-zapping and costly dryers, as one claimed: "I'm old-fashioned like that" and another explained:

> 'I'm a bit of a greenie, so I don't like using the dryer. … And I think it's something that they [OC] … I know [other] apartments don't like it. But I think it's crazy not using the sunshine to dry your clothing. It's just so bad to use a dryer. That's what my personal view is – it's bad here, in this building, the extent of washing on balconies – but I think it's insane [to use a dryer].'

Notwithstanding their willingness to flout by-laws, some residents were quickly discouraged from drying items on their balconies after finding their laundry was readily blown off, especially those living on higher floors and those with exposed balconies. Renter Aditya, who lived on the 9th floor of a middle-ring Melbourne condo, reported: "I've tried hanging it up outside on the balcony before, but it would just fly everywhere even if I put the pegs on. It's so high up that the wind is very strong." Others persevered, undeterred by the new challenges of their windswept balconies, finding ways to affix and protect their laundry.

Many 'rule-breaking' residents engaged in 'faux' compliance to meet their private interests, whether motivated by environmental concerns or spatial constraints or something else. They then rationalized their breaches by embracing a 'no harm, no foul' philosophy: since no one could see it and no one was hurt by it, they viewed their breach as immaterial. Many residents rationalized, just as 47-year-old Perth renter Tracey, did: "I do actually [hang washing on the balcony], you're not supposed to, but I figure no one can see it! No one can see it! Unless there was a drone …!" Balcony height, screening or surreptitious positioning ensured washing remained hidden, as residents such as 27-year-old inner-city Perth renter Vivian explained:

> 'I don't believe you're really meant to use the balcony in my apartment complex to dry the clothes, but it's quite a big balcony, and other people in the complex do it as well. And I keep it in the corner where you are least likely to see it. … It's got the couch in front of it, and I also move my fake plant to kind of cover it. And I position my high vis [fluorescent workwear], like my bright orange shirt in the back corner, so it's least visible. I haven't had any complaints as such.'

Most of these rule flouting residents described their laundering practices in terms that reinforced their view of this homemaking as non-compliant, for instance using expressions such as "being sneaky".

While some residents made some pretence of compliance, many residents appeared mostly nonchalant about their breaches, albeit some did fear being "caught" and reprimanded, especially renters. One reason for residents' nonchalance emerged later in residents' accounts of "illegal" laundering, which tended to follow a common pattern: first, residents would describe drying bans on their balconies and only later would they concede they had little or no knowledge of the actual by-laws governing their balcony. For a good number of residents their *impressions* of regulation regulated their laundering practices, rather than by-laws per se. So while comments such as "being sneaky" highlight how residents perceived their actions as non-compliant, most residents were poorly informed about the by-laws, including those governing their private balconies. In a similar vein, it is also worth noting that owners and renters alike often appeared to refer to the OC committee, building managers and facilities managers interchangeably and rarely distinguished between, and indeed often confused, the different roles and remits of each. Residents also often collapsed into 'the OC committee' all the responsibilities of the OC, including all contracted service providers (for example pool maintenance providers, cleaners and so on). This confusion reinforces how far-removed residents were at times from formal condo governance and its workings, with whom many had little interaction and whose workings were often unfamiliar or even opaque to them. This is also notable considering about half of all owners suggested they had some involvement with their OC committee at some stage.

Meanwhile, residents' observations of their co-residents' laundering practices helped them justify their own rule-breaking, as comments from Kevin, a 26-year-old Melbourne renter, capture:

> 'I will put the laundry on the basket, which you see here, and then take them out to the racks on the balcony to dry even though technically you're not supposed to do that. … I'm not sure, I haven't really checked for this building, but there were some [condo] rules where they don't want you to do your laundry on the balcony. We've been doing it. Haven't run into any trouble, so we're still doing it. Even with the buildings that you see out here, you can actually see the laundry on their balconies as well.'

Kevin's comments also highlight residents' perceptions of poor-policing, which was another common thread in residents' accounts, and which only added to residents' confusion about the terms of private restrictions. No residents admitted to receiving cautions about their balcony laundering, though several residents such as 47-year-old Melbourne renter Melinda suggested their neighbours had been cautioned, possibly because of the extent of their breaches. As Melinda reported, her neighbours "got in trouble because they hang their clothes there all the time; and it's very ugly". More frequently residents gave the impression of their building manager's "light touch" approach to laundry bans. In one high-end Perth condominium, 68-year-old retiree owner Marta referred humorously to the OC secretary as the "washing police" while repeatedly minimizing any impression that private rules circumscribed her home space:

Marta:	He just lets everyone know. He writes gorgeous notices in the lift for us all … funny pictures. He wanders around, and we call him 'the washing police'. He goes looking [for residents' washing] – 6am in the morning.
Interviewer:	Looking for their washing lines on the balcony?
Marta:	Well, he's having a walk [around], but he does tell people. But he's lovely. He's gorgeous, and he's so friendly, and if you ask him anything he gets it done, it's brilliant.

Discretionary and "soft" regulatory approaches such as those captured in Marta's account of the "washing police" show building managers complicit in residents' faux compliance. In such cases perhaps, as Cowan (2011) also observes, a 'soft-regulatory approach', such as enacted by a landlord leaving flowers for the incoming tenant, sets the tone for the working (landlord-tenant) relationship more effectively than the contract itself. Still, for all the focus on the way by-laws pertaining to private balcony use regulated how residents went about doing their laundry, residents' perceptions of their balconies as propertied home spaces were nonetheless complex. Residents talked about their balconies in ways that often conveyed very traditional propertied notions of ownership; they used possessive pronouns, such as "my" balcony or "our" balcony, for instance. When condo residents used their balcony they might only have been exercising exclusive use rights to common property, but the way many residents perceived and practised property on their balcony was with a sense of territoriality and ownership much akin to what we might expect from a homeowner discussing their private front yard: these were zones where residents felt relatively free to do as they pleased.

Yet these traditional propertied imaginaries and practices of the balcony were not the full picture. Further analysis revealed that in carrying out these mundane laundering practices, residents were not only attempting to reconcile their own private interests with private restrictions governing their balconies, as illustrated earlier; rather residents were additionally attempting to mediate social expectations surrounding balcony usage. For this laundry-drying prohibition was seen, as several residents related, as a both a "blessing and a curse". Residents were not always successful in "hiding" their washing and co-residents expressed frustration at the ugly aesthetics associated with other neighbours flouting washing bans. "We can't hang things out in the balcony and I get a bit annoyed when other people do because it is unsightly," 60-year-old Melbourne owner Max vented. So for all their frustrations, many residents also suggested the ban "made sense" and seemed appropriate: a facade adorned with flapping laundry after all, was unattractive some claimed – "very ugly", as Melinda put it. As Max elaborated: "[we're] not allowed to, nor should we be. I would pass the older tower blocks around here, and people occasionally leave their stuff out. It looks pretty unsightly. I don't like it". These social standards were also evidenced in buildings without bans, where large numbers of residents frowned upon balcony air-drying, viewing these as transgressive acts.

In trying to heed these often unspoken social norms, residents' laundry practices appeared to respond not solely, or even primarily in some instances, to any desire or impulse to comply or appear compliant with by-laws but rather to social standards and to their other-regarding impulses, including their pride in their building and a concern with keeping it from appearing "unsightly" for their neighbours' benefit. Conversely, even in buildings where residents believed balcony drying was permitted, residents spoke of hiding their washing behind balustrades and furniture and frowned upon their co-residents who left their washing in plain view, even though they would have been well within their rights.

Attempts to mediate by-laws and social norms were not frictionless. These tensions are illustrated by retiree owner Robin's commentary which captures both compliance, as Robin resorts to using her dryer and hanging things inside, but also the limits of this obedience, as private needs sometimes also trump formal restrictions. In this instance, Robin subsequently also engages in faux compliance, tucking her laundry out of sight on the balcony, so as to satisfy her private needs without compromising her building's aesthetics. Sixty-eight-year-old Robin, who lived on the 10th floor of an inner Melbourne condo, explained:

> 'When I first moved in, I found a problem because you can only use the clothes dryer. You aren't allowed to put any of your washing out on the balcony, which makes sense. I appreciate that. I wouldn't like it to look like a laundry on everybody's balcony … so I found that really difficult to deal with initially. I think if the laundry was perhaps a little bit bigger, there could be room for a drying rack or something which I think people would appreciate … because you know, how do you dry your lingerie and things [that] you can't put that in a dryer? So you really have to hang it somewhere. That's what I found difficult … because it's become difficult for me to get in and out of the big bath up there; I don't use it any more. I've put a clothes horse in the bath, so I hang them over that. Most days, the bathroom looks crappy because there's stuff hanging in the bathroom. Occasionally, I'll sneak something over one of the chairs on the balcony, and I'll pull it back so nobody can see it, something really heavy like jumpers and things which you don't put in the dryer either, that take a long time to dry in winter.'

These latter accounts begin to reveal, through the everyday mundanities of doing laundry, how condo homemaking is not singularly governed by private restrictions regulating balcony use nor by managers' policing of these restrictions. More commonly, rather, residents perceive various unspoken social expectations, including the aesthetic concerns of their co-residents and other publics, which, together with their other-regarding concerns, regulate how they do their laundry. As residents' homemaking is subsequently circumscribed, residents come to perceive limits to their own control over their private home spaces. Certainly by-laws banning the air-drying of laundry on balconies challenge residents' propertied expectations of their private home spaces as zones of control and autonomy. But as this snapshot of condo laundering illustrates, also of considerable importance to homemaking are local working rules. Those residents who complied with these formal and informal restrictions usually traded the creation of a public 'eyesore' with private, mostly small but nonetheless consequential practical and spatial inconveniences. Residents' compliance and self-regulation can compromise their sense of being 'at home', such as by creating visual 'ugliness' and undermining functionality by crowding lounges and bathrooms with laundry paraphernalia. It can also damage the condo home space by exacerbating condensation in bathrooms, worsening issues with damp and mould. By-laws governing condo balconies provides but one example of how private regulation intersects with social expectations within private condo units to circumscribe residents' homemaking. The significance of local working rules will remain a key focus in this chapter as we continue to explore the ways private regulations intersect with social expectations to circumscribe residents' homemaking.

Decorating by the book

As residents decorated their condos, they met with other regulatory constraints. Residents described strict rules governing what they could and could not do within their private unit; as an older outright-owner summed up: "they're fairly fussy about the rules". Some of these rules came to the attention of owners early on when they purchased their condo off-the-plan pre-construction and found that rules regulating floor finishes and window coverings, for instance, meant they were unable to select their preferred interior fit-out. Some of these rules inconvenienced and frustrated residents. Sometimes owners found rules wrong-headed, such as Robin, who we've just met, who reflected on her new three-bedroom condo where she has lived with her partner for the past two years:

> 'One stipulation of the builders, when we bought the apartment, is that all blinds have to be black on the outside. I really don't like that because I think that it makes the condo hotter. You're putting a black blind down and the sun's shining on it. It's very, very hot. So that's another negative about the building. … They want it all to be uniform and [but] why black? I don't know. It's supposed to be a green building because there's a lot of solar power used. All of the solar panels down there run all of the foyer lights, apparently, and passageway lights. … Yeah but we're wasting all this power for aircon because we've got these hot black-out blinds.'

Many owners similarly expressed a sense of being restricted within their unit and they variously echoed Robin's repeated refrains of "We're not allowed to! We have to get permission!" as they described decorating and personalizing their condo units.

Owners were often confused about their rights, as previous studies also identify (for example Easthope et al 2012), and this compounded owners' sense that they had limited control over their private home space. Lauren, a 67-year-old Perth owner, who was divorced and now lived with her adult daughter, wished to renovate the bathroom in her condo unit, where they had been living together for seven years. Lauren wanted to change the layout, toilet and sink and add a walk-in shower but exclaimed: "I don't know whether it's even possible to do anything differently." Lauren, who still had a mortgage, also worried she might overcapitalize too and was unsure of the added expense of such work in the condo setting. In the end, Lauren limited herself to cosmetic alterations elsewhere in the unit, such as painting and installing new carpets.

Owners who did attempt small renovations often met with complications, frustrations and unforeseen costs and timely administrative legwork. Several Perth owners in a 20-something-storey inner-city Perth high-rise had enclosed their balconies which were windswept and lay unused. Eloise, a retiree owner, and her partner had downsized to their condo four years ago, though they had purchased it some years prior as an investment property. She described a lengthy, ad hoc process:

> 'I paid nearly a thousand dollars to get [planning] approval. Then, when I came back to the council, it was different people … they said, "Oh, well, now, I've got to send a letter to everyone [her co-owners] to get permission from the other people." If one person scuttled on it, they can't go ahead. Well, that happened. One person didn't want it. "I'm denying it!" He couldn't [even] say why he didn't really want it, [they] just didn't want it! In the end, the [OC committee] said, "Look, we're quite happy for you to do it." So I thought, well, that was enough. So I had [the balcony enclosure] put up. But no one's even made a mention of it. Although I did get a letter the other day from the council saying, "It's been a year now. You were supposed to fill this form out". But I haven't even filled that out yet!'

Owners seldom anticipated such constraints; some were alarmed to find a co-owner could veto their plans. Residents' accounts echo research findings on homebuyers of private multi-owned residential buildings in England and New Zealand who similarly faced issues at the point of purchase including inaccuracies and incomplete information and a lack of transparency around contracts, including about future financial costs (Blandy et al 2006: 2376–8). Residents' accounts likewise corroborate how they fail to ask pertinent questions about their new building's operation and management and about their own responsibilities as co-owners (Blandy et al 2006: 2372–3). As such, condo residents' accounts similarly capture the way these factors then compound owners' experience of powerlessness over their private home spaces.

Those condo owners involved in formal governance suggested they were not always that much better informed, and many felt as powerless as other residents, if not more so, for their potentially greater awareness of some of the inner workings and governance of their building. These owners, moreover, often perceived formal restrictions in more ambiguous and ambivalent terms, both as something externally imposed by others *and* as something they had "insider" insights about and involvement in, albeit rarely a strong sense of control over. Christine, a 71-year-old Perth owner, made alternate references to the OC as "we" and "them", for instance, that disclosed these owners' contradictory sense of being simultaneously involved and uninvolved, and in control and powerless. Christine's ambiguous position as a formal governance agent is evident in much of her commentary, for instance:

> 'Quite a few people now are complaining that they want shade cloth or those screens that you can move [shutters]. … They're very strict. So now they're looking at that; they want the blinds done properly. … But we still haven't approved that yet. I've just gotten onto the council of owners now. It's all got to be done properly and looked at first.'

Moreover, while some owners complained about their diminished control, longer-term residents in particular also described regulation as reassuring; knowing their co-residents would be governed by standards of conduct, and policed accordingly, provided peace of mind. In this sense, residents could perceive private regulation as a means to de-risk condo living, but such comments often appeared somewhat contradictory as most owners also conceded a far from perfect governance system, with many complaining about a lack of transparency, frequent rule violations and inconsistent and untimely enforcement of by-laws, as we shall see. Many owners had a story along the same lines as Max, a 60-year-old inner-city Melbourne owner, who complained about regulatory oversight:

> 'When I had a [noise] issue with the floor upstairs, the building manager said – when I first raised it with him – he said there was a meeting that night of the committee [and] he'd raise it with them then. It appeared to me that he hadn't raised it. I had to follow him up quite a number of times and every time I talked to him he said he hasn't been able to talk to [resident living above] because every time he knocks on the door, they don't answer. I thought that's not a good enough reason. He can put a note in their letterbox. He's got their email address. He could have contacted them. I then got the impression that he probably hadn't raised it with the committee or else they would have followed up. It has been addressed now, but that's when I asked for the minutes, and I suspect that's why I couldn't get the [meeting] minutes.'

Residents' perception and experiences of the way private regulation restricted their homemaking, whether their decorating or their renovating, encouraged and reinforced residents' sense of reduced autonomy in the condo unit.

Residents' lack of control undermined their propertied expectations of their private home space as their 'castle'. For owners, especially those with longer-term plans to stay in their condos and the financial means, their inability to hang colourful curtains, install a timber floor or dry laundry on their balcony gave rise to lingering frustrations. As we saw with the discussion of laundering, some residents retaliated: they followed rules only loosely, they engaged in fake compliance and many admitted to occasionally flouting rules. Owners appeared relatively more brazen in shirking rules; one Melbourne owner had recently ordered a shutter for their bathroom window, for instance, and commented flippantly: "we'll see if we get into trouble for that one". For many owners for whom the condo unit was clearly perceived as their 'castle', their propertied expectations translated into a tangible sense of entitlement, and this appeared to reinforce owners' confidence about defying perceived rules in this brazen way. Such accounts suggest how owners sometimes came to view by-laws more as recommendations than inviolable rules and how they came to see building managers or their OC committee as empty threats rather than as domestic policing agents.

Renters, by contrast, appeared more conscientious and often far less at ease than owners in their rule breaking. For many renters, by-laws became yet another set of rules that overshadowed their home lives and home spaces and yet another set of conditions that could potentially jeopardize their tenancy. Renters' home decorating, for instance, was comparatively more constrained as a result, even aspects of home decorating that were permissible under by-laws. While less extensive decorating might well reflect private renters' relatively higher residential mobility, many renters also harboured concerns, and even deep anxieties, about being evicted or losing their rental bond. From that vantage point, every breach was potentially reckless and subsequently renters appeared far more frequently to seek formal OC approval. Accordingly, comments of this order were not uncommon: "I have to get permission for pretty much everything, and I don't want to take any chances with my tenancy. So I'm trying to do everything by the book." Exceptionally, renters undertook significant changes: they added a portable kitchen island when they found kitchen countertop space limited, they installed flyscreens and tinted windows using adhesive film, for example. As one Melbourne renter recounted:

> 'Being in such close proximity and directly opposite that high rise, one wants a little bit of privacy. I've gone to the lengths of changing these balcony doors to decrease the UV light that comes in and to deflect anybody looking in. It's a mirrored finish on the other side, and it reduces the UV light by 70 per cent. It's a tinting effect. … That's one thing I've done that has paid off to an extent. Once again, I was

told you have to leave it exactly the way you found it and tinting the windows isn't the way I found it. I went ahead and did it anyway!'

Frequently, the combination of tenancy regulation and by-laws hampered renters as they attempted to make the private unit their home. Many renters, like 53-year-old renter Rada, did little to personalize her unit but meanwhile "fantasized about making changes": she imagined repainting and recarpeting and installing shelving, TV mounts and picture hooks. Renters found landlords unreceptive or landlords' proposed "solutions" unworkable, such as Lui, a frustrated Perth renter, who hung picture frames using stickers specified by their rental agency, only for these to fall and smash. At the extreme, renters' anxieties severely restricted their capacity to make themselves comfortable in their units. One renter who lived in a pre-furnished inner-city Perth condo revealed they were so concerned with "ruining" their landlord's leather couches that they barely sat on them, protected them with throws when they did and cleaned them obsessively afterwards, retreating most days to their less anxiety-inducing bedroom. Some renters had limited means to invest in homemaking, and others were disinclined to invest time, energy or resources when they were unlikely to be able to stay for long. Reinforcing how private condo restrictions converge with the tenure insecurities that plague the Australian private rental market, 47-year-old long-term renter Tracey summed up: "We haven't touched anything. We haven't done artwork or anything. Yeah, because we're not here long enough."

While this evidence highlights how private regulation constrained how residents decorated and renovated their condos, tacit social expectations were also significant in governing residents' homemaking. In this regard, constraints on residents' decorating and renovating practices echoed my earlier account of the way routine chores such as laundering come to be circumscribed by local norms in everyday condo living. Craig, a 58-year-old outright-owner in Perth, for example, recounted how he and his wife had refrained from selecting their preferred timber flooring when they renovated their three-bedroom condo, even though by-laws did permit hard-wood flooring options. Craig explained their choice was driven by other-regarding concerns about noise-transfer to neighbours below: "I'm [now] a big advocate of carpet because [with] hard floors the noise transfers through these buildings badly. So although this complex allows them, we've managed to keep them to a minimum." Craig's choices were motivated by his own experience of nuisance noise produced by timber flooring, as we will see in the following chapter, and this suggests how such social expectations may take hold and be reproduced in everyday condo living through residents' cumulative experiences of high-rise condo living. For now, Craig's comments illustrate how local homemaking practices are governed neither by by-laws nor by self-interested motivations alone. Max, the retired Melbourne owner, described a similar level of personal restraint or self-regulation in choosing to have curtains fitted rather than blinds, even though he believed curtains offered less tailored protection against the significant sun glare his unit suffered during the day. Max elaborated:

> 'You can see that there's sort of built-in helmets, or whatever you call them, for the curtains on there, and all the bedrooms have there. … The only thing I could have done was get blinds, I think. … I do get a bit of sunlight coming in at times that's a bit annoying, but on the other hand, I just don't like the look of. … Some of the other apartments have put in blinds, and from outside it doesn't look very tidy. I'm not going to do it.'

Again, Max rationalized his private choice as partly dictated by the particularities of his condo's building design but also partly a decision motivated by other-regarding concerns about the *public* aesthetics of his window dressings as viewed by others on the external building facade.

Short on space

Limited space within private units, especially in Melbourne's condos, meant some residents had nowhere to store vacuum cleaners and no room for essential furniture, such as dining sets and bedside tables. Many had no linen cupboard and kitchens with little storage; at the extreme, one resident used their dishwasher to store pots and pans. Young families kept prams in their car boots as these blocked limited and narrow circulation spaces in their unit and rarely fit in their small bedrooms. Designs further limited how well the limited space residents did have could support their homemaking. Irregular-shaped living spaces doubled as circulation spaces connecting entryways, bedrooms and bathrooms, and oddly placed electrical sockets made furniture placement difficult. This resulted in sometimes dysfunctional furniture arrangements and required many households to do without a dedicated dining table. Comments from Trey, a Melbourne renter, illustrate a common spatial dilemma in condos' open-plan living zones: "I would like to have a table and chairs in here, but that just doesn't allow it. I've racked my brain about how I could reconfigure this lounge room." Meanwhile in flatshares, flatmates retreated to their small bedrooms for privacy, leaving dedicated living spaces unused. Other inefficiencies included barely used kitchens as residents ate out or ordered in. This accords with both Buys and Miller's (2012: 333) survey on higher-density dwellers in Brisbane, Australia which found residents' main design concern was space and with evidence on the small size and lack of storage in Melbourne condos especially, as compiled in Chapter 1.

Residents adjusted their expectations, adapted their household consumption and re-strategized their storage. These downsizing efforts could be rewarding, creating novel and pleasant experiences, reducing household clutter and minimizing housework. Some residents thrived. Scott, a 57-year-old Perth who had downsized from a suburban "McMansion" with his wife four years ago loved the new "efficiencies". He explained: "we didn't use 50 per cent of the rooms [in their previous house]. They had furniture or stuff in them – never used them! … Most people in their houses use three rooms: bedroom, kitchen, main living. Here, we just haven't got auxiliary." Christine, a 71-year-old recent widow who had recently moved from a larger property, had initial reservations: "I think I had 24 towels. So I had to get rid of 22. … I was worried sick that it was gonna be so tiny!" Christine, like several other downsizers, found downsizing emotionally taxing to begin with, but adjusted: "Hard to do initially but I'm fine now," Christine said. Renters seemed to tolerate such constraints more readily, often rationalizing these as a 'trade-off' for a better location and affordability. More generally, longer-term renters often appeared habituated to sometimes considerable constraints, both spatial and regulatory, over their home spaces. Owners meanwhile appeared more able and willing to invest in managing various spatio-regulatory constraints they confronted in their home spaces, and sometimes more innovative too. For instance, several owners invested in minor renovations, such as renovating their kitchens to secure additional storage, and one owner installed a bulkhead in their hallway to provide extra overhead storage in their ceiling space.

Still, many residents felt squeezed for space and this led most residents to engage in various forms of socio-spatial choreography and synchronizations so as to make their home in the condo. These micro-territorial practices took on heightened significance in relatively larger households comprising more than two people, such as families with young children or rental flatshares, for whom space was at an all-time premium in their small two-bedroom units. Earlier, we saw the inconveniences flatmates faced with laundries positioned in a flatmate's designated 'private' bathroom and the way flatmates retreated to their small bedrooms because measly living spaces made co-occupying these with their flatmates while also respecting each other's personal space and privacy difficult. Other accounts also emphasized how kitchens too small to accommodate more than one user required flatmates to schedule their cooking at different times for similar reasons. Poor sound insulation also undermined each flatmate's privacy, including in their ostensibly private bedrooms. Visual privacy was also an issue for 43-year-old renter Trey, for instance, who described how he was also disturbed visually by his flatmate when they used their kitchen at night, since Trey's bedroom 'borrowed light' from the kitchen through a high-level 'window'. As noted in Chapter 1, developers used this 'borrowed light' design strategy because it meant units could include 'bedrooms' with no windows – a practice now banned, but not before the buildings these residents live in were built. Many other residents faced similar visual and auditory disturbances, such as lounge lighting shining through frosted glass bedroom doors, which were providing 'borrowed light' to windowless rooms. Since house shares comprised of renters, it was condo renters again who navigated more delicate socio-territorial dynamics within their units. Some renters who had previously lived in high-rise housing suggested they were mostly habituated to the necessary socio-territorial 'dances' that enabled them to make the condo home, albeit they remained frustrated by these constraints. Other flatsharing renters who found themselves facing another set of flatsharing considerations above and beyond formal and informal restrictions, some of which we have touched on already, found their sense of being 'at home' considerably challenged.

Conversely, as I have described previously, children 'colonised' open-plan living spaces in condo units such that the paraphernalia of young family life – playpens, toys and prams, scooters and laundry-filled clothes racks – became permanent features (see Nethercote and Horne 2016). Young families often subsequently struggled to adjust to inadequate storage, impractical or inflexible condo layouts, limited bedrooms and lack of child-friendly private outdoor space. Parents adopted distinct dynamics of cohabiting and ordering children, as I have previously detailed, with open-plan designs assisting parents' juggling of chores with child-supervision, as others also report (Stevenson and Prout 2013). In families with older and adult children who required no or less intense supervision, however, desired physical separation and privacy between parents and children was difficult to achieve. Dowling and Power (2012) identify how parents and children achieve privacy and separation in detached houses through containment, exclusion of children and opportunities to undertake activities 'separately but together' within generous open-plan spaces. Without these options, parent-child negotiations in the condo home space could stall, complicating and challenging family life. Meanwhile young families' accounts corroborate prior studies which have underscored the subsequent pressures on young families living in condos (Nethercote and Horne 2016; Kerr et al 2018), with some voicing plans or a desire to abandon condo living. In migrant households in particular, space constraints also complicated expectations around accommodating family visitors, usually from abroad, for extended durations, often of the order of months rather than days or weeks. Guaraav, a young international student described, for instance, a recent two-month visit from their family abroad, in which eight family members stayed with him in his single-bedroom Melbourne inner-city condo. Although he recounted the family visit in mostly favourable terms, his revealed this substantive temporary overcrowding required intensive daily socio-spatial negotiations and synchronizations in which frictions were mostly minimized by relying on close familial bonds and shared cultural norms around intergenerational living.

Private storage cages became an essential strategy for many condo residents managing space constraints. Located in communal basement garages, these housed a plethora of possessions: seasonal items such as Christmas decorations; sporting and camping equipment; suitcases, artwork and heirloom furniture; filing cabinets; "boxes of miscellaneous rubbish" and other items residents could not bear to part with. For Mona's young family, who gained access to a storage cage late in their tenancy, this added storage captured the 'spill-over' of family life that could not be contained satisfactorily in their private unit. Thirty-three-year-old expat hairdresser Mona had rented her one-bedroom inner-city condo in Melbourne where she had lived for the past five years with her partner and, more recently, their newborn. The storage cage was transformative in enabling this new mother to regain her sense of control over her home, as Mona's account captures:

> 'When we got the cage, yeah, life was a little bit better. … My partner was like: "Oh, I've got a surprise, come downstairs." … And I saw the cage, and I started running out, crying, I was like "Oh my God! This is amazing! This is amazing!" And I ran back upstairs, and was like "We can put that down there! We can put that down there!" And all this stuff. Straight away, I wanted to fill it up. And he was like "Oh, you didn't even cry when we got engaged." But I was just like "Oh, it's gonna change our lives!"
>
> It's been amazing! Especially with a little one, we wouldn't be able to cope. All the bits you have with a baby as well. … Yeah, just things that he's gonna need in a few months are down there. Things he's outgrowing, we put down there. Yeah, the minimum up here. … So that's got lots of things [in the cage]: ornaments I have, and when he gets a bit more mobile, anything that's in the way I'll just put downstairs. We'll bulk buy boxes of nappies from Costco and keep them in the cage and bring bits up when we need them. … So if we didn't have that cage, we wouldn't have lasted here. I think because it's full to the roof. It's full! Suitcases, Christmas tree, sports things. You name it; it goes down in the cage.'

Many renters, however, went without such storage cages as landlords either leased these (as well as their designated car parking bay) separately to maximize rental yields or retained them for their own use. In any case, cages did not always provide ideal means to manage some space constraints in residents' private units with neither the relative security nor convenience of their private unit. Residents reported incidents where basement car parks flooded, exposing their storage items to water damage, and many highlighted that cages were prone to break-ins too, with car park entrances vulnerable to tailgating – security issues we return to in Chapter 5. Wary, residents refrained from storing valuables such as one Perth renter who, after having his costly carpentry tools stolen from his cage, started keeping his newly replaced tools in his unit, though lugging the tools back and forth between his car and unit each day for work was tiresome and inconvenient, and the tools also took up valuable space in his unit. Other residents conceded to renting private off-site storage or left items with local family or friends, especially those residents who had downsized but intended to upsize again, when they could afford a larger home or when their families expanded.

Even with additional storage, some condo families struggled to adapt, feeling the weight of traditional family ideals and the associated 'stigma' surrounding raising children in high-rise housing, as Kerr and colleagues (2020) also identify. As social expectations surrounding housing consumption and the spatial constraints of the private unit collide in everyday condo living, this could curb condo residents' desire to socialize at home, corroborating Kerr and colleagues' (2020: 433) findings and the sentiment expressed by condo parent Melanie, who remarks: "I feel almost embarrassed to invite people over, because especially friends with houses, because there's sometimes that little bit of rivalry, 'How can you live in a unit?' kind of thing, so I sometimes feel a bit like we can't really invite people over, unless they are also in a similar boat." Jason, a recently divorced father conceded struggling to personalize his children's bedrooms, for instance, since space constraints meant their rooms also functioned as a home office and housed lots of his possessions, including his bike, the latter due to inadequate security which we will get to in Chapters 5 and 6. Jason repeatedly compared his condo to his previous spacious suburban family home, revealing how the weight of social expectations, as well as personal housing aspirations, can work to undermine condo homemaking. For Jason, his struggles to "properly" accommodate his children undermined his level of attachment to the unit and his ability to feel much sense of ownership, as he doubted its longer-term viability to meet his homemaking needs. Meanwhile, the challenges of setting up an "acceptable" family home also diminished Jason's own sense of being a "good" father. Much like the parents in Kerr and colleagues' (2020) study, some tried to compensate, for instance, by buying small slides or cubby houses, many used infrequently, with the items described as "emotional baggage" by parents as they tried to ensure their children didn't "miss out" on the great Australian dream of having a private backyard.

On the other hand, for some, a sense of airiness and openness afforded by the high-rise condo's elevation and full-height glazing provided something of an antidote, or distraction at least, to the pressures of all these spatio-regulatory constraints on their homemaking. Corroborating emerging geographic literature on the affective atmospheres of vertical living cited in

Chapter 2, some residents living on higher levels described days where they felt 'caught' in the clouds and their surreal experience of looking out into white nothingness. Some, such as 32nd-floor resident Eddie embraced the sense of detachment from the city below:

> 'And it's interesting when you're up here, it happened to me last week. … I came home, and I walked in. I could not see a thing. It was white. Completely white. I was in a cloud. Completely white. I could not see anything outside the windows. It was wonderful. It was so unusual. It was like, my God! … The clouds come down, and all the tops of [nearby skyscrapers] disappeared. So that's interesting. Weird … and we can't really sense that it's raining here sometimes. There's no sense of it. … And you look down there, and you can see that all the footpaths are wet and stuff and so we know: it's raining. I know it's weird, but you might see specks of water on the glass, but we seem to be above it a bit.'

This appears to corroborate Baxter's (2017: 344) findings that those tenants living on higher floors were privy to a 'more expansive range and intensity of vertical practices' and were afforded 'the fullest expression of vertical homes'. Indeed the quirks of living high, including breathtaking vistas and novel perspectives and sensations contributed sometimes substantively to developing residents' attachment to their home space, to their home as subject-object belonging. For an inner-city Melbourne renter, their views were likewise a source of pride as well as delight: "When you walk into it, it's impressive. People always walk out and look at the view. You can see Luna Park all lit up at night. You can see all the lights. So people immediately come in and walk out to the balcony and start looking at landmarks." Even some residents who did not live especially high, such as 5th-floor Perth owner Marta remarked: "once we saw the view there was no other one [unit]. We used to come and park and look at where's the moon gonna be; it's just sensational!" On the other hand, residents could also find their great views changeable or short-lived, altered or blocked entirely by city development. Especially where residents described captivating vistas as defining features of their home spaces, they appeared to find their lack of control over their views unsettling. An owner's intention to live in their condo "forever" was thus sometimes qualified: they would move if their view were "built out".

For some, views were the "saving grace" of otherwise unmanageably small condos; Mona, the new mother we met earlier who had been struggling with space, commented:

> 'If it wasn't for that view, I don't think we would have stayed here so long … I think looking out onto the bay, I don't know, gives you that

> sense of openness, and just looking out there … looking out onto that every day, I'm like oh yeah, I can cope. I can cope a little bit longer in a tiny apartment.'

Even the smallest of balconies without much aspect provided some with physical and mental reprieve from the confines of claustrophobic or "cabin feverish" small private condo home spaces. Still, many found the balcony was far from the outdoor oasis marketed by developers. Some described their balconies as windswept, too shaded or too exposed and some suggested they used them infrequently or far less so than they had anticipated, especially those living on higher floors. For instance, a Perth renter had initially viewed their balcony as the "bonus feature" in their new rental, yet now never stepped foot on it except to clean up in anticipation of tenancy inspections. In another Perth condo, the balcony had become strictly their dog's domain.

These balconies were not redundant, however, to condo homemaking, often playing other practical functions, including providing additional storage space. While clearly not in keeping with their architect's design intent, residents used their balconies to stow away anything from old TVs, beanbags, charity bags awaiting donation, clothes racks, pot plants, brooms and dustbins and even, in one case, a surplus bed frame and mattress. For some, this makeshift storage solution was impractical, unsightly and frustrating. Other residents invested in integrated storage solutions, and this increased their satisfaction. Perth owners, as previously noted, had installed shutters to their balconies, and their screened balconies often functioned much like a domestic garage or shed, or like the basement storage cages, absorbing the 'spill over' of homemaking in spatially constrained private units. With their balconies now weatherproof, these Perth owners kitted these out with shelving to house camping equipment, tools, crates of wine, a spare fridge and so forth. These minor DIY jobs gave residents some sense of territorial autonomy and provided practical support for residents' homemaking by relieving pressures created by spatial constraints. Thirty-four-year-old renter Jasmine, who lived in a one-bedroom Perth unit with her partner described the storage as a "lifesaver because I was going nuts after moving from a four-bedroom [share] home, huge, big backyard…!"

However, even these industrious Perth owners who had successfully enclosed their balconies found the minor renovation process taxing and this had reinforced rather than assuaged their sense of limited autonomy and control over their private home space. Especially confronting was dealing with their OC committee and navigating private restrictions. Other residents likewise described how managing space constraints cemented their impressions of being powerless and hamstrung in their private home spaces. One reason for this was that residents perceived they had few space-making alternatives since expanding the condo was largely unfeasible beyond conversions of balconies and acquisitions of storage cages. Several residents implied or directly referenced a contrast between the sense of autonomy afforded to other homeowners, who are conceivably able to extend upwards or outwards. Condo residents were also unable or reluctant to invest in space-saving workarounds, such as smaller "condo-friendly" furniture. This was especially so for many renters for whom the condo was "just" a temporary home as well as for many younger owners who saw the condo as a form of "stop-gap" homeownership on their way to a "bigger and better" home. Homemaking in the context of the spatio-regulatory constraints we have reviewed here ranged from minor annoyance and mild frustrations to significant dissatisfaction and tension, reflective of processes of home unmaking. Long-time suburban homeowner Jason, who rented his condo in the wake of his divorce, told us: "I hate it! I absolutely hate it!", later claiming: "You take a liveability hit in the reduced size. I think everybody would feel that." For some, condo living had an expiry date – as one of several younger residents confirmed: "if we have kids, then the condo is not what we want … it's not enough space for kids or for pets". This perceived impermanence of the condo home likewise undermined some homemaking efforts, disincentivizing residents from personalizing their homes for instance, as we have seen, though such practices are otherwise known to deepen homemakers' sense of attachment. Even retirees who planned to be "carried out in a box", as they put it, harboured reservations about the permanence of their condo home. Eloise, a 69-year-old Perth owner revealed: "I always felt too claustrophobic. … Having come from a big house, a big yard. It took a while to … well … I don't know whether I'm even over it yet. I'm starting to have more thoughts of maybe we should move."

High maintenance

A low-maintenance carefree lifestyle was a big draw for many condo residents, providing domestic functionality and home comforts with minimal responsibilities. For some, this expectation was realized in everyday condo living. Owner Heath, a retired professor, who lived in inner-city Melbourne, struggled to recall any upkeep he had undertaken during ten years in his previous condo: "I think the concierge did it … replaced two fluorescent tubes and one-tap, I think. That was it!" Many relished their condo's 'lock-and-leave' convenience. Kaveh, a 38-year-old owner in middle-ring Perth commented: "I've gone off (travelling) for weeks at a time [and I] don't have to worry about anything." Forty-three-year-old renter Trey, who lived with a flatmate after downsizing from a large house in a regional town, described condo living as akin to a sea change. Less than a year in, he insisted condo living was "like living in a hotel" or "like I'm on holidays" due to the time freed up from home-maintenance. Trey wondered how long these feelings would last: "So would I feel that way in five years? I might say to you, 'Oh, I hate it. I feel closed in.' But for me, it's still new, and I still love it!" Many owners also seemed to turn a blind eye to their OC levies when they described maintenance as "cheap", with many echoing retiree owner Heath's assessment: "I've virtually no maintenance money at all. … I spend much less money, obviously, in maintenance." Again, this underscores residents' ambivalent and ambiguous impression of formal condo governance, including the way they manage to disassociate their home space from aspects of formal governance, such as the payment of levies.

Other residents, however, were less upbeat, emphasizing that "low maintenance" often translated to reduced control. They bemoaned the administration involved in getting things fixed or changed, chronicling their experiences of drawn-out processes and unduly delays. Perth owner Craig related: "Okay, let's have a meeting. Let's get three quotes, yadda yadda. So it takes three months to do what you'd do in your own house in a week." Some found OC fees excessive for the services provided. Others lamented how management only escalated "urgent" complaints. Residents oftentimes found maintenance more fraught than in previous homes and they emphasized the complexity of maintenance in large high-rise buildings where even minor issues often seemed to implicate numerous co-residents and often required the involvment of multiple other condo stakeholders to resolve too. Residents thus perceived their autonomy as limited, as 32-year-old Melbourne owner Pia explained:

> 'If your pipe burst and all that, it's a high cost. It's not something where you can tear it down and fix easily. You either get [the OC] involved … get your neighbours and all that. … So if anything goes wrong, you can't just make an executive decision and say, "I want to tear down my pipes." So I think that's the bad thing'.

Such experiences again chiselled away at owners' sense of autonomy, unsettling their traditional propertied expectations of their home as castle. On the other hand, some owners, particularly those who saw their unit only as a short-term proposition, appeared relatively less fazed. Conversely, most owners similarly brushed off longer-term building maintenance concerns, demonstrating neither much knowledge nor sense of responsibility about the longer-term maintenance of their building, including requisite upgrading. Their commentary frequently conveyed their finite and time-limited sense of ownership, as illustrated in remarks such as 60-year-old Melbourne owner Max's, who said: "that's down the track, it won't be an issue in my time".

Beyond routine maintenance, building defects caused residents headaches. Residents strategized: when condensation pooled on windowsills, for instance, as it frequently did in some buildings, they cranked open windows if they could, lay towels to catch the pooling water, hung laundry outdoors to minimize moisture, and kept watch for mould. Some residents used chemical desiccants or invested in dehumidifiers. Often residents depended on others, more so than they had in previous housing. Mark, a 66-year-old retiree owner bought a three-bed 30th-floor unit off-the-plan, and his regrettable experience since moving in two years ago illustrates well the issues surrounding the socio-spatial interdependencies of his home spaces on his co-residents' homes. Mark saw his purchase as a little risky, having never lived in a condo, but nonetheless reasoned "it might be pretty nice to live in something that's brand new and has nice views". He was at pains to point out that he had bought judiciously all the same, aware of the unfavourable reputation that surrounded Melbourne's condos by that time. Still, Mark harboured doubts:

> 'My apartment, including the balcony, is about a 130 square metres. … So, it is bigger than normal, and you pay for that, but I didn't want it to be pokey. And I'm appalled when I see some of the stuff they're building in Melbourne; I think it's terrible. I think they're the slums of the future, really. … I didn't want to get one of these pokey little apartments of which there are plenty around Melbourne. I've looked at quite a few of them and been quite horrified with what's being approved for construction these days. … They're shockers! They're horrible! And I wanted something a bit bigger and a bit nicer. You pay a bit of a premium for these apartments. I'm not sure it's totally justified in hindsight.'

Since moving in, Mark had faced a slew of defect issues: loud creaking noise in high winds, persistent smoke infiltration and water leaks. The OC and builder hand-balled his complaints back-and-forth; neither took responsibility. The builder eventually agreed to rectify the creaking issue but provided no timeline. Other issues remained unresolved. We will consider Mark's smoke infiltration issues more closely in the next chapter, but here, his general account of dealing with maintenance issues captures well his constrained autonomy over his home space:

> 'I don't know if they're going to fix it properly, cause there's no plans – [as] I understand – to take the tiles up in the lounge room. I'm concerned about that. I just don't know when [the builder is] coming. But he may, when he comes in to do the work I've said they'll do, like pull the walls down to fix the bad creaking – which is a problem they've encountered in other buildings, so they're familiar with this problem.'

Mark elaborated:

> 'I've spent a lot of money buying this place, and at times, it's virtually unliveable … I'm not using all the rooms because there's a number of problems I've got. [The builders] have been telling me for almost two years now that they would come in and pull the walls down. Three walls need to come down. And they're going to rectify one problem, which is terrible creaking when the wind's high. About a month ago, the building manager said he thinks they're coming sort of soonish. So, I got busy and cleared out the study/second bedroom. I've got a lot of things stacked up in the lounge room, so it's a bit hard. I'm sort of camping there, if you like. And it's been like that for a month and I still don't know when they're coming. They told me they were coming last November. They were coming December. They were coming January. They were coming February. Now March is gone. I still don't know when they're coming. And it's been almost two years. … So I'm basically camping out in the lounge room and using my bedroom and bathroom. And the bathroom, en-suite – I had to pack everything up into tubs there, too, because they apparently want to come in and patch up on some of the walls there for another problem.'

Alongside stress, upset and anger at his perceived powerlessness over his home space, this process consumed Mark's life:

> 'I haven't really felt like displaying the apartment to friends and inviting people up because I'm still camping. I tell them as much, and people must think I'm a bit strange – I'm not inviting people around. But I didn't expect to be having all these problems dragging on unresolved. I want things finished.
>
> If I get my apartment all fixed up, I might actually decide to stay forever, because there's a lot of positives. It's just all the frustrations that've taken the edge off for me. … I'm so frustrated living here at the moment. I'm just so frustrated; I don't know what to do.'

Mark knew of some co-owners who faced similar issues, though this provided little comfort or assistance as the builder shamed their attempts at collective remediation and co-owners received contradictory advice:

> '[But] I don't know how many people are experiencing this problem because you don't really get to know your neighbours. You're a bit isolated. … A few people that I talked to [suggested] that maybe I needed to do a leaflet drop to surrounding buildings and ask what

> the problems they're having are and get a bit of a group together and start to discuss common problems. Now I really only did this to try and get [the builder] to talk to me.
>
> So then [the builder] contacted me and they actually said: "Here, we've come downstairs." Two senior development guys from [builders], and they said, "I understand that you've been talking about us." And you sort of get a bit front footed, and I said: "Well, I don't actually like controversy. I did that as a tactic to try and get to speak to you and it seems to have worked. Here you are, talking to me." So that's the sort of desperate thing I've had to do at times, but it hasn't really led anywhere. And I don't know that it did me any favours getting them to respond like that. I did get to speak to them, but I'm still waiting.'

Although Mark faced serious defects issues, residents' struggles with defects were commonplace, rather than limited to a few isolated cases.

Residents' ability to maintain their private unit often relied heavily on the actions of external stakeholders including developers, builders, their OCs and committees and, in the larger condos which this analysis focuses upon, building and facilities managers. The relative complexity of the high-rise typology complicated routine and periodic maintenance. Technically, issues could be harder to diagnose by residents and building managers, as well as by qualified professionals. Operationally, owners could not action issues alone, relying instead on other stakeholders whose processes and procedures could be slow, haphazard and opaque. Managerially, the onus of responsibility could fall to multiple stakeholders, and OC actioning required accounting for all residents potentially affected, whether physically or financially by the issue in question and its practical remediation. Build quality issues exacerbated the dilemmas residents faced. Although owners were most disheartened by poor-quality design and workmanship and by their inability to independently action issues, renters were discouraged too. Renters found that cheap paint meant walls could not be wiped clean without causing damage, carpets scuffed more easily and so forth. Although renters like 22-year-old Aditya suggested that they tended to "just sort of live with [it]" they admitted they worried landlords might blame them for undue wear and tear and withhold their bond. This corresponds with findings on Australian private renters more broadly which identifies renters as both reluctant to pursue requests for maintenance and repairs out of fear their landlords will retaliate with rent increases or termination and also reluctant to invest time and money in personalizing, furnishings or making changes, such as painting, for a relatively short-term tenancy, knowing that all changes need to be 'reverted' at the end of their lease (Hulse et al 2011).

Local working rules

Private rules govern a range of homemaking practices that are essential to making the private unit a comfortable, functional and homely home. Residents entered their private condo units with largely traditional propertied expectations of this private home space as a place of relative autonomy, control and independence. Yet (their perceptions of) private rules regulated how they laundered, decorated, stored their possessions and undertook home-maintenance. And regardless of whether residents complied, faked compliance (as they did with air-drying laundry, for instance) or brazenly breached rules, navigating perceived restrictions could undermine their sense of the condo home as dominion. Residents' sense of powerlessness was compounded both by the high-rise condo's architectural and governance complexity, including its socio-spatial interdependencies and their reliance on condo stakeholders, and by significant design and construction quality issues since the meagre size of units, windswept balconies, a lack of storage, and windowless second bedrooms and so forth, could make it difficult for residents to meet their various needs for comfort and privacy, especially renters. Residents' limited sense of territorial control over their private home spaces led some to express misgivings about their condo purchase and to question their aptitude for condo living.

But besides private restriction, residents also self-regulated to meet a range of non-binding locally contingent working rules which, together with spatio-material and regulatory constraint, also substantively conditioned their homemaking.[3] These local working rules are implicit in residents' use of normative rather than legal frames of reference when detailing their own conduct and that of their co-residents. These informal rules variously replicate or replace by-laws with more, or less, stringent social expectations, the latter depicted for example in various normative discussions around the installation of timber flooring and 'shoe-free' living in the condo unit, for instance. Working rules can emerge from the chasm residents perceive between private restrictions and their own sense of what is locally appropriate.

[3] Note that residents also self-regulate in response to a wide range of other societal expectations, for instance regarding homemaking at various "life stages". This self-regulation is captured when condo families are observed refraining from socializing and hosting playdates within the condo to minimize social judgement about their perceived failings to adhere to traditional suburban family living ideals about space and parent-child separation and privacy. Similarly, retiree Mark refrains from having visitors to his defect-plagued condo out of a sense of shame that his living arrangements do not reflect the "proper" way of living at his advanced life-stage.

Returning briefly to the broader clothesline debate reveals the potential fallout of this misalignment between private restrictions and normative ideals, for it confirms how OC regulation can impact household chores as routine as laundry with sometimes far-reaching implications, not least amid a climate crisis and rising household energy poverty (Geoghegan 2010). Media reports from the UK suggest balcony air-drying bans may doubly inconvenience renters, for instance, where tenancy agreements additionally prohibit indoor drying to mitigate condensation and damp (Usborne 2016). In response to clothesline bans in private communities in the US, so-called Right to Dry advocates have rallied to rebrand the clothesline as eco-responsible and line-drying as desirable. From *Project Laundry List*, *Clotheslines for Change* to the 2012 documentary *Drying for Freedom*, this advocacy has been somewhat effective. In some states, such as California, it is now illegal for OCs to prohibit hanging clothes outdoors (Daum 2015). Likewise, in some Australian jurisdictions, OCs cannot ban where residents hang their washing so long as it is not over balcony balustrades in rulings that align with prohibitions on restrictions on sustainability infrastructure more broadly. The clothesline debate raises age-old questions about the collective rights of homeowners to regulate privatized communities, the contractual obligation of owners (and renters) to abide by such rules and the way these private rules support or undermine personal, private community and public interests, such as environmental imperatives. Whatever their genesis, working rules circumscribe homemaking above and beyond formal private restrictions as residents attempt to duly comply with what is deemed most appropriate locally.

While the ownership model primes us to expect that condo residents will operate as purely self-interested individuals, condo residents practise property in both privatized *and* other-regarding terms. Property scholars have long recognized that real property comes 'freighted' with obligations to others; so while we tend to think of the private garden only in terms of privatized interests such as pleasure, autonomy and seclusion, in practice privatized interests and proprietarian ends overlap (see Blomley 2005b; 2016b: 230). Condo residents using their private balconies, not unlike Blomley's gardeners, are alert to how their homemaking is seen or heard by other 'publics' including their co-residents, and they calibrate their practices accordingly, such as by maintaining an aesthetically pleasing building facade, free from "unsightly" washing.

That the balcony best illustrates this mediation surrounding homemaking comes as little surprise since the balcony, much like a private garden, is a liminal or edge space. This liminality means these spaces share a public visibility that engenders, for instance, aesthetic standards about what they should look like. Residents' responses to these aesthetic expectations recall Goffmanesque performativity, of which familiar examples abound. For instance, aesthetic concerns about Beijing's image and reputation are a possible reason why ordinarily ubiquitous balcony line-drying on its high-rise balconies was banned during the Beijing Olympics. Like the private garden, a condo balcony evokes questions of 'good taste', conformity and civic pride in a similar way to the private garden. Yet, its aesthetic qualities must be achieved collectively by co-residents in a similar way that the reputation or aesthetics of a street, neighbourhood or city relies on a collective response albeit at an even greater scale.

Beyond these liminal spaces, residents also practise property in other-regarding ways within the depths of the private unit when, for instance, often unbeknownst to their co-residents, residents disregarded favoured flooring choices as they self-regulate out of concern about their neighbours' peace and privacy. As this chapter details, whether laundering or renovating, condo homemaking requires that residents square other-regarding aesthetic or noise considerations with their own private interests, such as their desire to dry clothes sustainably, conveniently and cheaply or their preference for timber floors, which may be hardwearing, easy to clean and aesthetically pleasing but in a poorly insulated building are ultimately noisy for co-residents.[4]

This chapter shows how condo homemaking requires that residents mediate private rules and private interests, and local working rules and other-regarding concerns. Condo residents appear to recognize that 'it is necessary to develop a more collective and cooperative way of living to make the building "work"' (Blandy et al 2018: 86). Clarifying what this might involve, Blandy (2013: 167, 164) identifies, for instance, how relations between co-housing residents are based on reciprocity or the principles of 'give-and-take' as residents 'discovered what as a group we want to do'. However, this chapter also leaves largely unanswered questions about how residents cooperate and engage in 'give and take' over the appropriate use of their private home spaces. And indeed while property is inherently

[4] Blomley (2005b: 656) cautions against insisting on a false binary between privatized and other-regarding dimensions, arguing these can co-exist, for instance, in private gardening practices that 'mediate creatively between both extremes'. Blomley (2005b: 656) also encourages us to move away from thinking of privacy and propriety only in terms of antithetical extremes of 'narrow-minded individualism [privacy] … [or] stultifying conformism [propriety]' arguing this overlooks the more valuable and appealing dimensions of each such as 'autonomy and civic engagement' which are 'more immediately realised when privacy and propriety are set in relation to each other, rather than in opposition'. This is most tangible in visual examples. In the suburban garden, Blomley (2005b: 655) shows how propriety enacted in 'less conformist ways', in terms of local garden aesthetics that were 'more relaxed' enabled gardeners to garden without needing to 'conform to some rigid collective prescription'; these gardeners were 'no less proprietarian', in the sense of demonstrating 'some sense of obligation to community … though diverse, were not simply expressions of detached individuality'.

social and while residents are acutely aware of their co-residents' physical proximities, the infrequency of co-resident social interactions raises further questions. Complicating matters, informal rules sometimes appear unsettled, as evidenced by residents' different understandings of what was appropriate, perhaps because of the immaturity of Australian high-rise living and because of each building's material and design quirks. What happens to the condo home when residents do not or cannot comply with local working rules? These are questions and issues the following chapter will begin to explore as it turns to examine the private unit's borders as zones of co-resident contact and as it considers residents' border-marking and -maintenance, associated nuisance and its implications for condo relations and condo homemaking.

4

'I'll Close My Blinds'

In a luxury high-rise tower in London, owners felt like zoo specimens. A mere 34 metres away from their homes, on the Tate Modern's 10th-storey viewing platform the art gallery's visitors stared, waved and took photos and videos. Some used binoculars. A few made obscene gestures. Back in 2012, when the condo owners bought their multi-million pound units, plans for the Tate Gallery extension lay approved at City Hall. Only later, in 2016, when the museum's extension and viewing platform opened did these owners realize what this meant for them and, for some, the discomfort of this watchful gaze was such that it led them into the courtroom.

In a well-publicized court case, four of the high-rise tower's owners claimed an actionable nuisance and launched legal proceedings in the hope of securing an injunction to require the museum to close or screen parts of the viewing platform. The owners alleged a "relentless" intrusion on their privacy. One owner felt they must always be "properly dressed" and felt uncomfortable dining at their overlooked table. A mother did not allow her young daughter into the "exposed" areas of her unit. Another forbade their grandchildren from visiting. The onlookers' waving and gesturing left one owner "sick to her stomach". The QC for the owners claimed the breach of privacy was especially acute 'because visitors are on a viewing platform, they don't abide by the norms of behaviour that in everyday life protect the privacy of people in their home' (Press Association [PA] 2018: np).

The presiding judge conceded 'a significant number of people demonstrate a visual interest in the interiors of the flats' and held that 'a homeowner would reasonably regard [that] to be intrusive' (Morgan 2019: 274). Further, the judge reasoned that 'in principle, erecting a viewing platform to overlook a neighbour's land could be actionable in private nuisance'. He ventured that in the 'extreme' hypothetical in which a neighbour constructed a viewing tower to spy on their neighbour such overlooking would be deemed 'unreasonable', and therefore actionable (Morgan 2019: 274). Nevertheless, the high-rise owners lost their case.

The judge's ruling was damning. He argued the owners forfeited their privacy by choosing to buy units in a high-rise with floor-to-ceiling glazing. Mann, the judge, reasoned that their enchanting view 'in effect, comes at a price in terms of privacy'; owners had essentially 'created their own sensitivity' with this purchase (Brown 2019; Singh 2019). Legal scholar Morgan (2019: 276, emphasis added) explained the ruling:

> Yet although being spied on might in principle be actionable, Mann J. [the judge] held that the claims failed on the facts. Nuisance of course depends on *unreasonable interference* with the claimant's use and enjoyment of land, assessed in the particular locality. Mann J. designated the latter: 'an inner city urban environment, with a significant amount of tourist activity' (at [190]). In such a setting neighbours lived 'quite cheek by jowl'. They would therefore *have to put up with a considerable degree of being over-looked.* It was (given the judge's factual findings) a very considerable and intrusive degree in this case. But in his view, this was attributable as much to the *design of the claimants' flats* as to the defendant's erection of a public viewing platform. Had these flats had *normally sized windows*, it would not have been possible to see inside to anything like the same degree from the Tate's platform.
>
> As the judge noted at [203], the 'glass wall' architecture of the flats tended to draw the gaze of visitors to the platform. In the end, the claimants (by living in such open flats) *made themselves unusually vulnerable to this invasion of their privacy.*

Standing on the Tate viewing deck, one knows instinctively that these high-rise owners have *not* overstated their loss of privacy. The judgement acknowledges as much, but also deemed this *reasonable*; it was part and parcel of city living *and* encouraged by 'excessive' glazing. Owners were remiss, the judgement suggested, in disregarding countermeasures which 'could mitigate the "self-induced incentive to gaze"' and indeed this was deemed 'an important part of the "give and take" approach to a privacy-related nuisance' (Morgan 2019: 279). The judgement suggested that if the owners objected to this intrusion, they could draw their curtains, unfurl their blinds, adhere privacy film on their windows, hang net curtains, or judiciously position pot plants to screen themselves. Media commentary was mocking of the judge's suggestion that such 'achingly' modern units could have such impossibly suburban window dressings; owners 'would rather put their eyelids through a mincer' columnists only half-joked (Midgley 2019: np). The judge also suggested residents might more closely abide the architects' design intent, using the exposed 'winter gardens' as enclosed balconies and not, as the owners' furniture betrayed, as additional living spaces. This way, the judge argued, there might be 'less worth looking at' (Brown 2019). Morgan (2019: 276) recapped the judgement: 'Owners have to take the rough [diminished privacy] with the smooth [incredible vistas]. Hoi polloi can peer in to admire one's magnificent Arne Jacobsen chairs. Perhaps people who live in glass houses shouldn't stow thrones.' Meanwhile, new signage on the Tate's viewing platform coaxed visitors to engage in 'neighbourly behaviour' while security discouraged visitors from filming.

This chapter is largely *not* about actionable nuisance in the high-rise condo involving unlawfulness or even formal complaint. What this chapter is concerned with, however, and which this sorry story captures well, is the way that even as the tort of nuisance, as Morgan (2019: 276) argues 'may evolve to protect the expectations of modern living', crucially, in so doing, 'it still relies centrally on compromise, the spirit of "live and let live" between neighbours'. This familiar 'live and let live' dictum has lesser-known legal roots in an 1862 case, presided over by Judge Bramwell B.[1] Bramwell's judgement is often interpreted as being about balancing competing interests; as we see in Morgan's reference to 'compromise'. But the law on nuisance seeks to protect *both* sets of interests and rests on a moral question: what kinds of interference might be viewed as so unreasonable as to be unlawful? Bramwell's principle of 'give and take' comes into play, providing two necessary conditions for determining what is reasonable, and therefore inactionable (that is, lawful). They must be both 'necessary for the common and ordinary use and occupation of land and houses', and be 'conveniently done', namely performed with sufficient consideration of neighbours (Millet 1999: np).

Reasonableness by this account hinges on relationality. Lord Millet (1999: np) argues: 'It is not enough for a landowner to act reasonably in his own interest. He must also be considerate of the interests of his neighbour.' Playing loud music at 2am may well be reasonable if no one is around or if you live in the hinterland but unreasonable for the condo

[1] The 1862 case went as follows: a landowner was emitting noxious fumes as he fired bricks in his kiln, and these fumes were making surrounding landowners and their servants ill. The judgement held that the smoke was nonetheless reasonable because the bricks were expressly for building a home and it was in the public interest that this construction went ahead. This judgement was reversed on appeal: to be unlawful (that is, actionable), Judge Bramwell argued the nuisance needed to cause substantial harm and be unreasonable. Further, in determining what was reasonable, one could not disregard others: namely, the brickmaker should consider how his neighbours were impacted. Put differently, the test of reasonableness was relational: the brickmaker cannot determine what is reasonable in isolation of his and his land's connections to others. Bramwell presented a 'live and let live' argument for no liability in instances of common low-level intrusions with low-levels of harm. His appeal ruling emphasized the principle of reciprocity: give and take, live and let live. For discussion see Penner (2000; also Morgan 2019).

owner whose neighbours may be trying to sleep not two metres away. He further emphasizes: 'the governing principle is good neighbourliness and this involves reciprocity' (Millet 1999: np). This is the give and take to which Bramwell refers: neighbours are not asked to coordinate their activities to never annoy or inconvenience each other. But instead, to accept that in everyday life residents will likely face unintended nuisance, just as they will also likely cause nuisance for their neighbours (Penner 2000: 32).

These themes of give and take, reasonableness and relationality feature in this chapter, where I argue that, as residents interpret and practise property in their private units, residents repeatedly engage in give and take negotiations that can undermine their homemaking on occasion. One of the main difficulties residents encounter is that the borders of the private unit turn out to be relatively porous. These weak borders, coupled with extensive zones of neighbourly contact through their walls, floors and ceilings for instance, mean that residents' 'normatively personal, private activities' (Stokoe 2006: 2) readily transmit from one unit to another, such that even commonplace sights, sounds, smells and things of domestic life become unwanted incursions. Under these arrangements, and absent the 'buffer' zones of suburban gardens, private homemaking interests frequently clash with neighbouring expectations leading residents to perceive and commit frequent incursions across the borders of their private units. In this chapter, I trace a set of border incursions residents face, each involving a different sensory register. Although each of these sets of visual, acoustic, olfactory and material incursions might not usually constitute nuisance, in the strict legal sense, I show that these challenge the presumed territorial sanctity of the private unit that underpins the condo home as dominion and raise questions about reciprocity and tolerance in the context of high-rise homemaking. Along the way, this chapter also begins to consider how the socio-territorial dynamics across the condo unit's borders inform distinct neighbouring tensions and the construction of the 'bad' condo neighbour. These territorialities, subjectifications and social tensions all help understand the politics of belonging that sits centrally to the condo home as belonging and which also has consequences for residents' capacity to make themselves 'at home'.

'Like living in an aquarium'

Neighbours' windows could appear uncomfortably close: "there's zero privacy", Saanvi, a 33-year-old renter commented. Colin, a nearby renter, urged their balconies felt "too exposed" and "too open". At night, condo units lit by artificial lights broadcast residents' silhouettes to passers-by and onlookers. Residents sensed prying eyes; Colin rationalized: "if I can see them, they can see me". Across the country, Jason, a Perth renter who was new to condo living recounted:

> 'This is full-on overlooking. Like, "Oh, you can be seven and a half metres away." Seven and a half metres – if you've got good eyesight – you can see clear as day!... So, it's pretty crazy distances, whereas, everything I've ever lived in has been single-story, where you've kind of got that fence thing ... This is just overlooking! It's pretty crazy! This is the first time I've been in multi-story [housing] ever, in my life, so it's a bit of a new kind of thing for me. I'm kind of looking on that 30-degree angle [at neighbour's unit]: I go straight through one room, through the hall, straight into a bathroom – or something – I can see the state of the bathroom. There's a mirror, and it reflects a bit more. I can see clear as day what's going on! ... But yeah, they've gone into the bathroom, turned the light on, no blinds, clear glass, and yeah.'

Melbourne residents felt especially exposed in cheek-by-jowl towers in the inner city, with many emphasizing how neighbouring buildings were "very close". With a construction site adjacent to his home, Wei, a 26-year-old outright-owner felt his young family of three were living "in an aquarium, in a pet shop". He explained: "sometimes you just catch eyes with the builders – they look at you; you look at them, and then it's just awkward". Though some residents suggested they were unfazed, they nonetheless actively responded to the sense of being overlooked. Eddie, a 63-year-old inner-city Melbourne renter, lived with his partner and recalled a recent incident with "drunks" from the "Airbnb place up there". He commented: "Oh, I [felt] like a goldfish" but brushed it off, saying, "you just put the blind down. No, we just didn't care". To be sure, for some, living high afforded them a sense of total privacy, and some residents subsequently left blinds up day and night. Yolanda, a 30-year-old Perth renter commented: "I could sunbake out there naked, and no one would see. ... I think it's a very private space. We look over others. Others don't look over us, do they?"

But just as Yolanda's question partly intimates, many expressed a lingering unease over their visual privacy, which was evidenced in the way they sought to rationalize their privacy or the disinterest of onlookers to justify why they did not act as if they were overlooked. Nicole, a 48-year-old renter who shared her 33rd-floor condo with her partner in Melbourne's inner city rationalized: "I have to think it's very private. I hope it's very private because I wander around stark naked on some nights because it feels very private. I don't feel as if you've got anybody looking in...". Others spoke half in jest about being watched via telescope or drone. In a mid-rise condo in middle-ring Perth, condo owner Tom commented:

> 'We have side blinds and vertical blinds inside, which we have never used. We are high enough up not to worry about having to have privacy. We're very private and also there isn't an apartment opposite which can view straight in. The only thing we've got to watch for are little hovercraft. Drones.'

Throwaway remarks corroborated residents' anxieties; for instance, Aditya, a young Melbourne renter conceded: "sometimes you're just scared that someone's going to see what you're doing in your apartment". Residents' suspicions were sometimes confirmed. In Melbourne, Priya, a 21-year-old first-time renter and full-time medical student, recounted the "really creepy" experience of an acquaintance living opposite who sometimes texted: "Oh, I can see you in your apartment." In a more extreme example, Qing, a 41-year-old renter described being photographed by a co-resident in her inner-city Melbourne high-rise:

> 'When I first moved in here, there was a chick [girl] … on the floor above me and I was naked, getting ready to have an afternoon nap. And she was taking photos of me. So I had to report to [management] that there was a cheap … taking photos of me on the balcony above. They've left now, whoever it was.'

For some, the lack of privacy enabled opportunities for social interactions with neighbours, and thereby encouraged a sense of connection. A Perth owner, for instance, who lived on a lower floor, described how witnessing neighbours' comings-and-goings across their condo complex's inner courtyard provided visual cues to "go out and say hi", though they qualified: "there is [this] community element to it, but it comes with a loss of privacy". Less tangibly, lines of sight between condo units and busy city sidewalks made some residents on lower floors feel more connected to their city. Meanwhile, those with limited outlook or those living high up, such as Nicole, a 48-year-old renter living on the 33rd floor, felt detached from the city and instead "more connected to the clouds".

Many residents engaged in active attempts to reinstate their privacy. Residents relied on predictable tactics: they installed blinds or tinted windows using adhesive film and engaged in routinized practices of drawing curtains and blinds throughout the day to escape prying eyes. Rada, who rented on the 7th floor of a Melbourne condo tower, described this: "When my neighbour goes to her sink or cooks, she can see into my apartment. … it depends on what I'm doing, how much I want to slouch or feel sane as to how early in the day I'll put my blinds down so that [neighbour] doesn't get to see me." At dusk, when units glowed, some screened their windows, dimmed their lights or receded to more secluded zones away from their windows. In one building where visual privacy was particularly compromised, a few renters conceded defying their tenancy regulations and adhering privacy film to their windows, finding this necessary to make their condo functional. But often such strategies were less accessible to renters: they were less able or inclined to invest in blinds or privacy film due to costs, their temporary status and concerns about breaking rules. Meanwhile their landlords could be slow to address any tabled privacy concerns.

Some residents eventually accepted privacy breaches as part and parcel of city living. Rachael, a 30-year-old Perth renter explained: "I thought about it a lot, now I don't care." Others, such as 47-year-old renter Tracey, resigned themselves to being overlooked though this made them feel powerless: "I'm super aware of it. … I don't like it. I don't like to feel I'm overlooked. I'm sure no one's watching, but you know? – but I think that's city living." Others embraced a 'live and let live' mantra, as one owner reflected: "I can see straight across into three neighbours' windows, and they can presumably see into my living room as well. So I don't particularly mind it because I know that it's similar to that Dutch way of living: you just live your life and it's on display." Other residents found being "an overlooker" troubling too. Many mentioned or implied unspoken expectations about honouring others' privacy, often citing cultural and behavioural stereotypes. Ingrid, a renter living on the 16th floor of an inner-city Perth condo, rationalized that "in Australia … I think people just respect each other's privacy". Some, like retired owner Mark, explained this in terms of resisting the voyeuristic draw of observing others in their own homes and suggested "the novelty wears off". Others distinguished passive 'seeing' from active 'watching', to emphasize their intentional disengagement from their view into others' homes: as one resident put it, "I don't look, but I can see them."

Although residents' tolerance to being and feeling overlooked in their private unit varied, the various border-management practices these vision-related border incursions prompted, such as closing blinds during the day, could undermine residents' sense of control and impinge on their sense of being relaxed and feeling 'at home'. Additionally, a resident's private response to such border incursions could undermine other householders' enjoyment of the unit and create tension within the home. Jasmine, a 34-year-old renter, for instance, whose partner insisted on keeping the blinds down every day, found her home dark and unhomely; "I tell him he's keeping me in a cave!" she commented.

In everyday condo living, there appeared to be no hard and fast rules or 'straightforward dichotomies' between 'what counts as normal, innocuous and reasonable versus abnormal, proactive and unreasonable behaviour' (Stokoe 2006: 16). Not unlike Stokoe's (2006: 16) study of suburban neighbouring norms, which details how neighbours construe a man being frequently naked in his house as exposing himself, in everday condo living ambiguities often surround what counts as 'permissible and normal viewing/looking behaviour' and where the line is drawn between 'casual noticing' versus 'sought out prying'. But these ambiguities notwithstanding, residents also had some sense of 'what counts … as a transgression of normative neighbour relations' (Stokoe 2006: 2). For instance, residents often recounted homemaking practices that reflected unspoken attentiveness towards others' privacy and their commentary indicated how their being visible – their being "in public" or "on display" despite being in their private home – prompted self-restraint.

Condo residents moderated what they did, not (only) out of unease or embarrassment at being seen but also out of consideration and respect for those who might potentially see them. Jason, the 46-year-old renter and first-time condo resident we've met previously, described "reigning in" his behaviour after a half a lifetime of suburban living:

> 'There is a bit of a privacy issue because, if you look behind you, they're people's bedroom windows. … Not that I really care, it's probably more their problem. The way I have decided it is: in my bedroom, I have my blind down to kind of just above my knees. That offers enough light so I can see. So that means, on that half of the house, I can do whatever, wear whatever the hell I want, [but] when I come out in this half of the house, I at least put trunks on. And apart from that, it's their problem. … At first, I just had all the blinds open … doing what I wanted [but] then I just thought: maybe I gotta pull it back a little bit! So that's my compromise. I don't know what they think, but that's the compromise I've gone with.'

Similar self-regulation in response to unspoken social expectations around visual privacy and public exposure was also captured in comments made by Katya, a 49-year-old inner-city Perth renter. Katya sunbathed nude and was quick to justify that her 7th-floor balcony was secluded, urging: "I am not an exhibitionist! I promise!" Several intimated a clumsy 'dance' between neighbours as they avoided using their adjoining private balconies at the same time. Saanvi, a 33-year-old renter, lived in an inner-city Melbourne condo where a flimsy perforated metal sheeting was all that separated her balcony from her adjoining neighbours' balconies. Sanvi described the socio-territorial dynamics: "It's often awkward if you both go out there. I've noticed he'll quickly go back inside. What was the point of this barrier? You can see right through it. … It should've been solid at least so you can't see. It's just silly!"

Residents' enactments of privacy within their private units reveal how condo residents often 'presuppose an audience' (Blomley 2005b: 650) as they make their homes in the condo – a presumption not ordinarily reported in other housing typologies. Residents' self-regulation in response to visual privacy issues was not singularly or even predominantly about abiding by formal regulations to 'create a realm of acceptable tolerance within which they can get away with other offences' (Hilbrandt 2019: 361). Rather self-regulation, at times, appears motivated by less self-interested ambitions. Often residents' responses to poor visual privacy reflects their awareness and consideration of other publics, and often especially their co-residents. In such instances, even within residents' ostensibly private domestic domains, residents mediated their private interests with other regarding concerns. Much like the way residents conformed to visual aesthetics standards as they weighed up how to dry their laundry in the previous chapter, residents confronted with overlooking and exposure manage the borders of their private unit by observing tacit norms and etiquette surrounding visual privacy. As residents juggle homemaking in the context of these visual incursions, border-management within their private unit requires that they reconcile their own homemaking needs and their desire to minimize nuisance to themselves with more socially inflected concerns about the propriety of visual exposure and surveillance, including minimizing potential nuisance to others. If for the most part residents navigate satisfactorily this mediation when faced with overlooking and exposure, as we shall see, residents are not always as successful when it comes to other border incursions and subsequent struggles can jeopardize relations with neighbours, prompt the construction of the 'bad' condo neighbour and encourage the unmaking of their homes.

Teddy bears and cigarette butts

Material incursions into the private unit were by far the most tangible: residents faced cigarette butts, fly-away laundry, birds, curious cats and all manner of other intrusions onto their balconies and through their windows. In terms of incursions onto balconies, units on the highest floors of a building were least vulnerable with fewer balconies overhead from which things might fall or be thrown, and being higher also usually meant fewer flies, spiders, cockroaches and vermin too. But even balconies on higher floors attracted significant debris and dust, especially in Melbourne's inner city where ubiquitous construction sites expelled considerable dust. Private units suffered other incursions too such as water leaks permeating through party walls and ceilings. Indeed water quite regularly breached the unit's boundaries leaving residents with discoloured walls, damp issues and mould that were often difficult for residents to resolve and almost always implicated several other residents, as Chapter 5 elaborates. Mostly residents interpreted water leakages as unintentional, but there were plenty of exceptions too such as the owner who described a neighbour "drunkenly" turning on the fire station water supply, flooding several floors of units. These various material intrusions could surprise and frustrate residents, unsettling their homemaking, challenging their sense of territorial control over their unit and their capacities to make their condo homely.

Of all these material incursions, residents objected most vocally to cigarette butts. They were frustrated when balcony furniture was left pockmarked and fearful of worse. Recent Melbourne condo fires caused by a poorly extinguished cigarette did little to allay their fears. Describing their co-residents' behaviour, one resident exclaimed: "Oh, you're going to set our balcony on fire!" For some, these intrusions made balconies unwelcoming and discouraged their use, sometimes altogether. Jun, a 30-year-old Melbourne renter with a unit in the podium of a tall inner-city high-rise, vented: "It's really messy at the moment. Neighbours throw cigarette butts on it, and they water the plants up above, and so crap falls on our balcony. … And then it just lands on ours, and you just get sick of cleaning it up, so it's like, 'I can't be bothered'." With the condo tower's facades inaccessible to residents, some of this debris could prove near impossible for residents to clean, so some such incursions created lasting eyesores and this only amplified residents' frustrations. Full-time student and renter Lana, for example, complained about cigarette butts wedged between their windows and the balcony balustrading of their 21st-floor Melbourne condo: "I can't clean them!". Again, higher floors provided some reprieve from these incursions, as Rani, a 25-year-old Melbourne renter who lived with her mother on the top floor of a mid-rise condo, noted: "we're lucky we don't get anything … we have no one above us, we've never had any of those issues".

Unwelcome dust and debris, by contrast, impacted all residents regardless of how high up they lived. One resident described their frustrations both at the potential mess and the way keeping their windows and balcony door closed impacted their cat, who could no longer roam freely:

> '[The balcony door is] closed like this most of the time – it's open at night-time so [cat] can come and go out as she pleases – but in the day time, she's either in here and it's shut or she's out there and it's shut. Because the concrete, the dust and all of the rubbish, with the construction going on, that's all the dust that's all over the TV stand … it's ridiculous trying to maintain the cleaning in here, while all of that's going on over there [at adjacent construction site]! … It's not as bad now, because they're constructing. But before, when they were digging out for the foundation – that was when there was just dust every day!'

On account of these various border transgressions, balconies proved to be a disappointing feature of their high-rise condo for many residents. For residents living on higher floors, their disappointments were exacerbated by the discomfort and inconveniences of high winds. Eddie, a 63-year-old renter living on the 32nd floor of an inner-city Melbourne tower, explained:

> 'The balcony is probably the biggest gripe: it's small, in my opinion, and it's virtually windy almost every day. … I don't know why the wind is generated up here. You can go down to ground level and there's hardly any wind, but up here, it's very windy. It's hard to keep plants alive. Everything has to be tied down. You couldn't have any light furniture. Even those mats [on my balcony] have got Velcro underneath to keep them on there because they'll just blow away. … You couldn't have a barbecue cover just on there without the rope around it; otherwise, it would fly off.'

Despite the balcony's reduced functionality, residents generally valued access to their own private outdoor space. To make balconies more functional, residents had gone as far as permanently enclosing their balconies in one Perth complex, as described in Chapter 3.

Some non-human breaches of the unit's boundaries – such as one resident's daily visits from their neighbour's inquisitive cat who "kept coming to my balcony … just standing there wanting to come in" – proved less contentious, and indeed amusing, for residents who delighted in these unanticipated feline visitors. However, often incursions from uninvited animals were unwelcome and, like other incursions, these challenged residents' sense of territorial control. Multiple residents described recurrent encounters with wayward birds flying into their unit and these and other non-human intrusions eventually led residents to keep windows shut. Ana, a 33-year-old inner-city Melbourne renter, described a bug infestation after a restaurant opened below, causing them to be "bitten, like my whole body … I had to keep this closed". Again, higher floors could provide some respite from such incursions, as Sarah, a 58-year-old inner-city Perth renter enthused: "There's no cockroaches at all, here. I'm very happy about that. Very, very happy about that. I haven't seen one spider. You know, that's a biggie [big deal], for me." These non-human incursions were not readily ignored but rather required residents' active attention as they made and unmade their home, as Power (2009a; 2009b) similarly identified. As residents attempted to manage these incursions, renters' frustrations were compounded by dealings with tenancy managers. For instance, Qing, a Melbourne renter recounted how his landlord refused to install flyscreens: "I took photos and begged [tenancy manager], 'Can you give me fly screens?' And they said, 'No.' And I begged them and begged them. I took more photos of more birds that came."

Other residents reported additional incursions; as Perth owner Eloise summed up from her inner-city condo: "[I've seen] a fair bit of junk falling down and I've lost stuff over the edge too." Inanimate intrusions were of a cuddlier kind, on very rare occasions. In an upmarket 12-storey condo complex in Perth, homeowner Marta, who had downsized to her condo with her partner three years ago, described how her grandchildren played with another young child living directly above, calling out to each other from their respective balconies and, once, throwing a teddy between their balconies:

> 'when we first came here, a little girl hung over and said "hi". Little eight-year-old. We used to find the spot so she could talk to us, 'cause my little grandkids loved her. So they could find the spot. And I think once they even threw a teddy down to her – but that is against the rules, but you know … if you find the right spot you can.'

Residents acknowledged their own complicity in these incursions too, with many conceding they too had "lost things over the edge" and some admitting, as Marta did, to intentionally dropping or throwing things. Through these incidents, residents participated in bordering practices that likely disturbed their neighbours at times, and they sometimes acknowledged as much.

Even when material incursions did not strictly breach the bounds of their private unit per se, sightings of out-of-place objects 'in flight', flying by their windows or their balconies, could greatly unsettle residents' sense of territorial control over their home space. Katya, the 49-year-old who rented alone in inner-city Perth, made light of a disconcerting incident involving random possessions ejected from a neighbouring balcony:

> 'I had a friend here, not that I felt unsafe, but I had a friend here. She was in the bathroom, I was sitting out here and we both heard this bang and she's like, "Come here," and I'm, like … "Come here" [she said]. There were just things flying from someone's unit. They were just throwing things out and they were landing on the street. If you looked on the roof of that building down there, there's lighter panels where they've had to replace them. But there was a frying pan and a toaster then a chair and then a table. But there was no yelling. It was really weird. There was no yelling. No anything. Just these random things coming flying down. I was like "Oh my God." I had just been saying to her, "Nothing happens here. It's so quiet. It's really safe" blah, blah, blah and then … the police came. No, they couldn't find which apartment it came from. I was thinking, "Oh my God, a person's going to … they're like [going to] throw their partner off or something. We were like, "Oh shit." We were going out and my friend was like a … she can't let anything go; she's got to find out. We just happened to be going down the lift at the same time the police … were going

down the lift. She was giving them her opinion. It was funny. It was actually funny. It didn't scare me. She's, like, "Thank God no bodies have come over."'

Katya's and other residents' fears of falling bodies were realized in other condo buildings, where several residents reported witnessing suicides. Chapter 5 discusses residents' accounts of those tragedies as well as residents' perceptions and fears of other residents trespassing into their private unit. For this discussion of territorial incursions, however, I note just that residents did express fears about, and incidents of, others attempting to enter their units uninvited. Most concerns related to 'strangers' circulating in the building, which again Chapter 5 elaborates. However, residents did express concerns about intruders entering their units via their balconies on occasion too. Owner Cherese, who lived in a middle-ring condo, worried about her "drunken neighbours" using their balcony to access hers, suggesting the condo's design facilitated such escapades: "them jumping over the balcony and coming into mine – it's quite likely", she said. Cherese responded accordingly, with heightened attention to securing their private unit's borders, such as carefully locking balconies and doors, as did others with related security concerns.

Residents also evoked the porosity of their unit's borders through their accounts of basophobia and their fears of others falling, both of which made residents feel uneasy. Based on these concerns about the security of their domestic boundaries, many residents altered their property practices, sometimes in considerable ways. A retiree Perth renter, who worried her visiting granddaughter might fall, described how she refrained from hosting her family:

> 'So my daughter was here last week from [regional town], and my granddaughter's three, but we decided that they would stay in a hotel as much as I love them, and really love [having] them here. They stayed in a hotel in [nearby location] because of the balcony. The door … the front door doesn't have a lock on the inside. It's just a door that you can open. We … we're just worried about her because she's three that she would escape. … Whether she would … yes … I don't think she would … but we just couldn't live with that. It was just, like: no! [My daughter and granddaughter] did come and visit me [here], but of course, we're awake. We were just worried because she's three and she gets up in the morning … I was just like, "No." We just couldn't [have them stay overnight].'

Marta, the Perth grandmother we met earlier, conceded similar misgivings about her 5th-floor balcony and when their grandchildren slept over she described being sleepless with worry:

> 'When they first came, I couldn't sleep because: "My God! Are [the grandchildren] getting out?" But I mean, I've made sure we've locked that and I do lock that but you know … you just never. … And we couldn't have kids over who sleepwalked. So there is that. We have to be very careful that they're not getting out the window. … If there's kids here … well, I never used to sleep if the kids were here. Now, I mean they've grown up a bit.'

With her grandchildren growing up, Marta's fears had subsided somewhat, but she still kept her windows locked and admitted: "I'm [still] a bit scared about them going outside [on the balcony]." These fears associated with the porosity of the condo's borders do bring to mind earlier accounts of high-rise, and indeed pathologies of vertical housing, that linked the high-rise typology with the ejection from windows and roofs of various objects and, at the extreme, bodies in murders or suicides, and its unmaking of vertical homes (see Lees and Baxter 2011; Baxter 2017). Observing how residents perceive and respond to their porous private unit and its various incursions, however, reveals not only the wide range of incursions residents face and their nuanced perceptions of these, whether funny or fear-inducing, but also the more complicated and nuanced border maintenance practices these elicit.

'They're not meant to smoke'

Other incursions concerned olfaction. In the condo unit, a resident might smell their neighbour's curry or incense, the stench of cat urine or garbage, the miasma of damp or fumes rising from the traffic below. Cigarette smoke or the aroma of barbecued food sometimes drifted in from nearby balconies. Other odours travelled more discretely, penetrating the condo unit through unknown means, though residents speculated that air vents, loose light fittings, poorly sealed windows and even plug holes were to blame. With no cross ventilation and often ineffective mechanical ventilation too, these smells could linger in the private unit.

Residents' perceptions of smells were subjective and unpredictable. Co-residents' cooking aromas could be appetite-whetting while other lingering food smells were undesirable. Some residents subjected to unwelcome food smells cast aspersions on their neighbours' "different" cuisine, their commentaries brimming with casual racism. As with other unwanted incursions, residents (even renters) often blamed renters for olfactory nuisance. This racialized thinking was explicit as evidenced, for instance, in Melbourne renter June's commentary about their latest search for a condo to rent. June had rented in the inner city for years though she owned a suburban home too which she rented out in order to capitalize on rising property values. June explained an "odiferous" building was a "red flag" when hunting for a new condo home, alongside overcrowding and high residential turnover:

> 'So we looked around – across the river actually – at a few apartments in Docklands [inner city suburb], and none of them were quite suitable because it felt really rental-driven. So a lot of the buildings that we went to had a lot of people coming and going and some of the apartments that we inspected had like eight people living in one apartment, and the corridor stunk of cooking all the time, and it stunk of everything. It was not good!
>
> [June's tower] was actually the last one we were going to inspect that day. We started walking and we said, "Oh, it's so far [from the CBD], it'd better be good." ... The agent said that this area was more for owner-occupiers, so that was what drew us to this area because people tend to look after the building more, I guess, if they own it.'

Other residents faced with olfactory incursions embraced the spirit of live and let live, acknowledging how they too likely inconvenienced their neighbours with their smoking or repeated barbecues. Residents at times made generous concessions for their neighbours' incursions, including both when they thought their co-residents' practices were insensitive and when they thought they were rule-defying. Concessions made for practices deemed socially unacceptable or non-compliant with by-laws, were variously motivated. For instance, an owner forgave the fly-in-fly-out worker who lived next-door for his constant smoking because "[he] doesn't know all the rules or the etiquette" and was somewhat confident that this renter would move on "soon enough".

Second-hand smoke was by far the most contentious issue, raising health, property damage and property devaluation concerns. Even with windows and doors shut, residents found cigarette odours infiltrated their private home space. Sometimes residents were none the wiser as to the source or its infiltration points. Greer, a 24-year-old Perth renter pondered: "I do get cigarette smells into my bathroom. I don't know where that's coming from, but it's probably from one of the immediate neighbours that smokes – so you can smell it – into the vents." Balcony smoking bans potentially lessened the risk of such nuisance, but some residents took a lax approach to these private regulations. Lauren, a 67-year-old Perth owner living on the 9th floor, recounted:

> 'Since our last AGM nobody is even allowed to smoke any more ... one of my friends is [a smoker], and I'm not gonna stop her. ... You know, she goes out on the balcony. Anyway, it's one person and the smoke goes up, so nobody's bothered by it. I mean, I didn't agree with

> the vote, but … I think some people have some freedoms left, thank God! But if you've got a smoker next to you … I can imagine … or under you, and that smoke comes up all the time, that's horrible!'

Comments that at first appear riddled with double-standards and contradictions reflect the knotty tensions between by-law restrictions and personal freedoms, and between private interests and social norms. Lauren's justification, like that of several other residents, reflects an understanding of nuisance as relational, with visitors' smoking deemed harmless because no one can smell it. Lauren likewise downplays the occasional "cheeky smoke" while distinguishing it from the "horrible" nuisance of a neighbour who smoked frequently. The former was "no big deal", Narelle, a younger Perth owner, explained: possibly impolite, potentially banned but not unconscionable whereas a dedicated smoker with their persistent fumes would "have a real impact on myself".

While the expectation might be that residents might 'snitch' on their neighbours when faced with olfactory nuisance, residents infrequently reported their concerns to management. Certainly residents frequently criticized and blamed their neighbours, with accusations that suggested neighbours were not "doing their bit" or were failing to "do the right thing" – Why weren't they using the communal bin chute correctly? they challenged, for instance. Implicit in such comments was the way social standards governed residents' conduct. Yet residents seemed reluctant to snitch, with this reluctance appearing to stem from their sense that olfactory disturbances could be especially subjective and elusive. But there were other reasons too. Residents expected management to proactively maintain decent air quality, even in the absence of any complaints. An owner grumbled about pet urine and garbage smells seeping into their unit from shared hallways, making pointed remarks about the job remit of building managers: "I mean, if you're running this place as a hotel, I'm sure you would make sure that the building is presentable and it does not smell funny." But while it was within facility and building managers' remit to maintain garbage chutes and heating, ventilation and air conditioning systems, residents also felt management's powers were ultimately limited and their resources, authority and willingness to police residents only stretched so far. Ultimately management had no say over residents' culinary activities, for instance. Moreover, if poor design or construction encouraged smells to travel or linger, as residents believed they did, then managers could only do so much.

These limits on management's jurisdiction were illustrated by a serious nuisance case in which distraught Melbourne condo owner Mark struggled with intrusive cigarette smells for two years. Mark, a 66-year-old interstate downsizer, lived alone in his new three-bedroom condo on the 30th floor. When Mark first noticed the smoke smells soon after moving in, he assumed these were entering under his front door from his next-door neighbour's unit. His initial thoughts were: "I really wish he'd move out … smokes like a chimney!" But two years on, the smoke smells had not ceased, and so intense was the olfactory nuisance for Mark, and for several other co-residents too, that Mark had made a formal complaint. The developer investigated as Mark, a recent retiree, explained:

> '[The developer] thinks what's happening is smoke's travelling out the window of the offending apartment, along the facade, and going in. It's not an airtight building. The windows are not caulked as well as they should be. … So [the developers] don't finish it off. They don't do that. [The developers'] attitude is that these buildings have what's called make-up air and that's acceptable. That's the way they're meant to be. But as I say, some people with an apartment even higher than me have said that's not entirely believable. … The building breathes: in my bedroom, you can feel the draughts sometimes, up near the windows and you can see the blinds moving. That's apparently typical. Normal! … There's air travelling between the windows and apparently that's meant to be regarded as normal! They called it make-up air!
>
> But what's happening is that the cigarette smoke's coming in between cracks in the window frames from the outside and getting in between the walls … so they've [developers] been telling me. And then it comes out, in my case, in my en-suite, and then permeates the rest of the apartment.
>
> [The developers] haven't shown any appetite to do anything about it, notwithstanding that it's a health and safety issue. They've got my money. That's the attitude I think that exists … [Another owner] brought in a man and paid money to have all his windows caulked from the inside. … It's made it a lot more airtight. … So, that's another thing I might eventually have to do. Not good.'

Mark's dilemma demonstrates the classic clash between Mark and Mark's neighbour's own private interests and their – in this case, incompatible – expectations of home as dominion. Normative ideals about liveable home environments, such as about smoke-free homes, meanwhile, are Mark's prevailing frame for "judging" the nuisance the smoking is causing, as noted in Mark's emphasis on what is "normal".

While each of these residents' capacity to make their home in the high-rise is at stake, ultimately the developers take no responsibility for Mark's discomfort and the way the porosity of his unit's borders is unmaking his condo home. By emphasizing their compliance with building codes, the developers expect Mark to accept as 'normal' and therefore 'acceptable' poor airtightness while also attempting to shift responsibility back to the OC: "[The developers have] just said 'take it up with the Owners

Corporation.' Though they're just abrogating responsibility, saying, 'We've built the building to code. If you've got cigarette [smells] coming into your apartment: Too bad!'" This reflects the well-rehearsed complexities of condo governance, as described in Chapter 1, with its multiple stakeholders all with their own vested interests. While Mark disputed the developer's claim, the onus fell back on him to make his case to the developer in the hope of making his condo more liveable. Adequate air quality, Mark argued, was not a personal preference but a health and safety requirement that the developer's defective workmanship did not support.

This case of smoke infiltration calls into sharp relief the (in)ability of Mark and his neighbours to do as they please in their private units and equally to control what happens within their units. And yet at no point does Mark suggest that his OC should ban the offending smoker from smoking in their home. Indeed notwithstanding the intense nuisance Mark faces, he dismisses as unreasonable the idea that his neighbour should have to leave their unit to smoke, as too great an inconvenience. Mark's commentary captures how even as he seeks to reclaim control of his own home space, he remains acutely sensitive to respecting and preserving his neighbour's autonomy at home.

Mark is desperate nevertheless to regain control of his home space. The usual neighbouring dynamics of 'give and take' appear untenable, however, perhaps especially so in the absence of any sustained cooperation between these two neighbours who communicate infrequently and indirectly via the OC. It seems condo neighbouring relies upon – indeed perhaps requires – high-performing borders. For Mark, this translates to heightened expectations about the performance of the material fabric of his unit's borders:

> '[The OC] couldn't really help because, as the chairman said, how do you stop people smoking in their own apartment? The chap smoking is a tenant, and he's a nice bloke, and I've said to him. … [The OC have] asked him if he can go outside to smoke. But he won't, of course. He's on the 30th level, and he doesn't have a big balcony, so it's not an ideal apartment for him. He can't help it; he and his mates are [nationality]. They're heavy smokers, and so they try and open up their windows and do what they can. But really, they can't stop smoking. And you can't really expect people to go downstairs to smoke. So really the OC hasn't really been able to do all that much. I don't know what [the developers] thought [the OC would] be able to do.'

Indeed smoking represented a distinctly divisive type of clash between private interests and social expectations, though it was not unique in pitting concerns about health, wellbeing and safety – all arguably essential to making oneself feel at home – against regard for individual freedoms, with the latter essential to making the home as dominion. By-law smoking bans could and did protect residents and their assets to varying degrees, but only by simultaneously limiting residents' freedoms within their home spaces.

Often, residents appreciated the inherent tensions between protections to ensure the comfort and functionality of their unit and their autonomy on the other hand, and this complicated and nuanced their perceptions of olfactory nuisance. To be sure, many bemoaned smoke drift, lamented the health hazards it posed and viewed those who smoked as inconsiderate. But with smoking, perhaps more so than other forms of nuisance, residents also recognized this tension. Residents, seemingly quite reasonably, expected the condo designs to act as an adequate foil against foreseeable smoke nuisance, by, for instance, limiting smoke infiltration through air vents. But where design and build quality does not provide any such shield, the expectation that residents should be able to smoke in their private unit becomes far more contentious: ultimately it pits the liveability of one resident's home against the freedoms of another resident – in this instance, to smoke – within their home space. Mark's experience of being "smoked out" of his condo bears out this issue. Mark could not, independently, resolve the issues plaguing his unit and his home was ultimately sabotaged and unmade; Mark summed up:

> 'Living in an apartment where you've got cigarette smoke passively for two years is really, really bad. … Since I've lived here, quite often, before I go to bed at night, I open up all my windows for half an hour and just try and clear out the smoke. … I am a bit disappointed. I think it's a pretty serious issue, and it really affects how I live in the apartment. Hopefully, they'll eventually fix it. … I can't live with it forever.'

Vacuuming at midnight

Condos could be noisy places. The high-rise service infrastructures produced sounds that reverberated down corridors, up lift cores and stairs, through vents and between units, as others similarly note (Shilon and Eizenberg 2020). Lifts creaked and chimed, pipes echoed, air-conditioners hummed, evacuation alarms blared, gates buzzed and doors slammed and taller towers whistled and creaked, especially in high winds. Babies cried, children larked, neighbours stamped and talked, blasted songs and argued. They abluted and flushed, moaned and snored. Less frequently, residents found the condo deadly quiet. Unsettled by this silence, some residents contacted management only to find out, in a few cases, that they had no neighbours but were instead surrounded by units left vacant by investors.

Residents appraised these sounds: some were deemed appropriate, some were not. Opinions varied, sometimes wildly even within a single household. Intermittent and unanticipated sounds irritated the most: the thud and crash of bottle-banking below, weights dropped during a workout overhead, the echoey chatter of neighbours walking down the corridor and, especially in Melbourne's inner city, the chuff-chuff-chuff of helicopters from several nearby helipads and constant construction noise. But for others, even these sounds were unremarkable. Residents' noise tolerance was time-sensitive too, again reflecting unspoken norms. Vacuuming during the day was "normal", but inappropriate in the evening. Jason, the Perth renter we met with a 'live and let live' approach to visual incursions was more particular about noise: "I tend to be patient until 8:30pm during the week, [that] is reasonable, and then on the weekend, 10pm is my limit." But there were suggestions of double standards too: Jason was irate over his neighbour's evening blind-shutting rituals, with the clatter of their blinds being roughly unfurled reverberating through his unit, but then conceded watching Formula 1 so loudly he did not initially hear his neighbour banging on the door to complain.

Residents' tolerance changed over time too as they adapted to high-rise living: some lowered their expectations or became habituated to noise they had initially found irritating. Ali, a 33-year-old renter who lived alone was "pleasantly surprised" by their "quieter" condo, comparing it to a former condo where they had found it "impossible not to hear the kid or the dog above dropping its ping pong ball every five minutes". Some residents embraced the spirit of 'live and let live'; when they heard their neighbours argue, they recognized that "they've probably heard a few of ours", as Marta put it. Leniency was part of the "learning process" of condo living, as without tolerance frequent noise incursions would undermine homemaking. Ali, in his relatively quieter new condo, now rationalized: "[the noise is] annoying, but the other part of me just says: 'It's just normal. Accept it's not a big deal'. If you get worried about it, you would just end up enjoying yourself less". When these strategies failed to "tune that noise out", as Narelle phrased it, residents compensated: they closed windows, they used headphones and they drowned out the noise by creating some of their own, turning up the volume on their TVs or music.

Others baulked at inconveniencing a neighbour or having their own privacy compromised. At the first opportunity, Robin, a 67-year-old owner, sound-checked her 10th-floor three-bedroom condo, seeking reassurance about its soundproofing: "When the unit next door came up for sale, I turned my radio up really loud and I went in to have a listen – because [previous neighbours] assured me that they couldn't hear it, but I just wanted to make sure." As this begins to suggest, homemaking involved not inconsequential self-regulation, including minor adjustments to living practices to conform with unspoken social norms rather than formal regulation. In multiple condos, for instance, residents newly implemented a 'no-shoes' rule to minimize the sounds of their footfalls for neighbours living below. On the other hand, residents also altered their own homemaking practices in response to known incursions, so as to protect their own auditory privacy. Several residents refrained from socializing on their balconies for instance, not just to minimize noise to neighbours but also to avoid being overheard. Tracey, a Perth renter who lived with her partner, explained: "I don't actually want to be out there when we're talking because then other people can hear you really clearly." Somewhat counterintuitively, when householders wanted privacy from their own household, whether other family members or housemates, they often retreated to their balcony, such as to take a private call, again suggesting different 'publics' for private actions, even within the home space.

Some shunned the live and let live philosophy, convinced the noises they heard were unacceptable. They slipped notes under their neighbours' doors or into their mailboxes, banged on party walls and shouted, "Please be quiet!". These residents believed their expectations were appropriate, rationalizing, as Perth renter Sarah did, that "if you can hear me, that means I can hear you, right?" On the other hand, some on the receiving end could find this unreasonable and found being informally policed in their private home space by their co-residents could undermine their sense of being 'at home'. Aditya, a 22-year-old Melbourne renter living in a 9th-floor condo with her partner, recounted her frustration with being reprimanded by her co-residents:

> 'Our neighbour from under us would come banging on my door saying we're making noise. It would be about opening a door late at night – it was stupid things! We weren't allowed to wear shoes at home, *which was really silly!* Like how can someone tell me not to wear shoes when I pay rent for this place! … [The OC] had their own rules; they only told us after we moved in. Like they didn't tell us previously, which was really ridiculous. There was one night where our neighbour. … I left for work very early, like at three am in the morning. She got out on the balcony because apparently I woke her up by doing the smallest little things like opening the door, brushing my teeth, going to work. She got out on the balcony and started calling me names and cursing at me and whatnot. I'm just like: "What do you want me to do?" I mean, *I pay rent for this place. "You can't expect me to live by your rules and the way you live; I'm a human being, you know!"*'

While renters like Aditya were often unsure about by-laws, including because these were not clearly communicated to them, they remained convinced their conduct was appropriate. Still such interactions with their co-residents nonetheless unsettled them, including by making them anxious that co-residents would pursue their perceived misconduct through formal channels with the OC. Such lingering threats were sometimes realized. In more extreme but by no means unusual cases, poor conduct, such as inappropriate noise, might land condo residents in court. Legal scholar Sherry's (2008: 16–17) account of a fairly unremarkable Australian case concerning nuisance noise in a multi-owned property illustrates this well. In that case, the tribunal accepted the applicant's evidence that the hammering, banging, yelling and door-slamming of a neighbouring family would be 'difficult to tolerate' and were in breach of their by-laws, and the defendant was asked to 'make reasonable efforts to control it' (2008: 16–17). As Sherry points out, this noise would likely be a non-issue in a freestanding home and, in any case, a complainant living in a freestanding home would be without legal recourse, absent by-laws. Even while the judgement recognized noise disturbances as likely exacerbated by poor condo design and construction, the 'noisy' family was shouldered with fines and also ordered to pay OC expenses, including some $AUD3,000 for lawyer fees – 'penalties that have no counterpart in other housing' (2008: 16–17).

By contrast, other interactions between co-residents were civil and effective at ironing out noise-related tensions. Craig, a 58-year-old Perth owner, recounted:

> 'The one noise we do get is heavy footfall from the people above, and they're carpeted. And then two above, they've got wooden floors, and we had about an eight-month period of nightmares, of stiletto heels, kids with plastic wheels on their bikes and all sorts of things. So eventually, after pushing, pushing, pushing, the owner came down here while they made some noises, and he was very apologetic, and he put mats down. … So that was a drama!'

While the condo governance literature gives much weight to the role of by-laws and condo management in governing and policing everyday condo living, residents' accounts of managing frequent noise incursions across the borders of their private units underscore again the considerable role unspoken local norms play, including in how residents come to judge their neighbours' noise-making. Craig went on to explain how noise from balconies was managed in his large 20-storey high-rise. His account initially gives the impression that residents do, in fact, assess noise as reasonable or not based on what by-laws stipulate and that such stipulations are strictly policed. Craig recalled:

> 'At 10pm [security staff] come through. You can't use common areas like the pool room after 10pm. So the security company comes through and does a sweep: puts everyone to bed! We're not meant to use our balconies after 10pm, either. … And some people find that intrusive. If I was 30 years old and a party animal, this place isn't for me. But for us, at our stage, we're finished; we're burnt out at half-past eight.

> And if everyone's off their balconies at 10pm. ... You can still party in your apartment but ... because of the noise, there's a rule. Every now and then you get someone being silly. Usually ... usually, a renter. But generally, it's really good. And you can tell. Might be ten past, but people [notice]: "Look, it's ten past ten." They go in.'

Later in the interview, however, when Craig talked about using his balcony, he revealed that half an hour *after* the enforced balcony curfew, some residents, himself included, would still be out on their balconies. What became apparent was that there were informal working rules in Craig's building that determined the time at which retiring from balconies was considered necessary, and that time was later than the by-laws stipulated. And indeed not dissimilar accounts of residents' informal expectations surrounding the use of balconies were given by three other owners living in Craig's complex. While a seemingly minor point – 30 minutes is not much after all – the 'slippage' between by-laws and local working rules in this condo complex nonetheless challenges assumptions that by-laws strictly circumscribe how residents conduct themselves in their condo homes. It is this unspoken "10.30pm rule" which Craig and other owners abide by, which is the measure of appropriate and reasonable balcony use. As this illustrates, even while residents appreciate by-laws as more or less reasonable, locally contingent, informal working rules play an important role in governing everyday condo living. And while these local working rules may not be so dissimilar to local by-laws, they underscore how social norms circumscribe high-rise living. Craig's comments meanwhile also capture the pervasive everyday stereotyping of condo renters, who are blamed in this instance as in many others, for breaches of these unspoken working rules. This latter point is suggestive of the way all manner of sensory incursions across the private unit's borders, and related border-maintenance and management specifically, reproduces particular tenure-based politics of belonging within everyday condo living. We will continue to revisit these dynamics at other sites within the high-rise condo as the tour progresses.

Despite the emphasis on residents' self-management of various nuisance noises, residents do sometimes defer to condo management. By-laws certainly offered residents some protection against perceived nuisances, such as mandating volume levels for private AC units or regulating residents' balcony usage. Those residents who 'snitched' to the OC appeared foremost motivated by their desire to maintain social distance and privacy and minimize awkwardness with co-residents as they sought to protect their private interests. In some instances, residents' accounts suggested how by-laws could be weaponized against other residents, as we have previously seen and will see again, and a few accounts captured the sometimes insidious emotional and financial toll this had on residents, which Sherry's court case likewise intimates.

Other times, however, by-laws provided no protection against nuisance noise, especially when managers poorly or leniently policed by-laws and mismanaged complaints. Again, this highlights how the singular account of by-laws as oppressive private restrictions on residents' home lives requires nuancing in the face of evidence on everyday condo living. Remedial action by building management could be slow, ineffective, costly or altogether elusive, as I have described, compounding residents' frustrations. One owner, for example, criticized their manager's half-hearted efforts to address timber flooring which a co-resident overhead had installed with inadequate insulation. Recourse through formal channels could be expensive too for both parties, as intimated earlier. In a Perth condo, for instance, noise complaints regarding short-stay renters resulted in their non-resident landlords being taken to court: "It cost us," several owners complained.

The OC could prove powerless too in the face of nuisance complaints. Even as some residents advocated for *more* rules – rules for anything emitting or transfering sound: pets, AC units, flooring and so forth – some condo noises evaded regulation. Residents annoyed by dogs' yapping might find little recourse when they turned to managers and by-laws, for instance. Likewise, noise produced or exacerbated by poor design and build quality, such as the sometimes-piercing whistling described by residents in Melbourne's taller towers, evaded OC redress. Indeed subpar design and build, coupled sometimes with ad hoc maintenance, made it more difficult for residents to control their own noise production and exposed them to co-resident and building noise too. Residents criticized developers for "designing on the cheap", with "paper-thin" walls muffling few sounds, for example. When owners challenged developers over acceptable noise transfer levels through the walls and floors of their private units, they found developers quick to claim compliance, with insulation standards, for instance. Some owners remained unconvinced and grew exasperated as their homemaking was compromised. As Mark summed up: "what's acceptable to them [the builder] is not to me; I hear the guy using his toilet!". In some condos, build quality was better, sometimes considerably so. In her 30th-storey high-end three-bedroom condo, retiree Robin and her partner found the only noise they could hear was their neighbour's piano: "in the kitchen, just there, nowhere else. … I think that there might be some insulation missing up in that corner". For some, sound insulation was exceptional. In a middle-ring Perth suburb, several residents in another large high-end condo corroborated one owner's assessment; they stated: "We don't hear anything. It's like soundless; it's amazing!". A co-resident likewise recounted waking up to news of a fire in adjacent grassland. Such was their soundproofing, they had not heard multiple fire engines screeching into their street: "It's like you're in your own world," they explained. These owners saw this relative silence as a reflection of their judicious condo purchase from among a mass of otherwise "shoddy" towers.

Pinpointing where nuisance noise was coming from, especially in very large densely packed towers, proved another obstacle for condo stakeholders attempting to manage these noise incursions. Eloise, an older renter living in a large 20-plus-storey inner-city Perth condo described how "it sounds like it's next door, but it could be three stories up … you've no idea where it's coming from!" This confusion led residents to level false accusations at their co-residents, as Mona, the 33-year-old renter living with her partner and newborn baby who we met struggling with space in the previous chapter, recounted:

> 'The Christmas before, [we] came back to have these letters, you know, complaining about the noise from the landlord. … But it was the neighbour's bass [music] travelling through the wall downstairs because – it was underneath him … complaining. And we weren't even here! So we're like: "Nope, that's next door. We've complained about him! We can prove we weren't here – we got our passports stamped!"'

As this incident highlights, the high-rise tower's spatialities causes ambiguities and confusion in relation to nuisance noise production that sometimes inhibit spatially distanced residents on different floors from readily resolving property issues without third-party assistance. And moreover, even if management might investigate floor by floor to locate the 'offender', their assessments could be inaccurate and remedial steps unclear. In Mona's case, the manager's subsequent request that all parties involved "get together to resolve the issue … sit down and resolve it with him, on what was reasonable" captures well the unsettled nature of volumetric neighbouring standards in the high-rise, especially where building quality issues encourage excessive noise transfer between units.

We tend to assume noise in domestic spaces, and nuisance noise specifically, is something straightforward and readily identifiable, yet residents' accounts contradict such assumptions. Indeed some relatively louder noises, such as the sounds of children playing, were occasionally not only tolerated but welcomed with some residents describing these noises as providing a sense of conviviality. In Marta's mid-height Perth building, residents cheered a piano-playing co-resident whose music could fill their units. The 68-year-old owner explained: "A lot of people say, 'Can you please play today? You haven't played it for a while.' So he plays beautifully, and they love it." As this illustrates, assessments of noise incursions into the private unit are locally contingent social constructions 'that cannot be separated from its social production and interpretation' (Stokoe and Hepburn 2005: 648). Indeed this distinction is actually also evidenced in the legal case described by Sherry (2008) where everyday noise produced by children, such as crying, are legally considered 'part of "family noise"' and therefore not a breach, whereas other noise of a potentially similar volume, such as hammering, is. Additionally, and reflecting the way by-laws interact with local social expectations, Marta described this piano performer as adhering to stricter standards than those mandated by the by-laws: "so there's a curfew, you're not allowed to do it after 10pm, and I think after 9pm people wouldn't. And he doesn't play after 7 or 8pm unless he's had a request … he'd never play it late at night". This again challenges the common perception that it is private restrictions that do so much to constrain property practices within the high-rise condo by revealing informal working rules as sometimes – though not always as Craig's account of balcony norms illustrates – relatively stricter or more demanding controls on resident conduct.

These socio-spatial dynamics relating to noise production corroborate previous studies of vertical families that have highlighted the stress parents feel in managing the noise their children produce (Kerr et al 2020; also Warner and Andrews 2019). They also specify that the pressures residents perceive on their homemaking derive in substantive part from social expectations surrounding the production of noise rather than from a singular concern with breaching formal restrictions. These social expectations around noise production circumscribe homemaking in a range of different ways from encouraging the piano-practising adult to retire from playing in the early evening or encouraging parents to instruct their children not to run around during a playdate at home. And they circumscribe homemaking even when such adaptations are not legally mandated. Much of the time the ways local working rules constrain homemaking may be relatively inconsequential for most residents, but it can be significant. Families recount the heightened stress of hosting playdates, acutely aware of neighbours being potentially disturbed, alongside the very real practical and emotional challenge of trying to control children in this manner. This corroborates prior accounts, such as Kerr and colleagues' (2020: 12) vignette of a mother which captures how, even though her child 'knows not to run' during a playdate inevitably does, leaving the mother 'really stressed' in the face of the futile task of micro-managing their playdate, such that the occasion is 'not fun for anyone'.

Notwithstanding how ambiguous condo noise standards often appeared, noise incursions across the borders of the private unit nonetheless informed how residents viewed their co-residents *and* structured their relations with them. Residents could pigeonhole a "noisy" neighbour as "second-rate" with this then setting the tone for any future interactions. Residents, including renters, disproportionately blamed renters for noise incursions, perceiving them as "high-risk" neighbours: "you've only got to have one … that stuffs shit up", Gillian, a 62-year-old renter claimed. Max, another older owner, described the "second-rate" renter next door: "he was a door slammer", and despite Max asking him to close it softly, "he'd just keep doing it". The retiree, who lived alone in a 5th-floor two-bedroom unit likewise complained: "We could have been lousy about [closing] it too, but we weren't" – the "we" seeming to reference co-owners he otherwise shared his floor with. When the "door-slammer" vacated "really quite nice people" moved in, Max reported, revealing only later that his assessment was based solely on their quietness, having never met them.

Noise-related boundary incursions shaped resident dynamics in more subtle ways too. Sound transfer afforded residents voyeuristic insights into their co-residents' comings and goings and intimate home lives by rendering audible their intimate conversations, their music tastes and so forth. 'Knowing too much' about unfamiliar neighbours and, conversely, unease about what co-residents may have overheard of their own homemaking, in turn, could make for awkward interactions, given this obtrusive, 'unasked-for form of intimacy' (Gurney 2000: 39; also Stokoe 2006: 2). Many residents' accounts betrayed how they kept their co-residents at arm's length including to preserve some semblance of privacy in the face of their residential proximities and to minimize any potential embarrassment. These dynamics also recall Baker's (2013) account of Brisbane condo residents 'striking the right balance' between contact and privacy.

At the same time, neighbourly relations themselves also calibrated how residents perceived "nuisance" noise, illustrating again the complex and localized contingencies that surround border-management, this time in relation to noise incursions in the condo unit. Residents tolerated noise disturbances far better when they felt some sense of rapport with their co-residents. Marta, for example, insisted that "we don't get any horrible noise", instead framing her co-residents' loud music, for instance, in terms such as: "We think: 'Oh that's them having a party.' Doesn't worry us!" When social interaction was reported, residents also demonstrated more tolerance and leniency towards their co-residents' noise incursions. This perhaps is to be expected: residents better empathized with their neighbours when their circumstances were known and tolerated their inconvenience when they could "put a face" to the co-resident whose baby kept crying, when they knew the blaring TV was their partially deaf neighbour's or that the yapping dog was a recent widow's treasured companion. Ana, the 33-year-old renter, had been living in a large Melbourne condo for the past five years and explained this tolerance accordingly: "I think everyone just gives people a bit of leeway with things like that because it's not like it's every single night." Lui, an elderly renter in Perth articulated this tolerance in terms of the dynamics of give and take, including alluding to the potentially extended temporalities of this reciprocity: "People have got to live … I understand; when I was younger, we were always having parties." Relatedly, some stressed that genuine nuisance noise did not beleaguer their 'good' condo building as another resident explained: "It can be noisy without being truly antisocial.

There's a subtle difference. It's just inconsiderate rather than antisocial. But everyone here is good, so it works out well for us." Critically, however, the reverse dynamic also meant that unfavourable perceptions of renters encouraged residents to frame as antisocial what they might otherwise have deemed only inconsiderate. This was evidenced in residents' accounts of noise, as well as other border incursions. Likewise, when residents believed noise originated from short-stay rental units their tolerance immediately plummeted and virtually any noise was deemed inappropriate.

Territorial incursions

The private condo unit is far from impervious and impenetrable. In everyday condo living, incursions abound: pipes leak, cats trespass and a catalogue of inanimate objects land on or fall from balconies. Residents are overlooked by co-residents, passers-by, construction crews and even wayward drones. Cigarette smoke infiltrates via ventilation ducts and garbage odours seep under unit doors. Neighbours may be readily audible: their arguments, their TVs and their footfalls, when they wash the dishes, flush the toilet or have sex. The tower can be noisy too: elevator doors ping and the high-rise structures creak and whistle in high winds. These border breaches are by no means unique to the condo tower, but the 'porous' borders of these recently built private units make them likely and more intensive. These incursions may depart from strict legal understandings of actionable nuisance but as they impact residents in their most private home spaces they risk undermining the condo home.

Building on the previous chapter, this chapter reveals how local working rules govern across the sensory register, including what is seen, heard, smelt and felt from the private condo unit. Whether residents perceived auditory, material, visual or olfactory incursions as "crossing the line" between reasonable and unreasonable was locally contingent, including based on each breach's timing, duration and frequency in the distinct context of a building's spatialities and materialities. These contingencies complicated residents' appraisals of what was locally appropriate, meaning local working rules sometimes appeared unsettled, as the previous chapter also identified.[2]

[2] To be sure, the line between reasonable and unreasonable is not necessarily strictly delineated in other forms of neighbouring either where such designations can also not be 'be separated from [its] interactional context' (Stokoe 2006). However, the familiar taken-for-granted nature of suburban neighbouring norms, to the extent that this exists, is to be contrasted with volumetric neighbouring which takes place in the absence of the traditional propertied cues of gates, fences and gardens in low-density housing which still effectively communicate broadly accepted social expectations vis-à-vis domestic spatial territorialities, including by delineating 'buffer' zones for interactions between neighbours (Simmel 1971[1908]: 143–50; Stokoe 2006).

Where design and workmanship compromised the integrity of private unit boundaries, residents readily became nuisance-makers as their everyday homemaking practices, such as holding a conversation on the balcony, cooking an aromatic meal or walking around with shoes on, disturbed their co-residents. So as not to disturb their neighbours, residents self-regulated, engaging at times in the difficult work of 'literally and figuratively draught-proofing [their] homes' (Burrell 2014: 162). Subsequently residents practised property in other-regarding ways, including out of a sense of social obligation, even as this compromised their own homemaking. Residents queried whether high-rise condo living required different practices – more 'give' – especially those accustomed to freestanding homes or older (walk-up) flats with their solid double-brick construction. Is it the case then, as the judge in the Tate Modern's privacy case impressed, that diminished privacy is the price to be paid for full-height glazing? That judgement held high-rise owners responsible for purchasing units with full-height glazing, but what might be made of Australian condos with poor sound-proofing or inadequate window seals, where (new) working rules of volumetric neighbouring struggle to compensate for unsatisfactory build and design quality?

Residents' traditional propertied expectations for their condo home provided them with a specific 'vocabulary' to interpret manifold incursions across the borders of their private units (Blomley 2005a: 294). That vocabulary tended to be 'the moral logic of the "encroachment" … a privatised "taking", motivated by the desire to entrench upon another's rights' (on encroachment see: Blomley 2005a: 294; 2010: 48), but residents provided qualifications too based on local contingencies. As previewed earlier, residents' appraisals of border activity hinge on the relational character of nuisance: the way 'nuisance' necessarily implicates multiple parties and standards of 'good' neighbourliness. Property, after all, is inherently social and borders between neighbours are 'serious things, which required conversation, rather than assertion' (Blomley 2016b: 241–2). This is especially so in the condo tower where volumetric bordering is intensive, absent buffer zones such as gardens, and extensive in terms of physical contact. The illegibility, ambiguity and invisibility of the private condo unit's borders therefore matter for they impede how the boundary works as a 'zone of interaction' with neighbours (Blomley 2016b: 241).[3] Residents with few opportunities for social encounters at the border faced contextless 'takings' in the 'dark', with

3 Note the visual register is deemed essential to practising property, providing important visual cues and markers (Blomley 2005a; 2005b); as legal scholar Carol Rose (1994: 269) insists 'visibility runs through property law as perhaps no other legal area'. Yet the private condo unit's three-dimensional borders unfurl quite ambiguously, only clear to those who dig through the fine print of subdivision documents.

limited to no rapport and no 'history of positive and reciprocal relationships' (Blomley 2016b: 238) upon which to interpret or resolve these.

Far harder was it for co-residents to follow the 'subtle learned and improvised set of communications, understandings and actions that unfold over and help constitute a boundary relationship' (Blomley 2016b: 238); rather, in everyday condo living the 'interpersonal quality of the boundary fence' (Blomley 2016b: 238, 242) appeared on shaky ground. First, residents perceive border incursions without visual clues to interpret their neighbour's actions or intent; to borrow Blomley's analogy, residents cannot observe where the overhanging branch originated nor witness their neighbour's attempts at pruning. There is little context for interpreting smoke drift, leaking water or loud music when a resident cannot pinpoint their source. Second, neighbours cannot interact 'over the fence' with even fleeting encounters – a smile, a nod or handwave – unlikely and sometimes impossible with neighbours overhead and underfoot unreachable. Third, residents cannot readily manage their borders; they cannot easily 'mend the fence', no matter how poorly insulated, overly porous or overlooked that fence may be. So, while condo residents are especially dependent on their private unit's 'fences' to buffer noise, screen views and filter smells, their border-management is acutely circumscribed.

Volumetric neighbouring risks unmaking the condo home as (part-whole) belonging. In everyday condo living, it appears that subpar walls make for subpar neighbours, to rework Robert Frost's famous line. Namely, if neighbouring subjects are constructed *through* managing their shared 'fence' (Blomley 2013), then in everyday condo living, these manifold incursions figure centrally in the subjectification of the condo neighbour as risky and unruly. Certainly food aromas, a teddy thrown between children on neighbouring balconies or an impromptu piano performance were sources of delight for residents, but incursions were for the most part displeasing at best and stressful, unhealthy and unbearable at worst. As residents interpreted incursions, they drew on baseless stereotypes, sometimes of youths or families with children, but especially of renters, thereby reproducing pervasive tenure stigma and cementing growing disdain for short-stay renters. This subjectification and stigmatization were typically based on the pervasive assumption that owners, surely, would not be so careless or inconsiderate, rather than evidence of renters' culpability. Even renters succumbed to this stereotyping at times. Condo bordering thus frequently risked fracturing co-resident relations.

Incursions also unmake the condo home as dominion by denying residents (the sense of) control over their private home space that prevailing traditional propertied imaginaries have primed them to expect. Residents found their unit's 'porous' borders required repeated micro-mediations – to leave the blinds open despite being knowingly overlooked or to self-regulate and thereby forfeit their daylighting and views, for instance. Workarounds to mitigate these incursions often had time, cost and material implications, which made many of these options unviable for renters. Meanwhile, whether residents tolerated, retaliated or reported co-residents' incursions this impinged on their private condo home, as imagined and practised. Even co-residents' everyday homemaking was experienced as an incursion, for when co-residents' failed to remove their shoes to dampen their footfalls or socialized on poorly screened adjacent balconies, for instance, noise readily carried into residents' private home spaces. Residents temporarily surrendered a room, their balcony or their view in response to smells, out-of-place objects, watchful eyes or noise breaching their borders. On occasion, residents forfeited zones in their private homes for extended periods as incursions caused property damage and even health concerns, as was the case for Mark whose home was rendered almost uninhabitable by smoke infiltration. Meanwhile, in all but these most acute cases, formal condo governance restrictions, agents and procedures were noticeably out of frame in most residents' accounts. On occasion, residents did 'snitch' on co-residents as the literature on contractualized co-resident relations anticipates (for example Power 2015), including to maintain social distance from co-residents. Mostly, however, residents muddle through alone with their condo home compromised by inconvenience, frustrations, serious homemaking constraints and (perceived) social frictions.

Until now the private condo unit has taken centre-stage in this analysis, but this private home space is buttressed by a latticework of shared infrastructures. Lifts, stairs and corridors enable residents to access these private units, which cables, pipes and ducts illuminate, ventilate, cleanse and warm/cool in turn. This infrastructure moves people and things – parcels, rubbish, digital data, visitors, water and so on – around the condo tower's supposedly settled propertied landscapes, including across common/private property borders. This shared infrastructure is introduced in the next chapter, where we leave the condo's private property to explore how residents perceive and practise common property and how it shapes the making and unmaking of the condo home.

PART II

Shared Infrastructure and Amenities

5

'It's the Building's Wiring Problem'

Fred, a renter in a Melbourne condo, receives an exorbitant electricity bill. He is surprised and alarmed as he is rarely home. Unbeknown to Fred, his building has an embedded network for gas and electricity. But when he learns this, he is none the wiser as to its implications. As he exclaimed to reporters: "What is that? I don't know what that is!" (Farnsworth 2018; Hobday 2019).

An embedded network is essentially a private electricity network. A property developer or the owners corporations (OC) – the embedded network operator – contracts a company to bulk supply electricity, gas for stovetops, hot water or telecommunications at a single meter point who then on-sells at a profit to condo residents. This arrangement essentially locks Fred and his co-residents into a contract with the embedded network operator for the supply of that utility. It makes it nigh impossible for condo residents like Fred to 'shop around' for a better deal. The Australian Energy Market Commission (AEMC), the energy policy advisor to the Australian government, confirms that once contracted the embedded network 'often effectively becomes a monopoly electricity provider given the practical impediments to switching to a retailer of choice' (AEMC 2019: 21).

Over the past few years, the number and scale of embedded networks in Australia has increased significantly with condominium developments a 'primary driver' (AEMC 2019: ii). Data on exact numbers of embedded network customers do not exist, though figures likely exceed half a million Australian households (AEMC 2019: ii). As the AEMC makes clear, condo developers and other emergent businesses benefit by locking OCs into potentially lengthy, uncompetitive contracts for utilities.[1] Meanwhile,

[1] The AEMC (2019: 21) report on embedded networks states: 'The Commission understands developers now often choose to avoid the cost of establishing internal networks and metering by contracting a third party to fund and supply the infrastructure and the metering throughout an apartment [condo] complex. In return, the embedded network business is sometimes contracted to provide power to the whole building, which can tie

condo residents such as Fred can face a slew of problems: high-pricing and difficulties transferring to competitive providers, difficulties accessing rebates and concessions, lack of consumer protections, issues over accuracy of billing and excess charges, compliance issues, varying access to the ombudsman and poor connection standards (AEMC 2019: iv–v). In Fred's case, the OC faced a year-long battle to extract itself (and its condo residents) from their embedded network. In the interim, 'sky high' bills pushed frustrated condo owners to sell up and tenants such as Fred to try to break their leases (Hobday 2019).

This chapter sheds light on how residents like Fred perceive and practise common property as they navigate everyday condo mobilities associated with shared infrastructures. As Fred's account illustrates, much is shared between condo residents to make the private condo unit accessible and habitable: the structures to uphold it (columns, lift cores and so on), materials to clad it (aluminium composite panels, glazing systems, and so on), means to access it (lifts, automated doors, intercoms and so forth) and services to operate it (pipes, bin chutes, cables, ducts and so on). Much of this infrastructure is at least partially concealed from view. Moreover, as Fred's case illustrates, this sharing is potentially complex and the fallout shouldered by individuals. This chapter homes in on the movement of humans, non-humans, objects and matter through this shared infrastructure. It considers how the circulation of residents, visitors, building managers, pets, parcels, rubbish, water, gas and (informational) data around the condo's shared infrastructures is beset by a series of frictions, like the one Fred faced. These frictions configure residents' own mobility and their control over the movement of other people, things and matter. This chapter understands these frictions as forms of territorial constraint which I term *circulation frictions*, drawing loosely on geographic understandings of mobility frictions as one of the constituent parts of mobility. Namely, these frictions are conceived as: taking diverse forms, being 'variably distributed in space' (Cresswell 2010: 26) and, most significantly, as counter-forces to the otherwise seamless circulation of people, things and matter through the condo tower's shared infrastructures.

In considering how condo residents perceive of and practise mobility and attempt to assert control over the movement of other people, non-humans, things and matter through these shared infrastructures, I keep in mind Creswell's (2010: 26) question: 'what kind of friction does the mobility

a future owners corporation to lengthy contracts. These contracts are initially established before completion of construction and before strata schemes have been registered.' Embedded network providers meanwhile claim residents are 'only paying marginally more than the default price set by the Victorian Government' and while the industry peak body conceded regulatory reforms may be necessary, they also claimed the networks 'could offer good value and the opportunity for apartment dwellers to take advantage of renewables, such as rooftop solar' (Farnsworth 2018: np; Hobday 2019: np).

experience? … Is stopping a choice or is it forced?' I focus on everyday condo mobilities through entryways, through lifts and through pipes, wires and rubbish chutes and consider the multiple high-rise agents and security and digital technologies that mediate these mobilities. This foregrounds circulation frictions as another pressure point for condo homemaking, as residents variously mediate their private interests with local working rules. This chapter argues that while circulation frictions within the condo's propertied landscapes are not always harmful to condo homemaking, and indeed some are supportive and indeed necessary, they can be.

Pipes, cables and rubbish chutes

The mostly hidden transit of water, gas, electricity, rubbish and other matter around the high-rise was something residents quickly found they had little control over. Residents could not choose their utility providers nor their payment plans. Those without individual metres found, much like Fred, that they could not easily monitor their energy consumption nor control their bills. Some baulked at shouldering costs for overly heated or cooled shared lobbies and corridors, or resented subsidizing other residents' higher utility usage, labelling as freeloaders those co-owners who negotiated "excessive" gas appliances from the developer when they bought off-the-plan. In Melbourne, a retired senior manager and first-time condo owner recounted:

> 'It's an odd thing in this building: you don't pay for your own gas. … The gas bill comes into the building, and based on your body corporate [OC] share you pay a portion of the gas bill. So some of the apartments here have got people in there now, like some of the podium places, they have gas fireplaces, and you'll notice one in the lobby here. And they can have as much gas as they want; they don't have to pay for their own gas! So we – the rest of us – are subsidizing their heavy gas use, because they've been able to talk [the developer] into allowing them to put a gas fireplace in. It's not standard. It was like a special favour from [the developer].
>
> You don't know about these things when you buy and no one told me. If I'd known that was an option … it would have been wonderful! And gas is basically, pretty well … I don't use much gas, so what I'm paying for is basically other people's usage. … Why don't they just meter everybody's – what you use, metered like a house? But they don't. So the smart people are putting in extra gas appliances because they know they're basically getting it subsidized. That's strange.'

Indeed because resident consumption of utilities is 'hidden' by this lack of individually metering, condo buildings have been singled out as attractive places for illegal grow-ops, since their high-volume water and electricity usage is not as readily discoverable (Lippert et al 2017: 35–6). In Melbourne condos, utilities were also shared informally on occasion, with co-residents capitalizing on their physical proximity to share utilities provided privately to a single household, such as internet plans. In an inner-city condo, for instance, two neighbouring student households, who knew each other prior to renting adjacent units, described how they all accessed the internet off a single modem to reduce costs.

As residents shared infrastructures in everyday condo living, it was owners rather than renters who benefited from privileged access to information about the issues they encountered, albeit they frequently remained ill-informed nonetheless. Renters meanwhile were systematically omitted from OC digital communications, with few exceptions. This information advantage gave owners better context for interpreting and navigating issues including a better sense of the problem, who was managing it and what actions were being taken. As we shall see, owners received more information through formal communication channels, such as their OC committee or their building manager, and some benefited from formal involvement with their OC committee. Owners also received more information through informal owner-centric local social networks too. Owners also benefited, moreover, from relatively stronger personal relationships with building managers and co-residents than renters, with these relationships established during their relatively longer tenancies. Circulation frictions therefore relate not just to the mediated circulation of gas and other utilities through the condo, but also informational data as this chapter will illustrate.

Owners' relatively privileged access to information gave them a greater sense of control by better equipping owners to navigate everyday condo living and its frustrations. Being privy to information, as a form of power, afforded owners relatively more actual control over their homemaking too. Owners' informational advantage supported their homemaking in diverse ways. An owner who learnt that hot water was not individually metered after being on the OC committee, increased his usage, no longer constrained by concerns about soaring bills:

> 'Except I discovered, being on the committee, that hot water, you don't actually pay for. What you do: you pay your share. Hot water usage is not metered to you. If you are just using hot water all the time, and not cold water, then you're getting water pretty well free, really, in the sense that it's just a smaller share. They don't publicize that, but I think if you can get used to using hot water instead of cold water, you will, over time, I suppose, save a little bit.'

As this illustrates, residents did not perceive all circulation frictions as problematic and residents did not experience circulation frictions evenly, as suggested by the various ways residents responded when they understood utilities were collectively metered.

Some residents found ways to assert control over shared infrastructures, though this usually required know-how and time. Simon, a Melbourne owner who wanted cable TV, for instance, championed his building manager to install the necessary infrastructure. Simon explained how he "basically played the secretary for one of the building managers … providing finances and all the other documents, I basically did all the advocacy work". Renters perceived fewer options to take action. Facing cumbersome and expensive internet provision, 33-year-old Melbourne renter Saanvi, for example, eventually disconnected but was left wondering "how everyone else's internet had survived. … I have to go to my mum's or the library [to go online]. It's ridiculous!". Renters feared reproach from both the OC and their landlord and worried about being left out of pocket if they flagged issues to the OC committee or building management. A renter describes this triple threat when facing a wiring fault:

> 'It was only last week that we had a little incident with the [bathroom] switch. It blew, and it caught on fire, there was a bit of smoke and stuff going on, but it was 10pm. … And that was probably the most frustrating moment of moving into an apartment – that: the OC people didn't answer their numbers. The two building managers didn't answer their numbers. The real estate agent didn't, because it was 10pm; so it was out of the office hours. And the two emergency contact numbers that were on their agency website didn't answer either.
>
> So we had to call an electrician, a 24-hour one. … And even the electrician said, "This is the building's wiring problem, so they cannot possibly charge you for it." … I was afraid the OC would say, "Oh, you didn't use one of our electricians to fix it, so we're not going to pay you back." That was my biggest worry. … If it was your own house, like your land or property, you can just call anyone and fix it, and you know what you have to pay. But because we're only renting – and technically they're meant to take care of faults like this – I was worried that if we called an "outsider", they would say, "No, we're not going to reimburse you for that because you should've called one of our guys."'

Residents encountered other issues with the condo's smoke detection systems which caused additional inconveniences and frustrations. Many residents complained about "overly sensitive" alarms readily triggered by cooking, especially when coupled with ineffective kitchen exhaust fans.

Others, such as 66-year-old owner Mark, emphasized the "tips and tricks about living in an apartment that you have to learn … things that people do in apartments that they used to do in their own homes, and you can't do it". These "tips" included, for instance, not opening your front door when you burn your toast, so as not to trigger the building-wide smoke detectors. Again owners benefited from relatively privileged access to information. In Mark's case, these tips were gleaned from his involvement with the OC. He explained: "I'm on the committee here. It's been discussed because they've had a few incidents. They had incidents, like a bloke trying to use the fire hose to wash his car." As this suggests, access to information not only afforded owners a relatively greater sense of control over their home space than renters but also assisted owners' homemaking in mundane practical ways too.

As noted, owners had privileged access to information through informal channels too. Often information circulated only within exclusive subgroups of co-residents, with these groups typically comprising longer-term residents, and therefore generally owners, due to renters' tenure insecurity. Owner Scott's commentary captures well how groups of owners come to benefit from privileged access to information about everyday condo living and the way it potentially smooths over or lessens the frictions surrounding condo homemaking. Fifty-seven-year-old owner Scott, who shared a three-bedroom condo with his partner in Perth's middle ring where they had lived for the past four years, explained:

> 'We've got an "in group" community as well, people that have been there for a while. Like for example, ourselves, a guy that used to live next door to us. He's still in the same apartment. One above us that has been there since they were built … We communicate by email, by phone – watching out for each other. … If there's an issue – like the fire alarm went off the other day, I immediately emailed Strata and the body corporate [sic], include them all, cc'd. We just find out things like that. [Neighbour] will see something in the apartment, and she'll text me or ring me. "If you see the guys around with a pad, what are they there for?" – sort of thing. Or, "There's a boy running around. Why is he?" I'll have a look around. We look after each other.'

Scott elaborated, suggesting how larger groupings of co-residents could be awkward as relationships developed, including because co-residents couldn't "speak openly" about each other – they couldn't complain that "bloody [unit number] seven's dog was yapping last night". Scott commented, reflecting on these social dynamics:

> 'Unfortunately, it is a community within a community. We've got some 80 apartments. Now we've got single mums, we've got elderly

ladies whose husbands have died in the apartment block. We've got families. We've got people with young kids. We've got, I think, three babies at the moment. It's a mix, yeah.

There's not one social group. There's social groups within the group. Because being long-term residents now, we're older than two of them and we welcomed them. So they became very friendly, very quickly. Whereas Cara and Anthony, they were here first. We met them just because they drank a lot and we thought, "We may as well join in with them." … [Neighbour] will ring up, "What are you doing?" "Nothing." "Let's go downstair[s]." There's a coffee shop down on the corner. "Let's go and get a coffee." … So yeah, that all works well. This floor is a good community.'

Condo owners' privileged access to information, both through formal channels and through informal channels such as Scott's 'in group', take on heightened significance in the context of otherwise infrequent co-resident interactions.

On the other hand, issues surrounding shared infrastructure could themselves stimulate social interactions between residents. Renter Jasmine, a 34-year-old kitchen hand, who moved into her condo seven months prior, conceded: "Only, I think two times, the fire alarm would start and everybody went outside and [that] was the only times when you can say we speak with each other and we share our feelings." This was a surprisingly common refrain in fact. So infrequent were face-to-face interactions in many buildings that many residents cited evacuation alarms – when residents trudged down fire escapes together often in the middle of the night – as the most memorable and indeed for many the only occasions of social connection with co-residents. In Melbourne, 33-year-old Ana who, quite atypically, had rented the same inner-city unit for five years, told of how issues with her 12-storey building's hot water service "made the neighbours talk a lot". Ana described how by sharing information about the water problem, residents had bonded over their joint frustrations: "It was a blessing in disguise. … You got to speak to everybody … just in the lift: "Do you have hot water?". "No". "What's going on?".'

But in the absence of much social interaction and connection, circulation frictions associated with shared infrastructures often reproduced pathologies about renters as risky and careless, especially young renters. In the case of false alarms, for example, it was almost always renters who were blamed for the inconvenience, for wasting fire department resources and, through repeated false alarms, for creating dangerous complacency among many residents in response to these alarms. Wei, a 26-year-old owner and full-time student, criticized renters: "sometimes they just don't know how to use the stovetop exhausts … so they just cook and then they get fire alarms at 2am in the morning". Similar tensions also surrounded the use of communal rubbish chutes, which supposedly offered residents convenient rubbish disposal via a bin room on their floor, dumping rubbish into basement garbage skips. Residents frequently complained about co-residents who did not heed by-laws nor social etiquette. A renter described his "lazy" co-residents: "you'll see a pizza box stuck there and you're like 'obviously that's not going to fit in there! What are you doing?! … No! You're supposed to walk it down yourself [to the basement skips] and throw it into the bin!'" But while owners and renters alike complained, these residents almost always blamed renters for unacceptable waste practices.

Poor functionality and operational issues plaguing shared infrastructures compounded circulation frictions and their associated social tensions. For instance, the design of bin rooms and garbage chutes complicated residents' waste management, especially of recyclables, with many residents critical of their building's recycling infrastructure. One Melbourne renter commented:

> 'I'm very big on recycling. And in [previous house], I would recycle every toilet roll, every milk carton, every paper carton that biscuits come in. I was disappointed that when I came here: there's no room even to have a rubbish bin in the kitchen. … So I had two separate plastic bins on the balcony, one to put the recycling, one to put normal rubbish. And we have a rubbish chute in the hallway like most modern buildings: you pull down the door, and you throw the rubbish in and it goes down into a big bin downstairs. … And when I went down there one day, I realized that every item, no matter what it is, the recycling … it all goes into the one bin because we have the one waste company that comes and empties those bins. So that … I've stopped separating the rubbish now because it all ends up in the one bin.'

More commonly, garbage chutes only supported general waste with no on-level options for recycling. In some larger or taller condo complexes, travelling between private units and basement skips to dispose of recyclables took time and required motivation. Rebecca, who lived in a large 12-storey complex in inner-city Perth suggested "the whole trip itself could take ten to fifteen minutes". These frictions surrounding the removal of recyclables from the condo building were too onerous for some and many residents conceded they no longer recycled. Residents described being "pretty slack – sad to admit!" and "time poor". Others also blamed the fact that small kitchens left little space for collecting recyclables and looked "unsightly".

Yet even when owners expressed frustrations with such circulation frictions, they typically did not advocate for changes and upgrades to reduce these frictions. There were exceptions, to be sure, such as an owner who championed the OC to install a Nespresso recycler in their rubbish room, and such examples corroborate accounts of the importance of 'champion' residents in the formal governance literature. Mostly, however, owners and renters demonstrated a weak sense of ownership towards these common property elements, appearing poorly motivated to improve service infrastructure functionality and moreover resigned to its limitations. Contra prevailing propertied notions of home spaces as places where homemakers wield control and assert their territoriality, condo owners did not strongly emphasize their entitlements. Some suggested efforts to assert any control over shared infrastructures would be futile. Christine, a 71 year-old Perth resident, like many other owners, saw her building as comprising a large share of renters. This led Christine to believe, primed by prevailing pathologies of renters as careless, that the uptake of any recycling initiatives would be poor, for instance. Christine rationalized: "[it's] a shame [there's no recycling], but I think in a condo with tenants, very few of them would use it".

Meanwhile most owners associated resident passivity towards circulation frictions with the transience of residents, namely renters and, especially in inner-city Melbourne condos, student renters. Renters themselves also sometimes rehearsed the same stereotypes in their accounts, as identified in previous chapters. In Perth, 26-year-old owner Chris expressed regret about purchasing his one-bedroom unit off-the-plan; alongside his concerns about poor workmanship and his lack of control, he also thought poorly of his co-residents. "It's students galore," Chris complained of his 12-storey middle-ring building:

> 'Lots of students in this building. And there's a few AirBnBs here as well, so there's always travellers who come in and out ... it's described as "ghettos" of apartments ... [whereas] if the majority of the people who live in the building are all homeowners who live there, they tend to care more about it.'

Residents' limited territoriality over shared amenities is also partly explained by the territorial control asserted by other condo stakeholders. Even armed with comparatively more information than renters, owners often did not feel a strong sense of control over these shared infrastructures. Owners and renters alike could feel powerless when faced with resolving utility and service provision challenges. Retrofitting infrastructure could be costly, the logistics complex and the division of responsibilities between residents and OC ambiguous. Pia elaborated, expressing worries about leaking pipes: "your pipes are connected to others – so if anything goes wrong, you can't just make an executive decision and say 'I want to tear down my pipes'." Consistent with this sense of powerlessness, residents infrequently spoke of the OC as a self-governing body as typically envisioned in conceptual property models, or if they did it, it was in ambivalent terms as captured in Chapter 4. Melbourne renter Sophie distinguished between "some of the people involved in the OC [who] are really on top of all that stuff" and other residents who "kind of live off the spill-off ... [and] feel quite relaxed because someone else is taking care of it".

As this suggests, owners and renters alike often spoke of building managers, and surprisingly their OC committee too at times, as akin to third party service providers employed to deliver operational services. Residents usually had high expectations of condo management as a result and became frustrated in the absence of efficient and effective service or when they deemed these stakeholders' actions unnecessary, ill-advised or too costly. As their accounts often betrayed, residents felt that by paying levies they had relieved themselves of stewardship responsibilities and any accountability for the comfort, cleanliness and functionality of these shared infrastructures. Indeed, this was part of the appeal of the condo's presumed "low-maintenance" lifestyle. In Melbourne, 32-year-old owner Pia thus reflected:

> 'You tend to want to complain because you pay the OC fees each quarter for them to maintain the building to look presentable. So I guess if they're not doing their job, I guess I have the right to say, "Hey, I paid my OC fees every year or every quarter, and you're not doing anything about the upkeep of the building!"'

These condo actors, for their part, did intervene in managing circulation frictions. In the case of frictions surrounding waste infrastructure, for instance, private cleaning staff compensated for residents' carelessness by cleaning bin rooms and building managers scheduled additional cleaning contractors and helped residents dispose of larger items of rubbish.

As part of this process, residents also frequently felt disciplined by building managers, OC committee members and other residents. This disciplining oftentimes occurred at a distance without social interaction, such as through signs and notes, some patronizing in their requests that residents apply some common sense. For instance, retiree Lui reported "a constant flow of emails telling us that we should do this, we should be doing that". In some buildings, owners were complimentary of condo governance, but not perhaps in the ways usually assumed. Rather what residents valued foremost, their commentary often suggested, was the way these condo agents navigated administrative complexity and red tape, including by *avoiding* formal processes – by avoiding those very processes through which residents are usually imagined to assert their limited control. For instance, 58-year-old Perth owner Craig praised his "legend" OC secretary: "He's an action man; if it's less than 300 bucks, he just does it. He doesn't even wait – [there's] no muck around – for meetings and things. He apologizes after if he gets it wrong."

In/egress

The high-rise had two main entryways: a street-level lobby and an automated car park entry leading to the basement. These entries and exits were replete with security features: automatic boom gates and doors, key fob access, surveillance cameras and sometimes remote, app-accessible intercoms. Concierge, building managers and, in some buildings private security, monitored and policed who and what entered the condo building. This high-visibility security paraphernalia sometimes assuaged residents' safety fears and provided peace of mind. In other buildings, dedicated security or concierge staff similarly reassured residents of their safety. Indeed some felt so secure they admitted to rarely locking the doors of their private units. Greer, a 24-year-old Perth renter described how security cameras reinforced her sense of safety in her middle-ring condo: "There's 24-hour security, there's cameras that roll through the place, so it kind of makes me feel safe, in comparison to living in a house which doesn't have security." Residents trusted that CCTV was switched on and being monitored; as one resident of a Melbourne middle-ring condo rationalized: "There is a building manager constantly working, so I would assume that they're checking their cameras constantly." Other residents were not so trusting but believed security devices at least provided deterrents. Renter Yolanda who lived in a large 20-storey complex in inner-city Perth rationalized that even if "[security] didn't really do much, they made you feel better as a single woman, at the time, coming home" (also see Kern 2011).

With unstaffed lobbies, even *lawful* building access could be fraught. Rani, a renter in inner-city Melbourne explained for instance how her building was "sort of inaccessible in a way, to other people". Tom, an 88-year-old living in a 12-storey condo complex in middle-ring Perth, described how paramedic access was "a real problem". Tom explained that it was only after a concerned co-owner, a doctor, pressed the OC committee and went "through all the rigmarole" that emergency service access was resolved. Couriers tasked with parcel delivery to these high-rise condos faced an array of buttons, intercoms and sometimes multiple entrances and many residents in smaller or less upmarket buildings without permanent onsite staff frequently reported, as renter Rani described, that their building was not accessible. Couriers could insist that residents descend to the lobby to provide access or sometimes, by many residents' accounts, "don't bother attempting" deliveries at all. To avoid potential issues, a few residents paid for parcel boxes at their local post office and many others had parcels delivered to their workplace while expressing frustrations and recalling the ease of postal delivery in previous homes.

Residents' lack of control over the entryways and exits to their buildings challenged their sense of the condo home as dominion and could detract from their ability to feel 'at home', sometimes substantially. Residents reported all manner of incidents involving unlawful access to their buildings by "outsiders", some petty and others highly disturbing. In basement car parks, cars and bikes were stolen and storage cages burgled, as mentioned in Chapter 3. Tailgating was also a major issue despite the apparent sophistication of security technologies. Eddie, a 62-year-old Melbourne renter, described this: "a car follows you in, they just follow you in. So you can't stop that … there's nothing we can do about it", even if you wait for the boom gate to lower, "they'll just push their car up until it breaks the beam". When Trey, a 42-year-old renter in inner-city Melbourne reported a theft from his storage cage, police said it was "incredibly common" and "not to put anything in it". In some buildings, parcels regularly went missing from mailrooms. Intercom buzzers were sounded in the night, apparently by residents with misplaced keys or others just "mucking about".

In some buildings, usually those with unstaffed lobbies, "outsiders" could loiter, sometimes causing nuisance and property damage. Trespassing could be harmless, as renter Ana explained: "There are some homeless [people] that sleep on the seats downstairs, but they're okay. I went there. I was a bit nervous at the start, but literally, they're just sleeping." Other incidents were sadly humorous, albeit alarming too. Christine, a 71-year-old owner recounted an incident that had recently taken place in her middle-ring Perth condo building:

> 'I saw the police downstairs on the pavement. Three vans and I went down straight away to find out what had happened. And they were all laughing and joking. Then I walked up and asked, and he said, "I don't know if we can say" – it was a break-in, and it was on the first floor. And the young man came home from work. When he got home, his door was open, and then he thought he must have locked it. He's a single guy who doesn't do any washing, any dishes, doesn't clean the house … it was a tip. … He said, "I came home, walked in; everything had been vacuumed clean." His dishes were all done and put away; everything looked beautiful. So he immediately rang his mother. … He told her, "Don't ever come to my apartment without me knowing!" And she said, "I haven't been anywhere near your apartment; it is disgusting!" Then he said, "Well, it's not now. It's beautiful." So she said, "Well, you'd better ring the police." So he did. He rang the police, and he felt really stupid doing this. [He said:] "Somebody has been in my apartment and cleaned it all up." So the police came. … They knew who it was. She's an ice addict that lives in the apartment further up. She had been released that morning from jail. She'd gone straight to her dealer, but effects … came here and went to the same number apartment that she lives in, but up there.

> … He obviously must've left the door open because they don't know how the door got opened. And she apparently … she was absolutely horrified: the place was so terrible. So she got to cleaning it all up. … So community service went straight up there and arrested her. They didn't know what to charge [her] with!'

Other circulation frictions at the condo building's entry were unremarkable. For instance, untidy entrances and lobbies could detract from residents' sense of pride as a key public interface between the condo building and the local neighbourhood. Residents often felt they had little sway to have the cleaning "stepped up", as owner Christine hoped, for instance, or to have the "annoying" televisions in the lobby tuned to something other than a loop of "images of fuzzy people!", as renter Priya wished. Several owners, such as Melbourne owner Pia claimed that unless an issue was "severely impacting one person's unit" then managers and the OC "don't really care".

Poorly secured entry points into the condo building undermined residents' sense of home. Highly visible security equipment and warning signs posted by co-residents, such as "Hey, you can get tailgaters! You should be on the lookout!" as Chip, a 32-year-old Perth owner had stumbled across in his condo car park, together with rumours, all increased residents' fear of security breaches. Marta, a 68-year-old owner who purchased her unit after her outer suburban home was burgled "repeatedly", conceded feeling a "bit scared" with the condo garage pinpointed as a "weak point" in its fortification. Exceptionally, unchecked entry into the condo building exposed residents to horrific incidents: a female co-resident being thrown from a balcony, suicides, fatalities. Residents who witnessed these incidents were understandably distressed and the flashbacks unmade their homes for some time after. Eloise, a 69-year-old retired teacher described a tragic event in her 20-plus-storey condo in inner-city Perth where she had lived for some four years:

> 'I did witness a suicide from the top one time. … Yeah, just really awful. I was out on my balcony before I got the shutters. A poor young boy just came in; you could come in [to the building]. I mean, that is an issue too: people could just walk in [the front entrance]. … It was just awful. It took me years to get … it took me ages to get over that because …'

Circulation frictions reminded residents that control over entry to their private home space lay in the hands of multiple other high-rise stakeholders, including their co-residents. Despite this shared responsibility for border maintenance, residents often found themselves tasked as first-responders when these shared borders were breached, notwithstanding residents' expectations that building managers would be primary caretakers. Thirty-two-year-old renter Lani, a full-time student in Melbourne, frequently encountered "drunks" loitering in the lobby of her 12-storey condo and described feeling like she had no one to turn to: "I just don't know who to talk to about them because there's no security, there's no building manager. No one will pick up the phone … and I feel not safe." In staffed condo buildings, a building manager or concierge would usually take charge, at least during office hours. But still, residents who expected concierges to police short-stay renters arriving with suitcases in tow, for instance, were often left frustrated when concierges appeared to show little interest. Meanwhile, in unstaffed buildings and after hours, residents like Lani often did not know who was responsible or had authority to address issues from loitering to "lost" parcels and AirBnB nuisance.

Owners felt most comfortable turning to the OC committee to resolve such issues but could find its response slow and unsatisfactory and could begrudge the costs they might subsequently incur. When intercoms malfunctioned, for instance, defective devices within private units resulted in disputes over whether the owner was liable. Renters meanwhile felt relatively powerless to manage the various circulation frictions they encountered. Through these circulation frictions and border management, renters became acutely aware of the power differential between them and their co-resident owners. Richard expressed this in terms of recognizing that his co-resident owner "has a bit of pull, being an owner, and I think she gets some results … she seems to have clout". Together with renters' general concerns about their tenancy, this sense of powerlessness delimited how renters practised common property. Renter Richard confessed, for instance, that when faced with a "dangerous" safety matter, such as a recent issue with an anti-slip map that was "folded over, peeled over", he refrained from doing anything. He explained: "I thought, 'Oh no, I'm not [going to do or say anything]'" because, as a renter, "you don't want to make noise [a fuss]".

Circulation frictions surrounding the condo's entryways and exits also undermined residents' sense of belonging. The high-rise was not so highly fortified that "outsiders" could not sometimes enter and exert ownership claims. These territorializations were generally found, as we would expect, in those liminal spaces readily accessible to non-residents, including some ground-floor gardens, lobbies and entryways. A Perth resident, for instance, reported how homeless people and non-resident youths often came to use their shared courtyard, outdoor visitor parking bays or garden, marking out makeshift territories with a mattress, food and drink wrappers and the like. While the geography literature has tended to emphasize the tensions between outsiders and insiders, the latter withdrawn into privatized urbanisms behind fortressed facades, many condo residents did not baulk at this illegitimate territoriality of their condo's edge spaces. Mostly, residents appeared fairly tolerant, perhaps knowing management or private security would eventually intervene but also demonstrating their relative detachment from shared home spaces as Chapter 6 elaborates. One Melbourne resident described how homeless people frequented the private shared garden near the entranceway to their condo, gathering and sometimes sleeping there and often storing their belongings under its benches or garden shrubs. This tenant was disinclined to disturb these city residents and instead retreated to their private balcony.

The exclusionary dynamics the geography literature primes us to expect are not limited to insider-outsider dynamics, with some of the most fraught territorial dynamics – and those that impacted residents' sense of home most – often subtle and involving co-residents. While much of the focus on the peripheral borders of the condo centres on concerns over trespass by "outsiders", residents expressed as much if not more concern about "insiders", with co-residents often implicated in security breaches. Residents admitted harbouring suspicions about their co-residents. Melbourne owner Eddie, for instance, suggested a recent motorbike theft from his basement car park was possibly an "inside job" facilitated by knowledge that particular residents were currently on holiday; it appeared, he thought, "like someone has said, 'Look, those people have gone away…'." Residents also worried that co-residents' reckless approach to building security would compromise all residents' safety. Similar to the findings on border-management in the condo unit in Chapter 4, many pointed specifically at renters who residents, such as 38-year-old Perth owner Narelle, thought less likely to be "really mindful of who is coming and going" from the building and more likely to engage in careless boundary-maintenance. Mark, who owned a three-bedroom condo on the 30th floor of an inner Melbourne high-rise, similarly insinuated renters in reckless border maintenance: "People steal stuff, furniture, trash it. Half this building's tenanted, and half are owners, and some of the people don't respect things, common property like that, unfortunately. We've had things stolen from this lobby area." Accusations levelled at renters appeared baseless, and many residents conceded as much. Some residents, like 70-year-old Rory, who rented a one-bedroom unit with his partner, called out tenure prejudice they witnessed in interactions with co-residents: "[A co-resident owner] was almost arrogant … something happened, he said, 'Oh, they're just renters'. Some people in this building … like a two-class society: you've got renters and the owners!"

With limited social interactions between residents, fears about co-resident "others" meanwhile shaped residents' property practices in relation to common property. This in turn circumscribed their homemaking in sometime quite substantive ways, for instance curtailing their use of private storage cages and even their comings and goings from the condo building. Yolanda, the 30-year-old Perth renter, for example, no longer ventured out at night after witnessing an assault in her condo's lobby: "I just don't even go out late at night now … yeah, it was pretty scary", she remembered. Circulation frictions also encouraged subtle social frictions between residents as compromises and concessions were made for others' "nuisance" behaviour. When residents became annoyed at dog-owners who sometimes knowingly disregarded "silly" OC directives to take pets through their condo's back entrance, for instance, residents qualified their frustrations – "I don't find it's appropriate, but that's just me," suggesting again both the way private interests and social expectations could clash as well as residents' own uncertainties about prevailing working rules in their condo and about the level of tolerance expected of a 'good' condo neighbour.

Less tangibly, residents' collective border management reminded residents that the "community" to which they belonged comprised strangers. In stark contrast to the image of co-habiting residents who all know each other's business, many residents rarely saw, let alone recognized or felt any bond with, their co-residents. In attempting to collectively manage their shared borders these residents were mostly unable to distinguish those who lived in the tower from "outsiders". This reflects the large size of these condo complexes, comprising sometimes hundreds of residents, many of whom were renters who often relocated homes after 12 months. Eloise, the Perth owner we met earlier, reflected on the difficulties of controlling who entered their condo despite being attentive to security. Even after four years living in her complex Eloise recognized few of the co-residents that inhabited its some 150 units: "That was the big problem. … Because you'd see people, you knew that … well, you didn't definitely know that they didn't belong there, because you don't know anyone. They would come in with you. You can't turn around and say, 'What unit are you?'"

Notwithstanding residents' relative anonymity, condo renters were still repeatedly cast as illegitimate residents and bad neighbours by their co-residents. This was especially so for any short-stay renters who were sometimes scorned for traipsing through the lobby with suitcases in tow. Echoing reports on the detrimental impacts of short-stay rental platforms on longer-term homemakers, residents lamented these "strangers" in their home space: "different faces everyday – I mean, for me it's my home, you know? I don't want to be living in a hotel". Such comments are revealing of residents' complex relationship to common property: they were at once relatively disengaged, failing to assert the territorial authority associated with home as dominion, and yet some sense of ownership, however weak, clearly endured as implied by the possessive "my". Residents also associated the ostensibly private conduct of renters in their private units, such as perceived overcrowding, with circulation frictions surrounding the shared infrastructure including increased wear and tear and health and safety concerns.

Residents would not have always been aware that their co-residents perceived them as 'bad' neighbours since, in the absence of social interactions, there were limited opportunities for this hostility to be conveyed or perceived – a point I elaborate on in the next chapter. Guaraav, the international student renter we met in the private unit in Chapter 3, whose family of seven stayed for two months in his one-bedroom unit, reported that his co-residents had not noticed let alone complained about his guests. However, an account from one of Guaraav's co-residents who was also interviewed contradicts this. Lani had noticed the "overcrowding" in the building and described it as commonplace and acceptable: "they haven't given me any instructions about guests [and] I always see other people bring in their families; I think they stay a long time" she said. The ambiguities surrounding local working rules are intimated again here, suggesting in everyday condo living these can be less settled than assumed.

Resident WhatsApp groups and building Facebook pages provided residents with context for understanding circulation frictions. Alongside formal communication and in the absence of face-to-face interaction, this communication offered some reprieve from the difficulties of co-managing and co-maintaining shared borders and infrastructures by providing information, advice, reassurance and even camaraderie among often faceless co-residents. Indeed digital communication was often residents' first port of call when seeking to understand these frictions. As one renter explained: "If anybody sees anything suss [suspect] going on, immediately a message goes around on WhatsApp or Facebook saying, 'There's … someone's coming through the bike garage. Do we know this person?' Everyone's sort of … what do they call it? Passive surveillance." In a large Perth condo, 39-year-old renter Katya immediately turned to her building's online forum following an incident; contacting her building manager did not cross her mind. She recounted:

> 'Someone was trying to get in my door. … It really freaked me out, so I'm wobbling. … Whoever was still trying to get in and I said, "Who is it? Who is it?" They didn't answer and then still tried to get in. I just started knocking on the door. I didn't know what to do. … I heard the lift: so they'd left. So I went to the Facebook page for the building. I put on the Facebook page, "Someone just tried to get in my door. If it was an accident let me know because it actually scared me." The admin of the page didn't put it up until six o'clock, so everybody thought it had happened at six o'clock. They're all, like, "Oh, we're going to…" You know, you have some real overenthusiastic security people in this Facebook page, and they're like vigilantes that go out … and someone was … like, "Wow!"

> It hadn't occurred to me but someone said, "Let [X], the building manager, know." I was, like, "Oh, shit." So, I did, and he messaged me back straightaway and then said, "I will look at the [surveillance] video."

Katya went on to detail the particular appeal of digital networks such as these Facebook pages for condo residents as private sites where they could maintain adequate social distance, including preserving their anonymity to some extent. Shilon and Eizenberg's (2020: 133) research on the lived experience of high-rises in Israel similarly notes residents' use of digital communication technologies, such as building-level WhatsApp groups, to share building knowledge. Residents' accounts corroborate how these digital networks could encourage a sense of communality and social cohesion among otherwise socially distanced co-residents and, far more rarely, encourage some in-person social interactions such as by connecting condo mothers for playdates. This reliance on digital networks and digital forums contrasts starkly with the often presumed role of shared physical spaces in supporting social interaction in vertical living – a role which Chapter 6 will also challenge.

These digital forums, networks and 'communities', however, were rarely fully inclusive of all residents and those who were included were diversely engaged: some championed, some contributed, some merely observed. In each building, these digital networks and communities relied on administrators' and contributors' initiative and time, leading to marked differences between buildings in the importance of the digital register in residents' everyday condo living, including variation in the inclusivity and vibrancy of these online forums. These digital extensions of the condo home space could be exclusionary too and this exclusion was largely hidden. Online portals, Facebook pages and ad hoc messaging groups were not inclusive either because residents opted out, some struggled to gain digital access (for example elderly residents) or gatekeepers failed to invite them to join in the first case. High residential mobility also encouraged renters' exclusion. In Melbourne, owner Robin's partner had set up a residents' Facebook page when they first relocated to the brand new 200-unit 30-plus-storey condo tower some two year earlier. The Facebook page, however, only had 80–100 members, "which isn't everybody, but [it's] quite a few", Robin explained, of the digital network of owners who had been the first cohort of residents to move when the building opened.

Most digital interactions were at best transactional and gossipy: residents shared information, 'snitched' on 'bad' neighbours and vented about building issues. Many residents however, like Yolanda, were bystanders only, never contributing any information or updates to the Facebook page of their condos: "I'm on the Facebook page just for the sake of keeping up to date and stuff. You know, I don't post on there. And I prefer not to get to know people on there." Equally, and underscoring the dearth of in-person interactions, some residents felt they were "missing out" if they did not engage with these digital communities since these provided among the only updates about happenings around their buildings and among their co-residents. Sixty-nine-year-old Perth owner Eloise commented: "I do want to get back on it just for that reason, to see what's going on." Residents such as Yolanda, however, were far from alone in intentionally avoiding connections with co-residents to maintain their privacy. A Melbourne renter suggested condo residents fell into different categories: those "who really love to know everyone's business" and others, like Yolanda, who "appreciate not having that sort of incestuous apartment living".

Through digital networks residents perceived common property at a distance and in distributed ways, through devices in the palms of their hands. Crucially, being alerted digitally to border incursions into and through common property spaces, such as the "drunks" hanging out in the lobby or other circulation frictions such as hot water problems or stolen parcels, could unmake the condo home as dominion. These digital interfaces could reinforce residents' lack of territorial control and encourage feelings of dissatisfaction, fear and powerlessness, even when residents were physically removed from the incident in question. Consequently, the digital networks associated with everyday condo life played an ambiguous role in the making of the condo home. These technologies could support residents' sense of control and of community and went some way in compensating for co-residents' lack of face-to-face interaction. But these digital home spaces could also variously prompt the unmaking of home, such as through direct digital exclusion or through updates that made residents feel more unsafe, unsettled or dissatisfied with condo living, including by raising suspicions about their neighbours and by alerting them to issues they would otherwise have remained oblivious to, as Shilon and Eizenberg (2020) similarly identified.

Lifts

Lifts ferried residents, visitors, possessions and pets up and down the tower, offering speed and convenience. Lifts could be unpleasant at times, whether stuffy, crowded or litter-strewn. Moreover, various lift-related issues created circulation frictions that could undermine residents' sense of control over their home space, exacerbate their fears of living "high" and introduce practical challenges to condo homemaking. Especially in taller towers, lifts could prove slow: they could be slow to arrive and slow to travel up to higher floors as they stopped off multiple times along the way. Renter Eddie, who lived in a 30-plus-storey building, said: "we all gripe about the lifts. … It can be quite a lot of time before you finally get to the bottom".

Meanwhile, broken-down lifts were troublesome especially for families with prams and small children, residents unable to easily manage stairs and residents transporting items, such as furniture. Seventy-three-year-old Jeremy, who lived in a one-bedroom third-floor unit described being left virtually housebound after a recent operation when their lift broke down and the stairs were "almost an impossibility". Unreliable lifts also impacted residents. Twenty-six-year-old renter Kevin described the fallout of a broken lift in his large inner Melbourne condo tower:

> 'For two weeks, maybe a month ago, a lift was out service. There was only one lift servicing 30-plus floors of people in this building. That is crazy! There are maybe 10 units [on] each floor, so there are over 300 units of people and there are at least two people in each apartment. I know in some units they will have bunk beds for backpackers and students.'

When lifts malfunctioned or were deactivated during emergency evacuations, residents worried about escape routes. Owner Marta, who lived in a 12-storey Perth condo, specifically bought on Level 5 to be rescuable by a fire service ladder but remained fearful three years in: "that's the only little [thing] I can't get used to", she admitted. Some also worried about other practicalities, such as how paramedics might fit a stretcher in the lift cabin.

When lifts jammed, those stuck inside mostly found it slightly comical, at least to begin with. But others described incredible anxiety; Corina, a 24-year-old renter and international student panicked: "Oh. We're going to die!", she recalled of her experience. Neville recounted how a resident trapped in a lift in his inner-city condo required medical assistance:

> 'One young guy, he was stuck in the lift for over an hour and he went berserk. … He was an absolute nervous wreck. Poor guy. … He began to yell and scream. Somebody was walking in the corridor and heard this coming out of the lift. Said, "Are you all right?" … they got him out with the ambulance.'

Frictions inhibiting the functionality of lifts, including such incidents of vertical immobility, variously undermined residents' capacity to feel 'at home'. Residents' sense of agency was also diminished as building managers, CCTV and key fobs variously moderated who moved where, and when. A key fob was required to operate the lift and usually granted residents access only to the floor residents lived on and floors where shared amenities were located. Residents had to notify management about their plans to move in or move out or bring larger items, such as furniture, into the building so managers could commandeer a lift with protective coverings.

In many buildings resident had little say about such mobilities with their timing restricted, for instance to weekday office hours only, when building managers were available to oversee proceedings. Residents were also often banned from transiting larger possessions through the lobby which created added hassle in some buildings where residents first had to transport items from the basement to the ground floor in a goods lift then swap over to the commandeered passenger lifts. Lift capacity and dimensions meanwhile restricted what residents could bring into their units. Residents on lower floors sometimes innovated workarounds such as hauling large sofas up fire stairs or over balconies but higher-floor residents had no alternatives when they found larger furniture from previous homes could not fit in the lifts.

Local working rules meanwhile governed residents' conduct in the lift cabins: residents quietly manoeuvred around each other to maintain personal space, adopted hushed tones, suppressed coughs and closely supervised their children and pets. But not all residents self-regulated accordingly, and this too created circulation frictions. Melbourne renter Mona, who lived in a 200-plus-unit condo complex in inner Melbourne, complained about her co-residents: "Some people are idiots! They'll leave their McDonald's wrappers in the lift ... 'Can't you just take your rubbish? Why did you leave it in the lift?' But by Monday morning it's cleaned up. ... Just one of those things with sharing space, I suppose, with lots of other people." Mona's frustrations conveyed a limited sense of ownership towards the lifts, but at the same time no great sense of personal stewardship as is often associated with ownership. As this commentary captures, Mona did not pick up the litter but rather was relieved that contracted cleaners compensated for co-residents' apparent lack of care. In echoes of earlier accounts of circulation spaces, residents such as Mona rely on building management to manage and maintain the lifts even as this dependence on other condo agents introduces its own frustrations and further undermines residents' sense of control. Mona's final comment meanwhile conveys her reluctant acceptance of this conduct too, when she rationalizes this poor behaviour as part and parcel of sharing spaces with others.

Residents at times criticized building managers' inaction and poor communication. Renters in particular described being left "in the dark" about what management were doing to resolve various circulation frictions, such as lift breakdowns. Priya, a 21-year-old Melbourne renter, reported for instance the confusion about her building's broken lift: "So we don't know when it's getting fixed. We don't know what kind of problem it is. We don't know whether it's regular maintenance, or if there's a big fault." Residents also found fault with managers' slow responses and seemingly illogical actions. Lift capacity and wait times were problematic in one building, for instance, because a manager repeatedly scheduled lift cleaning during peak lift usage times, and in three other buildings because a manager had permanently designated one lift for deliveries and move-ins/outs only. Management handling of car-stackers, another mobility infrastructure, similarly frustrated residents who could wait up to ten minutes to park their cars when coming home at peak times. Meanwhile, when car-stackers malfunctioned after-hours, management was often of little help, as 23-year-old Melbourne renter Lani described, leaving residents temporarily stuck and inconvenienced:

> 'And the car elevator was broken, so they were stuck. They can't get their cars out and it was like maybe three or four of them that had the same problem! And they didn't know what to do, who to contact. And so I called the building manager for them but he wasn't picking up because it was night time. And so, the poor things, they were stuck there.'

Despite these circulation frictions, lifts also gave residents peace of mind by restricting and deterring "strangers" from circulating through the tower. Nicole, a 48-year-old Melbourne renter half-joked: "it feels 100 per cent safe and secure … There's only one, two, three … five units on this floor and so there's only five people who potentially could get in and rape and pillage us because nobody else can get in the lift!" Residents' sense of safety was often reinforced by their perception of vigilant management and extensive high-tech security systems and CCTV, that together were rigorously surveilling all lift cabins and lobby activity.

Several residents, such as 27-year-old Perth owner Georgie, also took comfort in the safety that came from being "invisible" in their large condo complex. Georgie lived with her fiancé in Perth's middle ring in a building containing some 200 other households and described how anonymity and privacy from these co-resident "others" made her feel safe:

> '[In my condo] no one would ever notice if you're there or not: they won't know! But then in a house, they can see from the outside, whether it's got lights on, firstly. And then, secondly, when you live [in] a house people can tell: they can see when you drive your car out so they can sort of know that "oh, this time of day, you usually drive out and this time of the day you come back home". But then when they don't see your car at all and then they sort of know maybe this person is on holiday, there's no one in the house, that kinda thing … security-wise. … I feel it's rather safe to lock-and-leave because no one will ever know that you leave anyway.'

Many condo residents' sense of privacy in their condo unit was therefore contradictory. Like Georgie, they felt their comings and goings were discrete, even hidden from view but on the other hand, as Chapter 4 illustrated, these same residents faced privacy breaches within their private units. Focusing on this former sense of anonymity and seclusion, residents such as 68-year-old Perth owner Marta, declared: "if you want privacy, that's the place to be: in an apartment building!" This idea of privacy differs from traditional propertied notions of privacy associated with the home as castle, which assumes personal privacy across the sensory registers. This privacy is much more inflected towards anonymity – a privacy among co-residents. In contrast, a minority of residents did not share Georgie's view and they emphasized instead the unavoidable publicness and visual exposure associated with circulating through their building, including being unable to depart unobserved from their private unit.

Residents' sense of security was full of contradictions too. Some residents rationalized that the threat of opportunistic burglaries was far lower in their securitized condo relative to a house, including because, as Georgie also believed, in a house trespassing was relatively more straightforward and the owner's absence was more noticeable, whether through the absence of cars in the driveway or lights in their windows. Residents did not, however, always feel safer in the condo than previous homes; their fears just differed.

Residents repeatedly noted that their security within the condo was distinctly contingent on their co-residents. Residents frequently intimated that they perceived the conduct of some co-residents and some of their co-residents' visitors as not only inappropriate but also a potential security risk. Residents told of countless incidents, such as 69-year-old owner Lauren who lived on the 9th floor in a middle-ring Perth condo with her adult daughter. Lauren's neighbour's unit attracted a steady flow of strangers: "we had a [prostitute] in the corner flat and all these strange guys were turning up in the lift, and even knocking on [our] door to ask where she lived". While most residents thought lift access was fairly secure with key fobs authorizing and restricting movement, the fire stairs could enable uncontrolled access to all floors in some buildings, causing some to worry about who was circulating unchecked. Retired Melbourne renter Neville, who lived alone in a one-bedroom unit in the inner city, described a co-resident who was apparently selling drugs from the unit above and who allowed their "unsavoury" customers to circulate unaccompanied through his building:

> 'The people selling the drugs [in the unit upstairs], they know that if they go downstairs and meet someone, they can bring them up [to their unit] and then the person's going to walk down the stairs [unescorted]. They can walk down … one floor and then go in and bother all of these people. I mean, for example, two weeks ago I had a knock on the door at a quarter past three, I had another knock on the door at four o'clock, I had another knock on the door at half-past four.'

This created a nuisance for Neville, heightening his security concerns. Residents openly admitted to subsequently feeling hostile towards their co-residents. For instance, India, a 24-year-old Melbourne renter, explained: "It's not 100 per cent safe. You still need to be aware of your neighbours on the same level". Heidi, a 50-year-old Perth renter, was even more direct: "you do need – when you're living in an apartment – security's not just from what's floating around outside, but security from those inside as well". With all these risks front of mind, a few residents conceded harbouring anxieties about travelling in their lift with others or letting children travel unaccompanied.

While these security concerns and safety fears contrast with condominium's engineered image of community as well as with propertied imaginaries of the fortressed castle home, they are in keeping with US condo research that highlights 'insider/hallway crime' occurring within the condo and committed by condo residents. For instance, alongside the prevalence of condo governance related white-collar crime, research identifies mischief, such as triggering false fire alarms, vandalism, assault and burglary, sexual solicitation and drug-related crimes (Lippert et al 2017: 35–6; also Lippert and Treffers 2016; Rollwagen 2016). Residents who felt their safety was contingent on their co-residents in turn often emphasized the perceived "reputation" of their building. This reputation, as previewed in earlier chapters, was largely based on the perceived tenure profile of its residents, as residents equated higher shares of owners-occupiers with increased safety.

As a propertied home space, the lift was a place where residents perceived OC and management territoriality, including through proprietorial and disciplining signage. Management posted messages restating by-laws about permitted conduct in the lift and other shared home spaces beyond, with these cautions framed sometimes as threats with references to punitive action for further breaches or, as in the bin rooms, with patronizing tones reminding residents of common sense etiquette. Wei, a 26-year-old owner and graduate student, described how multiple false alarms in his inner-city Melbourne condo led the OC to "start to educate the tenants using flyers in the lobby, in the elevator … they started telling tenants: 'You're going to get penalized $2,000 for it'." Some residents found signs excessively accusatory, rude and out-of-place in their home space. In Melbourne, 33-year-old renter and dental clinician Sergio described a recent incident of mail theft where the OC believed it was an "inside" job and management had "captured the pictures of the guy with a hoody and put it up on the lifts. Asking if anyone knew this person". Signage was at times variously perceived as intrusive, controlling, authoritarian and even dictatorial in the context of a domestic setting, with many expressing frustrations but also resignation at this perceived imbalance of power between residents and management. A Perth renter commented:

> 'At the moment the OC for the building sound very authoritarian with their notices. And for me, I know it's just typical – this is how it gets done because they don't have a better way of doing it – but surely there's a better way somewhere maybe. We haven't discovered it yet!'

In other buildings, signs were humiliating as well as accusatory, such as the Perth renter who found photos of himself stuck up in the lift, shaming him after he breached a by-law by erroneously parking his car in a visitor car park. Residents' perceptions of formal governance actors' territorial control of shared infrastructures such as the lifts were often compounded by poor communication from these actors about their intentions as well as residents' own uncertainties about their own entitlements. Renters, who were privy to relatively little communication, subsequently often experienced the fallout from OC decisions without any explanation. And indeed a fair share of owners conceded not engaging with communications from these actors in any case. Several owners said they were not receiving any OC correspondence and where owners had not chased this up, they appeared sheepish but unbothered by their information deficit. One Melbourne owner confided they had not received any correspondence from their OC for years; their OC had their now-defunct work email address that had been valid at the time of purchase and the owner was unsure who to contact: "So I know it sounds very stupid but yeah … I have no involvement, and I don't even know what's happening."

Property practices in the lifts provide further insights into residents' complex sense of ownership over common property elements and the unsettled nature of some local working rules. For instance, residents also reasserted their own territoriality in the lifts, including through signs of their own, for instance advertising meet-and-greets or other local events and relaying information or warnings about recent incidents. But residents held differing views as to whether their co-residents were acting appropriately by sticking up these notices. They questioned whether co-residents were asserting too much territoriality – were they being too proprietorial? – and whether (particular) notices were appropriate. Whereas some residents wished this communication would be delivered through other means, others frowned upon those who went ahead and took these notices down, challenging their co-residents' territorial claims. Illustrating the contested nature of both the territorial assertions (posting the sign) and its rejections (pulling down the sign), Kara, a Melbourne renter, described this: "people put letters or notes on the lift: 'Can someone help me with this, or someone help me with that?' And there's those vicious types that pull them off and don't believe that you're allowed to do that". Also evidenced here are glimpses of the way territorial contestations in shared spaces operate as means through which residents came to evaluate their co-residents as good or bad neighbours, as 'vicious types' – a thread we will pick up in the following chapter.

Note too that lifts could, by contrast, facilitate co-resident interactions, although not through face-to-face interactions as typically assumed. Lift signage provided a likely more inclusive communication channel than some of the digital networks and platforms described earlier and could counteract the information deficit that renters faced. Such signage could be inclusive, as Perth owner Eloise, whose 150-unit condo comprised only 23 owners, explained: "we just put that little notice in the lift to let other people know".

In contrast, in the lifts and lobbies residents rarely interacted with other residents nor observed much sociality between co-residents; residents described avoiding eye-contact and awkward silences. Many residents blamed high residential turnover among renters in particular. Colin, a 42-year-old insurance sales rep, described the frosty ambience in his relatively smaller, 75-unit inner Melbourne condo building, where he had lived with his partner for six years:

> 'People tend to keep to themselves. We've tried smiling and saying "Hi" and they get surprised by that kind of reaction. I think it's also because so many of the people that live here are short term. Whether it's a weekend, a week, a month, a few months, six months – they tend to just move through the space and don't acknowledge people [standing/living] beside them. It's strange sometimes. You're in the lift getting up to your floor and you may or may not know who's beside you. And you try to … but they're kind of like: "Oh, okay…" So, that's a pity. I thought we'd actually have more connection with people [living] beside us. But they're all renters beside us.'

Co-residents mostly appeared as "strangers" to residents living in these sizeable condo complexes. At worst, when residents frequently encountered people with suitcases in their lifts, this reinforced residents' impression that they were trying to make their home amid a highly transient group of short-stay renters. Renter Saanvi, a 33-year-old new mum and corrections officer, described her middle-ring Melbourne condo: "it's a constant turnover of different people … it's a bit hard to do a community. You just pass people in the lift or the lobby". Other residents found lifts and corridors always empty and openly wondered if they were living in a "ghost" building, making remarks such as: "This place is dead."

Sometimes accusatory signs and details gleaned from digital networks, which I detailed earlier, amplified residents' sense of social disconnection by increasing the frustration and suspicion they felt towards the few co-residents they did encounter in the lifts. On the other hand, frosty lift rides could conceal sometimes active engagements and connections between co-residents in the condo's digital home spaces, as described earlier. Indeed this online engagement could be formative in residents' impression of their condo "community", with residents such as Ying, a 53-year-old mother who lived with her partner and teenage daughter, assessing her co-residents on that basis: "Based on the forum, the Facebook group, everyone's friendly and helpful." In cases where residents engaged in especially vibrant forums or supportive condo messaging groups these exclusive digital communities enhanced their sense of part-whole belonging, including by dulling if not fully overwriting their otherwise negative impressions of intra-building sociality.

Circulation frictions

Shared infrastructure makes private condo units accessible, functional and comfortable home spaces. And yet the movement of people, things and matter through this infrastructure is far from seamless with various 'frictions' interrupting, stalling and obstructing everyday condo mobilities. Lifts break down, "outsiders" enter car garages unstopped, unstaffed lobbies hinder parcel deliveries, single-point utility metering disallows residents from swapping utility providers and waste management systems complicate residents' recycling practices. Indeed residents perceive various circulations frictions in everyday condo living. Residents are also implicated in producing these frictions, for instance by being inattentive to tailgaters, and conversely in easing these frictions, for instance by alerting co-residents to suspicious conduct via digital networks.

The concept of circulation frictions innovates by considering how mobility (not just of people-in-motion, but also of non-humans, things and matter) operates as another vector through which residents perceive and encounter territoriality in the condo's propertied landscapes. This concept represents an important departure from the usual focus only on movement and flows across borders without much consideration of how mobilities are differentially constrained and enabled across territory. Whereas Cresswell's (2010) account of mobility frictions centres around 'stopping' at borders, circulation frictions in everyday condo living involve interruptions, delays and discontinuities of people, things and matter not only at borders but in moving around common property elements.

Meanwhile, multiple high-rise agents and various security and digital technologies also mediate these condo mobilities. Security technologies and infrastructure, such as CCTV, programmed key fobs, automated doors and boom gates, and digital technologies, such as Facebook pages and WhatsApp groups, monitor and police mobilities into and around the condo building. These technologies, together with building managers, eased *and* exacerbated circulation frictions, slowing down and speeding up mobilities as in the case of managers scheduling lift cleaning during peak times or promptly servicing a broken-down lift. Together, these circulation frictions circumscribe condo homemaking, with the high-rise tower's residential density, scale and architectural form making frictions more likely, including as socio-spatial and governance complexities complicate collective attempts at managing condo mobilities.

Residents do not encounter circulation frictions uniformly, including due to their uneven positions in the condo's propertied landscape. Residents' capacity to respond to frictions is likewise uneven with owners better placed to navigate frictions, including because they typically benefit from better access to relevant information. Owners were privy to OC committee and building management communications about common property issues, such as updates about security issues or faulty infrastructure. Beyond formal communication channels, owners' tenure security, longer residencies and involvement in the OC provided more time and opportunities for owners to form social ties with co-residents and build rapport with condo actors, including managers. Renters appeared disproportionately excluded from informal digital communication channels, including because they were established prior to their tenancies and administered haphazardly by owners.[2] Digital communication technologies thus appeared to unevenly empower and disempower condo residents, including in relation to condo mobilities, thereby easing constraints on homemaking for some and not for others.

An information deficit impacted renters more generally too, with the workings of condominium, from by-laws to embedded networks, rarely well understood. Fred, who we met at the outset of this chapter, signed his lease none the wiser to his limited agency over his electricity provision and suffered financial costs and eventually terminated his tenancy as a result. The rise of embedded networks and associated complaints are shining light on this issue, with regulatory reform on the agenda (for example Lucas and Carey, 2018: np), but meanwhile renters like Fred who face these circulation frictions are relatively hamstrung, with breaking their lease often their only option. Owners by contrast are relatively better placed to navigate such frictions; if inclined, they can agitate for resolution through the OC, albeit this has limitations too with OC responses deemed slow, unforthcoming and potentially costly.

These circulation frictions contribute to the subjectification of condo residents as risky and unruly condo subjects, just as border incursions were shown to in the previous chapter. As residents observe and navigate issues surrounding condo mobilities, they classify residents associated with

[2] Given rising concerns with loneliness and social disconnection (also see Dorignon and Nethercote 2020), the function and fallout of intra-building digital networks in high-rise homes deserves further scrutiny.

smooth(ing) mobilities as 'good' neighbours. Conversely, and reflecting now familiar prevailing pathologies of renters, residents construe the "grubby" lift, the "stolen" mail, the misused rubbish chutes, the large collective power bill, and even the trespassing "drunk" in the lobby as condo renters' wrongdoings. Digital interactions between co-residents could sometimes ease tensions, as information sharing fostered understanding and tolerance, but it could also sometimes exacerbate tensions, such as by spreading hearsay and misinformation. At worst, residents came to view renters as illegitimate co-residents and poor neighbours. On occasion, associated social frictions escalated into face-to-face confrontations or accusatory messages left in lifts. Generally, however, civility prevailed though this should not be misconstrued as evidence of meaningful mutual respect or an ethic of care in everyday condo living (see Valentine 2008). The way circulation frictions inform co-resident relations is poorly captured in the usual emphasis on 'social interaction' and 'sense of community' in descriptions of resident relations. For these non-propertied concepts can obscure how a politics of belonging reflects *and* reproduces condo residents' uneven positioning in propertied space as everyday condo living (through circulation frictions, in this instance) contributes to the subjectification of the condo renter subject.

Circulation frictions undermine the condo home as part-whole belonging. Residents themselves perceive threats and nuisance within their home spaces that evoke fear and resentment. The threat of encountering a 'stranger' – an out-of-place figure in the domestic domain (Simmel 1908 [1971]) – is increasingly likely with towers often containing many hundreds of residents and with substantive residential turnover and short-stay lettings too. Residents' fears nuance prevailing imagery of condo residents cocooned away from the world below as conveyed through the emphasis on insider/outsider dynamics in domestic securitization, gating and urban verticalities literatures, with its suggestions of a relatively homogenous and cohesive community of co-residents. Equally, circulation frictions unsettle propertied imaginaries of private high-rise living which associate height with power, status and exclusivity, as forwarded in early verticalities research. Instead, this chapter builds on prior chapters in gathering evidence of housing tenure as a central stratifying device in volumetric urbanisms.

Circulation frictions can likewise undermine the condo home as dominion as residents come to understand their diminished autonomy surrounding everyday condo mobilities through their shared infrastructures. Residents grew frustrated when building managers failed to promptly fix broken lifts, expecting more accountability. Residents were unnerved when they realized their private safety was contingent on others and rattled when this led, in extreme cases, to major security breaches and nuisance. Residents, and especially renters, worried about being disciplined or being shouldered with unforeseen costs if they did not follow 'due process', such as when addressing an electricity fault after-hours. Residents could feel stressed when they received larger-than-expected utility bills or inconvenienced when their preferred fast broadband could not be installed. Circulation frictions thus became another means through which residents' capacity to feel 'at home' was compromised in everyday condo living.

Everyday condo mobilities and associated circulations frictions help reveal how residents perceive and practise common property in everyday condo living. Common property is not simply 'shared' as conceptual models of condominium imply since 'sharing' does not capture Fred's limited control over his electricity provision nor residents' limited control over their recycling practices. The practice of common property in everyday condo living is not accurately conceived either as something in stark opposition with practices of individual private property. For everyday condo mobilities involving common property elements raise practical and ethical quandaries for residents who again must mediate their private interests, including a need for control, privacy and comfort alongside social expectations. By sharing infrastructure, some homemaking practices undertaken in private units and assumed to be wholly private, such as taking long showers, impact other residents, for instance where utilities are not individually metered. Residents also practised common property in shared home spaces in caring and public-spirited ways, as illustrated by residents affixing signs in the lift cabins to alert co-residents to issues, for instance.

Additionally, the practice of common property in everyday condo living is also more complex than the exclusionary insider/outsider dynamics intimated in bird's-eye view accounts of condoization in the urban privatization and verticalities literature. To be sure, the condo's external boundaries communicate exclusion and operate in exclusionary ways, but this exclusion of "outsiders" is a somewhat fragile achievement. For as this chapter shows, the condo's external borders are susceptible to trespass, with break-ins, tailgating and loitering in the lobby not uncommon. The condo tower excludes only when its occupants are sufficiently conscientious about ensuring doors are locked, boom barriers are lowered, no "outsiders" tail residents into the lobby, and no tailgaters follow residents' cars into the car park. For all its security accoutrements, the safety and security of the condo home rely in no small part on a *collective* project of border management involving all building users. And still, residents remain relatively powerless to control the access and mobilities of co-residents' guests in their shared home spaces either.

Meanwhile, residents often displayed little attachment towards common property elements. They tended not to refer to their shared infrastructures using possessive terms such as "our bin system" or "my lifts" which might otherwise convey a collective or individual sense of ownership. Indeed, for all their frustrations, residents often appeared somewhat indifferent too about issues troubling condo mobilities. Whereas residents were demoralized and disturbed by incursions into their private unit and somewhat motivated to find workarounds, as documented in Chapter 4, residents regularly resigned themselves to circulation frictions, such as poor waste management systems. Still, residents did sometimes reassert their territoriality over common property elements, such as by confronting AirBnB guests in the lifts, and these territorialities, however small, are also important in piecing together how residents interpret and practise common property. These territorialities will be our focus as this tour concludes by taking in the more conspicuous common property elements – the shared amenities – in the next chapter.

6

'She's Sort of Made It Her Own'

On a well-trafficked Australian online forum, residents discuss the highs and lows of condo living. In one discussion thread, Carmel voices her concerns about the use of common property in her condo building. An absentee-owner-turned-AirBnB-host was using their communal laundry and then their letterbox to house a small key safe that enables the owner's guests to check in and out of their condo AirBnB independently. Carmel turns to the forum users to vent and to query the legalities of using common property in this way:

> 'We have quite a vexatious AirBnB host who, on her website, refers to herself as a "rule-breaker" and "disruptor". The "disruptor" attached the AirBnB key safe to her washing machine in the common laundry which has to be accessed with a security key. Residents began to disrupt the "disruptor" by making sure that the laundry door was always locked which meant that her AirBnB customers were not able to access the key. The "disruptor" made a complaint to the police that the secured common laundry door was being locked! She now has attached the key safe to her letterbox. My understanding is that letterboxes are common property: if the letterboxes are located within a brick wall which is located on the common property and clearly outside of a lot, then they [are] subject to the owners corporation's by-laws. So, my question is: can the AirBnB host modify common property (i.e. by attaching a key safe)?' (Carmel, FlatChat Forum 2018)

Carmel is not alone in being troubled by short-stay landlords' use of small key safes or lockboxes. These devices have begun appearing on public bike racks, staircase railings, parking meters and window grilles from Montreal to Edinburgh to Melbourne (Dow 2016; CBC News 2019; Scotsman 2019), and some city governments have recently moved to ban their use (for example City of Melbourne nd).

Public debate about this lockbox dilemma generally centres on the owner's territorial claims to public property adjacent to condo complexes. Property theorist Carol Rose (1994: 290) has previously referred to these kinds of provisional and extra-legal territorialities of public property as 'illusory property' or 'un-real estate' to capture the ways individuals (are perceived to) make claims to public spaces in the absence of legal rights. Green-fingered homeowners, for instance, who reclaim public sidewalks through their everyday acts of stewardship convey a layer of private ownership, with their weeding and planting asserting an 'unreal' proprietorship of public space (Rose 1994: 290) thereby creating complex informal property relationships with passers-by and their neighbours, irrespective of any overt agenda to gain formal ownership (Blomley 2004b). Carmel's lockbox query, however, while sharing similar concerns about the appropriateness of the condo owner affixing lockboxes to various things that are not hers alone, concerns, by contrast, *common* property in condominium rather than public property per se. This common property and its use and misuse is our focus in this final empirical chapter.

Through an abridged tour of the condo's shared home spaces, this chapter explores the different ways residents practise common property in the shared amenities of their condos. Together with the exploration of the condo's shared infrastructures in the previous chapter, its analysis extends our understanding of how common property is practised in everyday condo living and how this circumscribes condo homemaking. As explained in the Introduction, residents' shared amenities differed between buildings in terms of their designs, size, features and quality. In this chapter we take in some of the more standard inclusions, such as underground car parks, while recognizing that their distinct designs also condition how property is practised. I conceptualize the everyday and informal practices of common property elements by repurposing legal scholar Rose's concept of 'un-real estate', which referred to the extra-legal claims made to public space.[1] This chapter explores territorial dynamics of *annexing* and their counter practices of territorial *withdrawal* in an elevated shared courtyard, then on rooftop terraces, before descending into the car park to explore these dynamics further. This discussion highlights how practices of common property in everyday condo living are characterized by individualized territorial annexations which are sometimes countered by territorial withdrawals as other residents surrender their property entitlements and retreat from these shared spaces. Along the way, the analysis captures how building managers intervene in conditioning associated boundary work that demarcates the

[1] This is not to say that the potential for proprietary claims over other forms of property (Rose's 'unreal estate') has not been recognized. As Blomley (2004b: 636; also 2005b) writes: 'private spaces can also be laid claim to in the name of a local community' and equally, ' "private" owners can think of "their" land in relational and socialised ways'.

social boundaries of locally acceptable practices and how common property practices construct the condo renter as the risky and unruly condo neighbour.

Just as Carmel's forum post intimates, this everyday 'sharing' of shared amenities between co-residents has every potential to encourage frustrations and even escalate into confrontation. This chapter highlights these territorial annexations and withdrawals as another pressure point for condo homemaking. Residents' accounts capture their territorial apathy towards shared amenities and how many refrain from using these facilities, especially in the context of poor design and operational issues, but also how residents nonetheless demonstrate an ambivalent sense of ownership towards these shared home spaces. To explore this ambivalence further, the penultimate section explores how shared amenities figure as residents practise the condo home as a financial asset and emphasizes how their investor orientation means residents continue to value these sometimes little-used spaces for their perceived financial value. I suggest the anticommons thesis, which centres on the underuse of shared resources/spaces, provides a helpful way to conceptualize potential risks that underlie the sharing of common property elements in contemporary condos.

'You could watch their TV, for goodness' sake!'

In Qualia, a 10-storey 130-unit middle-ring Melbourne condo, residents shared a courtyard on Level 5. The courtyard was hemmed on three sides by private units. These adjacent private units had full-height glazing and sliding doors that opened directly onto a small strip of private terraces, with the courtyard beyond. All four unrelated residents we spoke with in this complex welcomed the idea of a shared courtyard but qualified their praise. Forty-eight-year-old renter Penny had moved in without viewing the courtyard and was taken aback when she saw its design, recalling: "I didn't realise … until I actually went down, once I'd moved in. I took that time to go down there and have a look. Those [private] balconies are *right* there!" she explained. As Penny noted, the private terraces adjoining the courtyard were not fenced off from the shared courtyard and in fact were only legible because of a change in surface tiling and well-spaced bollards and planter boxes along the courtyard's otherwise indiscernible border with these private terraces. Penny was taken aback by the proximity of the private units to the courtyard; she recalled: "You could watch their TV, for goodness' sake!"

Penny and two co-residents, none of whom lived on Level 5, suggested the courtyard was inconvenient to access and "too far" from their private units. But additional to this, Penny and her co-residents emphasized their lack of privacy in the courtyard, how they would be watched by residents living in units much like their own that overlooked the courtyard. For

Penny, being overlooked and potentially overheard by co-residents would compromise her capacity to feel 'at home' in the shared home space. She explained: "I wouldn't feel comfortable bringing family and friends out here, having a barbecue, sitting down and talking. You're not going to be yourself. It's restrictive … it's not private for anyone." Penny hated the idea of being "on display" to co-residents and suggested this was an important reason why most co-residents refrained from using the courtyard despite their legal entitlements and despite the fact that this was their only private outdoor space besides their small balconies. Penny elaborated: "I don't really see anyone using it … It feels a bit too public. So I don't think people would actually sit out there and do anything, because there's so many people overlooking that space. And I don't think it's a really relaxing, do-what-you-want space."

For residents such as Penny, the shared home space did not meet traditional propertied expectations of homely spaces, denying her both privacy and autonomy. Furthermore, Penny and her co-residents harboured concerns that through spending time in shared spaces they might establish rapports with their co-residents. This, the three residents similarly claimed, was undesirable when they were, as 42-year-old renter Ian explained, "already living in each other's pockets". Ian, who lived alone with his dog, explained how seemingly harmless casual interactions could lead to further intrusions on their privacy within the condo: "And it's kind of like, you lose your privacy once you befriend somebody in the apartment, because it's a lot easier for them to just come and knock on your door."

Beyond these mostly self-interested rationales for withdrawing from the courtyard, residents also expressed other-regarding concerns about encroaching on the privacy of co-residents who lived in the units adjoining the courtyard. Qualia's courtyard was designed in such a way as to make it difficult, if not impossible, for residents to satisfy their own homemaking needs, such as when socializing, while also respecting the private units and the propertied expectations of those living within. As Penny reasoned, socializing so close to these private units would be "disrespectful":

> 'And I just think, if I look at the environment that I'm in, to bring people from outside, even if it's four or five people, and put them in that area, that common area … I find for me – it could just be me … I think it's disrespectful to other people living here. Because you're going to be eating, other people's balcony doors are off of that [shared] living area. You're going to be drinking and socializing. If someone's [at a loose end], I mean, I'd include them, but some people would be shy and wouldn't. … So, I just find that from that point of view, I think it's just a little bit imposing on people's privacy. I really do. I actually don't think it is for me, really.'

With Qualia's courtyard accessible to over a hundred households, use of the courtyard did have the potential to encroach on the peace and quiet, security or privacy of residents in adjacent private units. Residents such as Penny perceive something of an imaginary buffer zone surrounding the private units that should be observed to help insulate their co-residents from any such intrusions. Similar socio-spatial dynamics were also evidenced in the case of 'spill out' lounges and other terraces and gardens. In Qualia, specifically, this buffer zone casts a shadow onto the shared courtyard, demarcating zones of inappropriate occupation. Penny's self-regulation recalls legal scholar Penner's (2000) thesis that there is an innate tendency to respect the property of others and illustrates the way the ownership model has conditioned how we interrelate with others through property.

As this suggests, legal entitlements to use and access shared spaces appear less consequential than local working rules in conditioning courtyard property practices. As Penny's account conveys, tacit social understandings establish the bounds of appropriate conduct in the courtyard. One unspoken objective of these rules is to protect the sanctity of individual private property and associated propertied expectations, such as for personal privacy for instance. Local working rules are therefore partly informed by architectural designs and especially adjacencies between shared home spaces and private units. The porous borders of the private units as described in Chapter 4, and the porous physical interfaces between private units and shared spaces specifically, delimit appropriate practices and zones of occupation in shared home spaces. By extension, residents trespassing this buffer zone were deemed to be acting out of line; they risked intruding on co-residents' privacy, creating potential nuisance and causing security concerns.

Residents could practise common property by withdrawing from these shared spaces, with such conduct at least partially driven by other-regarding concerns. In other buildings, residents similarly appeared to self-regulate in using shared amenities, though this did not always translate to residents refraining from using amenities per se, as it did in Qualia. Indeed on occasion in some buildings, similar other-regarding motivations prompted residents to *use* shared amenities. For instance, residents extended their private homemaking into shared amenities, for example by hosting their guests in resident lounges, including to protect the privacy and peace and quiet of the co-residents who lived around them. Far less frequently, shared home spaces functioned as a liminal space beyond the public sphere and private units, and were used by residents for instance when they had guests to maintain their own privacy at home, "if you maybe don't want to invite them over to your home", or to separate work and home life.

Meanwhile, as Penny and her co-residents adhered to these local working rules, they expressed ambivalence about territorializations they witnessed in their courtyard. Both Penny and Finn, a 57-year-old renter, disapproved of how residents living adjacent to the courtyard appeared to be "taking it over". Observing the courtyard from their Level 6 and Level 9 units, Penny and Finn interpreted the Level 5 residents as displaying proprietorial attitudes. They noted their personal possessions in the courtyard beyond their private terraces and similarly came to judge that these residents were behaving out of line. Penny recounted the questionable actions of one Level 5 resident in particular; as Penny saw it: "the woman that's taken over the whole of the courtyard!" Penny suggested this resident had appropriated a portion of the shared courtyard, interpreting her pot plants and a shade awning as an uninvited territoriality: "She's got a garden. … She's sort of made it her own!". This territoriality was all the more inappropriate and illegitimate, Penny thought, by dint of her co-resident's brief tenancy in the building; "She's not even [been] here that long; she's only been here for five months!", Penny exclaimed. Such dynamics demonstrate that co-residents can practise common property at a single site within their condo building in different ways.

In Qualia, perceptions and practices of common property around the shared courtyard inform the construction of the bad condo neighbour. Although property is inherently social, practices of common property observed by residents at-distance still clearly operate to construct the 'bad' condo neighbour in everyday condo living. In socio-territorial dynamics now familiar from previous chapters, Penny and Finn associate poor conduct with renting and their comments additionally seem to imply that longer-term residency may have given greater legitimacy to their co-resident's claims. If residency duration figures in determining legitimacy of territorial claims, this stands to impact renters in particular as relatively more transient residents.

This contested territoriality rarely translated to significant direct confrontations between co-residents at Qualia. This is at least partly because Penny and her co-residents were physically distanced from Level 5 residents, with social interactions unlikely without them expressly visiting the courtyard. Seeming to corroborate this, another co-resident claimed they *had* been verbally confronted when stepping into the courtyard, explaining: "I've gone down there, and she just abuses me … she believes that the entire courtyard is hers." These contested territorialities did, however, undermine co-residents' sense of part-whole belonging. Penny commented: "they're walking out [of their units] and talking … which is great", and "It's like another little community, I guess, down there with that. Good on them!" Penny jokingly hypothesized several ways she might "break in" to this Level 5 community. Penny imagined, for instance, how she might befriend a Level 5 resident so she felt less like an outsider, even speculating that some of her co-residents may have done precisely this.

Penny and Finn's interpretations of territorialities in the courtyard were nonetheless subjective. For when we spoke with Caitlyn, a Level 5 resident whose unit opened onto the courtyard, she revealed: "I've actually got access out to the courtyard out there. I used to go right out, but since this horrible obnoxious woman moved in next door to me … She's basically banned my cats from outside. They're not allowed outside in the courtyard any more." In response to this hostility, Caitlyn had modified her private terrace, attempting to create a semi-private outdoor "room" using pot plants and gauze screening to divide off her terrace from the courtyard. Caitlyn explained: "I've had to put pot plants all along and sort of block it off so the cats can go out" without roaming further into the courtyard. But due to tensions with her neighbour, Caitlyn refrained from entering the courtyard when she spotted her neighbour, abstaining even from what others saw as her own little "private" courtyard, to avoid further confrontation. What Penny and Finn had interpreted as her "colonization" of the shared courtyard, Caitlyn described as a feeble attempt to placate her adjacent neighbour while accommodating her cats.

Caitlyn's account provides a necessary counter perspective that establishes territorialities in the shared courtyard as more subjective and ambiguous than implied by Finn and Penny's interpretation of something of a social divide between 'insiders' on Level 5 and 'outsiders' living on other floors. We understand that property's meanings are produced as residents observe the 'material form of the site … to discern the intent of the space and thus shape a moral and aesthetic response to it' (Blomley 2016b: 240), and as empirical studies of property in everyday life preview, rarely if ever are these messages singular, coherent and cohesive. The messages residents 'read' from others' practices in courtyard do not emerge through some 'dyadic relation between thing and duty-bearer' (Blomley 2016b: 240; 2005b) but through attempts to understand the meanings of those users' property practices. But while property is inherently social, Penny and Caitlyn interpreted property practices mostly at a distance and in social isolation from each other, leading to Penny's misguided diagnosis of Caitlyn's territorial ambitions.

Qualia residents' accounts also convey complex expressions of ownership towards their courtyard. Neither Penny, Finn nor Caitlyn referred to their courtyard with personal or collective possessive pronouns (for example my, ours) but rather referenced "the courtyard" in neutral, non-possessive terms. Moreover, while these residents perceived co-residents' claims in collective terms, using collective pronouns (that is, comments such as: "its like it's *theirs*") to refer to others' occupation or territoriality, Caitlyn for instance did not describe her own territoriality or sense of ownership in collective terms. At the same time, Penny and Finn's frustrations about the courtyard being "taken over" nonetheless suggests residents feel some sense of entitlement, even while they do not feel any sense of attachment and even as they remain withdrawn from these spaces.

'It's always the same people using those areas!'

On a rooftop terrace in inner-city Perth, 30-year-old owner Cassie expressed frustrations about her co-residents' territorialities and carelessness. Cassie explained: "when I first moved in, I thought I'd use [the terrace] all the time"; it had "so much potential". Four years on, however, Cassie conceded that using the rooftop could feel awkward: "it's a shared space: it depends who's there; it's not super comfortable". For Cassie, "sharing" her roof deck with some 50 other households involved observing her co-residents making the deck their own. She had seen co-residents bring up personal possessions which later lay abandoned and she had observed their frequent property damage. On one occasion, co-residents had scaled onto the air-conditioning units beyond the designated terrace area to access better city views. When Cassie ascended to the deck, she never knew what she would find:

> 'I don't know what people did up there! … I think some people are just idiots as well though, because some people would leave their personal things up there. Someone left a barbecue up there for a really long time … someone had put two chairs out there [on the illegally accessed roof beyond the terrace] to sit on.'

Like many other residents, Cassie blamed renters for this uninvited territoriality, property damage and illegal conduct.

Design and operational issues compounded Cassie's frustrations. Rooftop access was circuitous ("I have to go down to the ground floor, across [to a separate lift], then back up"), use could be inconvenient ("every time anyone needed the bathroom, you've got to come all the way back to my unit, which wasn't as easy as it sounds") and the furniture was "weird" and "uncomfortable" and "the view's blocked – which is not ideal!" Rooftop maintenance was slapdash: tables and the chairs were broken, the vertical garden "wasn't well maintained [and] it looked terrible … it's been mismanaged". The deck was exposed, poorly furnished and short of a barbecue, accessible view or indeed anything much to entice Cassie. Describing the last time she ventured up, Cassie said: "I stayed up there for maybe three seconds and I was like: 'It's really windy!' and then I left." Cassie subsequently rarely used the deck; it has "been kind of wasted", she reflected, despite her initial interest.

Over time, residents considered such property practices as somewhat settled, as "the way things go around here". While resigned, residents sometimes appeared resentful too. Also in Perth, Scott, a 57-year-old owner, described not dissimilar territorial dynamics in his building's swimming pool. Scott's condo overlooked the pool where he observed the same "cast of characters" laying out towels on the deck chairs. "It's always the same people using those areas," Scott said: a young child, whom Scott and his partner had nicknamed "the dolphin" because they were "always there", and other youths who "like to have parties". Since moving in four years ago, whenever Scott ventured down to the pool he felt he was interrupting these regular users, intruding on their domain. Still, Scott persisted and described trying to carve out his own space at the pool: "like cutting through the line. They are having the party, and then you try to have some space". Rosie, an older resident in the same high-end complex, had also noticed the youths, describing how they had "taken over" the pool. She criticized their conduct: "I have an issue with the smoking and the drinking. It's pretty common knowledge you don't take glass into a pool area … unless you're a millennial … they don't seem to get it! They'll actually stand in the pool drinking out of a stubby or something." But like Scott, Rosie was resigned to these territorializations: "It's like, come on, guys! Seriously. … But that's what you have to live with," she said. Both owners assumed these younger residents were renters based on their age and their inconsiderate behaviour, though this was speculation and indeed perhaps unlikely given the pool-users' relatively longer residency.

In buildings with high rates of short-stay rentals, where residents similarly reported being discouraged from using their amenities, residents faced additional costs and inconveniences associated with others' usage. In inner-city Melbourne, Colin, a 49-year-old medical sales rep, purchased a high-end one-bedroom condo with his partner. Shortly after moving into the boutique 70-unit complex, Colin found out that fewer than 15 units were owner-occupied and that many of his absentee co-owners favoured lucrative short-stay letting. Six years in, Colin appeared resigned to the repeated "takeover" of their roof deck, day and night, by "really drunk" and "very rowdy" 18- to 25-year-old visitors. Colin and these temporary residents rarely exchanged words, but he saw them as "the worst of the worst". They made Colin feel like an uninvited guest in their shared home spaces: uncomfortable and not 'at home'.

Like other residents who found their shared amenities occupied by unknown 'others', the amenities lost their appeal. Colin and his partner barely used their rooftop deck: "It didn't have the same sort of appeal to us. So we thought, 'Let's just go outside instead.' So, we don't use it that much at all. In the beginning, we did; but now we don't…" Colin explained. Colin found, moreover, that the presence of these temporary visitors gave him the impression of living in a "rogue hotel" and, with no connection to his cohabitants, this too unmade the condo as home, undermining his capacity to establish any sense of "community" with his hyper-transient co-residents. The presence of these strangers cost Colin financially too, as he faced additional bills. Every New Year's Eve, for instance, extra building security were brought in to manage the influx of short-stay renters and their guests. Colin elaborated: "So they [building management] have to be careful around New Year's because it gets very rowdy upstairs. People get really drunk on the rooftop. So they generally have security there and make sure everybody leaves after midnight. ... There's always people that misbehave for whatever reason."

On occasion, these territorialities caused tensions. Cali, a young international student and renter in Melbourne's inner city described how over the past year he had become fed up with encountering short-stay renters in his home space and he admitted he had become increasingly aggressive towards them when he bumped into them in the lifts or the lobby. As Cali elaborated: "Sometimes we can see a group of people, just with a lot of luggage in the lobby. I don't know why they're there. I just go in there, and then I just go: 'What are you doing here?'" Cali's rhetorical question challenged the short-stay renters' occupation of his home space. He knew who they were since most short-stay renters were relatively conspicuous with their comings and goings, as Cali said, "you've never seen them before and you can clearly tell that they don't live in this building!" Such cases corroborate evidence of heightened hostility and conflict between short-stay renters and longer-term residents in condo developments and residents' growing frustrations, as tabled in Chapter 1 and Chapter 2. For the most part, however, longer-term residents, such as Cali and Colin, mostly acquiesced to these unchecked "takeovers" of their shared amenities, just as Penny and Finn had in Qualia, appearing variously worn down, unmotivated or unable to take substantive action.

Meanwhile, the way managers regulated residents' use of shared home spaces both directly and indirectly undermined residents' sense of the condo home as dominion. By programming key fobs, managers blocked residents' access to shared home spaces while routine or emergency maintenance or upgrades were carried out, just as they did with shared infrastructures, as detailed in Chapter 5. Managers also shut off residents' access to shared home spaces in response to misuse, accidents and reported damage, oftentimes (for renters especially) with little warning or explanation. Thirty-year-old renter June lived in a large Melbourne tower with some 200 units where residents supposedly enjoyed access to a lounge with a large television, games, a coffee machine and a "spectacular view". Initially, residents could come and go as they pleased using their key fobs to gain entry. But soon after moving in, June explained that "the place was trashed" and "a load of kids got in there and wrecked it". Again, renters or youths were blamed. Reprogrammed key fobs denied residents' access, even one year on. June was confused, suggesting renters like herself were "in the dark" without communication from the OC committee: "it's not open to residents … I don't know who it's open to, but building security … because it used to be open … I think something must have happened where they shut it and said 'we're not opening it any more!' So yeah, I don't know!"

Management action and inaction also indirectly conditioned how residents practised common property. Namely, policing or lack of policing partially informed which property practices residents understood as permissible. If Colin's short-stay renters partied on the roof deck without reprimand and if Cassie's co-residents' illicit wanderings on their rooftop deck and discarded possessions went unchecked, then residents such as Colin and Cassie tended to interpret these practices as accepted. Condo agents' role in legitimizing property practices in shared home spaces contrasts somewhat with dynamics observed in private units, where working rules were less obviously mediated in this way by management action and inaction.

Residents' lack of territorial control was most striking in a few buildings where residents were agitating to have shared spaces with ambiguous functions, such as "breakout zones" and large lobbies, repurposed. Although these spaces were ostensibly designed for "flexibility" and "spontaneity", residents conceded "barely anyone" used them. Condo governance ostensibly offered a means for owners to exert territorial control over shared amenities to address this, yet this proved fraught too. When Eloise, a 69-year-old owner, tried to have an idle "meeting room" repurposed into a family play space as part of lobby upgrade works in their Perth condo, for instance, her co-residents claimed children were already adequately accommodated for. In this and other cases, residents' attempts to build consensus among scores of diverse owners were fraught, including because of their diverse priorities for communal spaces, their differing enthusiasm to pursue other-regarding solutions and their differing means and willingness to commit to financial outlays. Owner Eloise grew frustrated. She queried: "Where can the children play? – there's nothing like that!", elaborating:

> 'I suggested ... because I know a couple of the young mothers here. They're crying out for somewhere to let their kids play. I thought, "Well, maybe make this into it." But I don't know what the architect ... they sort of said, "No. They've got this, that and the other." But then there's a couple of offices there at the end. [The tenancies] complained too when the [resident] mums have got their children playing out there, they have complained: "Oh, too much noise!" I'm thinking, Hmm! ... But there's nowhere for them to go to take their children!'

Owners like Eloise who did participate in condo governance met with well-rehearsed issues, corroborating extant condo governance research tabled in Chapter 1. Successful attempts to spur the OC committee into action usually involved a 'champion' with the wherewithal, skillset, time, motivation and tenacity to advocate. But such advocacy was time-consuming and energy-zapping and OC committee members admitted feeling worn out by the workload or worn down by the in-fighting, politics, hidden agendas and backbiting. Condo governance also carried an emotional toll, with its focus on something as intimate as their home and the intensity of managing conflict with those you may bump into in the lift. Many owners were not part of OC committees: some were unable, some were not interested and others had had their "fill of meetings". Others still, such as Wei, a 26-year-old Melbourne owner, failed to find any 'community' within the OC ecosystem and disengaged. Some forfeited voting rights too: "I used to come for the general AGM, back in 2014, but again … because 90 per cent of the owners are overseas, so it's more like a very small focus group. What I did, I gave my voting right to the building manager, so that's that!", Wei explained. Renters, meanwhile, who were formally disenfranchised from condo governance, were not privy to these discussions and moreover usually poorly informed of their content and outcomes, as previously noted.

Besides feeling they had little control over these shared home spaces, residents also often found these spaces unhomely. They expressed misgivings about their lack of privacy and struggled to 'be themselves' or feel 'at home'. In Perth's inner city, 30-year-old renter Rachael and her co-residents at The Vale, an upmarket 12-storey building with some 200 units, shared a large recreational area with a generous swimming pool, spa and barbecue facilities. These facilities were a drawcard when Rachael signed her lease, but after moving she discovered some 100 units directly overlooked the pool from their adjoining balconies. Rachael hated being "on display" and overlooked and struggled to feel at ease, describing how "your privacy is a bit non-existent [and] I'm not a very good swimmer and I feel embarrassed because everyone is looking at you. … No privacy at all – no, thank you! I don't want people watching me." In a nearby 22-storey condo, Katya, a 49-year-old mental health nurse, expressed similar misgivings. As Katya articulated, this unease arose not so much from being observed by others per se but rather being watched by her co-residents, in particular, with whom she desperately wanted to maintain social distance. Katya tried to explain: "I just feel uncomfortable with other people that I live in the building with going into the pool. I don't know why, but I just am."

Katya and Rachael faced other impracticalities and inconveniences using their pools in any case, and these only reinforced their withdrawal from these shared home spaces. Rachael described an exhaustive list of rules and regulations signposted poolside: prohibitions on drinking, eating, running and diving; restrictions on access hours and noise; limits on visitors; stipulations on showering before swimming; appropriate poolside attire; and the supervision of children aged 16 and under. As an aside, only exceptionally did residents associate such restrictions with city or public health regulations or insurance-related mandates. And while this reflects residents' relatively poor grasp on condo governance, it impressed on residents like Katya and Rachael the extensive control and heavy-handedness of condo agents in these shared home spaces. Like many Perth residents, Rachael and Katya also found their pools too cold, unheated and overshadowed (though conversely, inadequate shading was sometimes an issue too). Especially for parents, the lack of poolside bathrooms further inconvenienced residents who needed to chaperone children (or escort visitors) through multiple security doors and lifts to return to their private units, usually with personal belongings in tow since shared spaces were not deemed secure. Residents like Rachael and Katya were also aware of numerous construction defects from faulty pool gates and loose tiles to more serious issues; some prompting temporary closures of these facilities.

On top of feeling "crowded out" and "on display" in their shared home spaces, these various operational, regulatory, design and workmanship issues could be the final straw in dissuading residents from using the facilities. Some residents resorted to quick visits or, like Katya and Rachael, avoided their shared amenities altogether, as Katya confirmed: "I went with the intention of, 'Oh, I'll just figure out' … and it's just not me! … and I haven't used the pool at all!" These residents also rationalized the benefits of neighbourhood amenities, such as 50-year-old Perth renter Heidi who explained why she had not used her condo's elevated green space: you "may as well go to the neighbouring park" because in the condo you get none of the freedoms, privacy or convenience of a private backyard and less amenity, anonymity and privacy from co-residents than a public park affords. Anthony, a renter and father of a small child, likewise favoured his local park over a small shared green space in his Melbourne condo, explaining: "there's 30,000 trees all around, a playground, no OC oversight, no need to tell them I'm having a party, no nosy neighbours, and no bans on child-friendly activities such as biking, scootering, rollerblading, and skateboarding". Such comments highlight additional push factors behind condo parents' reliance on playgrounds, green space and other city amenities outside the condo tower to support family life (also see Andrews and Warner 2020), and beyond feeling unwelcome or poorly accommodated (Nethercote and Horne 2016), including condo residents' perceptions of compromised autonomy, control and privacy, alongside (and exacerbated by) design, regulatory and operational issues.

Residents, however, did not practise common property in uniform ways as the contrary territorial dynamics of annexing and withdrawing signal. A select set of residents – including co-residents like those Cassie, Scott and Colin observed "colonizing" their shared home spaces – considered shared home spaces as an extension of their private home. Rada, a 53-year-old renter who lived with her partner in a small one-bedroom condo in inner Melbourne, for instance, described using their shared rooftop terrace to escape the confines of their unit. Moreover, Rada explained how she used the terrace to do things that might otherwise take place in the private unit if space permitted. This included socializing, for instance, but also other intimate activities usually confined to private home spaces, such as arguments with her partner, as well as activities associated with some degree of privacy or solitude, such as "me time". Rada elaborated on her use of the terrace:

> 'Sometimes when I need to talk to my boyfriend not in apartment. Yeah. For argument, for sure. … And then we just go to the rooftop and just got the amazing views and the winds come over and then you calm down a bit. It's better than just stuck at home and "I hate you!", "No, I hate you more!" Things like that. Yeah. But still besides that, *I barely use it.* … It's really good especially sometimes *I need some me time* and just bring a glass of drinks there and just sit down there and it. … Enjoy some time. … Just like the city views and … you feel comfortable in there since there's barely [any] people … normally there's no people there.'

In contrast to other residents' earlier accounts, Rada could feel 'at home' on her shared terrace. On the other hand, this shared home space was usually vacant and therefore perhaps more amenable to serving Rada's propertied expectations of privacy. Most residents like Rada, for whom shared home spaces played a more important role in their homemaking, tended to live in small two-bedroom units with households of three or four people, usually flatshares. These shared home space dynamics were also most commonly seen in Melbourne's inner-city condos, where significant spatial and design constraints, as detailed in Chapter 1, acutely constrained the socio-spatial dynamics of homemaking *within* the private unit in ways that encouraged residents to pursue more intimate activities in shared spaces, as Rada described.

'You can park there all day and never get booked'

Communal car parks were also overlaid with territorial claims, some in breach of by-laws. Residents "borrowed" the visitor parking bays, for instance to park a rental car hired for an impending weekend trip and they "borrowed" other residents' private bays too when the need arose. Katie, a young Melbourne renter and new mum, explained how her mother "stole" a co-resident's spot when she visited her each week:

> 'My mum, who often comes, will just do the stealing of the spots. Because there's a lot of businesses also using the building, they don't work on weekends, for example, so we know where all their spots are. Those spots are all vacant, and you see everyone doing that. That's one option. Today my mum will be parked in one of those spots. Being in

> the building quite regularly, because of the baby, you tend to notice who goes to work – it sounds a bit stalker-ish – so you can borrow a spot. For sure I don't let someone park there for eight hours, [but for] a couple of hours … otherwise you've just got to circle on the street [looking for parking] unfortunately. There's not guest parking which is one downfall.'

Residents such as Trevor, an older Melbourne owner, were equally blasé about using others' designated parking bays; "of course, if you know that an apartment is vacant [I let them use their spot], because they'll only be there for four hours or something. Often I'll just zap them in", Trevor said of his adult children who visited frequently. Sometimes non-residents also made claims to the parking bays. In one Melbourne condo, brazen local business owners entered the insecure basement car park and used the visitor parking bays on a daily basis. A resident in the building recounted:

> 'I think [the visitor car parks] are full with people that work in the area that – some people are so sly! – because you see the same vehicles parked there day after day that I don't think are actually visiting people that live in this building. They can just park there, walk across the road to where they work, and they've got free parking all day!'

Katie, Trevor and other residents' perceptions about idle parking bays are corroborated by survey findings that indicate that some 25–41 per cent of private carparking spaces are left empty in Melbourne condos (Taylor 2018: 1) including because of the high number of car parks developers are required to provide in new condo developments.

In the carkpark, building managers used passive and non-punitive approaches to police these territorial claims. Residents sometimes received letters or saw warning notices posted in the mailrooms, in their lifts or on resident e-portals. Some building managers went further however. For instance, in several inner Melbourne condos, residents described how managers publicly "outed" offenders and their infringements, as owner Richard recounted: "They'll put pictures of illegal parking in everyone's letterbox." These punitive measures, and especially such public shaming, eliminated ambiguity about which parking practices were permissible. In several Perth buildings, meanwhile, parking officers were deployed, and again this eliminated ambiguity about permissible parking practices, albeit at a cost to residents.

Residents appeared mostly willing to defer to management to govern and maintain these shared car parks, even as they disagreed with some of their methods. For instance, while some residents welcomed the introduction of parking inspectors, others found their clamping practices variously "authoritarian" and "excessive"; they wanted greater recognition that this was a domestic setting and not a public or commercial parking lot. One Perth renter emphasized his expectation for more leniency:

> 'I've got one visitor's pass, but they are quite strict instructions on when it can be used and how long for. My ex-partner did get clamped twice. They were very quick at the clamping, which is obviously a little bit disappointing as well because it was just, like, you've got five hours and maybe he was there for six or seven, or he parked in the wrong spot, sort of thing, which … I guess he broke the rule … they've now stopped clamping as actively now, which I think is a good thing.'

Many residents seemed torn between reliance on management to challenge illegitimate claims and, more generally, maintain the car park, and the way such policing rendered these spaces unhomely: over-regulated and over-policed.

Residents' sense of ownership over their designated parking bays was complex. Unlike other shared home spaces residents *did* use possessive pronouns "my" and "ours" that are indicative of a greater sense of ownership. But if residents understood their own legal entitlements around these car parking bays, only rarely did they ever mention exclusive-use by-laws or specify that their car park was "on title", and generally only in vague terms. Instead, residents emphasized their very limited personal control as captured in 63-year-old renter Eddie's annoyance about the "very militant" rules that banned him from storing anything other than a motor vehicle in his parking bay. On the other hand, residents also appeared as reluctant stewards of these spaces. They expressed territorial indifference and overlooked potentially illegal parking practices, as reflected in comments such as "so long as I can park in my bay there, it doesn't really bother me what everyone else does". Others conceded condo car parks were difficult to police including due to the costs involved, with comments such as: "I don't know how you police that [visitor parking]. That's part of apartment living." Eve, a 30-year-old architect who lived with her sister, who owned their unit, described her realization that their parking bay was "theirs". Eve tried to explain:

> 'I think it's not part of the common area. It's actually … each bay is actually privately owned. … There's nobody to maintain it, so we end up cleaning it once in a while. But I don't know. People just end up dropping stuff there. There's no … we didn't even realize that. After a while, you think about it … you're like, yeah, yeah, it's actually privately owned cause it's part of the [private] apartment, but actually.'

As we might expect, given residents' territorial apathy, it was usually only residents who were directly inconvenienced who expressed much frustration at others' territorial claims. Residents described, for instance, how they had experienced multiple failed delivery attempts to their condo due to lack of available parking, how they had been forced to pay for on-street parking when another car kept parking in their designated bay and how their daily in-home care providers had nowhere to park because the visitor bays were always filled with the same few cars. Residents who were not directly impacted, meanwhile, typically expressed far less concern about these car park "sagas", as one resident called them, even if they breached by-laws. Notably, all residents' criticisms tended to use normative rather than legal frames of reference, with residents typically reflecting on what constituted reasonable or appropriate parking practices rather than showing much concern with what by-laws stipulated. Normative statements, such as: "it's 'not the right thing to do", were subsequently common. Residents' concern with propriety, in addition to and sometimes rather than legality, was also evidenced in how they justified their own parking practices.

Over time, as residents self-regulated their parking practices so as to not unduly inconvenience their co-residents, local working rules took hold, including in contradiction with by-laws. Unchecked "borrowing", for instance, became an acceptable practice as residents mimicked each other's unchecked claims. Residents' alluded to these tacit codes with mentions of their building's "culture" or the "way things are done around here" and other comments that implied a shared local understanding of how things are usually done. Local working rules were also shaped over time by residents' observations of the everyday policing of by-laws, as we observed on the roof decks too. When managers appeared to turn a blind eye to illegal parking, residents read managers' silence and inaction as passive endorsement of these practices and conversely, when building managers intervened, this delegitimized claims. This was frequently corroborated by remarks such as: "It says 15-minute parking, but you can park there all day and never get booked because it's not policed at all." Although this suggests working rules were somewhat fixed, many residents' accounts revealed that residents perceived working rules as somewhat unsettled. Residents' commentary often contained expressions of ambiguity and uncertainty, for example. When residents criticized each other's parking practices, for instance, they often qualified their disapproval with comments such as "but that's just me".

Confrontations over parking territorialities were relatively infrequent. For instance, Katie, whose mother "borrowed" an owner's vacant carparking bay revealed she had been confronted by the disgruntled owner: "They said: 'It's been reported to management! – I go away a lot for work – you've got to stop parking [here]!'" But if the owners did make such a report, Katie was never cautioned and her mother continued her "borrowing" as before. There were, however, confrontations that unsettled residents' sense of home and for renters, their security of tenure. Ethan, a middle-aged Perth renter, for instance, was approached by a co-resident after his adult daughter parked in an undesignated parking bay when she visited. Ethan recalled the incident:

> 'When I was first here, one of the owners was running around clicking away at me, and I didn't know what the rules were … because you had to agree with all [condo] rules, although you don't know what they are. … Well, I got that wrong because my daughter was just parked there and she got in trouble. And I had a guy from the apartments … he was watching me and taking photos, chasing me around about this car park. I thought, "What is your problem?" … And going off his head. … And then I had someone come up here, [and] say move your car. I thought, "What's going on here?"
>
> As it turned out, I got a breach notice from the tenancy agreement, because this guy breached me for parking this car there – which was my child's car. And it's more than one car there, so it's a breach!
>
> So I'm so scared … so I got in trouble for that. And then it was exacerbated when the owner, my neighbour in the complex, knocked on my front door and he told me to move the car. And I said, "Who are you?" He goes, "I'm [X], a homeowner, and I pay so and so much for my property." And I said, "My name's [Y], and I'm a tenant here so rag off!'

Ethan's incident highlights how practices of common property are implicated in the unmaking of the condo home. In the first instance, Ethan's incident illustrates again how property practices in shared home spaces are means through which renters are constructed as 'bad' condo neighbours in everyday condo living. Ethan, who like many renters was poorly informed about his building's by-laws, receives not only a warning notice from building management for his breach but also reported receiving a warning from his landlord. This incident jeopardizes Ethan's actual and perceived tenure security, as with each blemish on his tenancy record Ethan comes a step closer to losing his home. A poor tenancy record could have a more lasting impact too, potentially limiting Ethan's future renting options by sullying his tenancy record. In the second instance, Ethan's story captures how his co-resident, from his privileged position as an owner, draws on his relationship with his building manager which more readily enables him to act upon his racialized views of renters as second-rate condo residents. Ethan was not only extra cautious afterwards about where his children parked but was also acutely aware of his positioning within a tenure-based hierarchy in his condo. Along with the actual threats to his tenancy, this perceived exclusion also unmade his new condo home.

Other spaces in condo basements, such as communal bike storage facilities, similarly impacted residents' homemaking both by mediating residents' commuting practices and by cramping the private unit, as we shall see. Bike storage facilities varied between buildings but often included bike racks which were sometimes locked within a caged area or located in bike rooms with key fob access. Much like other shared amenities, some residents, like 22-year-old Perth renter Greer, questioned the very existence of these amenities: "Bike parking? Not one I know of … there may be, but I haven't really explored the building that much," she said, having moved in three months prior. But those who had used their bike facilities encountered issues that discouraged their use. Bike stores could be small with too few bays, as 30-year-old Melbourne renter June commented: "it's always packed" and "there's occasions where there's not enough bike racks for everyone". With inadequate space, residents found storing and accessing bikes troublesome and their bikes were sometimes damaged, as Melbourne renter Eddie explained about his large building: "The building, I don't know, probably has, guessing, maybe 60–70 parking spots for pushbikes, a particular room set aside. And that is completely overcrowded. Bikes get damaged by other users." Another owner, whose condo had a "first in, best dressed" bike storage policy described how the policy benefited owners who were the first to move in when the building opened: "I had the bike, and they said there were cages, but there's only, I think, 15 or 20 cages. So that was another one where I was lucky to get the one I got!" Other residents, especially renters, were not so fortunate arriving after these cages had been allocated. Besides space constraints and bike damage, many residents had or knew of co-residents who had had their bikes stolen. Alerts about these thefts circulated through the informal and formal digital communication channels discussed in Chapter 5. Multiple residents said they used their bikes less as a result and some stopped riding altogether.

When owners *did* attempt to regain some territorial control of these shared home spaces, such as by attempting to have some of these issues addressed, they described being met with perfunctory advice with limited follow-up from building managers or their OC committee paying lip-service to their problem. In several buildings, owners reported tabling and costing options for 24-hour security, spikes, CCTV and so forth. But action appeared sluggish and often only addressed some needs and interests, leaving other owners feeling powerless – although less so than renters who were fully excluded from formal governance matters. Ian, a 42-year-old renter, who wished to store his motorized scooter in the bike store, for instance, described having been overruled:

> 'Apparently, they did a survey and apparently, the majority of people use it for bikes. Unfortunately, it's one of those things where majority

> rules. To be honest with you, I don't think that's necessarily right because you … look, you can get a bike rack to store it on the wall or on the back of your door [in your private unit]. Yet, I don't have a bike; I have a more cumbersome vehicle, and I'm forced to store it in the condo. It doesn't really make sense, but sometimes you've got to pick your battles!'

When these attempted collective workarounds failed, residents faced with insecure or unsuitable communal bike storage fell back on individualized solutions. Some residents invested in more sturdy bike locks, and those more serious riders who owned several bikes limited their risk by leaving only their "cheaper" bikes in the basement. Many more bike riding residents who were aware of thefts, however, reasoned "why take the risk?" These riders instead stored their bikes on their private balconies, in the compact entryways of their units or in a second bedroom if they could. This satisfied their security concerns but proved impractical and contentious. Bikes trailed through lobbies, lifts and shared corridors attracted complaints from other residents who hated the congestion in the lifts and complained of undue wear and tear to carpets, scuffed walls and tracked-in dirt. Conversely, within these bike riders' private units, their bikes exacerbated space constraints, upset other homemaking practices and caused frictions within their households too. Nicole, a 48-year-old Melbourne renter, who lived with her partner in a two-bedroom unit on the 33rd floor and who was about to move into a new condo described how her partner stored his bike on their balcony: "That's not going to happen when we go to the new apartment! … I don't like it there!".

'They look so nice but…'

Residents' various territorial practices of annexing and withdrawal from shared home spaces demonstrate residents' ambivalent sense of ownership and attachment to these spaces. In this final section of the empirical analysis, this ambivalence towards shared home spaces is explored further by drawing into frame a less considered though important aspect of condo homemaking which is the way residents practise the condo home as a financial asset. As this section highlights, though homemaking in shared home spaces was oftentimes frustrating or at least not as rewarding or convenient as residents initially hoped, renters and owners alike nonetheless often still valued these amenities on financial terms. Given many residents' limited use of these amenities, this valorization had more to do with reputation, pride and distinction than with functionality or enjoyment. In inner Melbourne, 48-year-old renter Nicole described how her 30-plus-storey building was set apart from neighbouring condos, including by the aesthetics of its lobby: "the most elegant one … it's a really five-star hotel-feeling lobby". Nicole also delighted in her visitors' reactions of awe and "oh wows!" While clearly a source of pride and status for some, most Melbourne accounts revealed their large lobbies were barely used bar for circulation: "all very nice, but nobody ever sits in it", Nicole conceded of the multiple lounge spaces in her lobby. Other residents who lived in similarly high-end condo towers echoed similar sentiments, such as Robin, a 68-year-old Melbourne owner who commented: "The foyer's [a] lovely big area … nobody ever seems to use it. Nice for greeting guests though!"

Notwithstanding residents' limited use of these home spaces, most still saw these shared amenities as boosting the investment potential of their condo. Some owners anticipated they would rarely use them, maintaining that from the outset they had had limited interest in anything other than their private unit. Others had every intention of using these shared spaces, and even perhaps imagined using them a lot, but in fact did not. One Perth owner described how shared amenities were a condo investment "must-have"; a justifiable extra, even though they translated into higher OC fees and they did not intend to use them much or at all. Narelle, a 38-year-old owner who lived with her partner and dog in a two-bedroom unit in inner-city Perth reflected:

> 'I don't really use the gym all that much and maybe we use the pool in summer, but honestly not that much. My husband doesn't swim. We've never used the barbecue and I've never even been into the sauna area. … [But] I think in Perth for a property, it needs to have a pool from a resale value perspective. So even though I'm not using it, the pool and the gym were influences [in our purchasing decision].'

Kaveh, another Perth owner, who was also 38 and lived with his partner in middle-ring Perth, suggested their pool and gym were a drawcard – "just for lifestyle" – but also conceded that they considered buying in a "high-amenity" tower because they believed it would increase rental income in the future. Kaveh, who had recently purchased a home in suburban Perth to start his family as well as move back closer to his extended family, explained: "I thought: well, at some point I'll move out, and probably rent it out and so, they're features that are better to have."

A few residents suggested the condo presented a wise investment strategy, a "safer" investment than a house because, with management charged with the upkeep of shared amenities and neighbours (and specifically the upkeep of their properties) inconspicuous, "everything would look nice" come sale time. Scott, the 57-year-old Perth owner, who lived with his partner in a three-bedroom condo in middle-ring Perth made this point, emphasizing how the anonymity and obscurity of neighbours in condo developments could de-risk the condo investment relative to a house investment:

> 'Investment wise, I think you're better off with this than you are with a house. Cost-wise, I think you're better off with this than a house, because you don't have to keep. … You're paying [condo fees], but somebody else does the gardening. Somebody else cleans the pool. All that's handled in your levy. And it always looks nice. These days, a lot of people … you drive around the suburbs and see these houses. You could have a huge immaculate garden, and next door couldn't give a rat's [that is, care less]. So it's a big mess. That brings down the price of your house. Because people are gonna be, "Oh, I don't want to live next door to them." [In] apartment blocks, they look at the apartment, they don't even know who's next door! It all looks the same.'

While residents were frustrated by their diminished control over shared amenities, as noted earlier, they often also insisted on the attractions of having management charged with maintenance, often discounting the fact they paid condo fees for this service. Many appreciated, for instance, the peace of mind this provided: "It gave us that confidence" when they bought their condo, as one owner summed up, even as the OC offered less protection to the various territorial frictions and incursions in practice than most residents anticipated. A Perth owner commented:

> 'They're quite high [condo fees]. I remember talking to the real estate agent about that. I'm not sure exactly what the figure is, but it's maybe around 40 odd dollars a week, $45 a week, which I was told was high. I've only looked at one other place to compare it. … She did make a comment – but I don't know how they set those things, and how they justify it … I guess because they felt that it was a good complex, well maintained.'

Residents' emphasis on investment value may also represent a post-rationalization of their housing decision as they paid to upkeep amenities they seldom used or which were a source of frustration. By contrast, some owners were not convinced of the investment prospects of shared amenities. James, a 38-year-old separated father of one, who bought his one-bedroom unit less than a year prior, said amenities "weren't the be-all-and-end-all [in their decision to buy]", with the condo a "stepping stone" to buying a "proper" home for his daughter.

Renters meanwhile suggested that amenities were rarely a deciding factor in finding a rental, and indeed typically real estate agents used them to justify the high rents they were asking for. Some renters seemed to internalize that justification, however, describing how they felt their rental was better value for money relative to other condo units they had considered because it came with access to a host of amenities. If this private access provided tangible cost savings to renters, such as enabling them to forfeit a private gym membership, renters rarely mentioned those benefits. Rachael, the 33-year-old Perth renter who we saw earlier refraining from the pool, nuances her earlier comments about the pool being a drawcard, explaining:

> 'I really don't care about it [shared amenities]. I just consider it because of the price of the rent. I mean, when I'm looking for an apartment for me, it is: the number of rooms I need, the river view, the light, that's it. … But then because these apartments are quite pricey, I want to know, like, why is the rent so high? So in that sense, I do think: "Okay, they have a pool, they have this, they have that."'

For those same reasons, some renters also rationalized that shared amenities had or would assist in finding flatmates, especially when the rent "looked too high".

Other renters meanwhile had paid little or no attention to their condo's shared amenities when considering their new rental. This could lead renters to be pleasantly surprised, but also led to false hopes and disappointments in several cases. In Perth, 33-year-old Ali, a fly-in/fly-out worker on the mines who rented a two-bedroom unit alone, recalled seeing the gym after he moved in some five months earlier:

> 'The gym is probably worse than I realised. … It's older. It seems like some of the weights have gone missing over the years and not been replaced. There's not as much equipment as I thought there was, but I just took a quick glance before [signing lease], "Oh, cool. The gym looks good."'

Indeed, a surprising number of renters remained unfamiliar with their shared amenities, having never visited them, let alone used them. "I've never gone and figured out how to get there [to the rooftop], let alone how to use it," conceded 58-year-old self-employed Perth resident Sarah, who lived alone in a relatively smaller inner-city condo. Rory, a 70-year-old retiree who lived in a one-bedroom unit in a very large inner Melbourne condo with extensive amenities, revealed his own lack of familiarity: "I think there's also a small communal kitchen or dining room. … We've never used it … I think the facilities here are very rarely used." Remarkably, a few owners also conceded never having "explored" their building.

Meanwhile, a few owners and renters similarly suggested that in the future they would avoid condos on the grounds that the aesthetic appeal of amenities was mostly marketing gloss and did not translate to tangible benefits in their home lives. Sixty-nine-year-old Perth owner Eloise, who had first purchased her two-bedroom condo as an investment several years prior to downsizing, explained:

> 'I wouldn't go to another apartment. Although they're so … they look so nice but … they read up so nice … they do advertise all the amenities. … But yeah. I think that paying the strata fees … I mean, that's another thing that gets to you too because you sort of think, well, what are we paying for?'

Conversely, some residents, notably many of those who had previously lived in a condo, expressly sought out a high-rise with *limited* shared amenities to avoid the headaches and costs from higher purchase prices, condo fees or rents that they associated with these shared home spaces. One Melbourne resident described this: "No. I was not looking for a gym. I was not looking for a swimming pool. I wasn't looking for a general-purpose room. I was pretty much happy just being a condo in itself."

Such comments underscore the marked primacy of the private unit over the shared amenities in residents' perceptions of their condo home, and which bears out in most residents' condo property practices as preceding chapters have documented. Four years ago, Cassie's parents had bought her one-bedroom condo outright and now 30-year-old Cassie was repaying them. For Cassie, the attraction for her family of having "just" a rooftop terrace rather than an array of amenities was financial:

> 'The attraction for this [condo] was that it didn't have the extras, so the pool, the gym, etc. because they would have cost more and it was my first home, and I wanted something cost-effective for me. … So that was actually a proactive decision to choose to not have the pool, sauna, and so on.'

With the rooftop deck underwhelming despite its initial appeal, as detailed earlier, Cassie did not doubt her decision: "goes to show that maybe less shared facilities was the right choice for me!" Residents could struggle, however, to find new high-rise units without amenities, given the focus on amenity provision in condo development trends detailed in Chapter 1. Another Perth owner, 65-year-old Harriet, who lived alone with her cats in a two-bedroom unit in inner-city Perth, commented: "I would have preferred to be in a complex that doesn't have these facilities [pool, sauna, gym, barbecue, public bathrooms] because obviously, they're just a cost", but this was difficult because "nowadays, every complex of this size just has these things!", Harriet explained.

Annexing and withdrawing

Conceptual models of property in condominium anticipate shared amenities will be seamlessly 'shared' with the assistance of formal condo governance. Yet in everyday condo living this 'sharing' involves messy territorial dynamics and uneven and overlapping territorialities. This tour of the condo's courtyards, pools, rooftop terraces and car parks reveals 'sharing' comprises diverse property practices, some at odds with by-laws, and territorial withdrawals too, whereby residents forfeit the use of spaces they are legally entitled to, mostly voluntarily. Condo governance studies often highlight apathy among condo residents, for instance when describing residents' non-participation in formal governance, but this analysis suggests resident apathy also translates spatially to residents' diminished stewardship of, and even physical withdrawal from, shared spaces. In everyday condo living, it seems the 'sharing' of common property elements can invite a kind of territorial apathy towards shared home spaces that renders shared amenities susceptible to uneven use and at times infrequent use, with the latter a common characteristic of many of the shared amenities in the condos towers in question.

This chapter sheds further light on residents' everyday perceptions and practices of common property in condominium. It provides empirical evidence supporting Blandy and colleagues' (2018: 86) argument that everyday property relations can be 'inattentive' to formal legal frames. It illustrates that residents do not practise common property uniformly. Residents' diverse practices reflect, in part, the overlooked heterogeneity of common property itself, with its graduated entitlements, though residents rarely explicitly acknowledged such differences. In designated parking bays, nevertheless, residents expected and asserted more territorial control than in other shared spaces, for instance, and expressed a relatively stronger sense of ownership, including through possessive references to "my" car park bay, albeit without any strong sense of attachment.

However, diverse property practices were also identified in shared home spaces governed by similar legal entitlements to access and use. Residents practised common property to satisfy private interests and, on occasion, shared amenities were used as an extension of their private unit including to conduct intimate activities usually associated with private domestic domains. These practices of common property corroborate McKenzie's (2011) argument about the enduring 'calculus of private values' that riddles hybrid property forms such as condominium. However, many residents also self-regulated as they practised common property, including to satisfy other-regarding impulses and abide local working rules centred around respecting individual private property (that is, others' condo units).

Self-regulation also led residents to voluntarily withdraw from shared spaces though this was never a purely selfless act either, but rather also usually motivated by the residents' disappointment that shared spaces did not meet their traditional propertied expectations, such as for privacy. Conversely, on occasion, similar logics and other-regarding impulses motivated residents to *use* shared spaces. For instance, residents concerned about disturbing their adjacent neighbours as they entertained guests, relocated their socializing into shared spaces, including out of respect for their adjacent neighbours' peace and quiet.

Residents' territorializations of shared home spaces were rarely communicated through acts of stewardship. Rather, in shared spaces otherwise devoid of overt signs of their ownership, residents typically asserted their territoriality through physical occupation and, after vacating, through abandoned personal possessions, such as sunshades and pot plants and other propertied traces, such as their discarded personal furniture and rubbish. These artefacts provided visual cues through which co-residents could 'speak to each other, over time, about their relation to place' (Rose 1994: 268) but, without contextual information or social interaction, these objects usually conveyed ambiguous messages. Residents often (mis)interpreted co-residents' proprietary attitudes and practices as decidedly self-regarding. Just as Carmel saw her absentee co-owner's lockbox in the shared laundry as overly proprietorial, residents interpreted co-residents as 'taking liberties' with their 'inappropriate "private" behaviour' (Blomley 2005a: 288) in their shared home spaces. And indeed even plant pots were rarely seen as 'sharing with the community', as similar acts of stewardship vis-à-vis public property have been viewed on public property (Blomley 2005a: 291).

Residents' sense of ownership towards common property elements was complex: where residents are at once unhappy with others' territorial assertions, they were also nevertheless mostly relatively disinclined to assert much territoriality of their own. Residents' lack of stewardship stems both from residents' perceptions that caretaking was their manager's responsibility and because everyday condo living circumscribed opportunities for acts of collective stewardship, as the bike room vignette captured, for instance. However, while territorial withdrawals, in particular, appear to confirm residents' lack of attachment to these shared spaces, residents' sense of ownership was nevertheless ambivalent, including because residents perceived shared amenities as important to practising the condo home as a financial asset. Owners, for their part, valued these amenities as future financial rewards to be realized through capital gains or future rental revenue. Meanwhile, renters saddled with high rents associated shared amenities with "value for money", irrespective of their actual use-value. The way residents valued shared home spaces despite their often infrequent use suggests how an anticommons risk may take hold inside condominium's shared home spaces – a point elaborated in the Conclusion.

There was oftentimes slippage between the common property practices residents viewed as appropriate and those permissible under private restrictions. Each shared home space's material and spatial configurations, including its adjacencies to private units, informed locally contingent working rules that governed the use of each shared amenity. Meanwhile, as identified elsewhere in the condo building, design and construction inadequacies could also make these rules both difficult to adhere to and ambiguous. Building managers' action and inaction also informed residents' understanding of what was acceptable in each building. Managerial discretion therefore accounts for some of the slippage between by-laws and working rules governing these shared spaces. Additionally, snitching pushed management to police property practices they might otherwise have turned a blind eye to, property dynamics Hilbrandt (2019) similarly identified albeit in a different context. In such cases, those who 'snitched' could benefit from personal relationships with their building managers that enabled them to reassert some form of territorial control over shared home spaces. As illustrated with the case of 'illegal' parker Ian, renters risk being disproportionately sanctioned through inconsistent and discretionary management, in addition to being blamed for building nuisance, property damage and security issues (also see Reid et al 2017a; Lippert 2019).

Territorial annexations caused inconveniences, frustrations, tensions and exclusions that rendered shared spaces unhomely and uninviting. The analysis challenges the common assumptions that shared amenities operate as reliable incubators of social connection and conviviality. Social encounters between co-residents within shared spaces were not commonplace, by most accounts, notwithstanding sizeable populations living in each building. Moreover, as residents interpreted their co-residents' conduct as "crossing the line" in these spaces and as residents again blamed renters for these perceived transgressions, this further assisted in constructing the condo renter subject as an unruly and risky co-resident. This perception of a 'two-tier' community within the tower could, in turn, unmake the condo home as (part-whole) belonging for owners and renters alike. Territorial dynamics within shared amenities also undermined the condo home as dominion. Residents' sense of control was undermined as they struggled to reconcile their private interests with local working rules and other-regarding impulses, especially where design and construction issues and regulatory and operational issues made these near-incompatible. Many residents subsequently disengaged and many withdrew from these shared spaces. In this way, the territorial dynamics in shared home spaces undermined the condo home. All the while, the fallout from these socio-spatial dynamics was relatively less extensive than the fallout associated with border incursions into private units (see

Chapter 4) or the circulations frictions that constrained condo mobilities in or through shared infrastructures (see Chapter 5). This is explained, in part at least, because residents saw shared home spaces as subordinate to their private unit's functionality, security and comfort as the ownership model primes us to expect.

Conclusion: Securing Home in Verticalizing Cities

On 1 April 2020, the *New Statesman* published an article titled: 'Why we are living in JG Ballard's world'. Not an April Fool's joke alas, the author instead argued that 'much of our present reality now falls within the jurisdiction of Ballard's imagination' (O'Connell 2020: np.). High-rise housing, long vulnerable to dystopian depictions, had fallen prey to such characterizations yet again. As COVID-19 and lockdowns brought renewed scrutiny to the homes we live in, media commentary has sometimes portrayed these vertical towerscapes as cesspools of contagion and 'vertical cruise ships', the latter a nod to large outbreaks among cruise passengers as the virus first spread. In light of the significant health, social and financial consequences of the COVID-19 pandemic, government officials, lobby groups, condo industry representatives and condo residents have voiced a raft of concerns around the practical, ethical, legal and cost implications for high-rise condominium housing. These include concerns about ensuring safe and healthy living environments in the face of emerging medical knowledge and evolving public health guidelines. They include concerns about the management of local infections and concerns about (the need for) new private restrictions and revised social etiquette as residents spend more time at home. And they have included concerns about new financial risks whether from increased use and wear-and-tear of shared amenities and utilities, from compensation claims from owners frustrated by shuttered shared amenities or from risks associated with condo owners financially impacted by the pandemic and now unable to pay levies or who face foreclosure. These concerns are new in content, but they are variations on established themes and persistent anxieties that surround high-rise condo living.

What are the prospects then for securing the condo home in the verticalizing city? As the evidence in this book corroborates, there is no single universal set of practices through which the high-rise condo home is made or unmade. Instead diverse homemaking practices are identified within and across cities, across urban locations, and within different households and among residents of different genders, ages, life-stages, cultural backgrounds and tenures. Concurrent processes of homemaking and unmaking mean the condo home is riddled with contradictions too, such that exclusion coexists with belonging, attachment alongside frustrations and ambivalence, and freedoms alongside constraints and nuisance. Still, on the surface, all seems well enough with many condo residents appearing to make their condo home. Some residents revel in the novel experiences of living high, enjoying spectacular vistas, surreal experiences of "being in the clouds" and a newfound sense of seclusion from the city below. Many appreciate the relative safety of their private unit, the low-maintenance 'lock-and-leave' lifestyle it affords and its locational advantages, the latter beyond my focus here. Several viewed the condo as their "forever" home; as one retiree commented: "I've always wanted to live in an apartment ... We're here now, we love it. Nothing to me is negative. Nothing at all! Nothing...!" These are all commendable achievements for the high-rise condo. Other residents were disappointed, frustrated and inconvenienced with condo living falling short of their expectations, but this was often uneventful for their homemaking insofar as they adjusted and habituated. And many residents rationalized the ups-and-downs of homemaking as part and parcel of their circumstances, life-stage and the 'trade-offs' required of city living in the face of few housing alternatives.

Yet on closer inspection, several concerning risks materialize. Harnessing legal geography's potential to unpick 'often in granular detail, how unjust geographies are made' (Delaney 2016: 268), *Inside High-Rise Housing* exposes poorly recognized risks overshadowing the high-rise home. A perspective attuned to the relational dimensions of property draws attention to the way that condo property comes 'freighted' not just with entitlements but with obligations to others. Those obligations are captured as local working rules that ultimately circumscribe high-rise homemaking. Critically, as residents attempt to reconcile their private interests with local working rules condo homemaking can be compromised in various ways, including as breaches inevitably occur which help reproduce problematic condo renter subjectivities. Local working rules, with their emphasis on propriety, initially appear to suggest that condominium may engender a reorientation away from heavily individuated privatized property practices. Such a shift would be in keeping with property theorist Alexander's (2012: 1876, 1859) claim that the ownership of governance property such as condominium, more so than other forms of property, may help 'inculcate' virtues that promote human flourishing, including 'community, cooperation, trust and honesty'. Sidestepping Alexander's 'law first' approach, early condo researchers such as Wekerle and colleagues (1980: 171) did not so much as suggest condominium could or would instil such virtues, rather they argued that for condominium to become 'successful' it must precipitate changes in residents' ethics through 'major shifts in attitudes towards home ownership, shared responsibility, and increased involvement in community life'. Some 40 years on such change, however, is not apparent, not least of all because residents enter the condo with traditional propertied expectations that condition how they perceive and practise property in the condo's propertied landscapes. In this way, the roll-out of condominium appears not to singularly 'weaken an individualistic and detached sense of private property', as Harris (2011: 722) speculated the conversion of large tracts of urban land might, albeit nor does it appear to 'enhance [their] detachment by limiting the community to a defined group of owners'. Rather the private unit sits central to the high-rise home while common property elements remain secondary and indeed often marginal, viewed by residents with ambivalence even. Indeed, some shared home spaces may be seldom used, introducing potential anticommons risk.

This book concludes with some reflections on the prospects of condominium in urban futures. I start by synthesizing several risks to the high-rise condo home and then establish these risks as characteristic of contemporary condoization. The second half of this chapter then looks up from the intricacies of everyday condo living to consider the high-rise condo's future. Through a set of provocations, I consider how we might intervene to remedy problematic aspects of the territorialized workings of law behind these risks. The discussion homes in on the high-rise condo's design and built form and then on its social/tenure dynamics as two central areas of concern foregrounded by my analysis. These are provocations intended to promote discussion and action to secure brighter condo city futures.

Condo homes at risk

The making of the high-rise condo home is not seamless in everyday condo living. Two threats are identified: a threat to the condo *home as dominion* arises as local working rules governing everyday condo living significantly restrict and complicate condo residents' homemaking, and a threat to the condo *home as belonging* arises as residents' property practices are (mis)interpreted in ways that contribute to the subjectification of the condo renter as an unruly and risky condo co-resident. To these, we can add a third potential risk which is the anticommons risks surrounding the sharing of amenities raised in Chapter 6. Notably, as much as Perth and Melbourne residents struggle to make the condo home, their accounts tend to foreground physical deficiencies such as a lack of space, flexibility, self-expression or privacy (Kelly et al 2011) rather than taking issue with condo property per se. This suggests just how successful supply-side agents have been in scripting condo property. Conversely, despite these risks, many residents, including renters, nonetheless succeed in making the condo home for threats of home unmaking overlap, as prior analyses have shown, with homemaking practices that stabilize the condo as home, for a period at least. These risks and their contours are briefly reviewed in turn.

Threats to home as dominion

Residents perceived their homemaking as restricted. But homemaking is not singularly or even principally restricted by an obligation to comply with private restrictions alone or by the threat of being formally sanctioned by management, as much condo research suggests. Rather residents also, and often predominantly, perceive restriction on their homemaking in terms of the weight of social expectation, a desire to "do the right thing" and as a fear of being judged as a bad condo neighbour if they fail to comply. This analysis foregrounds the importance of local working rules, which are based on normative rather than big 'L' legal frames of reference and which are locally contingent. These informal social expectations can ask a great deal from co-residents as they make their home in close quarters and share spaces and essential infrastructure, especially when high-rise design and build quality is wanting. These working rules are wide-ranging including because they govern residents' homemaking deep within their private unit as described in Chapter 3, because they govern their homemaking in relation to shared infrastructure and shared home spaces as described in Chapter 5 and Chapter 6, and because they govern these homemaking practices across the full sensory register. These locally contingent rules of engagement may also be relatively unsettled, in part because of the added complexities and ambiguities surrounding volumetric neighbouring in the context of poor design and build quality and in part because of the relative immaturity of Australian high-rise living.

Homemaking circumscribed by local working rules requires residents to repeatedly reconcile their own private interests with often conflicting and sometimes incompatible social expectations. This is not to say that residents' mediation of private interests and local working rules was always especially consequential for their homemaking; it might only require that residents play their music more quietly or tuck their washing out of sight. Equally, private interests and social expectations need not be mutually exclusive either and indeed these rules could also be helpful in safeguarding the condo home. However, since residents mostly enter the condo with traditional propertied expectations of the home-as-castle and expect their units to be a 'place of maximum exercise of individual autonomy, [and] minimum conformity to the form and complex rules of public demeanor' (Rainwater 1966: 24), residents can end up torn between realizing their traditional propertied expectations and observing tacit social codes. Frequently, residents' mediation was less successful and whether the fallout was temporary or fateful these mediations could unmake the condo home, especially renters' condo home.

Local working rules are partly informed by private restrictions: they variously reinforce by-laws, counter by-laws or exceed by-laws by imposing more stringent expectations. These informal rules therefore emerge 'in the shadow of the law' (Blandy et al 2018: 102) in several ways in everyday condo living. Local working rules emerge as *(mis)interpretations of private regulation* as residents took cues from the local policing of private regulations, or its absence, to establish what was locally permissible. Residents, who often only had a hazy sense of their local by-laws, subsequently established working rules based on management (in)action and perceived leniency towards breaches. At times these working rules simply replicated and reinforced by-laws, in which cases these self-generated norms were not always 'contrary to the de jure right and duties' (Blandy 2013: 165), as residents (sometimes) assumed them to be, whereas other times working rules contradicted by-laws, sometimes unwittingly. For instance, as residents observed managers issuing warnings and barring access to certain home spaces and as they noticed managers turning a blind eye to unruly rooftop antics or misuse of the visitor parking bays, their management practices variously delegitimized and legitimized associated property practices. Accordingly, where residents repeatedly observed a by-law being weakly enforced in their building, such as a ban on walking dogs through lobbies, on casual borrowing of private parking bays or on affixing signs in the lift cabin, these practices came to be socially accepted despite being formally prohibited.

Local working rules also emerged *as substitutions for private regulation* as residents judged by-laws as too inconvenient, arbitrary or non-sensical and replaced these with less stringent expectations. As this suggests, residents assessed private restrictions on normative grounds and rejected some rules. In some buildings, therefore, air-drying laundry on balconies was tolerated despite breaching by-laws, for example. But while such practices might be considered socially acceptable, residents still sometimes engaged in faux compliance with washing bans by discretely positioning their washing, for instance, not just under the pretence of obeying by-laws but also sometimes to avoid bothering others with their "unsightly" washing. As Hilbrandt (2019) also emphasized, faking compliance in this way opens up room to manoeuvre. In the condo home, faux compliance provides scope to concurrently make the condo home in accordance with private interests *and* to perform the 'good' condo neighbour. As this suggests, local working rules did not always set stifling community standards nor diminish residents' autonomy, with the preservation of private 'caprice' and the protection of public values dually motivating some rules, such as local allowances made for the talented piano player practising into the evening with their windows open.

In contrast, where residents perceived formal rules as too lenient to protect their private interests and the sanctity of their private units other local working rules emerged as *an additive to private regulation*. Residents' adherence to these more stringent social expectations is evidenced repeatedly in the way residents self-regulated their property practices. In their private units, for instance, residents are seen to remove their shoes and turn their music down to reduce noise and withdraw from their balconies to observe informal weeknight curfews. Likewise residents are found to retreat from shared home spaces to protect the privacy of residents in adjoining units, as illustrated in shared courtyards. Contra Hilbrandt (2019), this latter self-regulation is far more about compliance with social expectations and respect for their neighbours than it is about compliance with any formal regulation. In some instances, local working rules could curtail not only opportunities for residents to pursue private interests but also opportunities for residents to engage in other-regarding practices.

Working rules are also informed by the tower typology and the specific spatialities and materialities of each condo building. Subpar designs and poor workmanship made territorial incursions across the condo's borders more likely, more intrusive and more detrimental to residents' homemaking. The design and build quality of each condo building therefore also conditioned how and where residents drew the line between reasonable and excessive property practices. Where housing quality was lacking, more demanding local working rules were required to govern the private unit so as to provide the conditions under which residents' traditional propertied expectations, such as for privacy and peace and quiet, could be met. After all, as Chapter 4 set out, the test for 'reasonableness' does not occur in a vacuum, but in specific spatial, material and social contexts. Paper-thin walls ask more of neighbours than well-insulated walls and whether residents judge their neighbours' music as "too loud" or their footfalls "too heavy" will depend on how sound is amplified or buffered by the condo's walls and floors, for instance. Equally, whether residents judge their neighbours' smoking as excessive or not will partly depend on how well the tower's mechanical ventilation system functions and how airtight its various fixtures and fittings are. At the same time, spatial and material inadequacies also unsettle working rules, making misunderstandings more common especially where social interaction between co-residents is limited.

In everyday condo living, these local working rules govern residents' volumetric neighbouring. These socio-spatial dynamics differ from 'suburban' neighbouring in at least three ways. Contrasts with 'suburban' neighbouring – neighbouring in low-rise, low-density housing typologies rather than in suburban locations per se – risk oversimplification, including downplaying how much all urban neighbouring has in common, especially given that a systematic comparison lies well beyond my scope. These reservations notwithstanding, such contrasts *are* productive since they help specify some of the distinct contours of volumetric neighbouring. In particular, such contrasts help specify why local working rules can be demanding in everyday condo living, especially in the context of poor design and build quality. First, volumetric neighbouring involves diverse, dispersed and digitized geographies of social contact and encounter between co-residents, whose interdependencies are formalized relative to traditional neighbours, and whose interactions are heavily mediated by third-party security and communication technologies. Second, these geographies make resident mediation of their private interests and neighbouring expectations more extensive *and* intensive, in ways I set out later. Third, the rules of engagement are established, as described earlier, by the interaction of local working rules with the localized policing of private restrictions and are additionally contingent upon local materialities and spatialities, alongside residential proximities and adjacencies typical of the tower typology. In the early days of condominium, it was claimed this novel form of housing might give rise to a 'new housing social dependence' (HUD 1975: v-3 cited in Wekerle et al 1980: 171). These noted points of difference provide clarity on what 'social dependence' looks like in everyday condo living and each is worth reviewing in turn.

Private units are typically flanked by other units: above, below and to each side. These private boundaries are fully three-dimensional sites of physical contact but often not sites of social encounter since from within the confines of their unit co-residents generally cannot see each other, let alone converse face-to-face. Residents are physically barred from forging social connections; they are stopped, for instance, from reaching their neighbours overhead and underfoot by securitized lifts and exit-only fire-stairs. In this arrangement, neighbouring is not choreographed around garden buffers, gates and porches but instead through walls, ceilings and floors. 'Suburban' residential borders, by contrast, can be more amenable to operating as 'zones of interaction', with this interaction allowing for 'practical decisions' about border management, wherein the answers to questions such as 'Do I pick the overhanging fruit?' or 'Who repairs the rotting fence?' is understood as highly contextual and intersubjective (Blomley 2016b: 235). While property is inherently social, however, the private unit provides few equivalent possibilities for social encounters 'over the fence'. Volumetric neighbouring is instead conducted 'in the dark' without the social cues or rapport built from a smile, hand-wave or impromptu chat at the front gate. Incursions over the private unit's borders, whether loud music, a water leak or smoke drift, are experienced in the absence of social context and often without visual clues as to the incursion's source. Yet context is everything: when a resident learns their neighbour is hearing-impaired, the blasting TV is interpreted differently even as the level of disturbance remains unchanged. If neighbouring is a calculative ritualized game of interaction in which participants 'feel each other out', as sociologist Erving Goffman (2013 [1961]) once described, condo neighbours are hampered despite their physical propinquity (also Manning 2013 [1992]; Valentine and Harris 2016). These complexities of border-management are all the more significant given manifold incursions detailed in Chapter 4. How well a border functions as a 'zone of interaction' (Blomley 2016b: 241) or as a 'site of contact and connection' (Blomley 2014: 232) matters for making the condo home, including because boundary breaches inform the construction of the 'bad' neighbour subject, as I detail later.

Beyond the private unit, the geographies of volumetric neighbouring in everyday condo living are also relatively more diverse and dispersed than other forms of residential neighbouring. Residents must co-manage not only the private borders of their units but also the sharing of other home spaces and essential infrastructures. A property perspective understands this 'sharing' as a territorial matter involving socio-spatial negotiations over the access, use and movement of people, things and matter through these shared spaces and other shared infrastructures. The territorialities of shared home spaces and infrastructures in everyday condo living often appear unremarkable and quotidian but unchecked territorialities repeatedly remind residents of their reduced control. Residents therefore perceive their diminished control in the pizza boxes dumped by the rubbish chute, a theft from the bike store or through messages about a tailgating incident. Residents also perceive their compromised territorial control when they must climb the stairs as lifts malfunction or when they struggle to transfer to a preferred utility provider or resolve their slow internet speeds. Residents likewise are made acutely aware of co-residents' unchecked territoriality when they encounter their roof deck left in disarray, receive a patronizing note about the visitor parking, find the now out-of-bounds resident lounge locked by management or notice personal pot plants placed in the shared courtyard.

Residents perceive and encounter territorial incursions, annexations and circulation frictions. These territorial constraints restrict their access and use and (control over) the mobility of people, things (such as parcels and rubbish) and matter (such as electricity and water) around the building. These territorial constraints have weak parallels in traditional neighbouring which involves the comparatively simpler task of staying 'between the lines' (Perin 1988; Blomley 2016b). Meanwhile, as residents navigate these territorial constraints the geographies of volumetric neighbouring delimit their control further, as evidenced by security technologies that constrain where a resident can go within their building. Certainly security gates and video-cameras also mediate more traditional neighbouring but in the condo these security technologies are operated by a third party who differentially regulates residents' access and mobility through the building, as Chapter 5 in particular showcases. In so doing, these technologies also limit the possibilities of in-person social encounter, such as between 'next floor' neighbours.

Face-to-face interactions between neighbours were surprisingly infrequent, and while largely civil these were generally cursory with residents keen to maintain social distance and privacy in the face of residential propinquity. Residents communicated through non-verbal and digital mediums including signs affixed in lifts, notes slipped under doors, and through emails, Facebook chats and WhatsApp messages. This contrasts with 'suburban' neighbouring where offline in-person, face-to-face interaction has been its dominant mode, at least traditionally. Digital communication was predominantly established and led by owners, and/or owner-centric. These technologies were used to connect both small and large groups of co-residents, many of whom had never met in-person. For many residents, this digital interaction was passive: they received emails, checked Facebook updates and followed chat and forum threads from afar, but never contributed. For some residents this was their sole social 'connection' to co-residents since, despite sometimes passing residents in the lobby or sharing a ride in the lifts, many conceded that they did not so much as acknowledge others with a nod or 'good morning'. Digital interaction generally, and the informal ad hoc way owners established these online groups, risked forging something of a 'digital divide' in which renters were excluded by dint of their relative residential transience. For instance, renters were often excluded from email, Facebook groups and WhatsApp messaging groups that had been set up in the first weeks of a condo building opening. Physically proximate, socially distanced condo neighbours often lacked both the means and opportunities for performing the 'good' neighbour, including social encounters through which to develop mutual respect (Valentine 2008). Given the politics of formal condo governance highlighted in prior governance-focused condo research, this lack of informal and ad hoc social interaction is problematic. When it occurs alongside tenure-based power asymmetries between renters and owners and prevailing renter pathologies, as I elaborate later, it is especially so.

As residents make their home in the condo, they mediate local working rules and private interests in the context of these distinct neighbouring geographies and the distinct propertied relationalities that come with the sharing of their condo home spaces. This mediation process can be taxing, encompassing moderating their practices in line with local working rules that circumscribe practices across the full sensory register and encompassing private and shared home spaces and physical and online modalities. To be sure, all forms of urban homemaking require mediating private interests with social expectations. In lower-density housing arrangements, however, the collision of private interests and social expectations registers foremost on a visual register: inasmuch as neighbours care about other people's private gardens, they are concerned foremost with how others' gardens look (Blomley 2004b). This concern with aesthetic standards can present issues for suburban neighbouring: a resident might be concerned that a neighbour's 'ratty' garden might lessen their property value, for instance. In fact, several condo residents suggested the absence of such risks – since from the faceless condo facade at least, the conduct of any 'deviant' condo neighbours would be indiscernible – was a distinct benefit of the high-rise condo home. But in lower-density housing, private and other-regarding interests traditionally overlap in the 'buffer zone' of the garden (Blomley 2004b; 2005b) leaving the private house itself relatively unburdened by social expectations. This is not the case in the condo. Certainly, social expectations regarding aesthetics are perhaps relatively less significant in the condo, absent any garden albeit the visual appearance of balconies matters as Chapter 4 shows. But instead, the condo unit's walls and floors and ceiling act as 'shock absorbers' buffering (or not) what can be seen, heard, smelt and felt across each neighbour's private borders. Furthermore, border incursions which can feature in all forms of neighbouring, intrude *directly* upon the treasured intimate private sphere in the condo in the absence of any garden buffer zone and are therefore more likely to disturb residents in their most private domains. Additionally, and unlike the suburban neighbour whose garden is displayed to a largely *public* audience, much of this 'public' audience for condo homemaking has a special relationship with the resident in question: as a co-resident and sometimes co-owner. It is an audience, therefore, who is distinctly invested.[1] For instance, to use water wastefully in a private condo unit is not simply a thoughtless but ultimately selfish private act and expense, rather it also amounts to a collective cost to be paid by all owners when the bill for the building's water consumption is settled.

At almost every turn, poor design and subpar build quality complicate homemaking in everyday condo living by making compliance with local working rules difficult to reconcile with one's private interests. Spatial and material deficiencies associated with the condo building risk turning everyday homemaking practices into nuisance, making residents both more vulnerable to experiencing nuisance in the form of incursions and circulation frictions and more likely to be implicated in creating this nuisance too. The borders of the private condo unit are highly pervious – sometimes acutely so. These borders are subsequently vulnerable to all manner of physical, auditory and olfactory incursions and visual breaches in the form of overlooking. So while condo neighbours may remain faceless, the aromas of their barbecue, snippets of their conversation and their washing drying on the balcony are all smelt, heard and seen. Accordingly, even deep within the private unit, social expectations can end up regulating how loudly a resident plays their

1 However, just as Blomley (2005b: 655) finds no singular homogenous 'public audience' for proprietarian gardening in suburban neighbourhoods, there is no single audience for 'other-regarding' home-making practices in the condo either. Rather 'multiple, interscalar publics were in evidence' (Blomley 2005b: 655) as captured when residents referred to their neighbours in terms of the 'private' public of immediate neighbours (above, below, next-door, on the same corridor), the larger cohort of sometimes-faceless co-residents and in terms of other neighbourhood residents (references to 'that' building, and people living 'across the street' for instance), and finally in terms of the neighbourhood in more abstract terms ('around here we do this/that').

music or when they draw their blinds, or even whether parents let their children run around or not.

In these residential settings, (perceived) nuisance should be understood as a design issue rather than a social issue. It is an issue with the potential to severely compromise residents' capacity to feel in control and to feel 'at home'. If 'good fences make good neighbours' then absent well-insulated walls and floors, 'good' high-rise neighbouring becomes an arduous task of compromise that may push residents to the edge of their tolerance. Adherence to social expectations and respect for physical boundaries may be hard to square with private interests or it might well be impossible. Adjacent co-residents, for instance, cannot socialize concurrently on their poorly screened adjoining balconies while also respecting each other's privacy. Where residents moderate their habituated homemaking to conform with local working rules, the relegation of their own wants and needs could also prove inimical to making the condo home. As local working rules circumscribe residents' homemaking, everyday condo living risks exposing residents to major nuisances, stress and even untenable living conditions. In the face of some building defects especially, these cumulative pressures amassed such that some residents wished to abandon their condo.

Homemaking in the context of significant territorial constraints undermines residents' sense of control over their domestic domain. Residents perceive territorial constraints first-hand, observe these constraints in the unchecked mobilities of other people or things, or learn of these constraints through digital mediums. Residents cannot readily, singlehandedly or cheaply rectify the constraints they face given co-residents' socio-spatial and financial interdependencies. Residents' relative powerlessness to navigate these territorialities is captured for instance in the issues they face when trying to navigate joint water metering or when trying to have an electrical fault dealt with after-hours. Renters felt even more powerless because of additional conditionalities and insecurities associated with their tenancies. And their impressions were not misplaced, as demonstrated by the case of renter Ian who received not just a reprimand for his 'illegal' parking, but also a strike against his tenancy record. Tenancy-related anxieties could also make condo renters more reluctant to snitch on owners and more hesitant to request assistance from the owners corporation (OC). Additionally, when renters did make such requests, they could not draw upon relationships with the OC nor with building managers as owners frequently did. To be sure, some renters appeared relatively unfazed by their diminished territorial control, including because they saw the condo as a temporary home and felt relatively uninvested in their home space and its community. But these renters were outliers and more commonly renters' lack of control could undermine their sense of ownership even as other qualities of everyday condo living, such as 'living high', encouraged a strong sense of attachment as Chapter 3 illustrated. Renters were not alone in this regard; as the later chapters convey, all residents could feel a sense of detachment and territorial apathy towards common property elements. Indeed, residents' sense of ownership was frequently ambivalent, since most residents still valued amenities mostly on financial grounds as they practised the condo home as a financial asset.

With breaches of working rules likely and their fallouts more acute, condo homemaking in the context of poor design and build quality risked heightening frictions and tensions between co-residents. Everyday condo living placed reciprocal demands on all residents to demonstrate more tolerance – more 'give and take' – including towards potentially nuisance noise, to compromised air-quality, to reduced privacy and so forth. And as this 'give and take' reached its limits, as it frequently could, residents property practices cast them as bad condo neighbours. Sometimes residents snitched on each other when faced with uninvited territorialities, but residents also frequently responded by withdrawing from parts of their home spaces. Residents, for instance, drew their curtains and forfeited their view and daylight and they withdrew from the shared courtyard and forfeited their only private open space.

Threats to home as belonging

Everyday condo living contributes to the subjectification of the condo renter and this has repercussions for the condo *home as belonging*. Territorialized expressions of law encourage the elision of the 'illegitimate' condo renter with the 'bad' neighbour, giving rise to the unruly and risky condo renter subject. A property perspective, which understands this subjectification as taking place through the performance of property, reveals how owners *and* renters were quick to blame any inappropriate, rowdy or untoward conduct on renters, often with little or conflicting evidence. This subjectification of the condo renter is relatively commonplace in everyday condo living because co-residents' property practices more frequently 'cross the line' in the context of poor design and build quality, as the previous section summarizes. This localized subjectification of the condo renter builds upon prevailing normative housing ideals and an historical record in which dominant property narratives have long denigrated renting as second-rate and transitional and renters as inferior to the responsible and impeccable homeowner (Ronald 2008). Formal law has always been critical to institutionalizing socio-political homeownership ideologies, such as through landlord favouring tenancy contracts. Condominium legislation further reinforces these embedded tenure-based hierarchies in urban housing systems by institutionalizing the privileging of absentee owners' interests over the condo renters' need for home. It does this in well-established ways, such as by disenfranchising the condo renter from formal governance of their domestic domain. In everyday condo living, the condo owners' relative position of privilege can garner a management response that further marginalizes condo renters. This was illustrated for instance in Chapter 6 by the case of renter Ian's errant car parking. The analysis corroborates the vital work of everyday condo living in reproducing renters' and owners' hierarchical position in property space and, by virtue of the depoliticized nature of territoriality in the condo's propertied landscapes, of reifying these unequal relations through everyday condo living. Moreover, it corroborates how, as subjects make their homes in propertied landscapes, those who conform with ideals and practices that reflect hegemonic understandings about what constitutes a 'proper' home find the property space 'holds up' their smooth 'orientation' in ways that supports their homemaking. Meanwhile, those who do not or cannot conform come face to face with various territorialized expressions of law, such that these subjects find themselves disorientated and their capacity for homemaking destabilized (see Nethercote forthcoming).

This account additionally corroborates prior condo research that suggests co-resident relationships are depersonalized (for example Power 2015). It captures how co-residents are typically strangers whose social encounters are infrequent and face-to-face social interactions even more so, despite being physically proximate. Co-resident relations are characterized by social distance, anonymity and sometimes hostility too. Co-resident relations also veer between tolerance and transactionality as Chapter 4's account of incursions and 'give and take' captures. The modalities of co-resident interaction warrant specification too. As this account identifies, while co-resident relations are devoid of much face-to-face interaction, volumetric neighbouring does entail a range of written communication both digital and analogue: residents sent each other emails, left each other notes and posted 'rants' on condo Facebook pages. Residents also engage in other verbal communication such as shouting through walls and sometimes non-verbal communication too, such as banging on doors, walls or floors. While 'meaningful' social 'encounters with difference' have every potential to encourage social transformation (Valentine 2008), the dynamics of volumetric neighbouring indicate that the propertied landscapes of the contemporary condo tower operate poorly as a site in which values might be contested and reworked. Moreover, in the context of prevailing renter pathologies, social tensions arising from the territorial constraints residents encounter in everyday condo living risk hardening and embedding these pathologies. The prospects for 'encounters with difference' to encourage any such social transformation are limited by structural conditions too, namely the way condominium's legal form assists in institutionalizing tenure-based inequalities between owners and renters. Accordingly, everyday condo living stands to enrol co-residents in a form of neighbouring that is, at best, characterized by civility and tolerance, rather than genuine mutual respect (on the distinction between these, see Valentine 2008).

Socio-spatial relations between condo residents have also previously been described as increasingly contractualized and less 'socially-inflected' (Power 2015), but this account suggests this characterization is likely incomplete. This analysis newly foregrounds the role of local working rules in circumscribing socio-territorial relations in everyday condo living. This finding suggests that if relations between co-residents are to be emphasized as increasingly contractualized, this contractualizaton should be understood as heavily based on social, not just legal, terms of engagement. And indeed the legal contract is not uncomplicated either for while condo owners' relationship is formalized through legal agreements as conceptual property models detail, there is no direct contractual relationship between a condo renter and the condo owners they live with, rather only a tenancy contract with their absentee condo landlord. Additionally, in making the condo home and in navigating socio-territorial constraints they encounter, residents do not singularly or strictly rely upon legal frames of reference. Certainly residents snitch on others and escalate some matters to building managers or the OC, including to preserve anonymity and minimize personal conflict with their co-residents. Yet residents also navigate a great number of territorial incursions, frictions and annexations that implicate their neighbours *without* resort to any formal governance mechanisms or any third party, at least initially. Moreover, the local working rules that circumscribe everyday condo living are informal and voluntary; residents conform not by force but rather of their own volition, including to preserve co-resident relationships and out of respect for others' private property. Resident actions and relations with their co-residents therefore remain 'socially inflected' at least to a degree, albeit residents' capacities to practise condo property in other-regarding ways is circumscribed, as established earlier. Meanwhile, emphasis on the contractualized nature of co-resident relations requires greater acknowledgement of co-residents' uneven positioning in the condo's propertied landscapes, especially the way the condo renter is unavoidably located in a position of relative vulnerability vis-à-vis condo owners.

The noted subjectification of condo renters through everyday condo living has significant implications for residents' homemaking, and especially the condo home as belonging. This subjectification of the condo renter risks fostering something of a 'two-tier' society within the condo tower in which renters are relegated to 'second-rate' citizen status and short-stay renters reviled. This risk does not lie in the future but rather is already perceived by residents, several of whom described their condo 'community' in these exact terms. This analysis subsequently corroborates earlier Australian condo research that identifies how residents' perceive a 'social divide' between owners and renters, 'a generalised prejudice towards renters' (for example Reid 2015: 443–4) and a 'palpable distinction' between owners and renters (Baker 2013: 274–5), as well as North American research which has emphasized the worrisome plight of the condo renter (for example Lippert 2019). Renters are directly impacted by associated stigmatization and exclusionary dynamics. A property-sensitive account of home, moreover, understands that condo residents' ability to feel 'at home' 'cannot exist outside the realm of power and its discourses and practices of socio-spatial inclusion/exclusion' (Antonsich 2010: 649) – after all, the formal/political belonging granted to condo renters by dint of a tenancy contract are insufficient to generate this sense of being 'at home' in the condo tower. As this account captures, these socio-territorial dynamics can compromise renters' ability to feel 'at home' (subject-object belonging) as well as their sense of being part of a condo community (part-whole belonging). The subjectification of condo renters as unruly and risky condo residents also undermines home for condo owners too. Recall Antonsich's (2010: 650) caution about the need for reflection 'on the extent to which our personal, intimate feeling [of being] "at home" in a place may derive from the comforting realisation of others' absence'. Regrettably, this tendency reveals itself in the condo where owners and renters express concerns about living in buildings with high shares of renters, with many residents openly admitting to actively seeking or preferencing an "owner-occupier" tower or a tower that was not "rental-driven".

An anticommons risk

Property scholars such as Michael Heller seem mostly to consider condominium an example of 'good' fragmentation of property ownership. Condominium provided an apposite legal architecture for avoiding under *and* overuse of land, they tend to conclude. It is not that legal scholars do not harbour concerns about these legal architectures; Heller (1999: 1184–5), for instance, identified how legal arrangements 'too weak to police governance failures' risked giving condo owners 'too much power to lock resources into low-value resources … [such that] each owner may have effective veto over certain socially valuable changes'. But, by and large, property theory posits condominium as well-designed to mitigate such risks. Mandated formal governance structures, such as the OC, provide mechanisms to 'promote *good* fragmentation while limiting its social costs' (Heller 1999: 1184; 2008: 160; 2005: 331; also Sherry 2016: Chapter 2).

Yet as Chapter 6 captures, many condo residents do not use their shared home spaces much, if at all – a phenomenon which is alluded to in earlier condo research (Hong Kong: La Grange 2014: 262). By many residents' accounts, their pools, gyms, resident lounges and roof decks were only used by a select handful of residents, some were barely used at all and some lay idle. Indeed some residents had never set foot inside their shared amenities and a few were unfamiliar with the amenities in their building, having never sighted these on their routine commute in and out of their tower via the lobby or basement car park. This contrasts with common renderings of private high-rise towers in urban verticalities research which anticipates condo residents cocooning in eyrie-like private vertical refuges, with access to a dizzying array of private amenities and services that enable them to retreat from the city below. Residents' limited uptake of shared amenities in everyday condo living also has some of the hallmarks of a tragedy of the anticommons.

The tragedy of the commons is familiar: if we all have access to a valuable asset, this opportunity frequently devolves into the asset's overuse, ruin or depletion. A canonical example is the mythical vacant city block which allows for free parking but which quickly ends in congestion and fights as self-interested drivers exploit this chance for free parking. This then deters drivers who eventually seek out parking elsewhere. The fallout of the commons' tragedy may be quite obvious: we *see* the overrun parking lot. While the tragedy of the commons is overuse, the tragedy of the anticommons is underuse. This underuse thesis anticipates how 'too much' ownership can result in the suboptimal use or under-consumption of valuable resources. It is an issue associated with ownership multiplicity, rather than a monopoly per se (Heller 2008), and this underuse is often harder to spot than overuse, with its visible signs.[2] Legal scholar Michael Heller's (1998; 2008) anticommons thesis states that the fragmentation of private ownership of a valuable resource between too many owners can have unintended consequences, chief among which is a 'gridlock' that inhibits efficiencies of use and innovation.[3]

2 Underuse is difficult to pin down; if use levels occur along a continuum, as property theorist Heller (2008: 35) argues, we are on a Goldilocks-style quest for optimum use – somewhere between not too little (underuse) and not too much (overuse).

3 This gridlock is ubiquitous across our economy from biotech patents to telecom, although much of it remains hidden since underuse is often invisible (Heller 2008: 4–5). When scientists identify a potential medical treatment, such as a vaccine, its commercialization requires access to numerous patents. One single patent owner demanding a huge sum of money can destroy the drug's manufacturing viability and the fallout is that the drug never enters the market (see Heller 2008: 4–5, Chapter 3). Similarly, 90 per cent of the airwaves in the US remain idle because thousands of owners with non-transferable licences hold the broadcast rights for tiny geographic areas as the remaining bandwidth faces high demand. In this case, reassembling the broadcast rights for new high-speed networks proves near impossible (Heller 2008: Chapter 4). Other instances of gridlock share these problems associated with fractionated private ownership, making it near impossible 'to reassemble the ownership egg'. The result is a 'Humpty Dumpty' gridlock characterized by underuse and inefficiencies (Heller 2008: 147). This gridlock has its roots in two different anticommons dilemmas. A spatial anticommons occurs when real estate is carved up to such an extent ('overly subdivided') that each owner is left with an unusable discrete lot. Property regimes generally avoid the tragedies of the spatial anticommons by dint of 'boundary rules' that limit over-fragmentation into 'wasteful' allotments. A legal anticommons, by contrast, occurs when 'substandard bundles of legal rights are allocated to competing owners in a normal amount of space', but, with too many owners with dispersed rights, its efficient use becomes more difficult (Heller 2008: 160, 163).

Urban scholars *have* previously identified condominium as a potential anticommons risk. But prior applications of Heller's thesis have typically centred around the condominium dissolution debate and focused on collective action dilemmas that arise when there is interest in redeveloping a condo complex. For instance, dissenting condo owners might exert their rights over their co-owners and so prevent ageing condo stock from being 'regenerated' into more 'efficient' (read profitable) uses. Beyond this, scholars such as Webb and Webber (2017) have directly referenced an anticommons risks associated with condo governance, for instance, noting how divergent stakeholder interests can threaten optimal long-term building maintenance outcomes. Most condo research, however, presumes that condo governance generally mitigates anticommons risks that might occur within the condo tower itself, just as property models suggest it will, notwithstanding the manifold issues that surround condo governance which Chapter 1 detailed. The limited use of shared amenities tabled in Chapter 6, by contrast, suggests shared amenities may sometimes present an unrecognized anticommons risk within the high-rise condo.

Chapter 6 identifies multiple drivers behind residents' retreat from their shared home spaces. Residents found shared amenities to be poorly designed, and sometimes even unfit for purpose, as well as overly regulated, mis-regulated or insufficiently regulated. These design, regulatory and operational issues often meant residents' propertied expectations were unmet in these shared spaces, and this discouraged their use. Residents also often wished to maintain privacy and social distance from their co-residents specifically, which was difficult in shared spaces. Residents with expectations of autonomy perceived amenities to be poorly operated and maintained (both due to overly strict or overly lax management), and sometimes also vulnerable to crime and security issues. Residents also wished to respect the private units of other residents, and this was not always possible in some shared spaces, leading residents to withdraw from these spaces, as evidenced with the shared courtyard example. Residents also had propertied expectations of comfort and convenience, and were subsequently dissuaded from using shared amenities because these were "too distant" from their private units. Residents were meanwhile also enticed by competing local amenities whether better-equipped gyms or big local parks, with bigger and better facilities, no by-laws, and privacy from co-residents' scrutiny. Residents also mentioned other personal factors, such as time and health constraints, which also determined their use of shared home spaces.

Evidence of how residents practise common property in everyday condo living suggests condo governance does not always eliminate so-called inefficiencies and under-use in the ways property models of condominium anticipate. These conceptual models, for instance, do not account for the way residents' practices of common property are conditioned by their propertied expectations of shared home spaces, by their respect for the sanctity of private property (that is, other residents' private units) and by sometimes onerous local working rules. Far from the equilibrium envisaged in property theorists' ideal types, common property is subsequently found to be sometimes dysfunctional, vulnerable to misuse and appropriation by select residents and underuse. This potential underuse challenges previous claims, such as by Webster (2002), that infrastructural efficiencies can be secured through the privatization of urban amenity that results from the conversion of land ownership to condominium and other analogous legal architectures.

Condo city futures

Recent optimism expressed over condominium's prospects rests on claims that condominium is flawed only on account of the political, economic and social system it operates within (for example Easthope 2019: 157–9). Negative assessments of condoization, Easthope (2019: 157) writes, such as those tabled at the outset of this book and in Chapter 1, have 'more to do with the political, economic and social systems … in which they operate, than it does with the condominium ownership and governance systems themselves'. Yet as legal scholars Britton-Purdy, Kapczynski and Grewal (2017: np) caution: 'law gives shape to the relations between politics and the economy at every point. It is the mediating institution that ties together politics and economics'. Many decades ago, condominium legislation gave shape to relations that existed between politics and economics at that time. Details of the advent of condominium legislation in Australia allude to those very relations. The commercial interest in condominium was crystal clear. The NSW Conveyancing (Strata Titles) Act, introduced in Parliament on 1 July 1961, was described as 'made in Australia, manufactured by Lend Lease' (Thompson 1986: 137). Civil and Civic Contractors Pty Ltd, a subsidiary of Lend Lease, led a committee tasked with finessing legislation which was set in motion, supervised and funded by Lend Lease and justified by both the difficulties of selling higher-density property ownership to residents under existing legislation and the redevelopment stimulus it provided for the inner city (Kondos 1980; Thompson 1986). Influential property developers meanwhile glossed over their own sizeable commercial stake in the proliferation of higher-density housing development (Thompson 1986). The political interest was relatively straightforward too: condominium was to extend the homeownership base and stimulate construction and, later, condoization also neatly aligned with prevailing compact city rhetoric. The distinct rights, collective responsibilities and private restrictions attached to condo ownership were meanwhile downplayed to the would-be consumer, as they continue to be today. Indeed this misrepresentation is an essential basis for the ongoing conversion of urban land and airspace to condominium and therefore in the interest of the state and all those who develop, market, service and insure condo developments. As this suggests, the political economies of condo development, even in its earliest forms, depended upon condominium's legal architectures – this much is as expected.

However, as condominium's legal architecture gave shape to the relations between politics and economics, they embedded within them an inherent tension between differing, and potentially irreconcilable, individual property interests. These tensions represent the so-termed 'lingering ailments' of condominium, present since its birth (Lippert and Treffers, 2020: np). Arguably the most critical of tensions between property interests in condominium is a conflict that turns on whether the primary function of a condo unit is to serve as a home for the resident owner or as an asset for the condo investor. Although this tension is not new,[4] it has been turbo-charged by the rise of buy-to-let and buy-to-leave investment which has seen growing numbers of condos re-envisioned as assets, with the former investment strategy increasing the number and share of renters seeking homes in condo housing. There are discontinuities in the contours of this tension too, these ushered in by the rise of digital property technologies, and especially 'home sharing' platforms such as AirBnB that enable condo landlords to extract maximum rents from their condo assets. Absentee owners' pursuit of these investment strategies has opened the condo's doors to short-stay renters and intensified profit-seeking activities within towers, often to the detriment of those attempting to make the condo home as this analysis captures.

This tension between homes and housing assets within condominium has considerable resonance for urban researchers: it is the knotty challenge faced by cities the world over as the financialization of housing intensifies (Madden and Marcuse 2016). However, the condominium form institutionalizes existing owner/renter power asymmetries within its propertied landscapes and it amplifies these power differentials by housing renters within privatized urban realms these condo renters can have no part in governing. This exposes condo renters to co-resident relations with resident owners with whom they are always in a property relation of relative vulnerability. As Chapter 1 reviewed, under contemporary condoization, the rise of the condo investor has paralleled a rise in subpar vertical built environments, many plagued by design and workmanship issues, including as developers have catered to investor markets for whom asset value trumped use value. Together, these material and relational realities pose potentially significant risks to the condo

[4] Soon after strata title legislation passed in Australia, investors entered the condo market. Resident owners took issue with these absentee owners, and more specifically their tenants, demanding legislation to enable the OC 'to control larrikanism and rowdiness from Tenanted Units' and blaming tenants for 'house management' disputes including noise, rubbish, parking and stairwells (Thompson 1986).

home. Lippert (2019), writing on the North American experience, captures some of the associated fallout. Lippert (2019: 237) describes how owners seeking 'community and building integrity' are pitted against absentee owners seeking 'low maintenance and a better aesthetic for profitable unit flips' and against renters 'with nowhere else to live'. This book expounds on this fallout by detailing the everyday homemaking of resident owners and renters, including the way units snapped up by investors, 'off-the-plan' and sight unseen, can be ill-suited and dysfunctional for renters trying to eke out a home.

Left unchecked, this inherent tension within condominium and the fallout associated with it threaten the high-rise condo home, especially for condo renters. These risks do not reside in some distant future: a significant number of owners and renters interviewed did not anticipate living in high-rise housing indefinitely: some had concrete plans to move and others aspired to alternative housing arrangements. Their future housing plans and aspirations give further weight to findings from a Grattan Institute (2013) survey of Perth residents which found a paltry 16 per cent of those currently living in condos expressed a preference to remain in a condo in the future. Resident experiences likewise corroborate local associations of condo living with noise, lack of privacy, size constraints, and concerns about 'problematic renters', the proximity of neighbours and the quality of condo stock.

These condo homemaking outcomes cannot be unyoked from the legal arrangements that make contemporary condoization possible – significantly but not exclusively, condominium's legal architectures. Recall that this tension is *inherent* to condominium's legal architecture and, as such, the outcomes associated with this tension should themselves also be seen as *indivisible* from the political economies of condoization. Given that power and law are two sides of the same coin – '(in)justice is constrained and enabled by what we call law' (Delaney 2016: 268) – the legal architectures behind condoization should be seen as complicit in generating the outcomes associated with everyday condo living. This unsettles the claim that condominium's poor outcomes can be attributed to externalities, with the legal form an innocent bystander. Easthope (2019: 88, emphasis added; also Easthope and Randolph 2018) appears to concede at least the genealogy of some poor condo outcomes when referencing 'a more fundamental tension *inherent* in the condominium: that between individual and collective needs and responsibilities'.

Given this diagnosis, the law-political economy connection also provides fertile ground for discussion and action towards brighter urban housing futures, raising questions for academics, policymakers and condo stakeholders. To be sure, law, geography, politics and power interlace in complex ways, providing us with no direct or linear relationship between 'changing law, re-configuring space and ameliorating injustice' (Delaney

2016: 268). Moreover, disrupting this status quo will forever be stalled by policy, practice and legal settings that valorize and protect real estate assets over city homes. While the combined impacts of the economic recessions and health crises wrought by COVID-19 have rendered urban futures more uncertain, the prominence of the high-rise condo in urban housing futures is not yet in question. In the final pages then I use the territorialized workings of law in everyday condo living documented in this book's pages as prompts for two sets of provocations. Examining the intimate business of how residents make their home shines the light on risks associated with (1) the systems of housing provision behind contemporary condoization, and it shines the light on (2) micro urban socio-spatial restructurings associated with these residential environments. My analysis by no means provides a systematic analysis of either of these macro issues, but by getting close up to these poor-quality homes and the sometimes-fraught renter-owner relations within them, it confirms just how much these issues trouble the condo home. These provocations are therefore intended to help move us from the intricacies of everyday homemaking to discussion about how these tabled risks might be mitigated to better secure the condo as home. The first provocation concerns how the workings of territory in everyday condo living might be improved through the provision of higher-quality, fit-for-purpose condo buildings. The second provocation concerns how the workings of law in everyday condo living might better manage renters' struggles over the right to a home in the city, especially as rentership numbers climb. Linking the book's findings into broader struggles over home and belonging in the contemporary city in this way acknowledges ongoing debate in critical geography concerning the disjuncture between academic research and practice (Kitchin and Hubbard 1999).

Better vertical homes

The condo home risks being severely compromised by the provision of poor-quality vertical living environments. The quality of condo housing clearly matters. It matters because the quality, functionality and comfort of this housing impacts the daily lives of those who live in it and it matters because these are the places where ever-greater shares of residents seek to make their home in the city. These new vertical landscapes have a daunting obduracy which warrants special attention, including in the face of our climate emergency. Upgrading and retro-fitting condo towers is logistically complex and costly, exponentially more so than lower-rise, lower-density housing due to the relative complexity of both its physical and legal architectures. Demolishing condo towers is likewise logistically complex, financially prohibitive and environmentally unsound. Warnings about creating the vertical 'slums of the future' caution us to take seriously the high-rise legacy condoization is delivering. The risks associated with poor-quality vertical homes mars condo development not just in Australia's capital cities, but in verticalizing cities from Vancouver to Manchester and many cities beyond.

The Grenfell Tower fire tragedy in London alerted many to the human risks wrought by the material realities of the privatization and deregulation of high-rise social housing (see Hodkinson 2019). Many, however, remain unaware just how much private high-rise housing is also beset by failings wrought by prioritizing profits over people, by pursuing an ethics of corner-cutting rather than of care. In South Sydney, cracks and structural issues in the 10-storey Mascot Tower led first to an evacuation order and then, months later, to the imposition of exorbitant levies on co-owners to cover rectification works to the tune of $AUD 20 million. These financial pressures combine with an unquantifiable emotional toll on residents forced to leave their homes and wait in limbo for resolution (ABC 2019; Casben 2019). This defects case is not exceptional and follows another well-publicized defect case in the Opal Tower, also in Sydney, that led to an evacuation order on Christmas Eve 2018. These cases are not outliers: an Australian survey of condo construction quality confirms systemic issues plaguing the national high-rise stock, with over eight in ten new condo buildings defective (Johnston and Reid 2019: 21). From water leaks and cracking walls, to malfunctioning fire systems and unsafe cladding, emerging evidence has since prompted an NSW parliamentary inquiry into construction standards. This is a story of split incentives and developer profiteering at the cost of quality functional homes. This is a story of vertical urbanization under market-led planning regimes and construction sector arrangements with inadequate controls and incentives to circumscribe the transgressions these forces wield. This is a story of thriving investor markets where undifferentiated 'investor grade' condos are marketed first and foremost as 'off-the-plan' investment opportunities' that are then snapped up by profit-seeking investors for whom liveability may be incidental (for example on Melbourne, see Nethercote 2019).

Siting much of this condo development in high-amenity areas not only defies metropolitan planning ambitions for medium-density, middle-ring development but, without affordable or social housing stipulations, this density is 'effectively "wasted"' (Dodson 2012: 29), since high land prices translate to relatively high-cost apartments that cater only to the housing and investment needs of relatively better-off households. This development then only worsens inequalities between those who can secure housing in these higher-amenity areas and lower-income households 'stuck' in job-poor suburbia, where lagging public transport infrastructure ensures car-dependency and limited access to jobs and services (Dodson 2012).

The political economies of condoization are shaping these vertical landscapes in other materially significant ways too, raising another set of concerns about functionality and benefit. As the so-dubbed 'amenities arms' race' has seen developers ratcheting up the provision of private shared amenities, this book uncovers the uneven use, abuse and underuse of shared amenities. This suggests condo governance does not adequately guard against such outcomes, at least not to the extent anticipated by idealized conceptual models of condominium; it suggests that common property in condominium may be far from the 'efficient form of urban enclosure' some suggest (Lee and Webster 2006: 41). As just discussed, the underuse of shared amenities – from rooftop decks, to resident gyms and swimming pools – represents a potential anticommons risk lying within condominium housing, especially when these are poorly designed. Under the standard build-to-sell model that underpins condo development, developers have little stake in how condos fare post-purchase, beyond managing reputational risks. In this context, developers have leveraged amenities to enhance their profits, using amenity provision to negotiate planning permission within discretionary market-driven planning regimes and to secure concessions for taller towers, denser sites or larger building footprints (for example in Toronto: Lehrer and Pantalone 2018). Amenity provision is also part of a marketing strategy in which statement offerings provide a point of differentiation and exclusivity as developers compete for buyers; it is a strategy condo buyers and condo renters in turn absorb as additional costs through price and rental premiums.

This anticommons risk is troubling at a household, building and municipal level on multiple fronts, especially at a time when developers are ratcheting up their provision of amenities. It is a risk that raises questions about condoization in the context of ongoing debates about the uncoordinated provision and privatization of amenities previously provided by the municipality, as discussed in Chapter 1. The potential for inefficiencies in the use of privatized urban spaces, while not unique to condominium by any means, raises evident ethical issues about wastefulness in the context of increasingly privatized cityscapes and amid a climate disaster. These inefficiencies are all the more troubling given that residents continue to value them, notwithstanding their patchy use, rationalizing them as offering 'value for money' when rents are high or contributing to their condo's asset value. As the analysis suggests, condo residents may seek out condos with amenities that many may never use, but which they believe assist in realizing the condo home as a financial asset. As private amenity provision associated with condo development is uncoordinated across the city, condoization risks delivering vertical neighbourhoods replete with countless often poorly frequented private gyms, private roof decks and private car parks. And, while this book has remained focused within the tower, these towers are also impoverishing surrounding public realm too, including through wind-tunnelling and overshadowing (Shaw 2013).

The poor uptake of shared amenities raises questions for planners too. Poor uptake presents a challenge to those who claim the ongoing privatization of the urban realm engenders efficiencies or for those who advocate for it on this basis. The uneven use of amenities also raises questions for those who endorse the provision of private shared amenities in lieu of public amenity provision based on well-rehearsed, albeit contested, claims about the role of shared amenities in forging 'community' and social cohesion or advocate for it on this basis. It also raises questions for those who claim private shared amenities support healthful recreation in higher-density housing or advocate for it on this basis. In terms of car parking specifically, data tabled in Chapter 6 corroborates prior concerns about the over-provision of car parking and associated cautions about the need to revise generous parking mandates for higher-density housing development (De Gruyter et al 2020; Taylor 2020). Relatedly, the everyday practices associated with parking and bike storage facility use warrant attention from supply-side actors who regulate, design and deliver these amenities including to account for actual uptake, functionality and security of these amenities and to address alternate transport modes, such as e-bikes, scooters and EV charging. Australia might also look to other cities which regulate for maximum rather than minimum car parking provisions, which better accommodate alternative transport modes, including cycling and which better future-proof designs for evolving transport patterns and modalities. Planners require, in the first instance, more systematic studies of shared amenity usage to begin to address these concerns.

One expects a tipping point. Australia is already witnessing a swelling crisis of confidence in its high-rise housing stock thanks to the publicity generated by its condo defects crisis, as the latest chapter in a longer story of condo design quality concerns (Horne and Nethercote 2015). The burden of responsibility is shouldered by those tiers and departments of government charged with regulating supply-side provision. Regulatory reform must be sufficiently robust to push build-to-sell developers to invest in quality, functional, sustainable, future-proofed designs that provide for diverse housing needs such that these vertical residential environments can withstand demographic and societal change and technological advances. This includes provision for adequate space, privacy, safety, affordable running and maintenance costs and comfort. Since the condo developments at the heart of this book were built, there has been some regulatory overhaul, including the implementation of 'apartment' design guidelines and stricter oversight of the design and construction of new buildings (for example *Design and Building Practitioners Act 2020* and the *Residential Apartment Buildings Act 2020* in NSW). These appear a step in the right direction, with evidence of their efficacy required.

A city home for all

The condo home also risks being severely compromised by fraught socio-territorial dynamics. Condoization is implicated in struggles over the right to the city (Lefebvre 1996 [1967]; for introduction: Mitchell 2003; Attoh 2011; Aalbers and Gibb 2014). This right is not just about city residents' access to particular urban resources but also about their power to remake the city in the ways they wish. The struggle over this right is about the unremitting concentration of that power in the hands of economic and political elites (Harvey 2008). One way condoization is implicated is through processes of socio-spatial restructuring, including neighbourhood gentrification. This is recognized inasmuch as the construction of faceless towers razes valued urban fabric and social networks and displaces local residents. Other ways condoization is implicated are not, however, as visible or well documented. They require looking away from this 'external life' of condo property and the associated insider/outsider dynamics. They require looking at the practices and relations of condo property within the tower in everyday condo living, as this book's analyses have ventured to do. With this granularity of socio-spatial data, other forms of social segregation and urban fragmentation become visible. As condoization privatizes the vertical urban realm, the right to the city falls into the hands of private interests, and while this sets in motion those familiar exclusionary insider/outsider dynamics extensively documented elsewhere, it also builds private communities which are themselves riddled with uneven power relations. Lippert (2019: 237, emphasis added) alludes to these dynamics when he argues that Mike Davis' concerns about 'a fundamental reorganisation of metropolitan space … which transcends traditional social segregation and urban fragmentation' are being realized *inside* the condo, including in the fraught social relations between resident owners, absentee owners and condo renters.

Focusing exclusively on relations between co-owners, legal scholar Douglas Harris (2019) shows us how these dynamics can play out and the risks they harbour. Specifically, Harris' analysis of a litigation case in Vancouver between condo co-owners captures how condo legislation can be weaponized by condo owners to control *from within* – namely, through private property relations – who has the right to the city. The court case between residential owners and their co-owner, a pharmacist and the owner of a street-level commercial condo lot, centred on an orchestrated campaign by the OC to hold the pharmacist responsible for 'chronic nuisance' allegedly caused by the pharmacy and its customers. The risk, in this instance, both to the pharmacist and the neighbourhood more broadly, derived from the way condominium legislation was designed only to protect private owners' interests, not its residents' interests and certainly not the needs of low-income community members who relied on access to the pharmacy. The judgement eventually saw fines issued by the condo board to the pharmacy owner for breaches annulled. Although this judgement ultimately turned on issues of procedural non-compliance within condo governance (related to the commercial owner's voting rights not being adequately administered), the judge did not accept that the nuisance was solely attributable to the pharmacy but was instead also part and parcel of life in Downtown Eastside Vancouver. The condo owners nonetheless clearly deployed 'the tools that private condominium government creates in their efforts to deal with the challenges of living in and owning a residence in Vancouver's Downtown Eastside' (Harris 2019: 385).

This book extends Harris' concerns over the way condominium is implicated in circumscribing city residents' right to the city through its emphasis on the way the socio-territorial dynamics of everyday condo living amplify asymmetrical power relations within the tower. At stake – and this time well before any litigation ensues – is the renter's chance of making a home in the city, as this book's analyses collectively show. To frame the condo renter's struggles in terms of the right to the city is to emphasize the *collective* nature of condo renters' struggle and to recognize this struggle as more than simply a struggle over renters' right to access a particular resource (Harvey 2008: 14). But while we can recognize the condo renter's relative vulnerabilities, a seemingly immutable challenge lies ahead in any attempt to mitigate the risks these pose to the condo home. For the legal frames of condominium offer only so much scope, given the sanctity of private property ownership in Australia and other property-owning democracies further afield. It goes almost without saying then that claims that condominium offers 'a ready-made structure for political action and engagement at the local level' (Easthope 2019: 159) require not simply significant qualification but far greater critical scrutiny of the very notion that a private government based on *property ownership* might ever provide means for *democratic* urban governance in the context of tenure inequalities (also see Barton and Silverman 1994; McKenzie 2011: 38).

And yet bettering the plight of private renters has never been a more pressing project given the marked rise in private renting across many Anglophone advanced liberal economies (Kemp 2015; Hulse et al 2018b). In Australia, the private rental sector grew at more than twice the rate of household growth between 2006 and 2016, with some one in four households nationally now renting privately and far higher rates in some urban neighbourhoods (Hulse et al 2018b: 8). This parallels expansion of the UK, Irish and US private rental sectors following the financial crisis, with divergent national drivers (Martin et al 2018; Byrne 2019). The UK private rental sector is valued at over $AUD 2 trillion, four times higher than 2002 and, in London, where a third of this value is concentrated, its private rental sector has nearly doubled since 2000 and, perhaps even more remarkably, the rate of growth has almost doubled since 2007 with private renters predicted to outnumber owner-occupiers by 2025 (Kemp 2015; Greater London Authority [GLA] 2018). In the US, over a third of households rent and rates are closer to 50 per cent in the high-cost urban housing markets of large cities such as Los Angeles and New York (Chan and Jush 2017). Such statistics herald the unravelling of the 'continuum model' of homeownership in which private renting was once a steppingstone (see Hulse et al 2018a). As the private rental sector grows, its renter households are becoming more diverse too, as noted in Chapter 1. Australia's private rental sector contains growing shares of lower- *and* higher-income renters, more longer- (ten+ years) and mid-term (five to nine years) renters, more midlife renters and more families with children than ever before (Hulse et al 2018b). Similar trends are found elsewhere too. In London, renter families with children increased by 86 per cent in the five years to 2011 (Kemp 2015: 610) and in the US, higher-socioeconomic households became increasingly likely to rent in the decade to 2015 (Chan and Jush 2017). Private renters have little security of tenure, live in often under-maintained properties and face involuntary house-moves. More renters, uncapped rents, weak tenant protections and COVID-19-related economic and health crises make for a potentially toxic mix of housing stress and financial risk for these households as they seek long-term homes in the city.

The risks confronting urban private renters can be conceived as arising from a social infrastructure deficit – a deficit of quality urban rental housing. Rental housing in higher-amenity, service-rich urban locations is limited, especially beyond the high-rise condo. Multifamily rental in North America and emergent build-to-rent sectors in the UK, Ireland and Australia present themselves as an alternative. Unlike the build-to-sell model behind condoization, the long-term investment horizons of build-to-rent's institutional investors potentially creates different priorities for tenancy and property management as institutional owners take an interest in operational efficiencies and tenant retention. These alternatives to renting in condos are marketed on the promise of rent and fee transparency, longer tenancy contracts, flexibility to up/down-size within the same building, allowances for pets and plentiful service and amenity offerings. The veracity of these claims still warrants critical evaluation (Nethercote 2020) and we know already that renters living in these homes will have no formal say over the governance of these domestic domains either. Beyond this, the earlier option for those who cannot or choose not to buy was public housing, but this exists today only in a highly residualized, sorely underfunded format. With appropriately funded public housing within a decommodified housing system that might also include the expansion of other forms of cooperative, communal or limited-equity co-ownership and community land trusts (Madden and Marcuse 2016) a long way off, city renters' options beyond the condo look set to be incredibly limited for some time yet.

The risks confronting the condo renter can also be conceived as a legal problem. This framing recognizes the crucial work of law in positioning renters in positions of relative vulnerability to owners in all propertied landscapes, and the specific work of condominium in amplifying this uneven relationship in the propertied landscapes of the condo tower. This tenure-based power asymmetry *is* partly addressed by provisions in landlord/tenant law that restrict the treatment of housing as a pure market asset. Through such provisions, the law acknowledges housing's foundational role in human flourishing. But the law currently only goes so far as enduring tenure inequalities corroborate (Christophers 2019).[5] Socio-political homeownership ideologies in advanced liberal economies have long traded on the idea that the lauded features of homeownership are intrinsic to homeownership and indeed exclusive to homeownership (Ruonovaara 1993; Doling 1999; also Blandy and Goodchild 1999; Marcuse 2020 and on tenure complexity: Hulse 2008; Arundel and Ronald 2020). But this conviction that homeownership is a precondition for achieving home has been challenged by a questioning of what is intrinsic or 'core' to any one tenure (while recognizing that tenure, like property, is a social construct) and what is socially and historically contingent. There is some agreement that homeownership differs from renting on some core rights, such as the right of disposition, and core relations: for instance, the renter cannot escape the landlord-tenant relationship. Yet other settings, so termed 'contingent rights' (Ruonavaara 2012) which govern the use and control of housing can and do vary across place and over time (for example see Easthope 2014). These contingent rights are neither inevitable nor unchangeable.

Those rights and attributes argued to enhance the experience of homeownership could, with the political will, be built into policies such as rent control and into tenancy contracts. In the housing system at large, regulation to support longer-term secure tenancies, to curb short-stay rentals and to limit speculation (for example ending negative gearing, increasing absentee/vacancy taxes and so on) could shift the private rental sector towards being a home-centric sector rather than an investment-centric sector. And with regards to condominium specifically, its legal architectures are not set in stone as their evolution over time and across jurisdictions confirms

5 To focus on the legal dimensions is not intended to downplay the economic dimensions of rentier capitalism (that is, the payment of rent, and relations between landlord and renter) but recall that the legal and economic dimensions of rent go hand in hand; how rent comes to be owed and paid depends upon the supportive institutions of private property (Blomley 2020).

(Dredge and Coiacetto 2011). Condo reforms could broaden renter's formal enfranchisement with participation and voting rights, although uptake of such reforms has been slow and underwhelming so far, including because these opportunities and their significance are not well communicated to renters. Progressive proposals also warrant consideration, such as suggestions that each private unit might be awarded two voting rights, shared between an absentee owner and their tenant (Altmann 2015). But the likelihood of revisions of condominium's legal architectures is limited, for we should not expect support, much less advocacy, among condo property stakeholders for any reforms that cede power to renters and, in any case, these reforms can only go so far.

Ultimately any reform that corrects for asymmetries between tenures will have implications for the social meanings of property ownership. Property scholarship understands well that renting and ownership are relational tenures; an owner's privilege and a renter's vulnerability are interconnected (Christophers 2019; Blomley 2020). Within the microcosm of condominium property, this interdependency between owners and renters is stark because it is so obvious that co-resident renters and owners cannot ever be evenly positioned in property space without diminishing the condo landlord's power, without diminishing the relative power of property owners. Lehavi (2015) writes of the challenges of devising private law reforms that conflict with prevailing socio-political orientations. Bringing housing tenures onto an equal footing inside the condo would require, as Brett Christophers (2019) writes of the housing system at large, 'nothing short of a major rethinking of certain core tenets of contemporary hegemonic Western political economy'. A property perspective, however, helpfully clarifies that the goal in securing a right to the city for all is not some kind of zero-sum game of turning property 'outsiders' (for example renters) into property 'insiders' (that is, owners) but instead a game of reconfiguring property relations so as to minimize vulnerabilities (Blomley 2020: 50).

APPENDIX

Fieldwork Notes

This book's empirical core derives from data collected between 2017 and 2019 under the auspices of an Australian Research Council funded project (LP150100089) on apartment development and high-rise living. *Project HOME: Housing Outcomes Metrics and Evaluation*, which is ongoing as I draft this, is led by Ralph Horne and comprises an interdisciplinary team of researchers across multiple institutions including RMIT University, University College London (UCL), The University of Western Australia and the University of Melbourne. The project also involved partnership and funding from external industry stakeholders involved in the design, development and regulation of 'apartments'. Project HOME set out to evaluate design quality in contemporary apartments in Melbourne, Perth, Barcelona and London using interdisciplinary methods that combine architectural plan-based analyses, lived experience perspectives attained through interviews with householders, and policy and practice context analyses complemented by supply-side stakeholder interviews.

An initial audit of new infill housing development in Melbourne, Perth, London and Barcelona identified all newly constructed 'apartment' developments built in the wake of the 2008/09 financial crisis and intervening years. Project HOME centred on 'apartments' which in the Australian context denotes residential developments comprising four or more storeys and also the units within them, as per the prevailing *Australian Bureau of Statistics* definition, with ownership form unspecified. The audit narrowed our focus to a set of 65 apartment buildings based on locational and design criteria, with this selection inclusive of a range of local housing market offerings in terms of architectural design, level of shared amenity, price-points, building scale and vertical profile. In each city, the research team then recruited residents living within each of these buildings using flyers posted in mailboxes and on resident noticeboards. Residents were selected to be interviewed such that the dataset roughly reflected local high-rise and household characteristics, including a range of housing tenures, household types and demographics and apartment typologies (for example studio, one, two, and three bedroom apartments).

In Melbourne, a total of 68 residents were recruited from within 14 buildings built between 2010 and 2016. These buildings ranged in height from four storeys to some 40 storeys, with over two thirds of these buildings seven or more storeys, and two buildings over 30 storeys. These buildings ranged in size from 24 units to some 290 units. Over two thirds of developments had more than 50 units and half had over 80 units. In Perth, a total of 60 residents were recruited from within 17 buildings built between 2009 and 2017. These buildings also ranged in height from two storeys to over 20 storeys, with more than half over seven storeys and a third over 12 storeys. These developments ranged in size from 15 units to near 200 units. While the Melbourne buildings were relatively taller, reflecting Melbourne's more intense verticalization, the Perth developments were often sizeable: the vast majority had over 40 units, two thirds had over 80 units and almost half had over 130 units. In-depth semi-structured 60–90-minute interviews were conducted in each resident's home and were complemented by observation of the resident's use of space and documented via photographs where residents consented. Interviews were audio-recorded and professionally transcribed.

These interviews were conducted together with Ralph Horne, Nicola Willand and Oenone Rooksby. This book would not have been possible without Ralph Horne's agile leadership on Project HOME, Nicola and Oenone's excellent assistance with conducting interviews nor the participation of residents who kindly spared their time and generously shared their personal housing experiences with us. Chapter 2 provides further details on this dataset, including my approach to preserving these residents' anonymity.

References

Aalbers, M. (2016) *The Financialization of Housing: A Political Economy Approach*, Routledge.

Aalbers, M. and Christophers, B. (2014) 'Centring housing in political economy', *Housing, Theory and Society*, 31(4): 373–94.

Aalbers, M. and Gibb, K. (2014) 'Housing and the right to the city: introduction to the special issue', *International Journal of Housing Policy*, 14(3): 207–13.

ABC [Australian Broadcasting Commission] (2019) 'Cracking Up', *ABC*, 20 August. Available from: www.abc.net.au/4corners/cracking-up/11431474

ABS [Australian Bureau of Statistics] (2010) 'A View of Housing Density in Perth, 2005–2009. Western Australian Statistical Indicators. 1367.5'. Available from: www.abs.gov.au/ausstats/abs@.nsf/Latestproducts/1367.5Feature%20Article102010

ABS [Australian Bureau of Statistics] (2011) 'Regional Population Growth, Australia, 2011. 3218.0'. Available from: www.abs.gov.au/ausstats/abs@.nsf/Products/3218.0~2011~Main+Features~Main+Features

ABS [Australian Bureau of Statistics] (2016) 'Apartment Living, Census of Population and Housing: Reflecting Australia – Stories from the Census, 2016, 2017.0'. Available from: www.abs.gov.au/ausstats/abs@.nsf/Lookup/by%20Subject/2071.0~2016~Main%20Features~Apartment%20Living~20

Acuto, M. (2010) 'High-rise Dubai urban entrepreneurialism and the technology of symbolic power', *Cities*, 27: 272–84.

AEMC [Australian Energy Market Commission] (2019) *'Updating the Regulatory Frameworks for Embedded Networks*, Final report', 20 June. Available from: www.aemc.gov.au/sites/default/files/2019-06/Updating%20the%20regulatory%20frameworks%20for%20embedded%20networks%20-%20FINAL%20REPORT.PDF

Alexander, G. (2012) 'Governance property', *University of Pennsylvania Law Review*, 160(7): 1853–88.

Alfasi, N. and Ganan, E. (2015) 'Jerusalem of (foreign) gold: entrepreneurship and pattern-driven policy in a historic city', *Urban Geography*, 36(2): 157–80.

Alterman, R. (2010) 'The maintenance of residential towers in condominium tenure: a comparative analysis of two extremes – Israel and Florida', in S. Blandy, A. Dupuis and J. Dixon (eds) *Multi-owned Housing: Law, Power and Practice*, Aldershot: Ashgate, pp 73–90.

Altman, I. (1975) *The Environment and Social Behavior: Privacy, Personal Space, Territory, and Crowding*, California: Brooks/Cole Publishing.

Altmann, E. (2015) 'Policy implications for governing Australia's apartment communities: tenants, committees of management and strata managers', in R. Dufty-Jones and D. Rogers (eds) *Housing in 21st Century Australia: People, Practices and Policies*, Farnham: Ashgate, pp 121–36.

Altmann, E. and Gabriel, M. (2018) 'Rights, restrictions and responsibilities in context', in E. Altmann and M. Gabriel (eds) *Multi-Owned Property in the Asia-Pacific Region: Rights, Restrictions and Responsibilities*, London: Palgrave Macmillan, pp 3–15.

Andrews, F.J. and Warner, E. (2020) '"Living outside the house": how families raising young children in new, private high-rise developments experience their local environment', *Journal of Urbanism: International Research on Placemaking and Urban Sustainability*, 13(3): 263–85.

Antonsich, M. (2010) 'Searching for belonging – an analytical framework', *Geography Compass*, 4(6): 644–59.

Arrigoitia, M. (2014) 'UnMaking public housing towers: the role of lifts and stairs in the demolition of a Puerto Rican project', *Home Cultures*, 11(2): 167–96.

Arundel, R. and Ronald, R. (2020) 'The false promise of homeownership: homeowner societies in an era of declining access and rising inequality', *Urban Studies*, 58(6): 1120–40.

Atkinson, R. (2019) 'Necrotecture: lifeless dwellings and London's super-rich', *International Journal of Urban and Regional Research*, 43(1): 2–13.

Atkinson, R. and Blandy, S. (eds) (2013) *Gated Communities: International Perspectives*, Oxon: Routledge.

Atkinson, R. and Blandy, S. (2016) *Domestic Fortress: Fear and the New Home Front*, Manchester: Manchester University Press.

Atkinson, R. and Jacobs, K. (2016) *House, Home and Society*, London: Palgrave.

Attoh, K.A. (2011) 'What kind of right is the right to the city?', *Progress in Human Geography*, 35(5): 669–85.

Baker, T. (2013) 'Home-making in higher density cities: residential experiences in Newcastle, Australia', *Urban Policy and Research*, 31(3): 265–79.

Ballard, R. (1975) *High-Rise* (2014 edn), London: Fourth Estate.

Ballard, R. (1978) 'J.G. Ballard Interview', *Search & Destroy*. Available from: www.jgballard.ca/media/1978_reprinted_1988_search%26destroy_newspaper.html

Barton, E. and Silverman, J. (1994) *Common Interest Communities: Private Government and Public Interests*, Berkeley: Institute of Governmental Studies.

Bauman, Z. (1993) *Postmodern Ethics* (Vol 34), Oxford: Blackwell.

Bauman, Z. (2005) *Work, Consumerism and the New Poor*, Maidenhead: Open University Press.

Baxter, R. (2017) 'The high-rise home: verticality as practice in London', *International Journal of Urban and Regional Research*, 41(2), 334–52.

Baxter, R. and Brickell, K. (2014) 'For home unmaking', *Home Cultures*, 11(2): 133–43.

Berger, C. (1963) 'Condominium: shelter on a statutory foundation', *Columbia Law Review*, 63(6): 987–1026.

Bhandar, B. (2018) *Colonial Lives of Property*, Australia: Duke University Press.

Birrell, B. and Healy, E. (2013) *Melbourne's High-Rise Apartment Boom*, Monash University Centre for Population and Urban Research Report, Monash University, Melbourne: Centre for Population and Urban Research. Available from: https://core.ac.uk/download/pdf/30675938.pdf

Birrell, B. and McCloskey, D. (2016) 'Sydney and Melbourne's housing affordability crisis report two: no end in sight', Canberra: The Australian Population Research Institute. Available from: https://tapri.org.au/wp-content/uploads/2016/02/Sydney-Melbourne-Housing-Report-No-2-No-End-in-Sight-6-Mar-2016-std.pdf

Blandy, S. (2008) 'Secession or cohesion? Exploring the impact of gated communities', in J. Flint and D. Robinson (eds) *Community Cohesion in Crisis: New Dimensions of Diversity and Difference*, Bristol: Policy Press, pp 239–57.

Blandy, S. (2013) 'Collective property: owning and sharing residential space', in N. Hopkins (ed) *Modern Studies in Property Law*, Vol 7, Oxford: Hart Publishing, pp 151–72.

Blandy, S. and Goodchild, B. (1999) 'From tenure to rights: conceptualizing the changing focus of housing law in England', *Housing, Theory and Society*, 16(1): 31–42.

Blandy, S. and Lister, D. (2005) 'Gated communities: (ne)gating community development?', *Housing Studies*, 20(2): 287–301.

Blandy, S. and Sibley, D. (2010) 'Law, boundaries and the production of space', *Social & Legal Studies*, 19(3): 275–84.

Blandy, S., Dixon, J. and Dupuis, A. (2006) 'Theorising power relationships in multi-owned residential developments: unpacking the bundle of rights', *Urban Studies*, 43(13): 2365–83.

Blandy, S., Dupuis, A. and Dixon, J. (2016) *Multi-Owned Housing: Law, Power and Practice*, London: Routledge.

Blandy, S., Bright, S. and Nield, S. (2018) 'The dynamics of enduring property relationships in land', *The Modern Law Review*, 81(1): 85–113.

Blandy, S., Nield, S. and Bright, S. (2020) 'Real property on the ground: the law of people and place', in H. Dagan and B. Zipursky (eds) *Research Handbook on Private Law Theory*, Edward Elgar, pp 237–53.

Blomley, N. (2004a) *Unsettling the City: Urban Land and the Politics of Property*, New York: Routledge.

Blomley, N. (2004b) 'Un-real estate: proprietary space and public gardening', *Antipode*, 36(4): 614–41.

Blomley, N. (2005a) 'Flowers in the bathtub: boundary crossings at the public–private divide', *Geoforum*, 36(3): 281–96.

Blomley, N. (2005b) 'The borrowed view: privacy, propriety, and the entanglements of property', *Law & Social Inquiry*, 30(4): 617–61.

Blomley, N. (2006) 'Homelessness and the delusions of property', *Transactions of the Institute of British Geographers*, 31(1): 3–5.

Blomley, N. (2013) 'Performing property: making the world', *Canadian Journal of Law & Jurisprudence*, 26(1): 23–48.

Blomley, N. (2014) 'Property, law, and space', *Property Law Review*, 3: 229–35.

Blomley, N. (2016a) 'The territory of property', *Progress in Human Geography*, 40(5): 593–609.

Blomley, N. (2016b) 'The boundaries of property: complexity, relationality, and spatiality', *Law & Society Review*, 50(1): 224–55.

Blomley, N. (2017) 'Taking up property: comments on Ananya Roy', *Geoforum* [online] doi.org/10.1016/j.geoforum.2016.12.013.

Blomley, N. (2020) 'Precarious territory: property law, housing, and the socio-spatial order', *Antipode*, 52(1): 36–57.

Blunt, A. and Dowling, R. (2006) *Home*, Oxon: Routledge.

Blunt, A. and Sheringham, O. (2019) 'Home-city geographies: urban dwelling and mobility', *Progress in Human Geography*, 43(5): 815–34.

Bonds, A. (2019) 'Race and ethnicity I: property, race, and the carceral state', *Progress in Human Geography*, 43(3): 574–83.

Braverman, I., Blomley, N., Delaney, D. and Kedar, A. (eds) (2014) *The Expanding Spaces of Law: A Timely Legal Geography*, Stanford: Stanford.

Brickell, K., Arrigoitia, M. and Vasudevan, A. (eds) (2017) *Geographies of Forced Eviction: Dispossession, Violence, Resistance*, London: Palgrave Macmillan.

Brighenti, A. (2010) 'On territorology: towards a general science of territory', *Theory, Culture and Society*, 27(1): 52–72.

Britton-Purdy, J., Kapczynski, A. and Grewal, S. (2017) 'Law and political economy: towards a manifesto', *The Law and Political Economy Project, Yale University*, 6 November. Available from: https://lpeproject.org/blog/law-and-political-economy-toward-a-manifesto/

Brown, M. (2019) 'Tate Modern Wins Privacy Case Brought by Owners of £4m Flats', *The Guardian*, 13 February. Available from: www.theguardian.com/artanddesign/2019/feb/12/tate-modern-wins-privacy-case-brought-by-owners-of-4m-flats

Bunce, S. (2016) 'Pursuing urban commons: politics and alliances in community land trust activism in East London', *Antipode*, 48(1): 134–50.

Bunker, R., Crommelin, L., Troy, L., Easthope, H., Pinnegar, S. and Randolph, B. (2017) 'Managing the transition to a more compact city in Australia', *International Planning Studies*, 22(4): 384–99.

Burrell, K. (2014) 'Spilling over from the street: contextualizing domestic space in an inner-city neighborhood', *Home Cultures*, 11(2): 145–66.

Buxton, M., Goodman, R. and Moloney, S. (2016) *Planning Melbourne: Lessons for a Sustainable City*, Melbourne: CSIRO.

Buys, L. and Miller, E. (2012) 'Residential satisfaction in inner urban higher-density Brisbane, Australia: role of dwelling design, neighbourhood and neighbours', *Journal of Environmental Planning and Management*, 55(3): 319–38.

Byrne, M. (2019) *The Financialization of Housing and the Growth of the Private Rental Sector in Ireland, the UK and Spain*, UCD Geary Institute for Public Policy, Discussion Paper Series, 10 January, Dublin: Geary Institute for Public Policy, University College Dublin. Available from: www.ucd.ie/geary/static/publications/workingpapers/gearywp201902.pdf

Carmel [Tiaeki] (2018) 'Using Common Property for AirBnB Key Safes', 12 December, Flat Chat [online forum]. Available from: www.flat-chat.com.au/topic/using-common-property-for-airbnb-key-safes/

Carroll, P., Witten, K. and Kearns, R. (2011) 'Housing intensification in Auckland, New Zealand: implications for children and families', *Housing Studies*, 26(03): 353–67.

Casben (2019) 'Mascot Towers' Residents Vote to Pay $7 Million in Levies as Repair Bill Blows Out to $20 Million', *ABC* [Australian Broadcasting Commission] *News*, 23 August. Available from: www.abc.net.au/news/2019-08-23/mascot-towers-repair-bill-soars-to-20-million/11439856

CBC News (2019) 'Montreal Cracking Down on Lock Boxes Affixed to Public Property', CBC News. Available from: www.cbc.ca/news/canada/montreal/montreal-cracks-down-on-lock-boxes-1.4967982

Chan, S. and Jush, G. (2017) *Renting in the Nation's Largest Metros: The 2017 National Rental Housing Landscape*, New York: Furman Center, NYU. Available from: http://furmancenter.org/files/NYUFurmanCenter_2017_National_Rental_Housing_Landscape_04OCT2017.pdf

Chang, C. and Peng, C. (2018) 'Urban renewal and affordable housing in Taiwan', in E. Altmann and M. Gabriel (eds) *Multi-Owned Property in the Asia-Pacific Region: Rights, Restrictions and Responsibilities*, London: Palgrave Macmillan, pp 137–51.

Charmes, E. and Keil, R. (2015) 'The politics of post-suburban densification in Canada and France', *International Journal of Urban and Regional Research*, 39(3): 581–602.

Charney, I. (2007) 'The politics of design: architecture, tall buildings and the skyline of Central London', *Area* 39(2): 195–205.

Cheshire, L., Walters, P. and Rosenblatt, T. (2010) 'The politics of housing consumption: renters as flawed consumers on a master planned estate', *Urban Studies*, 47(12): 2597614.

Cheshire, L., Easthope, H. and ten Have, C. (2019) 'Unneighbourliness and the unmaking of home', *Housing, Theory and Society*, 38(2): 133–51.

Christophers, B. (2019) 'A tale of two inequalities: housing-wealth inequality and tenure inequality', *Environment and Planning A: Economy and Space*, 53(3): 573–94.

City of Melbourne (2013) *Future Living: A Discussion Paper Identifying Issues and Options for Housing Our Community*, Melbourne: City of Melbourne.

City of Melbourne (2020) 'Median House Prices by Transfer Year from 2000–2016', *City of Melbourne.* Available from: https://data.melbourne.vic.gov.au/Property/Median-House-Prices-by-Transfer-Year-from-2000-201/67fb-mvax

City of Melbourne (nd) 'Maintaining Our Parks and Public Spaces', *City of Melbourne.* Available from: www.melbourne.vic.gov.au/community/parks-open-spaces/pages/maintaining-parks-public-spaces.aspx

Clapham, D. (2005) *The Meaning of Housing: A Pathways Approach*, Bristol: Policy Press.

Coleman, A. (1985) *Utopia on Trial. Vision and Reality in Planned Housing*, London: Hilary Shipman.

Cooper, D. (2007) 'Opening up ownership: community belonging, belongings, and the productive life of property', *Law & Social Inquiry*, 32(3): 625–64.

CoreLogic (2016) 'The profile of the Australian residential property investor', June, pp 1–46. Available from: https://www.corelogic.com.au/resources/pdf/ reports/CoreLogic%20Investor%20Report_ June%202016.pdf

CoreLogic (2018) *25 Years of Housing Trends*, CoreLogic. Available from: www.aussie.com.au/content/dam/aussie/images/general/rebrand-2020/property-report-graphs/aussie_25_years_report.pdf

Cowan, D. (2010) 'Housing and property', in P. Cain and H. Kritzer (eds) *The Oxford Handbook of Empirical Legal Research*, Oxford: Oxford, pp 331–52.

Cowan, D. (2011) *Housing Law and Policy*, Cambridge: Cambridge.

Cowan, D. and Hardy, B. (2019) 'Regulating home: a case study', *Housing, Theory and Society*, 37(5): 597–614.

Cowan, D., Carr, H. and Wallace, A. (2018) *Ownership, Narrative, Things*, London: Palgrave Macmillan.

Crabtree, L. (2020) 'Community land trusts: embracing the relationality of property', in J. Gibson-Graham and K. Dombroski (eds) *The Handbook of Diverse Economies*, Edward Elgar, pp 292–9.

Craggs, D. (2018) 'Skyscraper development and the dynamics of crisis: the new London skyline and spatial recapitalization, *Built Environment*, 43(4): 500–19.

Cresswell, T. (1996) *In Place/Out of Place: Geography, Ideology, and Transgression*, Minneapolis: Minnesota Press.

Cresswell, T. (2010) 'Towards a politics of mobility', *Environment and planning D: Society and Space*, 28(1): 17–31.

CTBUH [Council on Tall Buildings and Urban Habitat] (2019) 'CTBUH Year in Review: Tall Trends of 2018', *CTBUH*, Available from: www.skyscrapercenter.com/research/CTBUH_ResearchReport_2018YearInReview.pdf

CTBUH [Council on Tall Buildings and Urban Habitat] (2020) 'Cities Ranked by Number of 150m+ Completed Buildings', *The Skyscraper Centre: Global Tall Building Database of the CTBUH*. Available from: www.skyscrapercenter.com/cities

Dagan, H. and Heller, M. (2001) 'The liberal commons', *The Yale Law Journal*, 110(4): 549–623.

Daum, M. (2015) 'Column: Right-to-Dry Movement Gets its Day in the Sun in California', *Los Angeles Times*, 15 October. Available from: www.latimes.com/opinion/op-ed/la-oe-daum-right-to-dry-20151015-column.html

De Gruyter, C., Truong, L.T. and Taylor, E. (2020) 'Can high quality public transport support reduced car parking requirements for new residential apartments?', *Journal of Transport Geography*, 82: 102627.

Delaney, D. (2010) *The Spatial, the Legal and the Pragmatics of World-making: Nomospheric Investigations*, Oxon: Routledge.

Delaney, D. (2015) 'Legal geography I: constitutivities, complexities, and contingencies', *Progress in Human Geography*, 39(1): 96–102.

Delaney, D. (2016) 'Legal geography II: discerning injustice', *Progress in Human Geography*, 40(2): 267–74.

DELWP [Department of Environment, Land, Water and Planning] (2015) *Better Apartments: A Discussion Paper*, Melbourne: Victorian Government.

Dodson, J. (2012) 'Transforming Australia's "housing solution": how we can better plan suburbia to meet our future challenges', in R. Tomlinson R (ed) *Australia's Unintended Cities: The Impact of Housing on Urban Development*, Melbourne: CSIRO, pp 19–34.

Doling, J. (1999) 'De-commodification and welfare: evaluating housing systems', *Housing, Theory and Society*, 16(4): 156–64.

Dorignon, L. and Nethercote, M. (2020) 'Disorientation in the unmaking of high-rise homes', *Transactions of the Institute of British Geographers*, doi.org/10.1111/tran.12427.

Dow, A. (2016) 'Mysterious Padlocks Hanging in Melbourne's CBD a Telltale Sign of Short-stay Rentals', *The Age*, 10 June. Available from: www.theage.com.au/national/victoria/mysterious-padlocks-hanging-in-melbournes-cbd-a-telltale-sign-of-shortstay-rentals-20160609-gpfqgx.html

Dowling, R. and Mee, K. (2007) 'Home and homemaking in contemporary Australia', *Housing, Theory and Society*, 24(3): 161–5.

Dowling, R. and Power, E. (2012) 'Sizing home, doing family in Sydney, Australia', *Housing Studies*, 27(5): 605–19.

DPLH [Department of Planning, Lands and Heritage] (2019) *WA Tomorrow: Population Report No. 11: Medium-Term Age-Sex Population Forecasts, 2016 to 2031*. Population Report No. 11, Perth: DPLH. Available from: www.dplh.wa.gov.au/getmedia/c0a3f4c1-9ccd-439b-a133-6791149c87ef/LSD-WAT-Population-Report-No-11

Dredge, D. and Coiacetto, E. (2011) 'Strata title: towards a research agenda for informed planning practice', *Planning Practice and Research*, 26(4): 417–33.

Drozdz, M., Appert, M. and Harris, A. (2018) 'High-Rise Urbanism in Contemporary Europe', *Built Environment*, 43(4): 469–80.

Drying for Freedom (2012) [film] Available from: https://whitelantern.film/projects/dryingforfreedom/

Dyck, I., Kontos, P., Angus, J. and McKeever, P. (2005) 'The home as a site for long-term care: meanings and management of bodies and spaces', *Health & Place*, 11(2): 173–85.

Easthope, H. (2004) 'A place called home', *Housing, Theory and Society*, 21(3): 128–38.

Easthope, H. (2014) 'Making a rental property home', *Housing Studies*, 29(5): 579–96.

Easthope, H. (2019) *The Politics and Practices of Apartment Living*, Cheltenham: Edward Elgar.

Easthope, H. and Judd, S. (2010) *Living Well in Greater Density*, NSW: Shelter.

Easthope, H. and Tice, A. (2011) 'Children in apartments: implications for the compact city', *Urban Policy and Research*, 29(4): 415–34.

Easthope, H. and Randolph, B. (2018) 'Collective responsibility in strata apartments', in E. Altmann and M. Gabriel (eds) *Multi-Owned Property in the Asia-Pacific Region: Rights, Restrictions and Responsibilities*, London: Palgrave Macmillan, pp 177–95.

Easthope, H., Randolph, B. and Judd, S. (2012) *Governing the Compact City: The Role and Effectiveness of Strata Management*, Sydney: City Futures Research Centre, UNSW.

Easthope, H., Buckle, C. and Mann, V. (2018) *Australian National Strata Data*, Sydney: City Futures Research Centre, UNSW. Available from: https://cityfutures.be.unsw.edu.au/research/projects/national-strata-data-analysis/

Easthope, H., Warnken, J., Sherry, C., Coiacetto, E., Dredge, D., Guilding, C., Johnston, N., Lamminmaki, D. and Reid, S. (2014) 'How property title impacts urban consolidation: a life cycle examination of multi-title developments', *Urban Policy and Research*, 32(3): 289–304.

Elias, N. and Scotson, J. (1994) *The Established and the Outsiders* (Vol 32), London: Sage.

Ewick, P. and Silbey, S. (1998) *The Common Place of Law: Stories from Everyday Life*, Chicago: University of Chicago Press.

Farnsworth, S. (2018) 'Residents in Apartment Buildings Slugged Thousands to Change Power Companies', *ABC News*, 25 July. Available from: www.abc.net.au/news/2018-07-25/residents-in-apartments-slugged-thousands-to-change-power-supply/10029842

Fincher, R. (2004) 'Gender and life course in the narratives of Melbourne's high-rise housing developers', *Australian Geographical Studies*, 42(3): 325–38.

Fincher, R. (2007) 'Is high-rise housing innovative? Developers' contradictory narratives of high-rise housing in Melbourne', *Urban Studies*, 44(3): 631–49.

Fincher, R. and Gooder, H. (2007) 'At home with diversity in medium-density housing', *Housing, Theory and Society*, 24(3): 166–82.

Fincher, R. and Shaw, K. (2011) 'Enacting separate social worlds: "international" and "local" students in public space in central Melbourne', *Geoforum*, 42(5), 539–49.

Fisher, R. and McPhail, R. (2014) 'Residents' experiences in condominiums: a case study of Australian apartment living', *Housing Studies*, 29(6): 781–99.

Forrest, R., Koh, S. and Wissink, B. (eds) (2017) *Cities and the Super-Rich: Real Estate, Elite Practices and Urban Political Economies*, New York: Palgrave Macmillan.

Forster, C. (2006) 'The challenge of change: Australian cities and urban planning in the new millennium', *Geographical Research*, 44(2): 173–82.

Fox O'Mahony, L. (2012) 'The meanings of home', in S. Smith (ed) *International Encyclopaedia of Housing and Home (Vol 7)*, Amsterdam: Elsevier, pp 231–9.

Garvey, P. (2005) 'Domestic boundaries: privacy, visibility and the Norwegian window', *Journal of Material Culture*, 10(2): 157–76.

Geoghegan, T. (2010) 'The Fight Against Clothes Lines Bans', *BBC New Magazine*, 7 October. Available from: www.bbc.com/news/magazine-11417677

Ghosh, S. (2014) 'Everyday lives in vertical neighbourhoods: exploring Bangladeshi residential spaces in Toronto's inner suburbs', *International Journal of Urban and Regional Research*, 38(6): 2008–24.

GLA [Greater London Authority] (2018) *Housing in London 2018*, GLA, July 2018. Available from: www.data.london.gov.uk

Glaeser, E. (2011) *Triumph of the City: How our Greatest Invention Makes us Richer, Smarter, Greener, Healthier, and Happier*, United States: Penguin.

Glasze, G. (2003) 'Private neighbourhoods as club economies and shareholder democracies', *Revue Belge de Géographie*, 1: 87–98.

Glasze, G., Webster, C. and Frantz, K. (2004) *Private Cities: Global and Local Perspectives*, Oxon: Routledge.

Gleeson, B. (2008) 'Critical commentary. Waking from the dream: an Australian perspective on urban resilience', *Urban Studies*, 45(13): 2653–68.

Gleeson, B. (2017a) 'Market-driven Compaction Is No Way to Build an Eco-city', *The Conversation*, 10 July. Available from: https://theconversation.com/market-driven-compaction-is-no-way-to-build-an-ecocity-80199

Gleeson, B. (2017b) 'The metropolitan condition', in S. Hamnett and R. Freestone (eds) *Planning Metropolitan Australia*, London: Routledge, pp 195–211.

Gleeson, B. and Sipe, N. (2006) 'Reinstating kids in the city', in B. Gleeson and N. Sipe (eds) *Creating Child Friendly Cities: Reinstating Kids in the City*, London: Routledge, pp 1–10.

Goffman, E. (1961) *Encounters: Two Studies in the Sociology of Interaction (2013 edn)*, United States: Martino Fine Books.

Gorman-Murray, A. (2011) 'Economic crises and emotional fallout: work, home and men's senses of belonging in post-GFC Sydney', *Emotion, Space and Society*, 4(4): 211–20.

Graham, S. (2016a) *Vertical: The City from Satellites to Bunkers*, London: Verso.

Graham, S. (2016b) Vanity and Violence, *City*, 20(5): 755–71.

Graham, S. and Hewitt, L. (2013) 'Getting off the ground: on the politics of urban verticality', *Progress in Human Geography*, 37(1): 72–92.

Grattan Institute (2013) *The Housing We'd Choose: A Study for Perth and Peel*, Perth: Grattan Institute. Available from: www.housing.wa.gov.au/HousingDocuments/Housing_We_Choose_Summary_Report.PDF

Guilding, C., Warnken, J., Ardill, A. and Fredline, L. (2005) 'An agency theory perspective on the owner/manager relationship in tourism-based condominiums', *Tourism Management*, 26(3): 409–20.

Gurney, C. (2000) 'Transgressing private-public boundaries in the home: a sociological analysis of the coital noise taboo', *Venereology*, 13(1): 39.

Harris, A. (2015) Vertical urbanisms: opening up geographies of the three-dimensional city', *Progress in Human Geography*, 39(5): 601–20.

Harris, D. (2011) 'Condominium and the city: the rise of property in Vancouver', *Law & Social Inquiry*, 36(3): 694–726.

Harris, D. (2019) 'Condominium government and the right to live in the city', *Canadian Journal of Law & Society/La Revue Canadienne Droit et Société*, 34(3): 371–92.

Harris, D. and Gilewicz, N. (2015) 'Dissolving condominium, private takings, and the nature of property', in B. Hoops, E. Marais, H. Mostert, J. Sluysmans and L. Verstappen (eds) *Rethinking Expropriation Law II: Context, Criteria, and Consequences of Expropriation*, Portland: Eleven, pp 263–97.

Harris, E., Brickell, K. and Nowicki, M. (2020) 'Door locks, wall stickers, fireplaces: assemblage theory and home (un)making in Lewisham's temporary accommodation', *Antipode*, 52(5): 1286–309.

Harvey, D. (2008) 'The Right of the City,' *New Left Review*, September/October 2008(53). Available from: https://newleftreview.org/issues/II53/articles/avid-harvey-the-right-to-the-city.pdf

Hatherley, O. (2009) *Militant Modernism*, Hants: O Books.

Heller, M. (1998) 'The tragedy of the anticommons: property in the transition from Marx to markets', *Harvard Law Review*, 111(3): 621–88.

Heller, M. (1999) 'The boundaries of private property', *The Yale Law Journal*, 108(6): 1163–223.

Heller, M. (2005) 'Common interest developments at the crossroads of legal theory', *Urban Lawyer*, 37(3): 329–34.

Heller, M. (2008) *The Gridlock Economy: How too much Ownership Wrecks Markets, Stops Innovation, and Costs Lives*, New York: Basic.

HIFG [Housing Industry Forecasting Group] (2016) 'Forecast Dwelling Commencements in Western Australia: April 2016 Update', Perth: Housing Industry Forecasting Group. Available from: www.dplh.wa.gov.au/getmedia/ea5159e3-9167-43b6-b9a4-9116b07ced7b/HIFG_Update_April_2016

HIFG [Housing Industry Forecasting Group] (2019) 'Forecast Dwelling Commencements in Western Australia: 2018–19 Update', Perth: Housing Industry Forecasting Group. Available from: www.dplh.wa.gov.au/getmedia/c5c2de8f-3cca-452c-b600-64b2071ad380/HIFG_Update_May_2019

Hilbrandt, H. (2019) 'Everyday urbanism and the everyday state: negotiating habitat in allotment gardens in Berlin', *Urban Studies*, 56(2): 352–67.

Hilbrandt, H. (2021) *Housing in the Margins: Negotiating Urban Formalities in Berlin's Allotment Gardens*, Chichester: Wiley.

Hobday, L. (2019) 'Embedded Electricity Networks See Apartment Dwellers Paying Too Much for Power', *ABC News*, 30 October. Available from: www.abc.net.au/news/2019-10-30/embedded-electricity-networks-energy-customers-paying-too-much/11653730

Hodkinson, S. (2019) *Safe as Houses: Private Greed, Political Negligence and Housing Policy after Grenfell*, Manchester: Manchester University Press.

Holton, M. and Mouat, C. (2020) 'The rise (and rise) of vertical studentification: exploring the drivers of studentification in Australia', *Urban Studies*, 58(9): 1866–84.

Horne, R. and Nethercote, M. (2015) 'Life in a Windowless Box: The Vertical Slums of Melbourne', *The Conversation*, 18 May. Available from: https://theconversation.com/life-in-a-windowless-box-the-vertical-slums-of-melbourne-41181

Hulse, K. (2008) 'Shaky foundations: moving beyond "housing tenure"', *Housing, Theory and Society*, 25(3): 202–19.

Hulse, K., Milligan, V. and Easthope, H. (2011) *Secure Occupancy in Rental Housing: Conceptual Foundations and Comparative Perspectives*, AHURI Final Report No. 170, Melbourne: Australian Housing and Urban Research Institute.

Hulse, K., Morris, A. and Pawson, H. (2018a) 'Private renting in a home-owning society: disaster, diversity or deviance?', *Housing, Theory and Society*, 36(2): 167–88.

Hulse, K., Parkinson, S. and Martin, C. (2018b) *Inquiry into the Future of the Private Rental Sector*, AHURI Final Report No. 303, Melbourne: Australian Housing and Urban Research Institute.

Jacobs, J. and Smith, S. (2008) 'Living room: rematerialising home', *Environment and Planning A: Economy and Space*, 40: 515–19.

Jacobs, J., Cairns, S. and Strebel, I. (2012) 'Doing building work: methods at the interface of geography and architecture', *Geographical Research*, 50(2): 126–40.

Johnston, N. and Reid, S. (2019) *An Examination of Building Defects in Residential Multi-owned Properties*, Melbourne: Deakin University and Griffith University. Available from: www.griffith.edu.au/__data/assets/pdf_file/0030/831279/Examining-Building-Defects-Research-Report.pdf

Kaika, M. (2010) 'Architecture and crisis: re-inventing the icon, re-imag(in)ing London and re-branding the city', *Transactions of the Institute of British Geographers*, 35(4): 453–74.

Kaika, M. and Thielen. K. (2006) 'Form follows power: a genealogy of urban shrine', *City*, 10(1): 59–69.

Kärrholm, M. (2007) 'The materiality of territorial production: a conceptual discussion of territoriality, materiality, and the everyday life of public space', *Space and Culture*, 10(4): 437–53.

Kearns, A., Hiscock, R., Ellaway, A. and Macintyre, S. (2000) '"Beyond four walls". The psycho-social benefits of home: evidence from west central Scotland', *Housing Studies*, 15(3): 387–410.

Keenan, S. (2015) *Subversive Property: Law and the Production of Spaces of Belonging*, Oxon: Routledge.

Keil, R. (2017) *Suburban Planet: Making the World Urban from the Outside in*, Cambridge: Polity Press.

Kelly, J., Weidmann, B. and Walsh, M. (2011) *The Housing We'd Choose*, Melbourne: Grattan Institute. Available from: https://grattan.edu.au/wp-content/uploads/2014/04/090_cities_report_housing_market.pdf

Kemp, P. (2015) 'Private renting after the global financial crisis', *Housing Studies*, 30(4): 601–20.

Kern, L. (2010) 'Selling the "scary city": gendering freedom, fear and condominium development in the neoliberal city', *Social & Cultural Geography*, 11(3): 209–30.

Kern, L. (2011) *Sex and the Revitalized City: Gender, Condominium Development, and Urban Citizenship*, Vancouver: UBC.

Kerr, S., Gibson, C. and Klocker, N. (2018) 'Parenting and neighbouring in the consolidating city: the emotional geographies of sound in apartments', *Emotion, Space and Society*, 26: 1–8.

Kerr, S., Klocker, N. and Gibson, C. (2020) 'From backyards to balconies: cultural norms and parents' experiences of home in higher-density housing', *Housing Studies*, 36(3): 421–43.

Kitchin, R. and Hubbard, P. (1999) 'Research, action and "critical" geographies', *Area*, 31(3): 195–8.

Kondos, A. (1980) 'The hidden faces of power: a sociological analysis of housing legislation in Australia', in R. Tomasic (ed) *Legislation and Society in Australia*, NSW: Allen & Unwin/Law Foundation of NSW.

La Grange, A. (2014) 'Hong Kong's gating machine', *Housing Studies*, 29(2): 251–69.

Lasner, M. (2012) *High Life: Condo Living in the Suburban Century*, New Haven: Yale.

Laurier, E., Whyte. A. and Buckner, K (2002) 'Neighbouring as an occasioned activity: finding a lost cat', *Space and Culture*, 5(4): 346–67.

Lee, S. and Webster, C. (2006) 'Enclosure of the urban commons', *GeoJournal*, 66(1–2): 27–42.

Lees, L. (2018) 'Comparative urbanism in gentrification studies: fashion or progress?', in L. Lees with M. Phillips (eds) *Handbook of Gentrification Studies*, Cheltenham: Edward Elgar, pp 49–62.

Lees, L. and Baxter, R. (2011) 'A "building event" of fear: thinking through the geography of architecture', *Social & Cultural Geography*, 12(02): 107–22.

Lefebvre, H. (1967) 'The right to the city', in H. Lefebvre, E. Kofman and E. Lebas (eds and trans), *Writings on Cities* (Vol 63, 1996 edn), Oxford: Blackwell, pp 63–181.

Le Goix, R. (2005) 'Gated communities as predators of public resources: the outcomes of fading boundaries between private management and public authorities in Southern California', in G. Glasze, C. Webster and K. Frantz (eds) *Private Cities: Local and Global Perspectives*, London: Routledge.

Le Goix, R. and Webster, C. (2008) 'Gated communities', *Geography Compass*, 2(4): 1189–214.

Lehavi, A. (2008) 'Mixing property', *Seton Hall L. Rev.*, 38: 137–212.

Lehavi, A. (2015) 'Law, collective action and culture: condominium governance in comparative perspective', *Asia Pacific Law Review*, 23(2): 5–35.

Lehavi, A. (ed) (2016) *Private Communities and Urban Governance: Theoretical and Comparative Perspectives*, Springer.

Lehrer, U. and Wieditz, T. (2009) 'Condominium development and gentrification: the relationship between policies, building activities and socio-economic development in Toronto', *Canadian Journal of Urban Research*, 18(1):140–61.

Lehrer, U. and Pantalone, P. (2018) 'Negotiating height and density in Toronto's condominium boom', in K. Ward, A. Jonas, B. Miller, and D. Wilson (eds) *The Routledge Handbook on Spaces of Urban Politics*, Oxon: Routledge, pp 85–95.

Lehrer, U., Keil, R. and Kipfer, S. (2010) 'Reurbanization in Toronto: condominium boom and social housing revitalization', *DisP – The Planning Review*, 46(180): 81–90.

Leshinsky, R., Douglas, K., Condliffe, P. and Goodman, R. (2012) 'Dispute resolution under the Owners' Corporation Act 2006 (Vic): engaging with conflict in communal living', *Property Law Review*, 2: 39–63.

Lippert, R. (2012) 'Governing condominiums and renters with legal knowledge flows and external institutions', *Law & Policy*, 34(3): 263–90.

Lippert, R. (2019) *Condo Conquest: Urban Governance, Law, and Condoization in New York City and Toronto*, Vancouver: UBC Press.

Lippert, R. and Steckle, R. (2016) 'Conquering condos from within: condo-isation as urban governance and knowledge', *Urban Studies*, 53(1): 132–48.

Lippert, R. and Treffers, S. (2016) 'Legal knowledges and surveillance in the condo world', *Social & Legal Studies*, 25(4): 419–40.

Lippert, R. and Treffers, S. (2020) 'The Condominium's Grim Reapers: Coronavirus and Recession', *The Conversation*, 10 April. Available from: https://theconversation.com/the-condominiums-grim-reapers-coronavirus-and-recession-135662

Lippert, R., Treffers, S. and Bud, T. (2017) 'Condo crimes and legal prospects for confronting the unusual suspects', in A. Sarat (ed) *Studies in Law, Politics, and Society*, Vol 72, Emerald, pp 25–52.

Liu, E., Easthope, H., Ho, C. and Buckle, C. (2018) 'Diversity and participation in private apartment buildings: a review of the literature', *Geographical Research*, 56(4): 401–09.

Lloyd, J. and Vasta, E. (2017) 'Reimagining home in the 21st century', in J. Lloyd and E. Vasta (eds) *Reimagining Home in the 21st Century*, Cheltenham: Edward Elgar, pp 1–18.

Low, S. (2004) *Behind the Gates: Life, Security, and the Pursuit of Happiness in Fortress America*, New York: Routledge.

Low, S. (2008) 'Fortification of residential neighbourhoods and the new emotions of home', *Housing, Theory and Society*, 25(1): 47–65.

Low, S., Donovan, G. and Gieseking, J. (2012) 'Shoestring democracy: gated condominiums and market-rate cooperatives in New York', *Journal of Urban Affairs*, 34: 279–96.

Lucas, C. and Carey, A. (2018) 'Labor and Coalition Offer Rival Power Plans as State Election Looms', *The Age*, 26 October. Available from: www.theage.com.au/politics/victoria/labor-and-coalition-offer-rival-power-plans-as-state-election-looms-20181026-p50c25.html

Madden, D. and Marcuse, P. (2016) *In Defense of Housing: The Politics of Crisis*, London: Verso.

Maginn, P. and Foley, N. (2017) 'Perth: from "large provincial city" to "globalizing city"', in S. Hamnett and R. Freestone (eds) *Planning Metropolitan Australia*, London: Routledge, pp 124–47.

Mallett, S. (2004) 'Understanding home: a critical review of the literature', *The Sociological Review*, 52(1): 62–89.

Mandič, S. and Hrast, M. (2019) 'Homeownership in multi-apartment buildings: control beyond property rights', *Housing, Theory and Society*, 36(4): 401–25.

Manning, P. (1992) *Erving Goffman and Modern Sociology* (2013 edn), Cambridge: John Wiley & Sons.

Marcuse, P. (2020) 'Wealth accumulation through home ownership: the painful myth of housing tenure, and what to do about it', *City*, 24(1–2): 130–6.

Martin, C., Hulse, K., Pawson, H., Hayden, A., Kofner, S., Schwartz, A. and Stephens, M. (2018) *The Changing Institutions of Private Rental Housing: An International Review*, AHURI Final Report No. 292, Melbourne: Australian Housing and Urban Research Institute.

Massey, D. (1992) 'A place called home', *New Formations*, 17(3): 3–15.

Massey, D. (1994) *Space, Place and Gender*, Cambridge: Polity.

McFarlane, C. (2016) 'The geographies of urban density: topology, politics and the city', *Progress in Human Geography*, 40(5): 629–48.

McGuirk, P. and Dowling, R. (2011) 'Governing social reproduction in masterplanned estates: urban politics and everyday life in Sydney', *Urban Studies*, 48(12): 2611–28.

McKenzie, E. (2011) *Beyond Privatopia: Rethinking Residential Private Government*, Washington, DC: Urban Institute.

McKenzie, E. (2016) 'Rethinking residential private government in the US: recent trends in practices and policy', in A. Lehavi (ed) *Private Communities and Urban Governance*, Springer: Switzerland.

McNeill, D. (2005) 'Skyscraper geography', *Progress in Human Geography*, 29(1): 41–55.

McNeill, D. (2009) *The Global Architect: Firms, Fame and Urban Form*, New York: Routledge.

Mee, K. (2007) '"I ain't been to heaven yet? Living here, this is heaven to me": public housing and the making of home in inner Newcastle', *Housing, Theory and Society*, 24: 207–28.

Mee, K. and Wright, S. (2009) 'Geographies of belonging', *Environment and Planning A: Economy and Space*, 41: 772–9.

Merry, S. (1990) *Getting Justice and Getting Even: Legal Consciousness among Working-class Americans*, London: University of Chicago Press.

MFB [Metropolitan Fire Brigade] & City of Melbourne (nd) *Fire Safety on Balconies*, City of Melbourne and the Metropolitan Fire Brigade. Available from: www.melbourne.vic.gov.au/sitecollectiondocuments/fire-safety-balconies.pdf

Midgley, C. (2019) 'Net curtains Are a Crime Against Humanity', *The Times*, 18 February. Available from: www.thetimes.co.uk/article/net-curtains-are-a-crime-against-humanity-87gxgnwwn

Millet, P. (1999) Judgments – London Borough of Southwark and Another v. Mills and Others (A.P.); Baxter (A.P.) v. Mayor etc. of the London Borough of Camden, 21 October 1999. Available from: https://publications.parliament.uk/pa/ld199899/ldjudgmt/jd991021/mills-2.htm

Mitchell, D. (2003) *The Right to the City: Social Justice and the Fight for Public Space*, New York: Guilford.

Moos, M. (2016) 'From gentrification to youthification? The increasing importance of young age in delineating high-density living', *Urban Studies*, 53(14): 2903–20.

Morgan, J. (2019) '(Net) curtains for modern architecture? Privacy, nuisance and human rights', *Cambridge Law Journal*, 78(2): 273–6.

Morris, A. (2009) 'Living on the margins: comparing older private renters and older public housing tenants in Sydney, Australia', *Housing Studies*, 24(5): 693–707.

Munro, M. and Madigan, R. (1999) 'Negotiating space in the family home', in I. Cieraad (ed) *At Home: An Anthropology of Domestic Space*. Syracuse: Syracuse University Press, pp 107–17.

Murie, A. (2019) *Building on What We Know: Fault Lines for Housing Research?* Housing Studies Association. Available from: www.housing-studies-association.org/posts/144-building-on-what-we-know-fault-lines-for-housing-research

National Shelter [National Shelter, CHOICE, and the National Association of Tenant Organisations] (2018) *Disrupted: A Report into the Consumer Experience of Renting in Australia*, NSW: National Shelter.

Nedelsky, J. (2011) *Law's Relations: A Relational Theory of Self, Autonomy, and Law*, Oxford: Oxford University Press.

Nethercote, M. (2017) 'When social infrastructure deficits create displacement pressures: inner city schools and the suburbanization of families in Melbourne', *International Journal of Urban and Regional Research*, 41(3): 443–63.

Nethercote, M. (2018) 'Theorising vertical urbanisation', *City*, 22(5–6): 657–84.

Nethercote, M. (2019) 'Melbourne's vertical expansion and the political economies of high-rise residential development', *Urban Studies*, 56(16): 3394–414.

Nethercote, M. (2020) 'Build-to-rent and the financialization of rental housing: future research directions', *Housing Studies*, 35(5): 839–74.

Nethercote, M. (forthcoming) 'Racialized geographies of home: property, unhoming and other possible futures', *Progress in Human Geography*.

Nethercote, M. and Horne, R. (2016) 'Ordinary vertical urbanisms: city apartments and the everyday geographies of high-rise families', *Environment and Planning A*, 48(8): 1581–98.

Newman, O. (1972) *Defensible Space*, New York: Macmillan.

Nicholls, S., O'Neill, S. and Selvaratnam, N. (2019) 'A Legacy of Defects', *ABC Four Corners*. Available from: www.abc.net.au/news/2019-08-18/how-bad-could-the-apartment-building-crisis-be-in-your-state/11413122?nw=0

Nowicki, M. (2014) 'Rethinking domicide: towards an expanded critical geography of home', *Geography Compass*, 8(11): 785–95.

OCN [Owners Corporation Network of Australia Limited] (2015) *Adequacy of the Regulation of Short-term Holiday Letting in New South Wales: Submission to Parliamentary Inquiry (Submission No. 191)*, Sydney, Australia: OCN, 9 November. Available from: www.parliament.nsw.gov.au/ladocs/submissions/53808/Submission%20No%20191%20-%20Owners%20Corporation%20Network.PDF

O'Connell, M. (2020) 'Why We Are Living in JG Ballard's World', *New Statesman*, 1 April. Available from: www.newstatesman.com/2020/04/why-we-are-living-jg-ballard-s-world

Ong, A. (2011) 'Hyperbuilding: spectacle, speculation, and the hyperspace of sovereignty', in A. Roy, and A. Ong (eds) *Worlding Cities: Asian Experiments and the Art of Being Global*, London: Wiley, pp 205–26.

PA [Press Association] (2018) 'Flat Owners Take Tate Modern to Court over "Invasion of Privacy"', *The Guardian*, 3 November. Available from: www.theguardian.com/artanddesign/2018/nov/02/flat-owners-neo-bankside-tate-modern-court-over-invasion-privacy

Pawson, H. (2017) 'One in 10 Australian Dwellings Are Empty – and a Vacancy Tax Won't Solve the Problem', *ABC News*, July 2017. Available from: www.abc.net.au/news/ 2017-07-17/vacancy-tax-wont-solve-australias- empty-housing-problem/8709184

Pawson, H., Hulse, K. and Morris, A. (2017) 'Interpreting the rise of long-term private renting in a liberal welfare regime context', *Housing Studies*, 32(8): 1062–84.

Pawson, H., Milligan, M. and Yates, J. (2020) *Housing Policy in Australia: A Case for System Reform*, Singapore: Palgrave Macmillan.

Peck, J., Siemiatycki, E. and Wyly, E. (2014) 'Vancouver's suburban involution', *City*, 18(4–5): 386–415.

Penner, J. (2000) 'Nuisance, the morality of neighbourliness, and environmental protection', in J. Lowry and R. Edmunds (eds) *Environmental Protection and the Common Law*, Oxford: Hart, pp 27–50.

Perin, C. (1988) *Belonging in America: Reading Between the Lines*, Madison: University of Wisconsin.

Pow, C. (2009a) 'Public intervention, private aspiration: gated communities and the condominisation of housing landscapes in Singapore', *Asia Pacific Viewpoint*, 50(2): 215–27.

Pow, C. (2009b) 'Neoliberalism and the aestheticization of new middle-class landscapes', *Antipode*, 41: 371–90.

Pow, C. (2015) 'Urban dystopia and epistemologies of hope', *Progress in Human Geography*, 39(4): 464–85.

Power, E. (2009a) 'Domestic temporalities: nature times in the house-as-home', *Geoforum*, 40(6): 1024–32.

Power, E. (2009b) 'Border-processes and homemaking: encounters with possums in suburban Australian homes', *Cultural Geographies*, 16(1): 29–54.

Power, E. (2015) 'Placing community self-governance: building materialities, nuisance noise and neighbouring in self-governing communities', *Urban Studies*, 52(2): 245–60.

Power, E. and Gillon, C. (2020) 'Performing the "good tenant"', *Housing Studies*, DOI 10.1080/02673037.2020.1813260.

Probyn, E. (1996) *Outside Belonging*, London: Routledge.

PwC & ULI [PricewaterhouseCoopers & Urban Land Institute] (2019) *Emerging Trends in Real Estate 2019: United States and Canada 2019*, Washington, DC: PwC and the Urban Land Institute. ISBN: 978-0-87420-418-6. Available from: www.pwc.com/mx/es/publicaciones/archivo/2019/02/20190227-pwc-mx-emerging-trends-in-real-estate-2019.pdf

Rainwater, L. (1966) 'Fear and the house-as-haven in the lower class', *Journal of the American Institute of Planners*, 32: 23–31.

Randolph, B. (2020) 'Dimensions of urban segregation at the end of the Australian dream', in S. Musterd (ed) *Handbook of Urban Segregation*, Edward Elgar, pp 76–100.

Randolph, B. and Tice, A. (2013) 'Who lives in higher density housing? A study of spatially discontinuous housing sub-markets in Sydney and Melbourne', *Urban Studies*, 50(13): 2661–81.

Randolph, B. and Easthope, H. (2014) 'The rise of micro-government: strata title, reluctant democrats and the new urban vertical polity', in B. Gleeson and B. Beza (eds) *The Public City: Essays in Honour of Paul Mees*, Carlton, Melbourne University Press, pp 210–24.

Raynor, K. (2018) 'Social representations of children in higher density housing: enviable, inevitable or evil?', *Housing Studies*, 33(8): 1207–26.

Raynor, K., Matthews, T. and Mayere, S. (2017) 'Shaping urban consolidation debates: social representations in Brisbane newspaper media', *Urban Studies*, 54: 1519–36.

RBA [Reserve Bank of Australia] (2014) *Submission to the Inquiry into Affordable Housing, Submissions: Housing and Housing Finance*, Senate Economics References Committee, February 2014. Available from: www.rba.gov.au/publications/submissions/housing-and-housing-finance/inquiry-affordable-housing/

RBA [Reserve Bank of Australia] (2017) *Houses and Apartments in Australia*, Bulletin June Quarter 2017, Canberra: RBA. Available from: https://rba.gov.au/publications/bulletin/2017/jun/pdf/bu-0617-1-houses-and-apartments-in-australia.pdf

RBA [Reserve Bank of Australia] (2019) Financial Stability Review – April 2019: Box C: Risks in High-density Apartment Markets, Canberra: RBA. Available from: https://www.rba.gov.au/publications/fsr/2019/apr/box-c.html

Reid, S. (2015) 'Exploring social interactions and sense of community in multi-owned properties', *International Journal of Housing Markets and Analysis*, 8(4): 436–50.

Reid, S., Lloyd, K., O'Brien, W. and Guilding, C. (2017a) 'Power, ethopolitics and community relations: complexities of living in multi-owned properties', *Housing, Theory and Society*, 34(4): 439–57.

Reid, S., Lloyd, K. and O'Brien, W. (2017b) 'Women's perspectives on liveability in vertical communities: a feminist materialist approach', *Australian Planner*, 54(1): 16–23.

Richardson, J. (2018) *Place and Identity: The Performance of Home*, Routledge.

Robinson, J. (2006) *Ordinary Cities: Between Modernity and Development*, Oxon: Routledge.

Robinson, J. (2016a) 'Comparative urbanism: new geographies and cultures of theorizing the urban', *International Journal of Urban and Regional Research*, 40(1): 187–99.

Robinson, J. (2016b) 'Thinking cities through elsewhere: comparative tactics for a more global urban studies', *Progress in Human Geography*, 40(1): 3–29.

Roelofsen, M. (2018) 'Performing "home" in the sharing economies of tourism: the Airbnb experience in Sofia, Bulgaria', *Fennia-International Journal of Geography*, 196(1): 24–42.

Rollwagen, H. (2015) 'Constructing renters as a threat to neighbourhood safety', *Housing Studies*, 30(1): 1–21.

Rollwagen, H. (2016) 'The relationship between dwelling type and fear of crime', *Environment and Behavior*, 48(2): 365–87.

Ronald, R. (2008) *The Ideology of Home Ownership: Homeowner Societies and the Role of Housing*, Hampshire: Palgrave Macmillan.

Rose, C. (1994) *Property and Persuasion: Essays on the History, Theory, and Rhetoric of Ownership* (2019 edn), Oxon: Routledge.

Rose, N. (2000) 'Community, citizenship and the third way', *American Behavioural Scientist*, 43: 1395–411.

Rose, N. (2001) 'The politics of life itself', *Theory, Culture & Society*, 18(6): 1–30.

Rosen, G. (2017) 'Toronto's condo-builders: development approaches and spatial preferences', *Urban Geography*, 38(4): 606–25.

Rosen, G. and Walks, A. (2013) 'Rising cities: condominium development and the private transformation of the metropolis', *Geoforum*, 49: 160–72.

Rosen, G. and Walks, A. (2015) 'Castles in Toronto's sky: condo-ism as urban transformation', *Journal of Urban Affairs*, 37(3): 289–310.

Rowley, S., Ong, R. and James, A. (2017) *Perth's Infill Housing Future: Delivering Innovative and Sustainable Housing*, Perth: Curtin University. Available from: http://bcec.edu.au/assets/BCEC-Perths-Infill-Housing-Future-web-2.pdf

Roy, A. (2003) 'Paradigms of propertied citizenship: transnational techniques of analysis', *Urban Affairs Review*, 38(4): 463–91.

Ruonavaara, H. (1993) 'Types and forms of housing tenure: towards solving the comparison/translation problem', *Scandinavian Housing and Planning Research*, 10(1): 3–20.

Ruonavaara, H. (2012) 'Tenure as an institution', in S. Smith (ed) *International Encyclopaedia of Housing and Home*, Amsterdam: Elsevier, pp 185–9.

Sack, R. (1985) *Human Territoriality: Its Theory and History*, New York: Cambridge University Press.

Saunders, B., Kitzinger, J. and Kitzinger, C. (2015) 'Anonymising interview data: challenges and compromise in practice', *Qualitative Research*, 15(5): 616–32.

Saunders, P. and Williams, P. (1988) 'The constitution of the home: towards a research agenda', *Housing Studies*, 3(2): 81–93.

Schwartz, W. (1964) 'Condominium: hybrid castle in the sky', *Boston University Law Review*, 44: 37–55.

Scotsman (2019) 'Edinburgh AirBnB Hosts Using Key-storing Padlocks in City Parks to Avoid Legal Issues', *The Scotsman*, 11 February. Available from: www.edinburghnews.scotsman.com/news/edinburgh-airbnb-hosts-using-key-storing-padlocks-city-parks-avoid-legal-issues-122822

Searle, G. (2004) 'The limits to urban consolidation', *Australian Planner*, 41(1): 42–8.

SGS (2018) *Apartment Design Policy Economic Evaluation*, Final Report prepared for Department of Planning, Land and Heritage (Western Australia), Melbourne: SGS Economics & Planning. Available from: www.dplh.wa.gov.au/getmedia/bd90c8e7-7811-4df0-a374-4a97e614b6bf/DWA-SGS-ADP-Economic-Evaluation-and-Secret-Agent-Report

Shaw, K. (2013) 'Docklands dreamings: illusions of sustainability in the Melbourne Docks redevelopment', *Urban Studies*, 50(11): 2158–77.

Sherry, C. (2008) 'The legal fundamentals of high rise buildings and master planned estates: ownership, governance and living in multi-owned housing with a case study on children's play', *Australian Property Law Journal*, 16(1): 1–23.

Sherry, C. (2013) 'Lessons in personal freedom and functional land markets: what strata and community title can learn from traditional doctrines of property', *The University of New South Wales Law Journal*, 36(1): 280–315.

Sherry, C. (2016) *Strata Title Property Rights: Private Governance of Multi-owned Properties*, London: Routledge.

Sherry, C. (2018) 'Conflict between private and public restrictions, in E. Altmann and M. Gabriel (eds) *Multi-Owned Property in the Asia-Pacific Region*, London: Palgrave Macmillan, pp 105–18.

Shilon, M. and Eizenberg, E. (2020) 'Experiencing vertical living: affects, atmospheres, and technology', *Planning Theory*, 20(2): 121–42.

Simmel, G. (1908) *Georg Simmel: On Individuality and Social Forms* (1971 edn) Chicago: University of Chicago Press.

Singer, J. (2000) *Entitlement: The Paradoxes of Property*, London: Yale.

Singh, A. (2019) 'Tate Modern Neighbours Who Said Viewing Platform Made Them Feel Like Zoo Specimens Lose Privacy Battle', *The Telegraph*, 12 February. Available from: www.telegraph.co.uk/news/2019/02/12/tate-modern-neighbours-lose-privacy-battle-judge-says-put-net/

Sklair, L. (2017) *The Icon Project: Architecture, Cities, and Capitalist Globalization*, Oxford: Oxford University Press.

Soaita, A.M. and McKee, K. (2019) 'Assembling a "kind of" home in the UK private renting sector', *Geoforum*, 103: 148–57.

Somerville, P. (1997) 'The social construction of home', *Journal of Architectural and Planning Research*, 14(3): 226–45.

Stevenson, O. and Prout, A. (2013) 'Space for play? Families' strategies for organizing domestic space in homes with young children', *Home Cultures*, 10(2): 135–57.

Stokoe, E. (2006) 'Public intimacy in neighbour relationships and complaints', *Sociological Research Online*, 11(3): 137–57.

Stokoe, E. and Wallwork, J. (2003) 'Space invaders: the moral-spatial order in neighbour dispute discourse', *British Journal of Social Psychology*, 42(4): 551–69.

Stokoe, E. and Hepburn, A. (2005) '"You can hear a lot through the walls": noise formulations in neighbour complaints', *Discourse & Society*, 16(5): 647–73.

Stone, W., Sharam, A., Wiesel, I., Ralston, L., Markkanen, S. and James, A. (2015) *Accessing and Sustaining Private Rental Tenancies: Critical Life Events, Housing Shocks and Insurances*, AHURI Final Report no 259. Melbourne: AHURI.

Sullivan, E. (2018) *Manufactured Insecurity: Mobile Home Parks and Americans' Tenuous Right to Place*, California: University of California Press.

Taylor, E. (2018) *Transport Strategy Discussion Paper*, Melbourne: City of Melbourne. Available from: https://s3.ap-southeast-2.amazonaws.com/hdp.au.prod.app.com-participate.files/3815/2947/9994/Transport_Strategy_refresh_-_Car_parking.PDF

Taylor, E. (2020) 'Parking policy: the politics and uneven use of residential parking space in Melbourne', *Land Use Policy*, DOI 10.1016/j.landusepol.2018.11.011.

Thompson, R. (1986) *Sydney's Flats: A Social and Political History* [Unpublished Thesis], Macquarie University. Available from: http://hdl.handle.net/1959.14/90117

Thomson, J. (2018) 'Dirty Laundry of Strata Schemes Gets an Airing as Washing Rules Begin to Change', *Australian Financial Review*, 30 August. Available from: www.afr.com/wealth/dirty-laundry-of-strata-schemes-gets-an-airing-20180830-h14pwr

Treffers, S. and Lippert, R. (2019) 'Condominium self-governance? Issues, external interests, and the limits of statutory reform', *Housing Studies*, 35(6): 1025–49.

Troy, L., Randolph, B., Pinnegar, S., Crommelin, L. and Easthope, H. (2020) 'Vertical sprawl in the Australian city: Sydney's high-rise residential development boom', *Urban Policy and Research*, 38(1): 18–36.

Troy, P. (1996) *The Perils of Urban Consolidation: A Discussion of Australian Housing and Urban Development Policies*, Sydney: Federation Press.

Usborne, S. (2016) 'Washing-line Snobbery: Why Can't I Hang My Knickers Out to Dry?', *The Guardian*, 14 September. Available from: www.theguardian.com/environment/shortcuts/2016/sep/14/washing-line-snobbery-why-cant-hang-knickers-out-to-dry

Valentine, G. (2008) 'Living with difference: reflections on geographies of encounter', *Progress in Human Geography*, 32(3): 323–37.

Valentine, G. and Harris, C. (2016) 'Encounters and (in) tolerance: perceptions of legality and the regulation of space', *Social & Cultural Geography*, 17(7): 913–32.

Van Der Merwe, C. (ed) (2015) *European Condominium Law*, Cambridge: Cambridge University Press.

Van Eijk, G. (2011) '"They eat potatoes, I eat rice": symbolic boundary making and space in neighbour relations', *Sociological Research Online*, 16(4): 1–12.

Vesselinov, E., Cazessus, M. and Falk, W. (2007) 'Gated communities and spatial inequality', *Journal of Urban Affairs*, 29(2): 109–27.

Walks, A. (2006) 'Aestheticization and the cultural contradictions of neoliberal (sub)urbanism', *Cultural Geographies*, 13: 466–75.

Warner, E. and Andrews, F. (2019) '"Surface acquaintances": parents' experiences of social connectedness and social capital in Australian high-rise developments', *Health & Place*, DOI 10.1016/j.healthplace.2019.102165.

Webb, B. and Webber, S. (2017) 'The implications of condominium neighbourhoods for long-term urban revitalisation', *Cities*, 61: 48–57.

Weber, R. (2015) *From Boom to Bubble. How Finance Built The New Chicago*, Chicago: University of Chicago.

Webster, C. (2002) 'Property rights and the public realm: gates, green belts, and Gemeinschaft', *Environment and Planning B: Planning and Design*, 29(3): 397–412.

Webster, C. and Le Goix, R. (2005) 'Planning by commonhold', *Economic Affairs*, 25: 19–23.

Wegmann, J., Schafran, A. and Pfeiffer, D. (2017) 'Breaking the double impasse: securing and supporting diverse housing tenures in the United States', *Housing Policy Debate*, 27(2): 193–216.

Wekerle, G., Dragicevic, R., Jordon, R., Kaszyk, I. and Sorenson, M. (1980) 'Contradiction in ownership, participation and control: the case of condominium housing', in C. Ungerson and V. Karn (eds) *The Consumer Experience of Housing: Cross-national Perspectives*, Farnborough: Gower.

Wetzstein, S. (2017) 'The global urban housing affordability crisis', *Urban Studies*, 54(14): 3159–77.

Yau, Y. (2018) 'Efficacy beliefs and homeowner participation', in E. Altmann and M. Gabriel (eds) *Multi-Owned Property in the Asia-Pacific Region: Rights, Restrictions and Responsibilities*, London: Palgrave Macmillan, pp 231–50.

Yip, N. and Forrest, R. (2002) 'Property owning democracies? Homeowner corporations in Hong Kong', *Housing Studies*, 17(5): 703–20.

Yuen, B., Yeh, A., Appold, S., Earl, G., Ting, J. and Kwee, L. (2006) 'High-rise living in Singapore public housing', *Urban Studies*, 43(3): 583–600.

Yuval-Davis, N. (2006) 'Belonging and the politics of belonging', *Patterns of Prejudice*, 40(3): 197–214.

Index

References to endnotes show both the page number and the note number (231n3).

T